GLOBAL ISSUES

IMMIGRATION AND MIGRATION

GLOBAL ISSUES

IMMIGRATION AND MIGRATION

Rayna Bailey

Foreword by Lorenzo A. Trujillo
School of Law, University of Colorado

Viva Books

New Delhi | Mumbai | Chennai | Kolkata | Bangalore | Hyderabad | Kochi | Guwahati

First Indian Edition 2010

VIVA BOOKS PRIVATE LIMITED

- 4737/23 Ansari Road, Daryaganj, New Delhi 110 002
  E-mail: vivadelhi@vivagroupindia.net, Tel. 42242200
- 76, Service Industries, Shirvane, Sector 1, Nerul, Navi Mumbai 400 706
  E-mail: vivamumbai@vivagroupindia.net, Tel. 27721273, 27721274
- Jamals Fazal Chambers, 26 Greams Road, Chennai 600 006
  E-mail: vivachennai@vivagroupindia.net, Tel. 28290304, 28294241
- B-103, Jindal Towers, 21/1A/3 Darga Road, Kolkata 700 017
  E-mail: vivakolkata@vivagroupindia.net, Tel. 22836381, 22816713
- 7, Sovereign Park Apartments, 56-58, K. R. Road, Basavanagudi, Bangalore 560 004
  E-mail: vivabangalore@vivagroupindia.net, Tel. 26607409, 26607410
- 101-102 Mughal Marc Apartments, 3-4-637 to 641, Narayanguda, Hyderabad 500 029
  E-mail: vivahyderabad@vivagroupindia.net, Tel. 27564481, 27564482
- First Floor, Beevi Towers, SRM Road, Kaloor, Kochi 682 018, Kerala
  E-mail: vivakochi@vivagroupindia.net, Tel: 0484-2403055, 2403056
- 232, GNB Road, Beside UCO Bank, Silpukhuri, Guwahati 781 003
  E-mail: vivaguwahati@vivagroupindia.net, Tel: 0361-2666386

www.vivagroupindia.com

Published by arrangement with

Facts on File, Inc.
132 West 31st Street
New York 10001
USA

ISBN 978-81-309-1421-3

Published by Vinod Vasishtha for Viva Books Private Limited, 4737/23, Ansari Road, Daryaganj, New Delhi-110 002. Printed and bound by Anand Sons, Delhi - 110 092.

CONTENTS

Foreword

Understanding the history of immigration and migration allows us to better appreciate the world we live in today. Based on current news reports and political ads, one might get the impression that immigration in the United States is out of control. However, if the historical context is considered, the student will find that the problems that seem so very emotional and critical in America today are the same as those that have been experienced throughout history by many countries on all continents.

Global Issues: Immigration and Migration provides that indispensable historical context. In the United States, for example, immigration-related problems began as early as 1850, when the cities where many of the immigrants settled became overcrowded, public services were strained, and native-born citizens, who had once welcomed immigrant laborers, began to complain that newcomers were taking jobs and, because they were willing to work for little money, were depressing wages. Discrimination and prejudice against immigrants who had trouble adopting the linguistic, cultural, and social ways of America also increased.

Global Issues: Immigration and Migration is an insightful and unbiased study of immigration and migration from a historical and global perspective. It is presented in three parts. Part I begins with an introduction that defines what is at issue, outlines the global challenges involved, and provides a brief history of the subject of immigration and migration. Following the introduction are detailed case studies of the United States, France, South Africa, Mexico, and the Philippines that explore how immigration and migration have affected and still affect each country today, including a historical overview of immigration and the strategies, laws, and perspectives that each of them has pursued in response.

Part II presents significant U.S. and international primary source documents, such as excerpts from newspaper articles, speeches, relevant treaties and other legal documents, and scientific reports.

Part III is a compilation of useful research tools, such as brief biographies of key international players, facts and figures, an annotated bibliography, and a list of relevant international organizations and agencies. This is followed by a chronology, glossary, and index to provide additional resources for the researcher who wishes to pursue further studies.

The chapter on the United States, for example, includes a discussion of the fundamental question of why immigrants come to the United States, a balanced analysis of how the United States benefits from immigration, as well as a section on problems associated with immigration, followed by a review of immigration laws as they have evolved and continue to do so today. It also includes the rarely considered phenomenon of emigration, that is, why people leave the United States. The author has compiled an admirable amount of details and facts that provide a solid foundation to the reader who wants to explore the topic. Did you know, for example, that illegal aliens who get jobs with fraudulent Social Security numbers pay income tax, but they do not collect Social Security payments? It was reported in 2006 that, since the 1980s, the value of unclaimed Social Security benefits has more than doubled to about $189 billion.

From this book the novice will gain knowledge about terminology and concepts in immigration and migration. The professional will find it an invaluable resource of informed research and perspective for quality decision making. The reader will soon understand the many complexities that are involved in thinking about the issues that have impacted societies since the beginning of governments and borders.

Immigration and related issues have received tremendous attention in U.S. and world politics, which makes this volume a very timely one. Just about every person in the United States and in many other countries throughout the world has been touched by the issue, either directly or indirectly. Almost every person has an opinion on the subject. Ideally, these opinions should be based on factual and historical knowledge. Unfortunately, however, some of the most vocal people base their strongly held opinions on emotion rather than knowledge and reason, and some express them for political gain or other personal reasons instead of the common good.

For example, some political ads decry the possibility of making people who overstayed their visas permanent residents because, as these critics reason, overstayers are criminals by their illegal presence. Yet, at the same time, businesses and corporations benefit—and do not face criminal consequences—by hiring undocumented workers to perform work at low wages, and citizens enjoy the benefits of low-cost vegetables, fruits, and other commodities and services. Clearly, workers without employment authorization are in violation of national laws. But does that factor preclude revision of laws to more adequately meet the burgeoning needs of business, agriculture, and tourism?

In the United States the estimates of undocumented people range from 11 million to 20 million immigrants and children. Certainly, a law to force all undocumented people to return to their country of origin can be passed. This is a plan that is often heralded by anti-immigration activists. But what would the consequences be? How are these people, who live in the shadows of society, going to be identified? Will legal permanent residents and citizens who fit an immigrant profile be distinguished from undocumented workers? What type of force will be required to round up 11 million to 20 million undocumented workers and their families? Of critical concern for taxpayers is who will pay for the return travel and the army of bureaucrats and soldiers that will be required to handle the process? When and where will these roundups occur? When the United States is purged of undocumented workers, who will fill the jobs that are currently held by the undocumented workers? To further complicate the issue, who will fill the approximately 20 million new jobs that are estimated by the U.S. Department of Labor to be created by 2008? Once they are sent home, who will protect the borders to ensure that they all do not come back the next day?

Furthermore, immigration is not merely a policy debate. Rather, the questions we face are steeped in questions of morality. As Charles J. Chaput and Michael J. Sheridan wrote on July 6, 2006, in the *Denver Post*: "The measure of a just society is how it treats its weakest and most vulnerable members.... [T]he 'common good' is a fundamental and permanent principle of our social teaching.... [T]he common good requires legislation that enables both employers and workers to earn an adequate living without deceit or fear." As a just society we must direct ourselves to principled wisdom and leadership and to an understanding of our needs now and in the future.

Our form of government is dependent upon an educated citizenry. The United States is a country where the rule of law is the fundamental basis upon which its citizens are organized as a civilized society and it is the citizens' responsibility to make informed decisions about the laws they created and enforced in their name. We, as citizens, must see to it that those laws are based on sound reasoning and understandings of the impact of those laws on our lives and the quality of the society in which we live now and in the future.

The quick fixes that politicians might seek in response to the perceived immigration crisis often have long-term national and international consequences, many of them negative. Countries faced with an immigration and migration crisis must carefully review the underlying causes of such movements and seek to fully understand the results of decisions, actions, and laws before they are put into action.

Given the impact that these decisions have on the future well-being of a nation as well as millions of people we, as a society, are challenged to get beyond sensationalism, hyperbole, and fearmongering. The challenge is now. We are a nation of immigrants whose forefathers had the foresight and wisdom to establish a nation of laws under the Constitution. We hold the precious gift of our country's legacy in the decisions we make today. Let us make these decisions based on reason, factual data, comprehensive study, and a profound understanding of the world we live in.

I do not doubt that this book will provide an invaluable resource to all Americans and others throughout the world who must study immigration and migration.

—Lorenzo A. Trujillo
School of Law,
University of Colorado

PART I

At Issue

1

Introduction

From rioting by second-generation immigrants in France to protests by illegal immigrants in the United States, immigration has figured prominently in the news worldwide in the early 21st century. But immigration and migration are not practices that evolved with modern societies. Rather, immigration and migration are as old as civilization itself. And while much of the news about immigration focuses on the negative, over the course of history migrants have played a key role in spreading populations across the world and influencing the social, cultural, and economic fabric of countries, both those losing people and those receiving new residents. This chapter will offer readers an introduction to immigration and migration and its various aspects. It will provide information about the origins of population movements and the evolution of early human migrations into modern immigration and migration. Also included are an overview of the different reasons people immigrate or migrate, and the impact of immigration on countries receiving immigrants and those losing citizens. Although an overview of information on immigration and migration is provided in this chapter, because of increased globalization and the impact of cross-border immigration on both sending and receiving countries, the focus of this book is international immigration and migration.

WHAT ARE IMMIGRATION AND MIGRATION?

Immigration and migration are closely linked and often interchangeable terms, but there are differences between the two activities. In most instances immigration is the movement of people from one country to another with the intent of becoming permanent residents of the country to which they are relocating. Related terms are emigration and emigrant. While immigration is the act of arriving in a new country as an immigrant, emigration is the act of leaving one's homeland or becoming an emigrant.

IMMIGRATION AND MIGRATION

Like immigration, migration also is the movement of people from one location, country, or region to another. However, while some migrants eventually become permanent residents of the country or region to which they have moved, migration usually is the movement of people planning to remain only temporarily in the destination location. For example, in the United States an unskilled laborer from Mexico filling a job on a farm may remain only for a few months or until the end of the harvest, while a registered nurse from the Philippines working in a U.S. hospital may fill the job for several years.

Migration may be classified as either internal or international. Internal migration, or domestic migration, is the movement of people within a single country, either from rural to urban areas or in, reverse, from the city to the country. Throughout history all countries have experienced internal migration and the trend has continued to increase worldwide, according to a 2005 report by the International Organization for Migration. The report explains that push and pull factors, which are determined by a country's economic, political, cultural, and environmental landscape, played a key role in internal migration in the past and continue to do so in the present. Push factors are situations that push people to leave their native location, including food shortages, wars, or natural disasters such as flooding, whereas pull factors are those that pull people to new places, including better jobs, nicer weather, or stable governments. The International Organization for Migration report stated: "The classic push and pull forces that resulted in people from poor regions migrating to richer rural and urban locations still exist and may even be accentuated with rising population pressures and deteriorating land and water availability."[1] Internal migration may be temporary, as with migrant workers who move from one region within a country to another on a seasonal basis. Examples include migrant workers in the United States who have traditionally worked in agriculture and move from state to state as crops become ready to harvest, and people who live in the American Midwest or other areas with relatively mild summers and frigid winters who move to the warmer climates of the South or Southwest when cold winter weather arrives. Such seasonal migrants have earned the nickname *Snowbirds* in places like Florida, Arizona, and other Sunbelt states where they typically spend their winters. Internal migration may also be more permanent, as in Europe and the Middle East where migrant workers are more likely to leave a country's rural areas that are in economic decline looking for job opportunities in urban settings.

International migration is described in an article published by *Human Resources for Health* as "the movement of people from one country to another to take up employment, to establish residence or to seek refuge from persecution, either temporarily or permanently."[2] Much as internal migration has occurred throughout human history, so too has international migration. The United Nations specifically addressed the cross-border migration of people in its 2002 *International Migration Report.* Based on statistics, international migration is affecting ever-greater numbers of people as well as the economic and social climate of all nations. The United Nations report notes that, since 1970, the number of migrants worldwide has doubled and between 1990 and 2000 international migrants had increased 14 percent or by 21 million people.[3] In 2002 about 3 percent of the world's total population—approximately 175 million people—were living in a country in which they had not been born. By 2005 the total number of migrants around the world had increased to an estimated 185 million to 192 million with 75 percent of international migrants living in just 12 percent of the world's countries. The top three migrant-receiving countries in 2000 were the United States (35 percent), Russian Federation (13.3 percent), and Germany (7.3 percent).[4]

Article 13 of the Universal Declaration of Human Rights, which was adopted on December 10, 1948, by the General Assembly of the United Nations, addresses both internal and international migration. It states first: "Everyone has the right to freedom of movement and residence within the borders of each state," and second: "Everyone has the right to leave any country, including his own, and to return to his country."[5]

As more and more of the world's population join the ranks of immigrants or migrants it is important to consider that not all population movements are voluntary. Some people are involuntary migrants. Voluntary migration is the movement of people by choice, often by people from developing countries moving to industrialized nations in search of jobs and opportunities for a better life. In 2005 the British Broadcasting Corporation (BBC) described voluntary migration as "the movement of people from poor and failing states to rich and stable ones," and a movement "as inevitable as water running downhill."[6] The darker side of migration is involuntary or forced migration, which is the relocation of people from one country or region to another against their wishes. Involuntary migrants fall into several different categories. They are described by Stephen Castles in his report "Confronting the Realities of Forced Migration" as:[7]

- **Refugees.** Refugees are people living outside of their country of nationality and unable to return due to "well founded fear of persecution on account of race, religion, nationality, membership in a particular social group, or political opinion." A notable example of refugees includes Jews who migrated to escape anti-Semitism and persecution in Nazi Germany between 1933 and 1945. More recently, refugees have fled the war-torn countries of Angola, Vietnam, Somalia, Sudan, Afghanistan, and Iraq.

- **Asylum Seekers.** Asylum seekers are people who cross international borders seeking protection from wars and other dangerous situations in their homeland, but who are waiting for their claims for refugee status to be determined by the host country. Worldwide, as many as 90 percent of asylum seekers' applications are ultimately rejected by host governments, based on a determination that applicants do not face persecution. In addition, asylum seekers often live in a state of limbo in the host country, where they may not be allowed to hold jobs but cannot be deported because they have no passport or their home country refuses to repatriate them. While waiting for their appeals for refuge to move through court systems, which can take many years, asylum seekers may exist in an underground world often associated with illegal immigrants, including surviving on welfare handouts and money earned working off-the-books jobs.
- **Internally Displaced Persons.** IDPs are an example of involuntary internal migration rather than forced international migration. A historic example of forced international migration are the nearly 20 million Africans forcibly relocated from their homeland during the slave trade of the 16th to the 19th centuries. The United Nations defines IDPs as "persons who, as a result of persecution, armed conflict or violence, have been forced to abandon their homes and leave their usual place of residence, and who remain within the borders of their own country." Historic examples include African slaves in the United States who endured additional involuntary migration when more than 800,000 were forced to move with their white owners who migrated from Virginia, the Carolinas, and Georgia to establish residences in Mississippi, Louisiana, Arkansas, and Texas.[8] In 1838 the U.S. government forcibly removed nearly 17,000 Cherokees—whose tribal lands included the states of Georgia, Tennessee, and North Carolina—from their lands. The Cherokees were forced to migrate to Oklahoma in a 1,200-mile journey that became known as the Trail of Tears. In addition to the Cherokees, 2,000 black slaves owned by wealthy Cherokees, as well as members of the Chickasaw, Choctaw, Muscogee Creek, and Seminole Indian tribes also were part of the involuntary migration. More than 70,000 Native Americans were eventually forced off their lands and involuntarily migrated west following passage of the U.S. government's Indian Removal Act of 1830.[9]

According to Stephen Castles's report, in 2003 most of the IDP population lived in the African nations of Sudan, Uganda, and the Democratic Republic of Congo. As wars increasingly target civilian populations mass displacement of people has also increased. In 2006, for example, the United Nations High Commissioner for Human Rights reported that the number of IDPs in Iraq had increased to more than 1.2 million due to war and fighting between U.S.-led coalition forces and insurgent groups. The United Nations also estimated that in 2006 in Colombia there were more than 3 million IDPs due to a 40-year conflict between government troops and opposing paramilitaries and guerrillas.

- **Development Displacees.** This type of involuntary migrant is a person pushed from his or her home by their country's large-scale development projects, such as construction of dams, airports, and urban housing. While no specific data is available about the number of people displaced by development projects, the World Bank Environment Department estimates it as high as 10 million people each year worldwide. For example, the National Research Center for Resettlement in China estimated that over 45 million people in China were displaced between 1950 and 2000 by developments such as the Three Gorges Dam Project.[10] Development displacees, like IDPs, are usually relocated within their own country, but they may be eventually pushed by deteriorating circumstances into international migration.
- **Environmental and Disaster Displacees.** Victims of natural or man-made disasters fall into this category of involuntary migrants. Among the natural disasters that can force people to migrate are earthquakes, water pollution, desertification or deforestation, volcanoes, and weather events such as destructive hurricanes. Man-made disasters may include industrial accidents and radioactivity. An example of involuntary internal migration due to a natural disaster would be the thousands of people in New Orleans, Louisiana, and along the coast of Mississippi in the United States who were forced to migrate to other cities and states following the destruction of the region by Hurricane Katrina in late August 2005. A man-made disaster would be the April 1986 accident at the Chernobyl Nuclear Power Plant near Pripyat, Ukraine. The explosion at the plant spread radioactive fallout that contaminated large areas of Ukraine, Russia, and Belarus, and forced the displacement of more than 300,000 people.
- **People-Trafficking and Smuggling.** These are two aspects of the clandestine and, in the case of people-trafficking, involuntary movement of people across borders. The United Nations describes the difference as,

> "Smuggled migrants are moved illegally for profit; they are partners, however unequal, in a commercial transaction." Mexican nationals who pay *coyotes* to transport them into the United States illegally and Chinese nationals who pay *snakeheads* to smuggle them into South Africa illegally are examples of smuggled migrants. "The movement of trafficked persons is based on deception and coercion and is for the purpose of exploitation," the United Nations states. Women and children trafficked for the international illegal sex trade are common victims of this type of forced migration. An example is victims of the wars in Yugoslavia or Azerbaijan who were sold into prostitution in western Europe.

Other types of human migration to consider, although they fall outside traditionally held ideas of what constitutes immigration or migration, also involve people moving from one place to another either within one country or internationally. They include nomadism, tourism, and commuting.

Nomadism is the practice of people moving periodically rather than living continuously in one place. Early hunter-gatherer societies, which survived by taking advantage of available natural resources, practiced nomadism as they moved to follow food supplies or to assure fuel and shelter. All human societies were hunter-gatherers and practiced nomadism until about 10,000 years ago when the domestication of plants and animals began. While very few hunter-gatherer societies still exist today, the Bushmen of Australia are an example of people who continue to live as nomadic hunter-gatherers. The Rroma, a group of people who migrated to Europe from northwest India in the 1400s and now live throughout the world, also practiced nomadism. Better known as gypsies, the Rroma traveled seasonally to work as entertainers, fortune-tellers, or livestock traders. According to some estimates, by the early 21st century the number of Rroma had dwindled to between 2 million and 3 million worldwide. There is no clear estimate of how many Rroma still practice a nomadic lifestyle, but it is believed to be no more than 5 percent of European Rroma, due in part to modern influences such as integrated housing and financial independence that have eliminated their need to travel from place to place for survival.[11]

Tourism is loosely classified as a form of temporary migration because it involves a person leaving his or her home to spend time—a few days or longer—in another city, state, or country. Commuting, a way of life for many employees in the 21st century, is also loosely classified as a type of temporary migration because it involves people traveling for their jobs. The commute can be by automobile to a neighboring city or by airplane to another state or country; the time away from home may be just for the day or it may be for several days, weeks, or in some instances months or longer.[12]

A BRIEF HISTORY OF MIGRATION AND IMMIGRATION

Out of Africa: The Beginnings of Migration

The earliest human migrations, which began around 2 million years ago with *Homo erectus* moving from Africa north to Eurasia, were moves of necessity. As hunter-gatherers these ancient humans migrated in search of food and water, improved shelter, or, as their populations increased, to escape crowding and deterioration of the environment where they lived. Survival was the motivating factor for early migration rather than the goal of spreading people around the world. Research suggests that when human migration began there were between 10,000 and 20,000 people living on Earth and they were always on the move. This steady quest for survival continued and, as humans evolved, the migrations eventually spread populations to all corners of the Earth.

Homo sapiens evolved from *Homo erectus* around 400,000 to 250,000 years ago, and *Homo sapiens sapiens,* or what is described as the first modern humans, emerged around 80,000 to 120,000 years ago. Like their predecessors, *Homo sapiens sapiens* survived by hunting and gathering so they continued the migration habits of their predecessors for the same reasons. But besides the search for food, they were pushed farther afield by climate changes. Their developing use of fire for warmth and protection and stone tools also aided their migratory movements, making it easier for them to migrate to areas that were previously uninhabitable, such as the polar regions. Archaeological findings in a cave near the mouth of the Klasies River at the tip of South Africa indicate *Homo sapiens sapiens* appeared there about 100,000 years ago. The cave was an ideal setting for these early humans: it faces east so the rising sun would have provided light and warmth, and its location on the coast provided access to an abundance of shellfish when the tide went out.[13] Small bands of *Homo sapiens sapiens* probably established permanent or semi-permanent settlements in those areas where food resources such as fish were available throughout the year; others migrated seasonally, following the movement of the larger animals they hunted for food.[14] Some researchers also believe that climate changes, such as glacial activity that cooled the temperatures in Africa's Sahara region, may have made it possible for *Homo sapiens sapiens* to continue their migration into the Near East during that period. Advancing glaciers also created a land bridge across the Bering Strait that made movement from the area that is now northeastern Siberia into North America possible as early as 60,000 years ago. But some researchers speculate that poor weather conditions may have prohibited migration across the Bering Strait until much later, perhaps not until about 35,000 years ago.[15] Additional human migrations occurred probably in response to the harsh weather conditions during the glacial period, which sent people in search of shelter and food to warmer climates.[16] The areas encompassing Oceania (the islands of the central and south Pacific Ocean, including Micronesia, Melanesia, and Polynesia) were among the last to be populated when migrants began arriving in those areas between 20,000 and 15,000 years ago.

The Spread of the Indo-European Language Family

The practice of agriculture, that is, planting and raising crops, is believed to have started about 10,000 years ago in the Middle East in an area referred to by modern scholars as the Fertile Crescent. With the ability to raise their own food supply hunter-gatherer societies were no longer forced to migrate for survival. Thus the reasons people migrated began to change. Advances made by humans, such as improved tools, domestication of animals, and an ability to build seaworthy boats, also influenced human migration. Natural forces, such as floods, and human forces, such as invasions by neighboring tribes, began to impact human migration as well.

While it is uncertain where Indo-Europeans originated many scholars favor the theory that they began migrating out from the region between the Black and Caspian Seas into Europe, the Middle East, and India as early as 4000 B.C.E. At that time the Indo-Europeans were pastoral nomadic tribes that migrated in search of grazing land for their cattle, sheep, and goats. However, it also is possible that they moved to flee invasions by other migrating tribes. Domestication of the horse sometime between 4200 and 3500 B.C.E., followed by the invention of the wheel between 3300 and 3100 B.C.E., made it easier for people to travel and may have been responsible for the mass migration of Indo-Europeans that began in about 2900 B.C.E. As the evolving Indo-European people formed opposing religious, cultural, and social ideologies, tribes split and migrated in different directions. Information gleaned from the study of the evolution of languages suggests some Indo-Europeans, including those known as Aryans, "went south toward India. Others, who spoke early Celtic, Germanic, and Italic languages, moved west through Europe. Still others who spoke Greek and Persian, went to locations between those of the other groups."[17] Historians, using comparative studies of language, clothing, and cultural characteristics, have determined that most of the peoples of Europe, Iran, and India share a common Indo-European ancestry.[18]

Migrations in Medieval Europe and Asia

Major European migrations that marked the transition from ancient periods to the Middle Ages, often described by historians as Great Migrations, occurred in two waves. The first took place from about 300 to 500 C.E. with Germanic people leaving their homes in the Volga River region of Russia and migrating into the area that was then the Western Roman Empire. While some scholars believe this mass migration of Germanic people was caused in part by the invasion of their homeland by the Huns (pastoral nomads from Central Asia with warlike tendencies), others consider the reasons for the mass migration a mystery. Whatever the reason, the migration led to the Germanic conquest of the Western Roman Empire and contributed to the ultimate fall of the Roman Empire in 476. Richard Hooker, a professor at Washington State University, described the events as follows:

> *The Visigoths, one of the largest of the German tribes, probably did not number more than 100,000 people and could field probably no more than 25,000 soldiers at any one time. This is in comparison to the 60 to 70 million people living in the Empire and a standing army that outnumbered the entire population of Visigoths. Still, the Visigoths managed to enter Rome and assert administrative control over much of the western Empire.*[19]

Efforts by some of the Germanic invaders to maintain Roman culture and institutions failed, but "from these people would arise most of the major cultural and political groups of the later Middle Ages: the English, the French, the Scandinavians, Icelanders, and, of course, the Germans themselves."[20] The ongoing Germanic expansion led to the displacement of Slavic tribes in their path, probably triggering the second Great Migration between 500 and 900. There is also uncertainty about where Slavic tribes originated, but research suggests that during this period the Slavs split and groups migrated in several directions from what is now Russia west into the regions between the Odra River and the Elbe-Saale River line (an area between Germany and Poland); south into what is now Bohemia, Moravia, Slovakia, Hungary, and the Balkans; and north along the upper Dnieper River in Ukraine. Germanic movements also compelled Turkish tribes they encountered in southern Russia to migrate and establish settlements in the Eastern Roman Empire, including in Greece, Syria, the Balkans, Palestine, Egypt, eastern North Africa, sections of Italy, and Anatolia (modern-day Turkey).

Wars and invasions fueled by differing religious and political ideologies and a desire by leaders to possess more territory were often the driving force for migration during the Middle Ages, from approximately 476 through the mid-1400s. Those on the move during the Middle Ages included Saracens or Moors (North African Arabs and Berbers) who in 711 crossed the Straits of Gibraltar from North Africa and invaded Spain, which was under the control of the Germanic Visigoths at that time. Muslims also settled in southeastern Europe following wars between European armies and the Turks in the Balkans. Following the *reconquista* in 1492, in which the Spanish reclaimed control of Spain, the Moors fled to North Africa while Jews, who also were forced out of Spain, migrated to eastern Europe, Greece, and Istanbul.

Chinese expansion during the 11th century forced Seljuk Turkish tribes out of Central Asia west into the Volga River region and south into Persia, Armenia, Asia Minor, and Syria. In what is described as a military migration, beginning in 1219 Mongols led by Genghis Khan and his successors moved out of Mongolia and took control of parts of China, Central Asia, Iran, Mesopotamia, Syria, Asia Minor, Russia, and eastern Europe, setting in motion migrations of Turkic people that continued for several centuries.

European Colonialism

In the 15th century European explorers began discovering previously unknown lands and governments looked to those new regions to establish colonies and thereby expand their empires. Discoveries by Portuguese, Spanish, French, English, and Dutch explorers opened new opportunities for migration to the Americas, South Asia, Sub-Saharan Africa, and Australia.

Portuguese explorers, such as Vasco da Gama (1469–1524) led pioneering expeditions in discovering new routes to Asia by sailing around Africa.

Spain's foundations for empire were laid in the 15th century by explorers such as Christopher Columbus (1451–1506). By the early 16th century Spain had a colony on Hispaniola in the West Indies and achieved control of the Caribbean Islands with the 1515 occupation of Cuba. Spain continued its empire building by pushing into South and Central America, including conquering Mexico, Guatemala, and Nicaragua. Spanish settlers established colonies in Venezuela beginning in 1523. During the seven years from 1533 through 1540 Spain invaded and occupied Peru, Ecuador, Colombia, and Chile. Spanish explorer Ferdinand Magellan's (1480–1521) success navigating the Pacific Ocean opened the door for Spanish migration to the Philippines, with the first permanent Spanish settlement established there in 1564.[21] During this time Spain also established settlements along the east coast of North America in Florida. Spanish settlers, along with Mexican Indians, migrated north from Mexico into what are the present-day states of America's Southwest and West, namely, Arizona, New Mexico, California, and Texas, as well as Colorado.

In the 1600s, as the empires in Spain and Portugal slipped into decline, the Dutch pushed Spanish warships out of the Atlantic Ocean and claimed control of Portuguese ports in Brazil, Africa, and Asia. Many of the Dutch arriving in Asia came as temporary migrants, staying just long enough to make their fortunes from the spice trade before returning home. Dutch efforts to attract families or permanent settlers to their Asian colonies failed. Similar to outposts in Asia, Dutch colonies in Africa, the Caribbean, and Brazil were business ventures rather than permanent settlements. The Dutch were mostly unsuccessful at establishing colonies in North America as well. Despite the Dutch West India Company's founding of a colony on Manhattan Island (New Amsterdam) and the development of several frontier trading posts in the Hudson Valley, by 1660 there were only an estimated 5,000 settlers living in the colony of New Netherland. France's attempts at empire building by establishing permanent colonies in the New World also had limited success, and by 1663 just 2,500 French colonists had immigrated to the New World.[22]

Like other European nations looking toward the New World to expand and colonize, England's early attempts were limited; however, English efforts soon intensified. Circumstances in England, including a population that had swelled from 3 million to 4 million in the 70 years from 1530 to 1600, the persecution of some religious groups by the Church of England, and a growing business community looking for new places to invest capital, helped fuel immigration to North America and other places. The first English colony in America, the 1607 settlement of Jamestown in Virginia, opened the door for large numbers of English immigrants to make their way to the New World. Settling farther north, by 1642 some 25,000 people had migrated to "New England." English migrants also were settling in Africa and the West Indies, including in Bermuda, the Bahamas, and Barbados, which was uninhabited until English colonists established settlements there in 1627.[23] Within seven years the population of Barbados had increased to 37,000. The English also migrated to India and established trading posts on that country's west coast.[24]

Migration in the 19th and 20th Centuries

A study by the United Nations Department of Economic and Social Affairs, *World Economic and Social Survey 2004: International Migration*, reports that 52 million Europeans left their home countries between 1820 and 1932 and emigrated to destination countries in the Americas. Of those, 32 million immigrants arrived in the United States and 3.5 million migrated to Australia and New Zealand. Motivation for the population movements prior to World War I included "freer international movement of goods, capital and labour. . . . Innovations in both transoceanic shipping and transcontinental railways made possible major intercontinental flows of people seeking better lives in the expanding economies."[25]

Immigration during that period was not limited to Europeans. The UN study also noted that large numbers of people migrated from China and India to other developing countries. Modern migration slowed in the years prior to World War I and that trend continued after the war when nations that had received many of the earlier immigrants began putting restrictions on immigration. Following World War II immigration experienced an upswing, leading to the largest European migration of the 20th century, which included the emigration and resettlement in new homelands of nearly 20 million Germans, Poles, Ukrainians, and Jews. Also after World War II more than 6 million Muslims migrated to Pakistan and more than 5 million Hindus and Sikhs migrated to India following the division of the Indian subcontinent into two separate, independent states in 1947.

Migration and immigration stabilized worldwide well into the middle of the 20th century when it began increasing again in the 1970s. According to the United Nations study, in the decade from 1960 to 1970 the number of migrants worldwide increased from 76 million to 82 million; 10 years later in 1980 there were a reported 100 million international migrants and in 1990 the number had increased to 154 million. The United Nations estimates that 175 million people were living outside of their birth country in 2002 and, by 2005, the number was estimated at between 185 million and 192 million, or one in every 35 people. Based on the UN's data in 2005 the largest number of international migrants lived in Europe (approximately 65 million), Asia (approximately 54 million), and North America (approximately 44 million).[26]

A wide range of reasons motivate modern immigration or migration. They include:

- **Economic or professional.** Economic or professional immigrants and migrants leave their homes and move to a new location in search of a better life. They immigrate to escape poverty or to find jobs that are either unavailable or are available but pay lower wages in their home country. In the 21st century this has become one of the primary reasons for immigration and migration, with most migrants moving from developing to developed countries where opportunities are better. For example, unskilled Mexicans migrate to the United States to work as farm or construction laborers because the pay is better than what they can earn doing similar work in Mexico. Skilled professionals such as nurses, doctors, and teachers from the Philippines, South Africa, and India migrate to the United States where they also can earn much higher wages than those paid in their home countries.

- **Political.** People who immigrate or migrate for political reasons usually are pushed to leave their homelands to escape war, oppressive dictatorships, religious persecution, ethnic cleansing, and intolerable government policies. For example, people from Africa, including Nigeria, Gambia, Sierra Leone, and Liberia, migrate, many illegally, to Spain's Canary Islands to escape poverty and political turmoil in their homelands. Spanish officials estimated that "at least 31,000 African immigrants arrived in the Canaries" in 2006.[27] In 2002 an estimated 76,000 Africans immigrated to France, with 18,500 arriving from sub-Saharan Africa. Most arrive in France trying to escape poverty in their homeland and in search of work.[28]
- **Retirement.** Retirement migrants are typically older people who, after retiring from years of work, choose to move to a location with a better climate or lower cost of living than that of their home country, such as British retirees emigrating to Spain and American retirees emigrating to Mexico.
- **Natural disasters.** This type of migrant is a person pushed from his or her home by natural disasters that result in long-term damage and destruction to their home country or location, such as the earthquake-triggered tsunami in Southeast Asia in 2004 and the 2005 hurricanes in Louisiana and Mississippi in the United States.

CONSEQUENCES FOR THE COUNTRY OF ORIGIN

The consequences of immigration and migration are largely determined by whether a country is receiving immigrants (destination country) or losing its citizens (country of origin). According to the United Nations, the positive effects of immigration or migration on countries of origin include providing people opportunities to find work unavailable in their homeland and thereby helping to ease unemployment problems at home. The Philippines—with an unemployment rate of more than 11 percent in 2005 and where 21 percent of people held jobs for which they were overqualified—actively encourages economic migration of its citizens to manage its employment problems. The Filipino government began regulating emigration of its workers in the 1970s through licensing and support for recruitment agencies that help their overseas foreign workers (OFWs) find jobs and through the establishment of methods for protecting its workers while they are employed in foreign countries. Nearly 10 percent of Filipinos, about 8.1 million people, were OFWs at the end of 2004.[29] Mexico, despite boasting a low unemployment rate of 3.7 percent in 2005, still loses thousands of its citizens each year to economic migration due to underemployment (an estimated 25 percent of workers are filling jobs for which they are overqualified), and extremely low wages (farm laborers or factory workers in Mexico may earn as little as $8.50 per day or less).[30] By 2006 an estimated 10 percent of Mexico's population had emigrated for jobs with most going to the United States. Although Mexico embraces the economic migration of its citizens, unlike the Philippines, the country lacks formal government programs supporting economic migration and its migrant workers.

The governments of both the Philippines and Mexico as well as other countries with large numbers of economic migrants have long recognized a key benefit of their citizens working abroad is *remittances,* or the practice of sending a portion of the money earned from jobs in another country back to family remaining in the homeland, which also can help the country of origin's economy. The Migration Policy Institute estimates that in 2003 remittances paid by migrants worldwide totaled $100 billion annually.[31] In 2003 remittances paid by Filipino OFWs were $7.6 billion while Mexico's remittances totaled $12 billion. Available 2006 data estimate that remittances sent home by Mexico's economic migrants reached $20 billion, passing oil revenues as a source of income. The Philippines expected to receive $11.8 billion in remittances by the end of 2006.

An increased movement of trade between the receiving country and the country of origin and the potential to increase human capital in the country of origin when the migrant returns to the homeland with new skills acquired while living in the receiving country are also noted as positive aspects of migration.

Possible negative effects include the loss of highly skilled workers, or brain drain. In countries like the Philippines and South Africa the loss of doctors, nurses, and teachers has reduced the quality of essential services such as education and medical care. Between 1996 and 2006 nearly 100,000 Filipino nurses and doctors emigrated to work in other countries, particularly the United States, where salaries are much higher. As a result, just 700 of the Philippines's 1,600 hospitals remained open in 2006 and the patient-to-nurse ratio increased to just one nurse to care for each 55 patients. The ratio for optimum care is one nurse for four patients.[32] Similarly, as South Africa's nurses emigrated for better paying positions the country reported a shortage of about 32,000 nurses in 2003.[33] While reliable data from South Africa regarding emigrating medical professionals is limited, health professionals with the country's National School of Public Health at Medunsa reported that 23,400 doctors and nurses had emigrated between 1994 and 2004, citing South Africa's economic instability, poor working conditions, and the impact of HIV/AIDS as reasons for leaving.[34] South Africa's minister for education reported that the country's teachers were following medical personnel and also leaving for jobs elsewhere. In 2004 as many as 5,000 South African teachers were working in the United Kingdom in London schools alone. It was noted, however, that while emigrating teachers contributed to the brain drain the country was not experiencing a teacher shortage.[35] The exodus of a country's workers, especially highly skilled workers, may ultimately lead to declining growth and reduced productivity in all areas requiring a well-trained labor force, including business and technology, possible financial problems related to the loss of taxes on employees wages, and the potential for revenues from remittances to decrease over time.

CONSEQUENCES FOR THE DESTINATION COUNTRY

Destination countries also experience both positive and negative effects of immigration and migration. On the positive side, destination countries receiving highly skilled workers, or brain gain, reap the benefits of adding professionals such as doctors, nurses, teachers, and others to the workforce, thereby helping to reduce labor shortages. The United States has benefited from the influx of highly skilled immigrants, for example, by encouraging the immigration of nurses and doctors from the Philippines to help reduce U.S. shortages of medical professionals. Studies suggest that by 2020 the United States will have a physician shortage of as high as 200,000 and a nurse shortage of 800,000 or more. To boost its supply of available nurses, in 2005 the U.S. government created 50,000 new green cards for immigrating nurses with allocation of the cards to begin in 2007.[36] Great Britain, which is struggling with a teacher shortage, especially in London and other large cities, is looking to South Africa to recruit teachers. Brain gain also occurs when students travel to another country to complete their college educations or earn advanced degrees, then choose to remain in the host country to put those newly earned skills to work after graduation. A host country reaps the benefits of highly skilled foreign students trained in its universities staying on to fill jobs as doctors, engineers and scientists, among others, rather than leaving to take those skills to their homeland.

Receiving countries benefit from unskilled immigrants joining the labor force as well. Unskilled immigrants often take jobs in the receiving country that native populations are unwilling to fill, such as Mexican migrants who work in U.S. fields harvesting crops. The value of unskilled migrant laborers filling jobs in a receiving country was noted in the United States in 2006 when the government cracked down on illegal immigration from Mexico, leading to shortages of workers to harvest crops ranging from fruit orchards in California to farms in Michigan. California farms and orchards, which typically hire 450,000 people during the harvest season, reported a shortage of 70,000 workers. Losses in the millions of dollars resulted as fruit and other produce went unpicked and rotted on trees or in fields. A California company that grows and markets vine-ripe tomatoes said that efforts to attract American workers had failed. "Americans do not raise their children to be farm workers," a company spokeswoman told the *New York Times.*[37] The U.S. Department of Agriculture (USDA) predicted that the prices of fruits and vegetables would increase about 4.3 percent in 2006 due partly to the shortage of migrant workers to bring in the crops.[38] A 2007 study by the USDA found that in 2006 the prices of fruits and vegetables actually increased 4.8 percent and the agency was predicting that prices would increase between 3.5 percent and 4.5 percent in 2007. Most receiving countries use unskilled immigrants as a source of cheap labor and to fill jobs native workers do not want to do. Unskilled immigrants in many receiving countries can be found laboring on construction sites, serving on the housekeeping staffs of hotels and resorts, picking crops in fields, working in meat processing plants and factories, and more.

Other positive effects of migration include building populations in countries that are experiencing declining demographic growth. The United Nations reported that without the addition of 5 million migrants in the five years from 1995 to 2000 Europe's population would have decreased. "Even with about 5 million immigrants in this period, its population increased by only 600,000," noted the UN report.[39] In North America, which is not experiencing a population decline similar to that in Europe, migration still accounted for 43 percent of the total population growth during that same five years, according to the United Nations.

In addition to compensating for a shortage of employees in both skilled and unskilled jobs, other benefits of immigration and migration for destination countries include economic growth due to the added demand for products and services created by migrants as well as increased revenues through additional taxes paid by migrants on purchases and wages. Receiving countries also benefit from the social and cultural contributions immigrants make in their adopted communities.

On the downside, destination countries may experience problems integrating immigrants into their society. The United Nations cites two methods of integration: assimilation, in which migrants adopt the language, culture, values, and beliefs of the destination country, and multiculturalism, which promotes diversity by encouraging migrants to maintain their ethnic, racial, and cultural characteristics distinct from those of the destination country.[40] While most destination countries have embraced multiculturalism since the 1970s, the UN study notes rising problems as some receiving countries are beginning to expect migrants to adapt to the accepted social and cultural norms, including learning the country's local language and acquiring civic knowledge. Other receiving countries have begun prohibiting migrants from practicing some of the customs from their homelands. Muslim immigrants in France, for example, have increasingly experienced pressure to set aside the traditions of their homelands. In 1989 three Muslims girls were suspended from school for wearing Islamic headscarves, an act the school claimed violated the country's law of separation of church and state. The suspension was overturned and the girls returned to class, but the controversy continued. Teachers in a school in Nantua, France, went on strike in 1993 to protest against students wearing Islamic headscarves in class. More than 10 years later, in 2006, the debate not only raged on but also had spread to other European nations. It also reached beyond the headscarf to include the Islamic face veil and the *burqa,* a type of garment worn by some Muslim women that covers their entire body and face except their eyes. Britain's former foreign secretary began asking Muslim women at meetings to remove their veils to allow better communication. Prime Minister Tony Blair described the veil as a "mark of separation," and another government official called for a teaching assistant who wore an Islamic veil to be fired, stating she was unable to do her job properly while wearing the veil. Italy's prime minister stated that women should not "hide behind" full veils, and the Netherlands began considering a ban of the *burqa.*[41] As the examples in the preceding paragraph show, cultural differences between countries and often a lack of understanding of those differences may result in discrimination toward immigrants by a country's natives and hinder the immigrants' ability to assimilate or fit into the social fabric of their new homeland.

Another universal complaint by immigrant-receiving countries worldwide is that immigrants will take jobs from native workers and drive down salaries since they are usually willing to work for less pay, especially in unskilled and lower-end jobs. Fears of Chinese immigrants taking jobs from native workers were so great in the United States in the 1800s that in 1882 the government passed a law banning all Chinese immigration. In 2006, the United States was planning to build a fence along stretches of the U.S./Mexico border to try to stop the increasing numbers of Mexican nationals entering the United States illegally looking for work. South Africa has actively tried to discourage economic migrants from entering the country for jobs, especially unskilled migrants from other African nations. A 2003 law allowed South African businesses to hire skilled immigrants but banned the hiring of unskilled immigrants. It also limited permanent residency for foreigners to those who had been offered a job no South African was qualified to fill.

Amid fears that immigrants will change the historical fabric or identity of the receiving country many immigrants encounter hostility, racism, exploitation, and marginalization. The disenfranchisement of North African immigrants in France, including unemployment or being pushed into the lowest paying and most menial jobs, led to labor riots in 1994. Their circumstances having improved little some 10 years later, groups of unemployed or underemployed youths, most of them the children of North African immigrants, went on a nine-day rampage through working-class and low-income Paris suburbs in 2005.[42] Immigrants to the United States have also experienced intolerance and distrust from both natives and other immigrants who had been in the country for a long time. In the past, newly arrived Irish, German, Italian, and Jewish immigrants all experienced discrimination, racism, and alienation as they struggled to find a place in American society. Since the September 2001 terrorist attacks, Muslims in the United States have increasingly been targeted for discrimination and hate crimes. Due to an increase in illegal immigration to the United States, most of it from Mexico, Mexicans bore the brunt of most xenophobic attitudes in 2006.

CONCLUSION

Receiving countries worldwide struggle to balance the problems of increasing numbers of arriving immigrants and migrants with the benefits these would-be new citizens provide. When creating immigration policies and laws, receiving countries have much to consider, such as what happens to unskilled immigrant workers when the low-paying jobs they have filled dry up? For example, in the United States in 2007 migrant laborers, many in the country illegally, accounted for 7 percent of the construction workforce, but then the home-building industry took a downturn and many of those laborers were left without jobs.[43] How can governments protect their citizens from potential terrorists trying to enter the country without closing the door on legitimate immigrants? What social services—such as education, health care, welfare—should countries provide immigrants, including those arriving illegally? How can countries enforce existing immigration laws without alienating legal immigrants or the governments and people of sending countries? How much influence should immigrants, legal and illegal, have in developing related immigration laws and policies? What can or should be done to help immigrants assimilate into their new countries? The list of challenges is seemingly endless and the answers can be as diverse as the immigrants and the countries receiving them.

Harvard International Review's explanation of the attitude toward immigrants and migrants in the United States could easily describe the scenario in other immigrant-receiving countries as well:[44]

> *Immigration has always generated ambivalence during the best of times and hysteria during the worst. Historically immigrants in the United States are loved but only looking backwards: celebrating their proud achievements after the fact, while remaining deeply anxious about any further migration in the here and now, has been the constant pattern from the end of the 19th century to the end of the 20th century. One hundred years ago there were apoplectic responses to large-scale immigration from Ireland, Eastern Europe, and the Mediterranean countries. Eastern European Jews, the Catholic Irish, and the Italians were especially suspect on cultural, religious, and security grounds. There were endless debates as to whether Jews and Catholics could ever succeed in the ethos of a predominately Anglo-Saxon Protestant America.*

The information outlined in this introduction will be expanded and treated in more depth in focusing on the specific countries under discussion in Chapter 2 (the United States) and Chapter 3 (Mexico, France, the Philippines, and South Africa). While each country's immigration/migration experiences are unique, they are also similar in many ways. Keeping in mind the different types of immigration/migration, the push/pull factors that trigger migration, and other information provided in this chapter should help readers place immigration and migration in a global perspective. "As the French remind us, the more things change, the more they remain the same."[45] This is particularly true of immigration and migration over the course of history worldwide.

---

[1] Priya Deshingkar and Sven Grimm. *Internal Migration and Development: A Global Perspective.* Geneva: International Organization for Migration, February 2005.

[2] Barbara Stillwell et al. "Developing Evidence-based Ethical Policies on the Migration of Health Workers: Conceptual and Practical Challenges." *Human Resources for Health.* London: BioMed Central, October 28, 2003.

[3] *International Migration Report 2002.* New York: United Nations Department of Economic and Social Affairs, Population Division, 2002.

[4] International Organization for Migration. "Section 3: International Migration Data and Statistics." In *World Migration 2005*, p. 397. Available online. URL: http://www.iom.int/jahia/webdav/site/myjahiasite/shared/shared/mainsite/published_docs/books/wmr_sec03.pdf. Accessed April 26, 2007.

[5] *Universal Declaration of Human Rights*, Resolution 217A (III). New York: United Nations General Assembly, December 10, 1948.

[6] BBC News online. *Migration: "A Force of History."* May 18, 2004. Available online. URL: http://news.bbc.co.uk/1/hi/world/3523208.stm. Accessed October 23, 2006.

[7] Stephen Castles. "Confronting the Realities of Forced Migration." *Migration Information Source.* Washington, D.C.: Migration Policy Institute, May 1, 2004.

[8] Eric Foner and John A. Garraty, eds. "Internal Migration." *Reader's Companion to American History.* Boston: Houghton Mifflin Company, 1991.

[9] Studyworld. *Indian Removal Act of 1830.* Available online. URL: http://www.studyworld.com/indian_removal_act_of_1830.htm. Accessed October 24, 2006.

[10] Jason Stanley. "Development-Induced Displacement and Resettlement." *Forced Migration.* January 2004. Available online. URL: http://www.forcedmigration.org/guides/fmo022/. Accessed October 24, 2006.

[11] *The Religion and Culture of the Roma.* Ontario, Canada: Ontario Consultants on Religious Tolerance, October 10, 2005. Available online. URL: http://www.religioustolerance.org/roma.htm. Accessed October 24, 2006.

[12] *Population Index* 66, no. 1 (Spring 2000). Princeton, N.J.: Princeton University, Office of Population Research, 2000.

[13] "In Search of Human Origins Part Three." Transcript, Public Broadcasting System, NOVA, June 17, 1997. Available online. URL: http://www.pbs.org/wgbh/nova/transcripts/2108hum3.html. Accessed October 24, 2006.

[14] Joseph D. Sneed. *Technology, Environment and Human Adaptation: Part I Early Peoples in the New World.* Golden: Colorado School of Mines, Division of Liberal Arts and International Studies, 2006.

[15] Joseph D. Sneed. *Technology, Environment and Human Adaptation: Part I Early Peoples in the New World.* Golden: Colorado School of Mines, Division of Liberal Arts and International Studies, 2006.

[16] Joseph D. Sneed. *Technology, Environment and Human Adaptation: Part I Early Peoples in the New World.* Golden: Colorado School of Mines, Division of Liberal Arts and International Studies, 2006.

[17] "Indo-European Migration." *Kids Discover,* May 1, 2003.

[18] "History of Iran, Chapter 2: Iranians before Iran." September 15, 2005. Available online. URL: http://www.iranologie.com/history/history2.html. Accessed October 28, 2006.

[19] Richard Hooker. "European Middle Ages: The Germans." *World Civilizations.* Pullman: Washington State University Press, June 6, 1999.

[20] Richard Hooker. "European Middle Ages: The Germans." *World Civilizations.* Pullman: Washington State University Press, June 6, 1999.

[21] "History of the Spanish Empire." *HistoryWorld.* Available online. URL: http://www.history world.net/wrldhis/PlainTextHistories.asp?historyid=ab49. Accessed October 31, 2006.

[22] "Beginnings of North European Expansion." *International World History Project: World History from the Pre-Sumerican Period to the Present.* Available online. URL: http://histo ryworld.org/beginnings_of_north_european_exp.htm. Accessed October 31, 2006.

[23] "Barbados." *World Fact Book.* Washington, D.C.: U.S. Central Intelligence Agency, October 17, 2006.

[24] "Beginnings of North European Expansion." *International World History Project: World History from the Pre-Sumerican Period to the Present.* Available online. URL: http:// historyworld.org/beginnings_of_north_european_exp.htm. Accessed October 31, 2006.

[25] *World Economic and Social Survey 2004: International Migration.* New York: United Nations Department of Economic and Social Affairs, 2004.

[26] *World Economic and Social Survey 2004: International Migration.* New York: United Nations Department of Economic and Social Affairs, 2004.

[27] BBC News Online. *Waring over Canaries Migration.* January 20, 2007. Available online. URL: http://news.bbc.co.uk/1/hi/uk/6281167.stm. Accessed April 17, 2007.

[28] "Towards Development-Friendly Migration Policies and Programmes: Some Concrete Examples from European Member States." Report. Conference on Migration and Development, Brussels, Belgium, March 15–16, 2006. Available online. URL: http://www.iom .int/jahia/webdav/site/myjahiasite/shared/shared/mainsite/policy_and_research/research/ CMD15160306.pdf. Accessed April 17, 2007.

[29] Maruja M. B. Asis. "The Philippines' Culture of Migration." *Migration Information Source.* Washington, D.C.: Migration Policy Institute, January 2006.

[30] Michael Marizco. "Abandonment. Plenty of Jobs, Not Enough Pay: Economic Forces Push Mexican Workers North." *High Country News,* May 15, 2006, p. 4.

[31] Kathleen Newland. "Migration as a Factor in Development of Poverty Reduction." *Migration Information Source.* Washington, D.C.: Migration Policy Institute, June 1, 2003.

[32] George Nishiyama. "Philippines Health Care Paralyzed by Nurses Exodus." *Reuters,* February 28, 2006.

[33] "Immigration of Doctors and Nurses Two-Edged." Press Release, University of Illinois Extension, Dekalb, May 30, 2006.

[34] "Exodus of Medical Staff Continues." *The Mercury (South Africa),* August 10, 2004.

[35] Kader Asmal. "South Africa's Brain Drain Dilemma." *BBC News,* April 19, 2004.

[36] "Immigration of Doctors and Nurses Two-Edged." Press Release, University of Illinois Extension, Dekalb, May 30, 2006.

[37] Julia Preston. "Pickers Are Few, and Growers Blame Congress." *New York Times,* September 22, 2006.

[38] "Raids Cause Migrant Worker Shortage, Michigan Farmers Say." *Detroit News,* October 20, 2006.

[39] *World Economic and Social Survey 2004: International Migration.* New York: United Nations Department of Economic and Social Affairs, 2004.

[40] *World Economic and Social Survey 2004: International Migration.* New York: United Nations Department of Economic and Social Affairs, 2004.

[41] Kathleen Moore. "Islam: Europe Grapples with the Veil." Radio Free Europe/Radio Liberty, October 18, 2006.

[42] Craig S. Smith and Ariane Bernard. "Angry Immigrants Embroil France in Wider Riots." *New York Times,* November 5, 2005.

[43] Eduardo Porter. "Housing Slump Takes a Toll on Illegal Immigrants." *New York Times,* April 17, 2007.

[44] Marcelo M. Orozco-Suárez. "Stranger Anxieties: U.S. Immigration and Its Discontents." *Harvard International Review,* July 30, 2006.

[45] Marcelo M. Orozco-Suárez. "Stranger Anxieties: U.S. Immigration and Its Discontents." *Harvard International Review,* July 30, 2006.

2

Focus on the United States

With its long history of immigration and migration, the United States is known worldwide as a social melting pot built by immigrants. The first explorers who came to the New World from Europe in the late 15th and early 16th centuries opened a floodgate for the immigration that would soon follow. Whether they came to escape religious persecution, wars, poverty, in search of jobs and other opportunities, or to join family and friends who had already immigrated to America, new immigrants came by the millions. The first census in the United States, completed in 1790, listed nearly 5 million foreign-born residents. Between 1820 and 1930 some 60 percent of the world's total immigrants arrived in the United States, and data indicates that from 1820 to 1975 more than 47 million people immigrated to the United States. The trend of immigration to the United States has continued and increased in the 21st century. According to the Center for Immigration Studies, in 2005 foreign-born people living in the United States constituted slightly more than 12 percent of the population, or 35.2 million people. Further, based on the 2005 U.S. Census Bureau's Current Population Survey about 7.9 million people immigrated to the United States between 2000 and 2005, which was "the highest five-year period of immigration on record."[1]

Topics discussed in this chapter include: where immigrants to the United States have come from historically; why they come; why some immigrants come to America illegally; the economic, social, and cultural impact immigrants have on America; and how the U.S. government has managed immigration through policies and laws. Also discussed is emigration from the United States, the flipside of immigration, including why Americans choose to leave the country and where they go when they emigrate.

HISTORICAL BACKGROUND

First Immigrants

When the first Europeans set foot on American soil, rather than finding only unpopulated lands boasting pristine forests and sparkling rivers, they were greeted by people who some scholars suggest may have arrived in North America somewhere between 60,000 to 35,000 years ago; the oldest officially documented Indian cultures in North America date back to about 15,000 B.C.E.[2] These first immigrants to North America are believed to have traveled to the new land during the last ice age across a land bridge from northeastern Siberia into Alaska. The name *Indian* came into use when explorer Christopher Columbus landed in North America and thought he had arrived in India. By the time the first European settlers arrived in North America there were an estimated 10 million Native Americans living in communities that reached from north of present-day Mexico into Alaska. As more and more Europeans immigrated to and settled in the New World the indigenous population suffered the consequences. Native Americans caught and died from diseases carried by the colonists, such as small pox and measles, for which they had no natural immunity, and they lost their lands when the colonists claimed the country for their own. By 1890, the first year that the U.S. census officially counted American Indians, the Native American population had decreased to 325,464 people. Most also had been forced off their lands and were living on reservations in the West.

Early Settlements and the Colonial Period

THE ENGLISH

From the youngest ages American children are taught stories of the hardy and adventurous souls who braved all odds to climb aboard the English ship the *Mayflower* and cross the ocean to reach the untamed shores of America. Known as Pilgrims, America's first immigrants from England came by way of Holland and arrived in Plymouth, Massachusetts, in 1620. But English immigrants began arriving in America more than 30 years before the Pilgrims. In 1584 explorers dispatched by Sir Walter Raleigh (1552–1618) reached the outer islands of North Carolina. Impressed with Raleigh's journeys and his discoveries, Queen Elizabeth (r. 1558–1603) gave Raleigh ownership of all the lands he could occupy in the New World and she named the whole of the new land Virginia in honor of the Virgin Queen. Raleigh enlisted 100 men, including soldiers, craftsmen, and scholars, to build a settlement and a fort on one of North Carolina's outer banks islands, Roanoke Island. By 1586 the fort and settlement were abandoned when the men's supplies ran low, Native

Americans occupying the area grew hostile, and other problems made staying on the island almost impossible. Undeterred by the setbacks of the earlier immigrants to the New World, 117 men, women, and children emigrated from England to Roanoke Island in 1587 to establish a permanent colony, The Cittie of Raleigh, near the site of the original settlement. But the entire colony disappeared within three years, leaving behind the remnants of their settlement and a mystery about what happened to the colonists that endures today.[3] Despite the mysterious disappearance of the Roanoke Island colonists and failed earlier attempts by the English to immigrate to the New World, a group of 108 intrepid English settlers set sail from London in 1606 for the New World to establish a settlement in Virginia. Under the leadership of Captain John Smith (1580–1631), the immigrants landed on Jamestown Island in 1607 and established the Virginia English colony along the banks of the James River in the Chesapeake Bay region of Virginia.[4] While the Roanoke Island colonists, the Jamestown settlers, and the Pilgrims can be counted among America's early immigrants, and perhaps the best known, they were not the first Europeans to reach America's shores.

THE SPANISH

About 70 years before the arrival of the English in America Spanish explorer Juan Ponce de León (1460–1521) forged a path for Spanish people wishing to immigrate to the New World when he reached America in 1513. Ponce de León named his landing place on the Atlantic coast La Florida in honor of the Spanish name for the Easter season, *pascua florida*.[5] Like some of the first English immigrants' attempts to settle America, Ponce de León's attempts to establish a colony of Spanish immigrants in La Florida in 1521 failed, but that did not deter future immigrants from leaving Spain for the New World. The first Spanish immigrants settled at St. Augustine, Florida, in 1565.[6] The Spanish established a Jesuit mission in the Chesapeake Bay region of Virginia in 1570, 37 years prior to the arrival of Captain Smith and the establishment of Jamestown in 1607. Spanish migrants also traveled inland and reached the Appalachian Mountains, the Mississippi River, the Grand Canyon, and the Great Plains within 30 years of Ponce de León's arrival. During the period from 1528 to 1536 a group of Spanish explorers journeyed across the continent from Florida to California. Under the leadership of Francisco Vázquez de Coronado (1510–54) in 1540 Spanish and Mexican Indians crossed into the present-day United States in the area that is now the border between Arizona and Mexico and made their way into the region that is now central Kansas. In 1598 Juan de Oñate (1550–1630) founded the first successful long-term European settlement in New Mexico at San Juan de los Caballeros, nearly a decade before the English founded their first permanent settlement at Jamestown, Virginia. Historians believe Spanish immigrants established a colony at Santa Fe, New Mexico, about the same time (1607–08) that the English settled Jamestown. Spanish immigrants also established settlements in San Diego, California (1602), San Antonio, Texas (1691), and Tucson, Arizona (1699).[7] By the mid-1600s the Spanish in America numbered more than 400,000.

THE FRENCH

In the years between 1534 and 1542 French explorer Jacques Cartier (1491–1557) traveled to the shores of North America three times. Cartier established the first French colonies in North America in 1550 near Beaufort, South Carolina, and Jacksonville, Florida. Around that time the French also claimed a colonial territory they named Acadie that encompassed the entire northeastern section of North America, reaching from eastern Quebec in Canada, into what is now New England and as far south as Philadelphia. In 1588 King Henry III (r. 1574–89) began financing French colonization in North America by issuing fur-trading monopolies to French citizens willing to immigrate to the New World and establish settlements there. Pierre du Gua de Mons (1560–1630), who received one of the trading monopolies, sailed with 120 French settlers to North America in 1604. The new immigrants established a colony near the St. Croix River in what is now Maine. Due to illness and hardships caused by harsh winter weather the colony relocated to Port-Royal in what is now Nova Scotia. The attempt at colonization failed, in part because Pierre du Gua de Mons's fur-trading monopoly was revoked, and in 1607 the struggling immigrants returned to France. A new group of French immigrants attempted to resettle Port-Royal in 1610 and additional French settlers established a second colony in 1613 at St. Sauveur, also in what is now Maine. Within one year English colonists from Virginia had destroyed both of the French settlements, but the settlements were returned to the French through a treaty with the English in 1632. By 1650 there were more than 400 French immigrants living in the area.[8] By the time of the Revolutionary War (1775–83) some 70,000 French immigrants had arrived to settle in Louisiana, the Mississippi Valley, the area of the Great Lakes, and farther north in Canada.

THE GERMANS

Other Europeans who emigrated from their homelands to settle in America during the period from 1600 to 1700 included German Mennonites who settled in Pennsylvania in 1683 and established a colony, Germantown, outside of Philadelphia. Protestant Germans, such as Anabaptists and Calvinists, settled in southeastern Pennsylvania and northern Virginia. An estimated 150,000 Germans immigrated to North America during this period, many of them as indentured servants.[9] Other groups of Germans emigrated to escape the consequences of various wars—including the Thirty Years' War (1618–48) and the War of the Spanish Succession (1702–14)—as well as poverty, starvation, and illness. An estimated 150,000 Germans arrived during the colonial period and by 1775 German immigrants and their descendants made up approximately 10 percent of the population of the English North American colonies.

THE AFRICANS

Perhaps one of the largest groups of early immigrants—nearly 12 million Africans—began arriving in North America in the 1500s, first as colonists with the Spanish and then as unwilling slaves.[10] It is noted in *The Peopling of America* that an African captained one of Columbus's ships during his first voyage to the Americas and a Spanish effort to establish a colony in North Carolina in 1526 ultimately failed after the African colonists in the group fled to establish homes with the Native Americans living in the region. However, the status of Africans as free colonists soon changed and the nearly 12 million Africans who immigrated to North America from the mid-16th century into the 19th century were forced immigrants, brought to the new land against their will as slaves by English, French, Dutch, Spanish, and Portuguese traders.

THE SCOTS-IRISH

Scots-Irish, people from Scotland who had settled in Ireland, began emigrating from Northern Ireland to the United States in large numbers around 1718. By 1790 more than 320,000 had arrived. The first group of Scots-Irish immigrants settled in Boston, and, as more came, they made their homes in New Hampshire, Pennsylvania, Virginia, and the Carolinas. Most of those who came to America did so willingly, many to escape poverty and religious persecution, but others were prisoners in Ireland who were deported while some came as indentured servants and others, who were serving in the British army, chose to remain in the colonies rather than return home.[11]

The Revolutionary and Civil War Periods

Historically, periods of war and economic declines in America led to significant downturns in the number of people immigrating to America. Immigration slowed and then went into a decline during and following the Revolutionary War (1775–83), but it resumed and continued increasing at a steady pace beginning in the mid-1800s. Among those who arrived in the post–Revolutionary War period were immigrants from Ireland, who came by the thousands fleeing the effects of famine and poverty in their homeland. In addition, immigrants from England, Germany, and southern and eastern European nations continued to arrive in search of jobs and a better life.

IRISH IMMIGRANTS

Unlike the Scots-Irish who began immigrating to the United States in the mid-1700s, Irish immigration to the United States did not begin until almost 100 years later in the 1800s. The mass emigration was attributed to the country's changing politics and economics. After 1815 at the end of the Napoleonic Wars, Ireland's population was burgeoning, which led to job shortages and rampant poverty. Circumstances for many Irish citizens, especially rural peasants, were aggravated by the Irish Potato Famine, which began in 1845 and continued for six years, causing the starvation deaths of more than a million impoverished Irish peasants. Additional millions, including poor tenant farmers without the financial resources to pay their landlords, had no alternative but to emigrate to avoid starvation and to find work. Religious persecution by Protestants against Ireland's Catholics pushed others to emigrate. In the 1840s approximately 2 million Irish immigrants arrived in the United States in search of work, improved economic conditions, and religious freedom.[12]

During the decade of 1840 to 1850 most immigrants who flocked to America settled in New York City. According to statistics, New York City had 200,000 residents in 1830. Within 20 years that number had jumped to over 500,000 and 10 years later in 1860 the city had a population of over 1 million with more than half of those residents being immigrants.[13]

SOUTHERN AND EASTERN EUROPEAN IMMIGRANTS

Following the Civil War (1861–65) America needed workers to fill jobs created by the country's growing economy and its move toward industrialization. Although large numbers of immigrants continued to arrive from England, Ireland, Germany, and Scandinavia, by the 1880s the majority of new immigrants were arriving from the southern and eastern European nations of Italy, Austria-Hungary, Poland, Greece, and Russia. While the Irish immigrants arriving before the Civil War were poverty-stricken, many of the earlier immigrants arriving before and after the Civil War from Europe were educated and possessed some financial resources. However, the later immigrants arriving from southern and eastern Europe were as a rule poor and uneducated. Without the resources to buy land for farming these later immigrants settled in large cities and sought out employment in factories. By 1890, a majority of the populations in large American cities were foreign-born, including 87 percent of Chicago's population, 80 percent of New York's population, and 84 percent of the populations in Detroit and Milwaukee.[14]

ASIAN IMMIGRANTS

The Chinese were the first Asian immigrants to arrive in the United States. While their numbers were small in the beginning, the discovery of gold in California in 1848 prompted a large number of Chinese to immigrate to the country in search of work. By 1851 an estimated 25,000 Chinese immigrants were working in California, and another 30,000 were working as laborers and in service trades in states outside of California.

Another group of Asian immigrants, those from Japan, began migrating to Hawaii in search of work in the island nation's booming sugar industry. From 1885 and continuing through 1894 more than 28,000 Japanese immigrated to Hawaii. By 1899 Hawaii's plantation owners had brought in an additional 26,000 Japanese contract laborers.

An 1882 treaty between the United States and Korea opened the door for immigration from that Asian country, but only small numbers of Koreans immigrated at that time. Large-scale immigration by Koreans did not begin until 1903, when 100 Korean immigrants arrived in Hawaii to work on the sugar plantations. By 1905 more than 7,000 Korean immigrants were in Hawaii. Most Korean immigrants left Hawaii by 1908 and returned to their homeland, leaving an estimated 2,000 behind. Of those, some 1,000 moved to the American mainland to work in California's rice fields.

Prior to World War I, emigration from Asian nations to the United States was curtailed and ultimately stopped for a variety of reasons. Beginning in 1882, rising complaints by American citizens and other immigrant groups that the Chinese were taking jobs and depressing wages led the government to pass laws that closed the door to immigration from China and banned Chinese immigrants from entering the United States. This Chinese Exclusion Act was the first law to deny entry to the United States on the basis of race. Annexation of the Hawaiian Islands by the United States in 1898 and the "Gentleman's Agreement" between the United States and Japan in 1908 ended immigration from Japan to the United States. Moreover, in 1905 the Korean government, under pressure by Japan's government, ended the emigration of Koreans to Hawaii. The U.S. government passed legislation in 1917 that created what became known as the "Asiatic Barred Zone." All migration to the United States by Asians and non-Asian born descendants of Asians was prohibited by the legislation.

World War I

After the United States entered World War I in 1919 immigration dropped, due in part to the U.S. government's increasingly restrictive immigration policies that established quotas on who could come to America and from where. Even though immigrants from southern and eastern European nations, including Russia, Poland, and Italy, were welcomed in America following the Civil War, they were among those excluded or restricted by policy from immigrating to the United States at this time. Also because of the war, immigrants from the Asian Pacific Triangle nations, including Japan, the

Philippines, India, and Korea, were excluded from the United States. In addition, the ongoing restrictions toward immigrants from China, also an Asian Pacific Triangle nation, that began in 1870 continued and effectively prohibited emigration from that country.[15]

MEXICAN IMMIGRANTS

The largest number of immigrants during World War I came to the United States from Mexico. Based on statistical data, between 1911 and 1929 an estimated 1 million Mexican refugees migrated across the border into the United States to escape the Mexican Revolution. The timing was perfect. The United States was suffering through a labor shortage due to the military draft taking American men to fight overseas, and Mexican workers stepped in to fill jobs in mining, agriculture, manufacturing, and on the railroads.

For many Mexican immigrants at that time their stay in the United States was only temporary. Most returned to their homeland in the 1930s, including at least 100,000 who returned willingly to Mexico during the Great Depression and another 400,000 who were deported by the U.S. government when jobs became scarce.[16] Some of those deported included U.S. citizens.

JEWISH IMMIGRANTS

Despite fluctuations in immigrants arriving on its shores, the United States received 60 percent of all immigrants worldwide from 1820 through 1930, including more than 2 million Jews who immigrated to the United States from Russia, Poland, Galicia, and Romania, as well as Turkey and Syria beginning in 1880 to escape religious oppression. Jewish refugees continued to arrive in America until 1924 when the U.S. government adopted a policy of restricting immigration.

The Great Depression and World War II

Immigration remained at low levels through the Great Depression (1930s) and World War II (1939–45), except for large numbers of immigrants arriving from Mexico. Similar to the situation in World War I, during World War II millions of men signed on for military service and America needed workers to fill jobs. Migrant workers from Mexico once again stepped in to meet the need. Mexican immigrants aside, during World War II U.S. doors were not generally open to immigrants. In 1939 the U.S. quota for Germans wishing to immigrate was set at 27,370, but a year earlier 300,000 Germans, mostly Jewish refugees, applied for permits to enter the country. Just 20,000 entry permits were approved. The government quotas were supported by public sentiment. Opinion polls in 1938 indicated that 82 percent of Americans were opposed to admitting large numbers of Jewish refugees. American paranoia during the war, including fears that spies and other undesirables would enter the country as immigrants, led the U.S. government to impose tighter immigration restrictions, further limiting immigration at that time.[17] But at the end of World War II immigration to the United States took an upswing and has continued to climb ever since.

Modern Immigration

ASIAN AND LATIN AMERICAN IMMIGRANTS

In the 1960s immigrants arriving from European nations declined while those from Asia and Latin America increased in numbers. Asian immigrants accounted for 28 percent of the total number of immigrants arriving in the United States from 1966 to 1979. Immigrants from the Philippines numbered about 6,000 in 1965 but jumped to more than 41,000 in 1979. The rapid increase in Filipino immigrants as well as those from other Asian and Latin American nations was driven by wars, failing economies, and political instabilities in those regions. Changes to U.S. immigration policy in 1965, including abolishing the nation-of-origin quota system, also opened the door to increased immigration from non-European nations.

IMMIGRANTS FROM INDOCHINA

Emigration from Indochina increased beginning in 1965 as well. A total of 130,000 Vietnamese refugees fled to America in 1975 following withdrawal of the U.S. military from South Vietnam and the collapse of its capital city Saigon at the end of the Vietnam War. This first wave of refugees from Vietnam continued through 1977 and was comprised primarily of military and government officials who had worked for the U.S. government during the war and their families. Chinese, Cambodians, and Laotians also immigrated to the United States at that time due to growing pressures on their homelands by Vietnam's government. Known as boat people, nearly 268,000 refugees from Cambodia, Laos, and Vietnam entered the United States between 1978 and 1980.[18] By 1985 Indochinese accounted for more than 700,000 immigrants to the United States.

CUBAN IMMIGRANTS

When Fidel Castro's (1926–) revolutionaries overthrew the regime of Fulgencio Batista (1901–73) in 1959 some 200,000 Cubans refugees, most of them highly educated members of that nation's middle class, immigrated to the United States to escape the Cuban government's shift to communism. An additional 360,000 Cuban refugees followed in 1965 when the Cuban government granted them permission to leave. Between 1980 and 1981 Cuba's government allowed another 130,000 refugees in the "Mariel group," named for their departure point, the Port of Mariel, Cuba, to immigrate to the United States. Most arrived in boats, earning the mass movement of Cuban refugees the name "Mariel boatlift."

MEXICAN IMMIGRANTS

After 1965 one of the largest group of immigrants came to the United States from Mexico. Almost 38,000 Mexican immigrants arrived in 1965 and by 1978 that number had increased to more than 92,000 annually. During the decade of 1976 to 1986 approximately 720,000 Mexicans immigrated to the United States to escape poverty in their homeland and to search for work in America's agricultural and manufacturing industries.

In 2000 the U.S. Census listed the top 10 countries of birth of immigrants and the number of immigrants from each country residing in the United States, as well as the projected growth in immigration by 2010. The largest increase in immigrants, 23.7 percent, is predicted to come from Mexico. It is expected that 9.6 million Mexican immigrants will be living in the United States by 2010. Other projected increases and the number of immigrants from each country living in the United States in 2010 include:

TOP 10 COUNTRIES OF ORIGIN FOR U.S. IMMIGRATION

COUNTRY OF ORIGIN	NUMBER OF IMMIGRANTS RESIDING IN THE UNITED STATES, 2000	PROJECTED NUMBER OF IMMIGRANTS, 2010	PROJECTED INCREASE, 2000–2010
Mexico	7,800,000	9,600,000	23.7 percent
China	1,400,000	1,900,000	4.7 percent
Philippines	1,200,000	1,700,000	4.2 percent
India	1,000,000	1,600,000	4.0 percent
Cuba	952,000	1,100,000	2.7 percent
Vietnam	863,000	1,200,000	3.0 percent
El Salvador	765,000	1,100,000	2.7 percent
Korea	701,000	880,000	2.2 percent
Dominican Republic	692,000	941,000	2.3 percent
Canada	678,000	920,000	2.3 percent

Source: U. S. Census, 2000

WHY IMMIGRANTS COME TO THE UNITED STATES

Although the reasons people choose to immigrate to the United States can be as diverse as the people themselves, generally people immigrate for only a few reasons: religious freedom, economic opportunity, and political stability. Other reasons include escaping areas damaged by natural disasters, such as floods, earthquakes, or volcanoes, and reuniting with family members who emigrated at an earlier time.

Religious Freedom

The Reformation, a religious movement that began in the early 1500s in Europe, was fueled by protests against the doctrines and corruption in the Roman Catholic Church at that time. Christianity ultimately splintered into two groups, Catholic and Protestant. The Reformation itself was characterized by great diversity of opinion and included groups such as Lutherans, Reformed, Anglicans, and radicals.

As a result of this split in Western Christianity, which led to religious wars and persecutions across Europe, the Pilgrims and French and German Protestants were among the first groups of people who immigrated to America in search of religious freedom. The Pilgrims left England after Queen Elizabeth I organized the Church of England and proclaimed Anglicanism the only religion of the country. Unwilling to conform to the new Anglican religious order and abandon their Calvinist faith, the people became religious dissenters known as Separatist Puritans. Tired of suffering persecution by the Anglicans, one group of Separatists, who had taken the name Pilgrims in reference to their "idea of life on earth as a pilgrimage towards heavenly bliss,"[19] left England in 1609. The emigrating Pilgrims' first stop after leaving England was Holland where they found more tolerance for different religious beliefs. But Separatist Pilgrims did not believe the Dutch showed sufficient respect for the Sabbath and they feared absorption into Dutch society. They immigrated to America where they could practice their faith freely.[20]

Religious persecution was severe in Germany in the 1600s as well and many members of German Protestant sects, such as Mennonites, immigrated to America. Much as the Pilgrims before them had immigrated to Holland prior to their final move to America, Germans first fled to England, joining the large numbers of Germans who had established homes and businesses in Great Britain beginning in the 1400s. By 1700 there were four German churches in London and a German population in that city totaling as many as 15,000. But the increasing numbers of Germans in London was followed by increased persecution,[21] and stress on that country's infrastructure caused by the large influx of German immigrants led Queen Anne (r. 1685–1714) to fund ships and supplies for Germans willing to immigrate to America.

In France, Protestants known as Huguenots grew rapidly and members became targets of persecution by Catholics. In 1594 King Henry IV granted political and religious rights to the Huguenots, but in 1685 King Louis XIV revoked those rights. The loss of their religious freedom and political rights caused thousands of French Huguenots to immigrate to North America.

The rise of Nazi Germany in the 1930s forced many to flee and seek refuge in other countries, including the United States. Between 1938 and 1939 some 85,000 Jewish refugees arrived in America. However, the United States's restrictive immigration policies at that time prohibited more Jews from entering the country. In 1939, the U.S. government refused entry to 900 Jewish refugees, forcing them to return to Europe where many ultimately died in Nazi concentration camps.

Political Stability

In the 1800s another large wave of German immigrants came to the United States. Most came in search of political asylum in 1848 following the failure of the German revolutions. More Germans, predominately Jews, homosexuals, Social Democrats, and other dissidents, immigrated in the years 1933 to 1945 to escape persecution during the Nazi regime.[22] Eastern Europeans displaced after World War II, including 205,000 people and 17,000 orphans who were unable or unwilling to return to their countries, immigrated to the United States in 1948. Many of the displaced persons were survivors of Nazi concentration camps, laborers forced to work in German factories or farms, and those fleeing communism.[23]

After 1965 the face of immigration changed. As the politics of European countries stabilized fewer immigrants were coming to the United States from Europe and more were coming from Asia and Latin America, where many countries were in political turmoil. Just as European immigrants after World War II were displaced persons or refugees, so too were many of the immigrants arriving in the United States from Asia and Latin America. Since Fidel Castro's rise to power in Cuba in 1959 about 1 million Cuban refugees have fled the country, and 300,000 of those have settled in Miami, Florida.

Following the fall of Saigon at the end of the Vietnam War in 1975 nearly 130,000 Vietnamese refugees immigrated to the United States. As communism continued to spread through Southeast Asia thousands more refugees from that region immigrated to the United States in search of asylum. The sometimes clandestine U.S. wars against the Sandinistas in Nicaragua and the guerrillas in El Salvador and Guatemala drove people from those regions to emigrate in search of safety from the violence in their homelands.

The Soviet invasion of Afghanistan (1979–89) forced thousands of refugees to flee, with many coming to America. The rise of the Taliban in 1996 increased the outflow of refugees. Although it is difficult to estimate the number of Afghans now living in the United States, according to U.S. Immigration and Naturalization Service estimates, in 2002 the numbers had reached 60,000 or more.

During the first Persian Gulf War (1990–91) and continuing through 2002, some 32,000 Iraqis were given refuge in the United States. Following the U.S. invasion of Iraq in 2003 more displaced Iraqis looked to the United States for refuge from the war. Despite that, the U.S. government set an annual quota of 500 for immigrants from Iraq, severely limiting the number who could come to America and forcing them to flee to other countries. As the war continued in 2007, the U.S. government changed its position on refugees from Iraq, lifting the quota and agreeing to accept 7,000 refugees in a resettlement program.

Economic Opportunities

Early immigrants to America also came for economic reasons. The Pilgrims were struggling financially and slipping into poverty due to a difficult labor market in Holland. The Jamestown colonists had instructions from King James I not only to colonize Virginia but also to "find gold and a water route to the Orient."[24] Spanish explorer Francisco Vásquez de Coronado made his 1540 journey as far into America as Kansas in search of the "fabled riches" in the New Land that he had heard about, and the Spanish established St. Augustine on the coast of Florida in 1565 as a fort to protect ships sailing to Spain laden with treasures discovered in America. Among the first French immigrants were those planning to establish what was believed to be lucrative fur-trading monopolies in the New World.

After the Civil War and continuing into the mid-1900s most immigrants to the United States were described as economic migrants. Many of the new immigrants were poor and uneducated and the United States, with its rapid industrialization and expanding economy, was seen as a land of opportunity. Business growth in America created jobs for which there was a limited supply of native-born American workers. Immigrants, approximately 25 million between 1866 and 1915, provided a badly needed labor force in the cities.[25] America's westward expansion also created work opportunities for immigrants. Chinese and Irish immigrants working as laborers are credited with building the Central Pacific and Union Pacific Railroads, which crossed the continent in 1869. Mexican immigrants worked as laborers on farms and for the railroads, particularly in California.

But not all immigrants arriving in the United States were poor, uneducated, unskilled laborers. Some who left their countries for economic reasons were skilled professionals or craftsmen who took advantage of opportunities in America and used their expertise to start businesses of their own. Amadeo Gianni (1870–1949), a second-generation immigrant who was born in America but whose parents had emigrated from Italy, opened the Bank of Italy in San Francisco in 1904. Despite the devastation of the 1906 San Francisco earthquake, Gianni's bank thrived, boasting several branch offices by 1916. He became a leader in the city's banking community and in 1928 Gianni's Bank of Italy merged with the Bank of America, Los Angeles. The institution's name became Bank of America and today it is the largest commercial bank in the United States.

German piano maker Heinrich Steinweg (1797–1871) immigrated to the United States with his family in 1850 when instabilities in his homeland began to negatively impact his business. Some three years later, in 1853, Steinweg and his sons launched a piano manufacturing business in the United States under their Americanized name, Steinway. The first Steinway and Sons grand piano was presented to the White House in 1903.

Another German, Adolphus Busch (1839–1913), immigrated to join members of his family in the United States in 1857. He brought with him a college education and a desire to succeed. Although he owned and operated a successful wholesale business, following his marriage to Lily Anheuser he went to work in his father-in-law's business, the E. Anheuser & Co. brewery. The company became known as Anheuser-Busch and the rest is American beer-brewing history.

Other immigrants started businesses ranging from restaurants offering foods from an immigrant's homeland to barber shops, retail establishments, repair shops, construction companies, and more.

In the 1960s, when new policies created a more favorable climate for immigrants, an increasing number of immigrants coming to the United States were skilled urban professionals from India, the Philippines, and South Africa who were encouraged by the U.S. government to come and fill jobs going unfilled due to a shortage of American professionals.

Despite an increase in highly skilled immigrants arriving in the United States to fill jobs, Mexicans remained the largest group of immigrants coming to the United States in search of work after 1965. An estimated 60,000 Mexican workers, most of them unskilled, arrived annually during the 1970s. According to statistics, employment opportunities increased by

645,000 jobs in Los Angeles County, California, in the 1970s with about 22,000 of the available positions filled by Mexicans who were in the country both legally and illegally.[26] Problems in Mexico during the 1980s, such as the collapse of oil prices and devaluation of the Mexican peso, drove even more Mexicans to immigrate to America for jobs. A defining moment in economic immigration from Mexico occurred in 1994 when the North American Free Trade Agreement (NAFTA) took effect. The agreement, while intended to be beneficial, eventually caused an economic crisis in Mexico that included a stock market crash in that country and further devaluation of the peso. As Mexican businesses and farms failed thousands of rural peasants abandoned their communities and flocked to America in search of work.[27]

In the 2000s, the United States continued to struggle with shortages of professionals to work in fields such as technology, medicine, and teaching, causing the country to look beyond its borders to find people to fill the jobs. Many of the new immigrants responding to America's call for workers were nurses, teachers, technology experts, and other educated professionals enticed to immigrate to the United States by the promise of much higher wages than they could earn in the countries they left behind.

HOW THE UNITED STATES BENEFITS FROM IMMIGRATION

Over the course of history the impact of immigration on the United States has had positive and negative consequences, sometimes both at the same time. Immigrants helped solve problems, such as building the population and providing a labor force, but they created problems as the population or labor force outgrew cities and available jobs.

Unskilled Workers

In the 1600s, when the number of immigrants was small, averaging about 6,000 annually, newcomers were welcomed with open arms by the settlers who had established colonies in the New World. An estimated 950,000 immigrants arrived in America over the 130-year period from the 1600s through the years prior to the 1790 census, increasing the country's population to 3.9 million.[28] By 1850 the population had increased to 23 million.[29] The early immigrants provided an unskilled workforce to harvest crops, work as servants, staff factories, build railroads, work in the mines, and more. Continuing into the mid-1900s and through the present unskilled workers have been in demand to fill factory, construction, and service jobs such as hotel services that native-born American workers typically will not do.

As increasing numbers of America's baby boomers reach their 60s unskilled immigrants may be needed to fill another low-paying job that many Americans do not want to do: caring for the United States's aging population. In 2006, according to a *Wall Street Journal* report, "Immigrants, whether legal or undocumented, make up a disproportionate share of those who care for the elderly—and the need for such workers is set to explode in the coming years."[30] The U.S. Department of Health and Human Services noted that in 2000 the workforce of people caring for America's elderly was 1.9 million. By 2050 more than 5 million workers will be required to meet the need. Noting the value of immigrants to fill unskilled jobs in nursing homes and other elder-care institutions, the American Health Care Association and the National Association for Home Care lobbied Congress "for a new visa that they hoped would annually admit 400,000 low-skilled workers—the grist of the home-care field."[31]

Highly Skilled Immigrants and Brain Gain

In addition to low-skilled laborers, highly educated and skilled professionals were also needed to make up for labor shortages in America's workforce. Beginning as early as the 1950s U.S. businesses benefited from the brain gain resulting from the growing number of highly skilled immigrants filling jobs in health care, teaching, and technology. The U.S. government implemented Medicare in 1965, leading to a shortage of health care professionals to meet the program's requirements. As a result, America began looking beyond its borders to fill medical positions. In a nine-year period between 1965 and 1974 approximately 75,000 foreign-born physicians immigrated to the United States to fill jobs. More than 13,000 medical professionals from Korea, primarily nurses, also immigrated to the United States at that time in search of work, and by 1974 there were more than 10,000 Filipina nurses working in the United States.[32] To further encourage professionals to come to America, in 2000 the U.S. government increased its quota on highly skilled professionals wishing to immigrate for employment from 115,000 to 195,000, with the new level in effect until 2003.

Economic Benefits

Based on statistics from the U.S. Congressional Budget Office, immigrants are vital to the American economy. In 2005 immigrants comprised 12 percent of the total U.S. population, but they accounted for 14 percent of the country's workers. In the decade from 1994 to 2004 "the number of foreign born workers grew to 21 million from 13 million, a rise that accounted for more than half of the growth of the U.S. labor force."[33] A study by the American Immigration Lawyers Association found that 40 percent of farming, fishing, and forestry jobs; 33 percent of building and grounds maintenance jobs; and 22 percent of food preparation and construction jobs were held by immigrants.[34] In addition, immigrants, both legal and illegal, contribute to the national tax coffers as well as the tax receipts in the communities where they live. Immigrants pay sales tax on goods purchased and income and payroll taxes on job earnings. A Public Broadcasting System *In the Mix* program, "Teen Immigrants, Five American Stories," reported that while immigrants collect about $5 billion in welfare annually, "immigrants collectively earn $240 billion a year, [and] pay $90 billion a year in taxes."[35] Illegal aliens who get jobs with fraudulent Social Security numbers also pay income tax, but they do not collect Social Security payments. It was reported in 2006 that since the 1980s the value of unclaimed Social Security taxes has more than doubled to about $189 billion.[36]

Cultural and Social Benefits

Although the United States has encouraged immigrants to assimilate into the communities where they settle, historically the country also has embraced the cultural contributions newcomers make. Consider the variety of ethnic foods now available in America because immigrants introduced favorite foods from their homeland to American appetites. The National Restaurant Association study reported that in the year 2000 Italian, Mexican, and Chinese food had "become so ingrained in American culture that they are no longer foreign to the American palate."[37] Holidays from the homelands of immigrants have been integrated into the broader American culture as well. For example *Cinco de Mayo,* celebrating the victory of Mexican soldiers over the French army in 1862, and St. Patrick's Day, honoring the patron saint of Ireland, are national holidays in Mexico and Ireland, respectively, but both are widely celebrated in the United States by people of all ethnic backgrounds. December in the United States sees multiethnic celebrations that include Christmas (Christian), Hanukkah (Jewish), and Kwanzaa (African American).

PROBLEMS ASSOCIATED WITH IMMIGRATION

Early Immigration

Most of the population growth in the United States from the first census in 1790 through 1820 occurred internally, that is, due to a high birth rate among people who had been in the country for generations rather than to the arrival of people from outside the country; perhaps as a result there were few conflicts among immigrant groups and native-born residents.[38] However, as war with France threatened in 1798 the federal government passed its first laws related to immigration, allowing the government to deport aliens suspected of being dangerous to the country's peace. Between 1820 and 1850 immigration to the United States exploded, climbing from a total of approximately 60,000 immigrants through the 1820s to a total of 1.7 million living in the country by the 1850s. Along with the influx of immigrants came problems, such as periods of nativism—the belief that new immigrants would undermine the accepted way of life in America—leading to racism and discrimination against groups of immigrants. After 1850 the cities where many of the immigrants settled became overcrowded, public services were strained, and native-born citizens, who once welcomed immigrant laborers, complained that newcomers were taking jobs and, because they were willing to work for little money, were depressing wages. Other problems increased, such as discrimination or prejudice against immigrants who had trouble adopting the language, culture, and social ways of America.

An influx of Chinese immigrants after 1850 led to a rise in racial tensions, particularly in California, as they vied for jobs with native-born Americans and European immigrants. As visible minorities, they suffered from racism as well as nativism. Since they were prohibited from becoming citizens, the Chinese made little effort to assimilate, planning to eventually return to China once their financial position had improved. Thus they often maintained the customs, style of dress, and other practices from their homeland. Animosity toward, and discrimination of, Chinese became so virulent that the federal government passed the Chinese Exclusion Act in 1882 forbidding immigration of Chinese.[39] The act only served to create one of the country's first groups of illegal immigrants: Chinese who continued to come to the United States outside of the law.

Despite an ongoing need for a larger workforce, especially unskilled laborers to work in the fields, mines, and factories, the government responded to concerns that immigrants were taking jobs away from native-born residents by passing laws prohibiting companies or individuals from bringing aliens to America to work through a prearranged labor agreement. To help control rapidly growing immigration—nearly 25 million immigrants came to America between 1865 and 1915—the government established the Bureau of Immigration in 1891.[40]

In the early 1900s, problems increased along with the number of immigrants arriving in the United States. Although many immigrants came to escape poverty and to take advantage of employment opportunities not available in their homelands they often found circumstances equally difficult in America. Immigrants were vulnerable to unscrupulous factory owners and other employers who took advantage of them by paying substandard wages. Not only did immigrant men go to work, women and children did as well, either to support themselves if they were single women or to supplement the inadequate earnings of their husbands or, in the case of children, their parents. Employers hired women and children for even lower wages than their male counterparts. In the 1900s more than 20 percent of women (about 5 million) worked, which represented a fourfold increase of women in the workforce over the 30-year period beginning in 1870. In addition, 1.7 million children under age 16 worked in factories and fields for minimal wages. As more and more immigrants took up residence in cities, apartments became overcrowded and deteriorated into slums. Building owners added to the problem by squeezing as many people as possible into the smallest spaces available in order to collect more rents.[41] To stem the rising tide of immigrants flocking to the United States, in 1921 the government implemented quotas limiting the number of people from each country who were allowed to enter the United States. The quotas led to increased illegal immigration because as each country's quotas were filled and the front door was closed on people wishing to immigrate, they came anyway by entering illegally through the back door. To ease the perceived overburden on the country caused by immigrants, in 1935 the government undertook measures to encourage some immigrants, specifically Filipinos, to return to the Philippines and promise not to come back to America.[42] Also in the 1930s some one-half million Mexican workers were deported because it was believed they were taking jobs away from native-born people during the Great Depression.[43]

Although it was evident that the United States generally benefited from immigrants in adding to the labor force, measures taken to prohibit admission of some immigrants were often racially motivated, while the government took measures to attract others. After ejecting 500,000 Mexican workers in the 1930s the government created a guest worker program in 1943 known as the Bracero Program to entice agricultural laborers from Mexico and other Central and South American countries to work in America's fields. The program was discontinued 21 years later in 1964 amid complaints of racism, discrimination, and exploitation of migrant Mexican agricultural workers. The program ended also due both to an excess of so called illegal workers and to technological advancements in farm equipment.[44] Canceling the Bracero Program helped trigger the creation of yet another and even larger group of illegal immigrants, namely, Mexicans.

Illegal Immigration

The number of illegal immigrants entering the United States every year is staggering: 11 million to 12 million foreign-born people illegally lived in the United States in 2005, according to the Pew Hispanic Center. Although illegal immigration to the United States, especially from Mexico, was a hot-button issue in 2006, the practice has a long history that can be traced back to the country's first laws restricting immigration (1882) and establishing country quota systems (1920s). Faced with legislation that closed the door to all but a fortunate few and long waiting lists for obtaining proper documentation to immigrate to America, people found alternate, albeit illegal, back-door ways to come in.

Who Are Illegal Aliens

The Pew Hispanic Center reported that an estimated 6.2 million illegal aliens in America in 2005 were Mexicans. In 2005 there were a total of 10.5 million legal immigrants and 11.5 million foreign-born naturalized citizens.[45] Foreign-born people in the United States without proper documentation are generally described as immigration law violators, illegal aliens, or undocumented aliens, rather than immigrants.[46] And despite popular belief that illegal aliens always enter the country by slipping across the border between Mexico and the United States, in 2004 approximately 40 percent of illegal aliens were nonimmigrant overstays, that is, foreign-born people who legally entered the United States with temporary tourist visas, work visas, border crossing cards, or green cards and stayed once the documents expired. An estimated 2.3 million Mexicans who entered the country legally in 2004 as nonimmigrants with authentic documents slipped into illegal status after they failed to leave when their documents expired. Those who enter the United States with forged or fraudulent documents are also classified as nonimmigrant overstays.[47] For example, in 2006, a Filipino immigrant was charged and indicted for stealing passports from the Micronesian embassy in Washington, D.C., where he was an employee. He made necessary adjustments to the passports and then sold the forged documents to other Filipinos wishing to enter the United States. Use of Micronesian passports was essential because unlike passport from the Philippines, which require an accompanying U.S. visa to enter the United States, people with Micronesian passports may enter without a visa.[48]

Mexico also is not the only source of illegal aliens living in the United States, but Mexico is often the gateway through which illegal aliens from other countries enter America. As early as 1908 it was reported that illegal aliens from Syria, Greece, Japan, and China entered the United States by way of Mexico.[49] Noting the connection of illegal aliens with the 2001 terrorist attacks, it was reported that four of the terrorists involved were visa overstays.[50] By 2003 increasing numbers of illegal aliens from South and Central American countries, including El Salvador, Guatemala, Colombia, and Honduras, were entering Mexico as illegal aliens and then making their way illegally across the border into the United States. Top countries accounting for illegal aliens living in the United States in 2003, according to the Immigration and Naturalization Service, were China, the Philippines, Brazil, India, Peru, Korea, and Canada.

Human Smuggling

Illegal aliens often turn to human traffickers for help immigrating to the United States. In 2006, 22 Chinese nationals were caught illegally entering the United States at the Port of Seattle, Washington, after they were spotted climbing out of a cargo container in which they had stowed away before the container was loaded on a ship in Shanghai.[51] Human smuggling across the U.S./Mexico border also has become a big business for smugglers and can be a costly and often dangerous adventure for the smuggled. In 2006 some 4,000 Mexicans arrived each day in Sasabe, a town situated near the U.S.-Mexico border. From there they illegally cross the border into the United States. Many who tried to walk across were caught by U.S. Border Patrol agents—200,000 in one six-month period—were handcuffed, put in vans, and driven back into Mexico. Others died trying to walk across the scorching hot southern Arizona desert. A reported 200 Mexican aliens perished in their attempt to cross the Arizona desert in 2005. Still others, those who have saved enough money to pay, wait for smugglers known as *coyotes* or *polleros* to transport them into the United States. Smugglers have an intricate network of border observation posts, cell phone connections, and fleets of vehicles ready to drive people into America. The price is high considering the average daily earnings for a Mexican worker may be as little as $6. Smugglers charge Mexicans as much as $1,500 per person, meaning a coyote may earn as much as $30,000 per van load of illegal aliens driven across the border. Aliens from Central America, who are already in Mexico illegally, must pay $5,000 each for help continuing on illegally into the United States. The highest price, as much as $50,000 per person, is paid by Asians illegally moving through Mexico into America.[52]

Smuggling and Illegal Drugs

An early problem in the United States linked with illegal aliens was liquor smuggling. The U.S. government's implementation of prohibition in 1920 led to stepped up enforcement along both the U.S.-Mexico and U.S.-Canada borders not only to catch illegal immigrants but also to catch whiskey bootleggers. With the 1933 repeal of prohibition, whiskey smuggling ceased to be a problem, but it was replaced by drug smuggling. The U.S. Department of Homeland Security reported that Border Patrol agents confiscated 1.4 million pounds of marijuana and more than 30,000 pounds of cocaine in 2002. In 2006 a 2,400-foot-long smuggling tunnel was found along the U.S.-Mexico border that linked a warehouse in Tijuana, Mexico, to one in San Diego, California. At the time of the discovery no people were in the tunnel, but searchers found 2 tons of marijuana.[53] It was one of 35 such smuggling tunnels discovered that linked the United States and Mexico, enabling the undetected passage of people and drugs between the two countries.

The Border Patrol

Amid concerns in the 1920s about the increase in the number of illegal aliens entering, living, and working in the United States the government created the U.S. Border Patrol in 1924 as a division of the Immigration Service to enforce immigration policies and apprehend and deport those entering the country illegally. In the 1950s concerns were again raised about the growing number of illegal aliens in the United States, notably Mexican farm workers but also others believed to be "criminals, communists, and subversives," leading to increased enforcement along the borders. The government created a special task force of 800 Border Patrol agents in 1950 to apprehend and return thousands of illegal aliens to Mexico from California. The effort was expanded to include Texas in 1954. It was discontinued in 1956 after nearly 50,000 illegal aliens had been returned to Mexico.[54] At that time there were 2,000 Border Patrol agents whose efforts significantly reduced the flow of illegal aliens into America. They proved so successful that in 1955 the Immigration Service issued a report stating, "The border has been secured."[55]

Private aircraft also began to be used as a means to smuggle illegal aliens into the United States and, with the onset of the Cuban missile crisis in 1962, the Border Patrol was charged with preventing unauthorized small-aircraft flights by Cuban defectors living in Florida. As illegal immigration exploded in the 1980s and 1990s the Border Patrol improved its technology and increased its manpower in an attempt to stop the flood of aliens crossing the border. Projects included Operation Hold the Line in 1993 in El Paso, Texas, and Operation Gatekeeper in 1994 in San Diego, California. The Border Safety Initiative was launched in 1998 with the Mexican government promising to support the project.[56]

Illegal Immigration 2000 and Beyond

Despite earlier successes at securing the border and a burgeoning staff of Border Patrol agents—11,000 in 2006—working to enforce immigration laws and control illegal immigration, illegal aliens continue to pour into the United States in ever increasing numbers. They are estimated at 850,000 annually. The growing tide led to concerns that native-born Americans and legal immigrants were losing jobs to illegal aliens, and that the infrastructure of public services such as health care facilities, schools, social welfare programs, and law enforcement were being strained by the increased population, especially in states that received the highest number of illegal aliens: California (estimated as high as 2.7 million), Texas (up to 1.6 million), Florida (up to 950,000), and New York (up to 650,000), according to the Pew Hispanic Center.[57] Other states, particularly those in the South, also experienced an upsurge of Mexican illegal aliens locating there. It is estimated that from 1990 to 2005 illegal immigrants living in Georgia increased from 35,000 to between 350,000 and 450,000.[58] Rising crime rates that many attributed to illegal immigrants also raised concerns. The U.S. Department of Justice reported that in 2005 as many as 270,000 illegal aliens spent time incarcerated in local jails and state prisons. It further noted that 19 percent of the 35,000 inmates in federal prisons were immigrants. According to the Department of Homeland Security an estimated 302,000 immigrants who should have been deported in 2006 were going to be transferred instead to state prisons and local jails.[59]

In response, the government once again began rigorously enforcing existing immigration laws in 2006. The National Guard was called up in June 2006 to begin assisting Border Patrol agents along the U.S.-Mexico border. Billed as "Operation Jump Start," National Guard members were expected to monitor surveillance cameras, build roads, install fences along the border, and perform other non–law enforcement activities. By the end of 2008 the government expected to have a total of 18,000 Border Patrol agents in place to manage the U.S.-Mexico border.[60] Also in 2006 companies that hired illegal aliens began to feel the crackdown as the government enforced the 1986 law putting in place fines of up to $11,000 for knowingly hiring illegal aliens. Enforcement of the law resulted in 140 indictments, 127 convictions, 165 criminal arrests, and 980 civil arrests against employers.[61]

Terror's Impact: Immigration after September 11, 2001

When terrorists attacked the United States in 2001 the perceived dangers associated with immigration were intensified. Similar to the United States's response to immigrants in the country during previous international conflicts that threatened security and safety in America—the internment of German Americans during World War I, the deportation of eastern Europeans during Russia's Bolshevik Revolution and the subsequent Red Scare, and the internment of Japanese Americans during World War II—the reaction to the terrorist attacks was swift and initially targeted specific immigrant groups believed linked with the terrorists. Because information indicated that the 9/11 terrorists were associated with al-Qaeda, a Sunni Islamist organization, most of the U.S. government's actions were aimed at members of Muslim-American communities.

The government used immigration laws as a key weapon to fight terrorism. Approximately two weeks after the attacks U.S. Attorney General John Ashcroft reported that 480 aliens had been picked up and detained. Little more than one month later Attorney General Ashcroft announced that antiterrorism investigations had resulted in nearly 1,000 people being arrested or detained. All immigrants living in America of Muslim ethnicity were considered suspect and discrimination against them swelled. Hate crimes against Muslims jumped 1,500 percent and the federal Equal Employment Opportunity Commission received more than 700 September 11–related employment discrimination complaints in the year following the terrorist attacks.[62] John Tirman, director of the Massachusetts Institute of Technology Center for International Studies, stated: "Muslims in America, about equally from South Asia, the Middle East and North Africa, and Southeast Asia, were targeted along with their institutions. . . . Muslim charities were targeted by the FBI, with many of them closed down and a number of them prosecuted. Transnational labor migration was sharply curtailed. Student visas were more difficult to obtain. Mosques were under constant surveillance."[63] The Migration Policy Institute (MPI) further stated, "The government has selectively enforced immigration laws based on nationality since September 11. . . . The U.S. government has imposed immigration measures more commonly associated with totalitarian regimes."[64]

Various actions related specifically to immigration were taken by the government after 9/11. On September 17, six days after the attack, the Immigration and Naturalization Service (INS) increased the amount of time an alien could be held without being charged for a crime or immigration violation from 24 hours to 48 hours plus an additional "reasonable period of time for an emergency or other extraordinary circumstance." On October 1 the "Snitch Visa" law was enacted granting special visas to nonimmigrant aliens who possessed information about terrorist organizations and would share the information with law enforcement officials. The following day the U.S. government passed the Uniting and Strengthening America by Providing

Appropriate Tools Required to Intercept and Obstruct Terrorism Act of 2001, better known as the USA PATRIOT Act, which provided additional powers to law enforcement to conduct searches, use electronic surveillance, and detain suspected terrorists. On November 19 the Aviation and Transportation Security Act passed into law, which established the Transportation and Security Administration (TSA). As part of the new law, the TSA was authorized to "use information from government agencies to identify individuals on passenger lists who may be a threat to civil or national security." Further, the TSA could "prevent identified individual(s) from boarding an aircraft." According to the INS, on December 6 the Alien Absconder Initiative began in which more than 300,000 names of aliens remaining in the United States despite deportation orders were sent to the Federal Bureau of Investigation for inclusion in the National Crime Information Center's database. Antiterrorism efforts by the government continued in 2002, including using the Absconder Apprehension Initiative to locate some 314,000 aliens under final deportation orders who had not turned themselves in for removal. Operation TIPS, the Terrorism Information and Prevention Program, in which ordinary U.S. citizens could act as informants reporting "suspicious activity" was announced on the Department of Justice Web site in July. In August a new entry-exit system known as NSEERS (National Security Entry–Exit Registration System) was put into place requiring "certain nonimmigrants" considered to be a national security risk to register and submit fingerprints and photographs upon entering the United States. Additionally, they were required to report to an INS field office within 30 days of arrival and re-report to the INS annually during their stay. When leaving the country, nonimmigrants were required to notify an INS agent. Through the program, by November the INS had fingerprinted and registered more than 14,000 visitors to the United States, resulting in 179 arrests. The Interim Student and Exchange Authentication System (ISEAS) was implemented by the State Department's Bureau of Consular Affairs on September 11, 2002, one year after the terrorist attacks. ISEAS stated that nonimmigrant visas would not be issued to foreign students wishing to attend school in the United States unless sponsoring schools notified overseas consular officers that students applying for visas had been accepted for admittance by the educational institution.

As the government intensified its efforts to stop terrorists, attention became focused on the country's borders and enhancing security in an area that many considered a weak link in the war on terrorism. Fears grew that al-Qaeda operatives could enter the United States by way of the loosely guarded land border with Mexico and launch another attack. As a result, immigrants from Mexico and Latin America joined Muslims being scrutinized by the government's watchful eye. Mexican immigrants migrating illegally across the border in search of jobs were especially hard hit by the government's ongoing efforts. According to John Tirman, "[M]easures such as electronic fences, deployment of national guard troops, roundups of unauthorized workers in places of employment, and expanded border patrols are advocated to keep illegal immigrants out and provide an added shield against al Qaeda."[65]

POLICIES AND LAWS

Early Government Regulations

Throughout its history the United States has tried to control immigration and to manage associated problems, both perceived and real, with government regulations. Although increasing numbers of immigrants were moving to America, actions taken by the government in the late 1770s restricted opportunities for immigrants to become citizens and made it possible to deport immigrants perceived as undesirable. The 1790 Naturalization Act limited naturalized citizenship to "free white persons" who had lived in America for two years and in their state of residence for one year. In 1795 the required time of residency was increased to five years plus three years after notice of intent to request citizenship. The time period was increased again in 1798 to 14 years residency and five years notice of intent. Also in 1798 the Alien and Sedition Acts were passed, giving the president authority to deport any foreigner believed to be dangerous. Additionally, the act made it a crime to speak, write, or publish "anything of a false, scandalous, and malicious nature" about Congress or the president. The first federal legislation specific to immigration passed by Congress, the 1819 Steerage Act, called for the continued reporting of immigrants arriving in the United States.[66]

Early efforts to control immigration were limited, however, and immigration in the United States was relatively unregulated until the mid- to late-1800s. Prior to that time, most people wishing to immigrate to the United States were encouraged to do so, often by the governments of their homelands that planned to establish colonies in America, viewed emigration as a way to rid their countries of perceived troublemakers such as religious dissenters, or aimed to solve other problems such as overpopulation leading to land or job shortages. The government leaders and business people in colonial America encouraged immigration as well due to a need to increase the population. There was ample land to settle and farm, and there were an abundance of jobs in developing cities and on new tobacco plantations but a shortage of laborers to do the work. Because of the United States's open borders and welcoming policies, more and more immigrants flooded into American cities and rural areas in search of jobs and, with them, the possibility of a life better than what they had in their homelands. Despite the influx of immigrants, federal immigration legislation was limited until 1862 when the government passed the Homestead Act. Designed to further encourage immigration and migration, the act granted 160 acres of public land to anyone willing to live on the property five years and make improvements such as building a home and planting crops.

Early State-Implemented Laws

In an attempt to manage the growing tide of immigrants and accompanying problems, such as worsening economic conditions in some areas, several states began passing their own immigration laws. They included California. Due to the cries of "gold" and promises of instant wealth, the state experienced a population boom of American migrants from the East and foreign immigrants, many of them Chinese, during the gold rush of the 1850s. In response, California imposed a "Foreign Miner's Tax" on any miner who was not planning to become a citizen. California implemented a $50 tax on newly arrived miners in 1855 using the same criteria for exemption as the Foreign Miner's Tax: The new miners had to be planning to become citizens. The catch to the laws lay in the stipulation that only white immigrants were eligible for naturalized citizenship. In 1862 California imposed a $2.50 per month tax on Chinese immigrants living in the state.[67] Laws passed by the state of California during the 1870s directly targeted the Chinese, including laundry-operation fees, which limited the ability of Chinese immigrants, many of whom opened laundry businesses, to work. Anti-Chinese propaganda promoting the idea that Chinese immigrants "worked cheap and smelled bad," further aggravated tensions. Despite the federal exclusion act and California laws, Chinese still managed to immigrate to America, but they did so illegally. The ongoing influx of Chinese immigrants led the city of San Francisco in 1910 to build a detention center—Angel Island—where all incoming immigrants were screened and officials deported questionable newcomers.

Supreme Court Intervention and Increased Federal Control

Efforts by individual states to control immigration encouraged the Supreme Court in 1875 to formally declare that immigration regulation was the responsibility of the federal government. Regulation of immigrants by the federal government followed the Supreme Court's action when in 1875 an earlier law prohibiting the admittance of criminals, prostitutes, convicts, and other undesirables was reinstated.

Congress followed its 1875 legislation with the 1882 Immigration Act, implementing a 50-cents-per-immigrant head tax and placing restrictions on entry of immigrants to the United States. Excluded were people who were in poor health, uneducated, or those who were identified as "idiots, lunatics, convicts, and persons likely to become a public charge." The list of undesirables was lengthened in 1903 to include "polygamists, persons suffering from a loathsome or a dangerous contagious disease, and those convicted of a misdemeanor involving moral turpitude." Also in 1882 Congress passed the Chinese Exclusion Act, which banned Chinese immigrants from entering the United States for a period of 10 years. In 1892 the act was extended an additional 10 years by the Geary Act, and it was made permanent by the Extension Act of 1904. The act remained in place until it was finally rescinded in 1943. The Chinese Exclusion Act was enacted in response to racial tensions between Chinese immigrants, who flocked to California during the California gold rush, and miners, prospectors, other American citizens, and white immigrants who claimed the Chinese were taking away jobs and reducing overall wages. Problems persisted over an approximately 30-year period before passage of the act, with segregation of Chinese along with rampant persecution by American citizens and white immigrants.[68]

As anti-immigration sentiment and nativism increased nationwide, fueled by the perceived threat that immigrants were taking away jobs from Americans and dragging down wages, the federal government passed Alien Contract Labor laws in 1885, 1887, 1888, and 1891, which prohibited immigrants from entering the United States as contract laborers unless they were working for other immigrants or were doing jobs that did not already exist in the United States.

Post-1800s Laws

In the early 1900s Congress implemented additional immigration and naturalization legislation. In 1901 the Anarchist Exclusion Act was passed to exclude known anarchist agitators from immigrating to the United States. The 1906 Naturalization Act mandated that immigrants wishing to become naturalized citizens must speak and understand English. A 1907–08 action by the government, called the Gentlemen's Agreement, constituted an informal agreement between the United States and Japan designed to limit Japanese immigration. Under terms of the agreement Japan would stop emigration of its laborers to the United States by refusing to issue them passports and, in return, schools in San Francisco would stop discriminating against Japanese students. In addition, the agreement added to the excluded list Korean immigrants and "imbeciles, feeble-minded persons, unaccompanied children under 17 years of age, and persons who are found to be and are certified by the examination surgeon as being mentally or physically defective, such mental or physical defect being of a nature which may affect the ability of such aliens to earn a living." The immigrant head tax was also increased to $5 from 50 cents per immigrant. Literacy became a requirement for immigration with the passage of the Immigration Act of 1917, which required that all immigrants be able to read and write their native language.

Immigration from European nations slowed to a trickle following the outbreak of World War I, but it resumed at the war's end. Responding to the increased number of people wishing to come to America, Congress established an immigrant quota system with the passage of the 1921 and 1924 immigration acts. Under the 1921 Quota Law, immigrants allowed into the United States from each country in Europe were limited to 3 percent of each individual country's representation on the 1910 census. Immigrants from most Asian countries continued to be excluded from admission. The 1924 act, known as the Johnson-Reed Act, built on the earlier act by setting a numerical limit on total immigration to no more than 165,000 immigrants annually and it reduced the quota to 2 percent of each country's representation in the United States in 1890. Further, the act excluded all people from the Asian Pacific Triangle, including Japan, China, the Philippines, Laos, Thailand, Cambodia, Singapore, Korea, Vietnam, Indonesia, Burma, India, Sri Lanka, and Malaysia. The severe restrictions placed on legal immigration by the 1924 act led to an increase in illegal immigration. As the Great Depression raged and the U.S. economy collapsed with hundreds of thousands of people out of work, in 1932 the State Department closed off most immigration to the United States. Consequently, between the start of the depression in 1929 and through 1933 legal immigration dropped from 236,000 to just 23,000.

Under the 1934 Tydings-McDuffie Act the Philippines became a Commonwealth, and, under terms of the act, people in the Philippines not born in the United States were declared to be aliens. It also set an annual quota on the number of Filipinos allowed to immigrate to the United States at 50. Additional reductions in the number of Filipinos in the United States came with the 1935 Filipino Repatriation Act, which gave a one-way ticket back to the Philippines to any Filipino living in the United States under the condition they agree not to return to the United States. Records indicate that about 2,000 people accepted the offer, but 120,000 refused to go.[69] In 1946 the Philippines became independent and the Luce-Cellar Act was passed, allowing Filipinos and Asian Indians living in the United States to become naturalized citizens.

Laws Passed from World War II to 1965

With the threat of World War II looming, immigration began to be perceived as a national security problem rather than an economic problem. Following the outbreak of the war in Europe in 1939 Congress passed the Alien Registration Act in 1940, which required all aliens living in the United States to register with the federal government through post offices. Registration of aliens soon became a permanent part of the routine immigration procedure with all aliens registering at U.S. ports of entry. Those entering as permanent residents received a small green card that identified them as lawful permanent residents entitled to live and work in the United States indefinitely.

Billed as a guest-worker program, the Mexican Farm Labor Agreement was signed by Congress in 1943. Commonly referred to as the Bracero Program, it encouraged impoverished farm workers in Mexico to legally migrate to the United States on a temporary, seasonal basis to work in the fields and then return to Mexico. Among the program's requirements were a guaranteed minimum wage of 30 cents per hour and humane treatment of migrant workers that included adequate food, housing, and sanitation. The program was under the supervision of independent farmers associations and the American Farm Bureau Federation. To avoid program restrictions, such as the required minimum wage, farmers and growers in some border states chose not to participate. Rather, they bypassed the program and hired workers, known as *wetbacks,* directly from Mexico and brought them to the United States illegally.[70]

In 1945 the government passed the War Brides Act to enable foreign-born spouses of U.S. citizens who had served in the U.S. military to immigrate to the United States. The act was extended the following year to include foreign-born fiancées of American soldiers. Besides extending the War Brides Act, America began admitting immigrants fleeing persecution in their homelands through the 1948 Displaced Persons Act. The act opened the door for 205,000 refugees from European countries, including Germany, Austria, Czechoslovakia, and Italy, as well as orphans under 16 years old from the approved areas who had been displaced by the Nazi regime and World War II to enter the United States. Displaced persons from Palestine, China, and India were not included in the act, nor were 90 percent of Jews.

Congress adopted numerous immigration-related laws during the 1950s. Passage of the 1950 Internal Security Act made green cards, which began to be issued in 1940, even more valuable to immigrants as proof that they were in the country legally, especially since the act prohibited admission into the United States of any foreigner who was a communist or might participate in activities that could be harmful or dangerous to the "welfare and safety of the United States." Revisions to the immigrant quota system occurred with passage of the 1952 McCarran-Walter Immigration Act, which restated the 1924 national-origin quotas and set limits on total immigration at one-sixth of 1 percent of the population in the United States in 1920, or a total of just 175,455 immigrants worldwide. Non-Europeans were able to immigrate as refugees following passage of the 1953 Refugee Relief Act.

Another 12 years passed before the federal government took further action regarding U.S. immigration policies. In 1965, at the height of the civil rights movement, the Immigration and Nationality Act Amendments were passed, which made significant changes to the 1952 McCarran-Walter Act. The amendments eliminated the discriminatory nation-of-origin quota system and replaced it with a preference system intended to reunite immigrants with their families and attract skilled immigrants to the United States rather than just unskilled laborers. The 1965 act liberalized immigration and opened America's doors to immigrants from every country in the world. Following passage of the act, immigration to the United States reached one of its highest levels in history. Nearly 18 million legal immigrants and an unknown number of illegal immigrants, with many coming from Asian and Latin American countries, arrived between 1965 and 1995.[71]

Laws Passed 1970s–2000

In 1978 the number of immigrants, worldwide, who were permitted to enter the United States was increased to 290,000 annually. Refugees were removed from the preference category and new criteria were established for their admittance with passage of the 1980 Refugee Act. The 1980 act also reduced the number of people allowed to immigrate to 270,000 from 290,000.

Another attempt by the federal government to control illegal immigration occurred with passage of the 1986 Immigration Reform and Control Act. Key elements of the act included imposing a system of fines on employers who knowingly hired undocumented workers and granting amnesty to some 2.7 million illegal immigrants, most of them from Mexico, who had been living in the United States continuously since 1982, giving them legal status and allowing them to eventually apply for citizenship.[72] With the door presumably closed to illegal immigrants by the 1986 act, Congress improved the opportunities for those wishing to immigrate to the United States by passing the 1990 Immigration Act. The act increased the number of people allowed to immigrate for the purpose of seeking employment to as many as 700,000 and established H-1B visas, which enabled U.S. employers to bring highly skilled foreigners to temporarily fill positions in professional occupations for a period of up to six years. It eased the limits on family-based immigration, changed exclusion and deportation regulations, and gave temporary protected status to refugees from countries at war.

Other federal legislation passed in the 1990s included the 1996 Illegal Immigration and Immigrant Responsibility Act, which reduced legal immigrants' eligibility for federal benefits such as food stamps and welfare payments, raised the income requirements for sponsors of immigrants, and simplified the process for deporting illegal immigrants and those convicted of committing crimes; and the 1996 Personal Responsibility and Work Opportunity Act, which placed restrictions on the eligibility of legal immigrants to receive public assistance such as food stamps and Supplemental Security Income, and increased restrictions on public benefits for illegal immigrants. When a new Congress convened in 1997 it reversed some of the 1996 restrictions, calling them "overly harsh." Additional reversals of the 1996 restrictions were completed in 1998, including partially restoring eligibility for some public benefits to legal immigrants.[73] At the end of 2000 a bill known as the LIFE Act was passed, allowing illegal immigrants who were otherwise eligible for a green card to remain in the United States while their status was adjusted to that of legal immigrants.

Legislation after the September 11, 2001, Terrorist Attacks

In January 2001 the time period during which an illegal immigrant could apply for legal residency without returning to his or her homeland and waiting for a U.S. visa to reenter the country, as established by the 1965 act, was extended by four months until the end of April of that year. However, an estimated 200,000 illegal immigrants failed to meet the deadline. Therefore, on September 6, 2001, the federal government began a process to extend the deadline until April 30, 2002. The effort was sidelined five days later on September 11 when terrorists attacked the United States. On October 26 the "Uniting and Strengthening America by Proving Appropriate Tools Required to Intercept and Obstruct Terrorism Act of 2001" (the PATRIOT Act) was signed into law.[74] Elements of the act that deal with immigration include:[75]

- Enhanced enforcement by the Border Patrol along U.S. borders with Mexico and Canada
- Expanded terrorism-related inadmissibility and deportation of immigrants
- Mandatory detention of immigrants certified as terrorists for up to seven days rather than two days before bringing immigration or criminal charges

- Implementation of an automated entry-exit control system at all airports, seaports, and land border points of entry
- Granting Special Immigrant Status for family members of immigrants who were attack victims.

Anti-immigration sentiment increased across the United States following the terrorist attacks, particularly against those entering the country illegally. In 2005 President George W. Bush urged Congress to pass immigration legislation that, among other things, would tighten security on the U.S. border with Mexico to stem the growing tide of illegal immigrants pouring into the United States—estimated at 11 million people—and implement a guest worker program reminiscent of the Bracero Program of 1943.

Despite growing cries from the American public and pressure from the president for increased enforcement of, and upgrades to, the country's immigrations laws, Congress became mired in discussion and disagreement about what new immigration legislation should include. The split in Congress over how best to respond to the problem of illegal immigration became evident when the House passed a bill in December 2005 that excluded a guest worker program and a path to citizenship for undocumented aliens and focused on tightening border security and enforcing immigration laws already in place.[76] In May 2006 the Senate followed by passing its own version of an immigration bill, the Comprehensive Immigration Reform Act of 2006, which tightened the borders but also created a guest worker program and offered citizenship to most illegal aliens who met specific criteria much as the 1986 act had.[77] The conflicting measures led to a stalemate in Congress and the government's failure to implement any new immigration policies in 2006.

Post 9/11 State-Based Immigration Action

In response, the states, just as they had done 130 years earlier in the late 1800s, took immigration legislation into their own hands. According to the National Conference of State Legislatures, in 2006 more than 500 immigration-related pieces of legislation were introduced by state legislatures nationwide with 57 bills enacted in 27 states. Most legislation focused on illegal aliens and policies related to employment, public services such as education, and law enforcement. Legislation passed in 2006 included: Arizona (April), stated illegal immigrants may only receive emergency medical services; Kansas (March), prohibited unemployment benefits and employment protections for illegal immigrants; Nebraska (April), became the 10th state to allow long-term illegal immigrants who were students and met certain requirements to qualify for in-state tuition; Colorado (May and June), implemented a $50,000 civil fine for counterfeiting identification documents and made smuggling humans a class 3 felony, prohibited state agencies from issuing contracts to contractors who knowingly employ illegal immigrants and required contractors to verify the legal work status of all employees; Idaho (March), denied unemployment benefits to illegal aliens; and Florida (June), required proof of legal immigrant status on driver's license applications.[78]

Law Enforcement

Early immigration laws were enforced by the state boards of commissioners under the guidance of U.S. Treasury Department officials. U.S. Customs collectors were responsible for collecting immigrants' head taxes at each port of entry, and Chinese inspectors enforced the Chinese Exclusion Act. But as immigration laws became more complex and difficult to enforce, the federal government passed its first comprehensive immigration act in 1891 and established the Bureau of Immigration as a division of the U.S. Treasury Department. To aid the Bureau of Immigration in undertaking its duties, in 1892 a new federal immigration facility opened in New York harbor on Ellis Island. By 1893 Ellis Island had a staff of 119 Immigration Service employees in addition to civilian staffers. The facility also had hearing and detention rooms, a hospital, cafeterias, administrative offices, railroad ticket offices, and representatives from numerous immigration aid societies. Other immigration stations were built at traditional immigrant ports of arrival, including Boston and Philadelphia.[79]

To reduce the number of immigrants entering the United States illegally and further enforce the immigration laws, in 1924 Congress created the U.S. Border Patrol to operate under the jurisdiction of the Immigration Service.[80] Responding to the rapidly growing number of illegal immigrants from Mexico attributable to some employers circumventing the Bracero Program—a 6,000 percent increase from 1944 to 1954—the government implemented Operation Wetback in 1954 to force the return to Mexico of Mexicans in the United States illegally. Although formal estimates of how many illegal Mexican immigrants were deported are not available, the Immigration and Naturalization Service claimed as many as 1.3 million were apprehended and returned to Mexico. Other statistics indicate the number of deportees reached as high as 3.8 million.[81] Some of the deportees were U.S. citizens whose ancestors had come as early settlers of the southwestern United States. These U.S. citizens suddenly found themselves in a foreign land.

Following the 2001 terrorist attacks, legislation creating the Department of Homeland Security, which included merging the Immigration and Naturalization Service with all or parts of 21 other federal agencies, further enhanced the government's immigration law enforcement abilities. Additionally, the U.S. Departments of Justice and Defense reached an agreement that permitted the Department of Defense to help the INS patrol the country's borders. The Enhanced Border Security and Visa Entry Reform Act became law on May 14, 2002. The act required that intelligence agencies, the INS, and the State Department share information related to the admissibility and deportability of aliens.[82] In 2003 the INS proposed that all travelers using airlines and ships, including U.S. citizens, be required to provide personal information such as name, date of birth, citizenship, and passport number when entering or leaving the United States. The information was to be matched against security databases. Operation Liberty Shield, designed to enhance "security and readiness" in the United States, was launched in March. Also in March it was reported that FBI agents and U.S. marshals had been authorized to detain foreign nationals for alleged immigration violations when evidence of criminal charges was missing.[83]

EMIGRANTS

Given the number of people who immigrate to the United States from all corners of the world every year it is easy to forget that the road runs both ways. The numbers may be small by comparison, but each year people leave the United States, that is, they emigrate. Many foreign-born residents return to their homelands and native-born citizens leave to live in other countries. Due to the United States's immigration laws, information about people legally immigrating to the country is widely available and accurate. However, the United States stopped collecting information about people emigrating from the country in 1957 so contemporary statistics and estimates about emigration are usually based on data gathered in the countries receiving immigrants from the United States. As a result, the numbers vary widely. Information published in the U.S. government's *2000 Statistical Yearbook of the Immigration and Naturalization Service* indicates that since the 1950s emigration from the United States has grown at a steady pace, surpassing 100,000 people annually in the 30 years between 1970 and the 2000 report. According to the *Yearbook*, in the years between 1900 and 1990 some 38 million people immigrated to the United States while an estimated 12 million foreign-born people emigrated from the United States and returned to their homelands.[84] The report also noted statistics published by the United Nations and the Economic Commission for Europe that estimated as many as 200,000 U.S. residents, both native and foreign born, emigrated from the United States annually between 1995 and 1997. Further, the U.S. Census Bureau estimated that 311,000 foreign-born U.S. residents would emigrate in 2005. Estimates by the U.S. State Department, which gathers information through its Registration of U.S. Citizens Abroad program, suggested that 48,000 native-born Americans would probably emigrate each year.[85]

Why They Leave

Regardless of what country they choose as an immigration destination, like most immigrants, people emigrating from the United States often cite economics and politics as top reasons for making the decision to leave the United States behind. A 2005 study by the Migration Policy Institute (MPI), *Placing American Emigration to Canada in Context,* found dissatisfaction with the U.S. government's political policies the reason most given by emigrants. Between 1968 and 1978 Americans opposed to the Vietnam War and young men wanting to avoid being drafted into U.S. military service emigrated by the thousands. U.S. policies after 2002 continued to encourage some disgruntled Americans to look toward other countries, such as Canada, that had more liberal views regarding equal rights for gays, lesbians, and same-sex couples, opposed the war in Iraq, or offered legalized use of medical marijuana.

Americans also are increasingly emigrating following retirement. But rather than political factors, retirees typically cited economic reasons for emigrating, with the lower cost of living in the destination country of choice being a key factor. Responding to questions, retired emigrants often mention the high cost of health care or an inability to qualify for health insurance in the United States, doubts that Social Security or job pensions and private savings will be an adequate income source to maintain their lifestyle in the United States, and cheaper transportation and technology costs as reasons influencing their decision to emigrate. As noted in the MPI study: "A lower cost of living in some other countries allows retirees to enjoy amenities that would be nearly impossible to afford in the United States, while communications technology and increasingly efficient air travel allow them to stay in touch with family and friends in the United States." Many U.S.-born emigrants also continue to consider U.S. government policies when planning to emigrate, citing health policies that have failed to control explosive medical care costs and policies implemented following the September 11, 2001, terrorist attacks that many believe interfere with their civil liberties. Climate and population often plays a role in the decision as well. A snowy December in Chicago may be replaced with a sunny beach in Mexico; a crowded city in Florida may be replaced with a less-populated town south of the border. Foreign-born emigrants also leave for a variety of other reasons, including deportation by the U.S. government, racism or discrimination by Americans, a lack of employment opportunities, or simply a longing for their homelands.

Where They Go

CANADA

In 1956 about 9,800 people emigrated from the United States to Canada. The numbers have increased steadily and, in 1966, about 17,500 people emigrated across America's northern border into Canada. During that 10-year period more than 400,000 Americans immigrated to Canada, 50,000 of whom were men of draft age. Many others who emigrated were family members of draft resisters or people opposed to the U.S. foreign policies of the time. Even after President Jimmy Carter granted amnesty in 1977 to Vietnam War draft resisters who had emigrated, more than half of American emigrants chose to remain in Canada. The years after 1978 saw American immigration to Canada drop significantly from a high of 10,559 in 1981 to a low of 4,323 in 1995. In 2002 about 5,300 Americans immigrated to Canada. The war in Iraq also led a small number of U.S. soldiers to seek refugee status in Canada much as their Vietnam-era counterparts did in the 1970s. Although the United States no longer had a military draft, some active-duty soldiers wanted to avoid fighting in Iraq or Afghanistan. In addition to soldiers, in 2004 more than 100 Americans applied for refugee status in Canada for reasons that included the right to use medical marijuana.[86]

MEXICO AND SOUTH AND CENTRAL AMERICA

U.S. Citizens

In a twist on the norm of Mexicans and others from South and Central America immigrating to the United States, Americans are immigrating to Mexico and beyond. "In recent years a steadily increasing stream of Americans has been heading south to Latin America, particularly for retirement," states the opening sentence in *America's Emigrants: U.S. Retirement Migration to Mexico and Panama,* an in-depth study by the MPI.[87] Although the U.S. Census Bureau no longer tracks information on people emigrating, until 1999 the U.S. Department of State made attempts to estimate the number of Americans living abroad. According to its data, in 1999 approximately 1 million U.S. citizens were living in Mexico. Other countries with large numbers of American emigrants as reported by the State Department include Brazil, with approximately 46,000, Colombia, about 31,000; Argentina, nearly 28,000; and Venezuela, an estimated 25,000. However, based on census data from Mexico and Panama, which are believed to be more accurate than the 1999 figures released by the U.S. State Department, between

1990 and 2000 Mexico reported only 358,614 U.S.-born immigrants of all ages, including children, living in Mexico in 2000. The number of U.S.-born seniors, people aged 55 and older, living in Mexico increased 17 percent between 1990 and 2000. The U.S. embassy in Mexico estimated 600,000 American expatriates lived in Mexico in 2004. Panama reported 5,113 U.S.-born immigrants of all ages living there in 2000 with the number of U.S. seniors living in Panama accounting for about one-quarter of the total. As the first of America's baby boomers reached age 60 in 2006 and began planning for retirement, the number of those choosing to emigrate was expected to increase.[88]

Mexicans and Mexican Americans

The first large wave of Mexicans and Mexican Americans emigrating from the United States occurred in the late 1920s. Many returned to Mexico to escape the discrimination and racial biases they experienced in the United States. In 1929 some 79,000 Mexicans emigrated. As the Great Depression sent the U.S. economy into a downward spiral in 1930 at least 70,000 more Mexicans and Mexican Americans chose to return to Mexico. Statistics from the Mexican Migration Service recorded an additional 125,000 returned to Mexico in 1931. Camille Guerin-Gonzales noted in her book, *Mexican Workers and American Dreams: Immigration, Repatriation, and California Farm Labor, 1900–1939,* that 80 percent of Mexican emigrants at that time returned to Mexico due to a lack of jobs in the United States.[89] However, many Mexican-American emigrants returned to Mexico unwillingly, deported by the American government, despite being U.S.-born and legal residents of the United States. The deportation effort was described by a University of Chicago immigration history expert as "a racial removal program" that targeted anyone of Mexican ancestry. Known as *repatriados,* the returning Mexicans encountered obstacles as difficult in Mexico as they had been in the United States. Besides finding few or no opportunities for employment, Mexican-American emigrants found themselves considered foreigners in Mexico much as they had been considered foreigners in the United States. Additionally, *repatriados* who were American citizens and wanted to return to the United States often were unable to do so because they had been forced to leave the country without the documents necessary to prove citizenship.[90] To avoid repeating the past, in 2006 when another group of *repatriados* were deported by the U.S. government and returned to Mexico, the Mexican government began taking steps to help them repatriate. However, most of the returning Mexican emigrants had been living in the United States illegally. To receive help from the Mexican government through the country's Repatriados Trabajando in Mexico program an emigrant had to prove he or she had been recently deported from the United States and had to be a Mexican citizen at least 18 years old. They also had to prove they planned to stay in Mexico and not return to the United States. Help came in the form of cash ($173), employment training and jobs, and housing.[91]

CONCLUSION

As the United States struggled with managing immigration in 2006—from attempts to adopt immigration reform laws to building a 700-mile-long fence along the U.S.-Mexico border to stop the flow of illegal immigration—the issues facing the country concerning immigration remained the same. Citizens from around the world continued to look toward the United States as a place of refuge and as a country in which to make new beginnings. They continued to make their way to America as legal immigrants while, at the same time, illegal immigration continued to be a problem in 2006 much as it was more than 100 years ago. Federal policies and laws are adjusted to either accommodate immigrants or reject them, again depending on the nation's state of affairs. Comparing historical attitudes toward immigrants with those of Americans in 2006, especially toward Mexicans, Lawrence Downes stated in a *New York Times* editorial, "The Terrible, Horrible, Urgent National Disaster That Immigration Isn't": "If you could find a 250-year-old American to discuss this, he or she would tell you how familiar it all sounds. Identical arguments were once made about Chinese laborers, Japanese-Americans, Roman Catholics, the Irish, Italians, and the original unloved—though fully documented—outsiders, African-Americans."[92]

[1] "U.S. Immigration Boom Hits Record Levels." *Associated Press*, December 12, 2005. Available online. URL: http://www.msnbc.msn.com/id/10440110/. Accessed November 7, 2006.

[2] "Native Americans—American Indians—the First People of America; History of Native American Tribes." *Native Americans*. Available online. URL: http://www.nativeamericans.com/. Accessed July 20, 2006.

[3] Eric Hause. "The Lost Colony: Roanoke, N.C." *CoastalGuide's Packet*. North Carolina Tourism, 2006.

[4] "History of Jamestown." *Jamestown Rediscovery*. Richmond, Va.: Association for the Preservation of Virginia Antiquities, 2000.

[5] M. C. Bob Leonard. "Florida of the Conquistadors." *The Floridians: A Social History of Florida*. Tampa, Fla.: Hillsborough Community College. Available online. URL: http://www.floridahistory.org/floridians/conquis.htm. Accessed July 20, 2006.

[6] M. C. Bob Leonard. "Florida of the Spanish." *The Floridians: A Social History of Florida*. Tampa, Fla.: Hillsborough Community College. Available online. URL: http://www.floridahistory.org/floridians/spanish.htm. Accessed July 20, 2006.

[7] "Early Cities of the Americas." *Common-Place* 3, no. 4 (July 2003). Worcester, Mass.: American Antiquarian Society. Available online. URL: http://www.common-place.org/vol-03/no-04/. Accessed July 18, 2006.

[8] "First Acadians." *Acadian Culture in Maine.* Fort Kent: University of Maine, 1994.

[9] Marlou Shrover. "European Expansion." *History of International Migration.* Leiden, the Netherlands: Leiden University, 2006.

[10] Jason H. Silverman. "The Peopling of America: A Synoptic History." *Americans All Resource Materials.* Beltsville, Md.: People of America Foundation, 2000.

[11] Kyle J. Betit. "Scots-Irish in Colonial America." *The Irish at Home and Abroad* 2, no. 1 (1994/1995). Available online. URL: http://www.ireland.com/ancestor/magazine/articles/iha_scotsus1.htm. Accessed April 23, 2007.

[12] "The Irish." *Immigration: The Journey to America.* ThinkQuest Educational Foundation Library. Available online. URL: http://library.thinkquest.org/20619/Irish.html. Accessed July 18, 2006.

[13] Lewis Sitzer. *American Immigration Past and Present: A Simulation Activity.* Beaver Falls, N.Y.: Beaver River Middle School/High School, 2006.

[14] Alan Brinkley. "The Age of the City." *American History: A Survey.* Vol. 2, *Since 1865.* 9th ed. New York: McGraw-Hill, 1995, p. 509.

[15] "Chapter II: Immigration Policy." *American Immigration: An Overview.* Washington, D.C.: U.S. English, Inc., 2006.

[16] Wendy Koch. "U.S. Urged to Apologize for 1930s Deportations." *USA Today,* April 5, 2005.

[17] "United States Immigration Policy and Hitler's Holocaust." Los Angeles: Constitutional Rights Foundation, July 2000.

[18] "Asian Refugees Welcome." *AsianWeek,* March 2–8, 2001.

[19] R. Walton. *Pilgrim History.* Available online. URL: http://www.richmondancestry.org/pilgrim.shtml. Accessed July 20, 2006.

[20] R. Walton. *Pilgrim History.* Available online. URL: http://www.richmondancestory.org/pilgrim.shtml. Accessed on July 20, 2006.

[21] Kory L. Meyerink. *Germans in England.* Progenealogists Family History Research Group. Available online. URL: http://www.progenealogists.com/germansengland.htm. Accessed April 25, 2007.

[22] "Waves of German Immigrants Embrace America." *Infocus: German Americans.* Washington, D.C.: Embassy of the Federal Republic of Germany, 2006.

[23] "Displaced Person Transports: Cargos of Hope." *The Mast Magazine,* 1948. U.S. Maritime Service Veterans. Available online. URL: http://www.usmm.org/dp.html. Accessed July 20, 2006.

[24] "History of Jamestown." *Jamestown Rediscovery.* Richmond, Va.: Association for the Preservation of Virginia Antiquities, 2000.

[25] Lewis Sitzer. *American Immigration Past and Present: A Simulation Activity.* Beaver Falls, N.Y.: Beaver River Middle School/High School, 2006.

[26] Nathan Glazer, ed. *Clamor at the Gates: The New American Immigration.* San Francisco: Institute for Contemporary Studies, 1985, p. 118.

[27] Jeff Faux. "How NAFTA Failed Mexico." *The American Prospect* 14, no. 17 (July 3, 2003).

[28] Loretto Szucs Dennis. *The Source: A Guidebook of American Genealogy.* Provo, Utah: Ancestry.com, 1996.

[29] U.S. Census Bureau. "Population, Housing Units, Area Measurements, and Density: 1790 to 1900." Available online. URL: http://www.census.gov/population/censusdata/table-2.pdf. Accessed April 11, 2007.

[30] Barry Newman. "Who Will Care for U.S. Elderly If Border Closes?" *Wall Street Journal,* July 26, 2006, p. B1.

[31] Barry Newman. "Who Will Care for U.S. Elderly if Border Closes?" *Wall Street Journal,* July 26, 2006, p. B1.

[32] Mark E. Steiner. "Immigration Law from 1943–1965. Asian Americans and the Law." Houston, Texas: South Texas College of Law. Microsoft Powerpoint. Available online. URL: http://www.stcl.edu/faculty_pages/faculty_folders/steiner/aal/aal1943-1965/1943-1965.ppt. Accessed November 7, 2006.

[33] Lawrence Downes. "The Terrible, Horrible, Urgent National Disaster That Immigration Isn't." *New York Times,* June 20, 2006.

[34] Lawrence Downes. "The Terrible, Horrible, Urgent National Disaster That Immigration Isn't." *New York Times,* June 20, 2006.

[35] "Teen Immigrants, Five American Stories." *In the Mix.* Public Broadcasting System, November 2006.

[36] Lawrence Downes. "The Terrible, Horrible, Urgent National Disaster That Immigration Isn't." *New York Times,* June 20, 2006, p.

[37] "International Cuisine Reaches America's Main Street." Press Release, National Restaurant Association, August 10, 2000.

[38] *Historical Statistics of the United States, Colonial Times to 1970.* Washington, D.C.: U. S. Census Bureau. Available online. URL: http://www.census.gov/prod/www/abs/statab.html. Accessed July 20, 2006.

[39] Michael Brody. "Chinese Exclusion Act: A Black Legacy." Atherton, Calif.: Menlo School, 2006. Available online. URL: http://sun.menloschool.org/mbrody/ushistory/angel/exclusion_act/. Accessed July 20, 2006.

[40] Marian L. Smith. "Overview of INS History." *A Historical Guide to the U.S. Government.* New York: Oxford University Press, 1998.

[41] Alan Brinkley. "Industrial Supremacy." *American History: A Survey.* Vol. 2, *Since 1865.* 9th ed. New York: McGraw-Hill, 1995, p. 492.

[42] "Chapter II: Immigration Policy." *American Immigration: An Overview.* Washington, D.C.: U.S. English, Inc., 2006.

[43] Camille Guerin-Gonzales. *Mexican Workers and American Dreams: Immigration, Repatriation, and California Farm Labor, 1900–1939.* New Brunswick, N.J.: Rutgers University Press, 1994, pp. 97–101.

[44] "The Bracero Program." Sin Fronteras Organizing Project, 1999. Available online. URL: http://www.farmworkers.org/bracerop.html. Accessed July 31, 2006.

[45] Philip Martin. *The Battle over Unauthorized Immigration to the United States.* Washington, D.C.: Population Reference Bureau, 2006.

[46] George Weissinger. *The Illegal Alien Problem: Enforcing the Immigration Laws.* Central Islip, N.Y.: New York Institute of Technology, 203.

[47] "Modes of Entry for the Unauthorized Migrant Population." Fact Sheet. Washington, D.C.: Pew Hispanic Center, May 22, 2006.

[48] Ronald Smothers. "Ex-Embassy Driver Is Indicted in People-Smuggling Scheme." *New York Times,* May 13, 2006.

[49] "U.S. Border Patrol History." Washington, D.C.: U.S. Department of Homeland Security, Customs and Border Protection, July 15, 2003. Available online. URL: http://www.cbp.gov/xp/cgov/border_security/border_patrol/history.xml. Accessed July 24, 2006.

[50] Mark Krikorian. *Visa Overstays: Can We Bar the Terrorist Door?* Washington, D.C.: Center for Immigration Studies, May 11, 2006.

[51] "22 Chinese Are Held in a Smuggling Case." *New York Times,* April 6, 2006.

[52] Michael Marizco. "Perseverance, an Immigrant's Journey: Dust, Flies and the Long Walk." *High Country News,* May 15, 2006, p. 6.

[53] "Drug Haul in Secret Border Tunnel. U.S. Border Officials Have Unearthed the Longest and Deepest Tunnel Ever Gouged under the Country's Mexican Border." *BBC News,* January 27, 2006.

[54] "U.S. Border Patrol History." Washington, D.C.: U.S. Department of Homeland Security, Customs and Border Protection, July 15, 2003. Available online. URL: http://www.cbp.gov/xp/cgov/border_security/border_patrol/history.xml. Accessed July 24, 2006.

[55] John Tierney. "Securing the Border (Again)." *New York Times,* June 6, 2006.

[56] "U.S. Border Patrol History." Washington, D.C.: U.S. Department of Homeland Security, Customs and Border Protection, July 15, 2003. Available online. URL: http://www.cbp.gov/xp/cgov/border_security/border_patrol/history.xml. Accessed July 24, 2006.

[57] "Estimates of the Unauthorized Migrant Population for the States." Fact Sheet. Washington, D.C.: Pew Hispanic Center, April 26, 2006.

[58] Rachel L. Swarns. "In Georgia, Immigrants Unsettle Old Sense of Place." *New York Times,* August 4, 2006.

[59] Julia Preston. "New Scrutiny of Illegal Immigrants in Minor Crimes." *New York Times,* June 20, 2006.

[60] Randal C. Archibald. "Tasks Are Workaday for Guard Troops on Border." *New York Times,* August 7, 2006.

[61] Steven Greenhouse. "Going after Migrants, but Not Employers." *New York Times,* April 16, 2006.

[62] Muzaffaar A. Chishti and Stephen W. Yale-Loehr et al. *America's Challenge: Domestic Security, Civil Liberties, and National Unity after September 11.* Washington, D.C.: Migration Policy Institute, 2003.

[63] John Tirman. "Immigration and Insecurity: Post 9/11 Fear in the United States." *The Audit of Conventional Wisdom.* Cambridge: Massachusetts Institute of Technology, 2006.

[64] Muzaffaar A. Chishti and Stephen W. Yale-Loehr et al. *America's Challenge: Domestic Security, Civil Liberties, and National Unity after September 11.* Washington, D.C.: Migration Policy Institute, 2003.

[65] John Tirman. "Immigration and Insecurity: Post 9/11 Fear in the United States." *The Audit of Conventional Wisdom.* Cambridge: Massachusetts Institute of Technology, 2006.

[66] "Chapter II: Immigration Policy." *American Immigration: An Overview.* Washington, D.C.: U.S. English, Inc., 2006.

[67] "Chapter II: Immigration Policy." *American Immigration: An Overview.* Washington, D.C.: U.S. English, Inc., 2006.

[68] Michael Brody. "Chinese Exclusion Act: A Black Legacy." Atherton, Calif.: Menlo School, 2006. Available online. URL: http://sun.menloschool.org/mbrody/ushistory/angel/exclusion_act/. Accessed July 20, 2006.

[69] "From the Pages of Time." *AsianWeek,* August 25, 2006.

[70] Fred L. Koestler. "Bracero Program." *The Handbook of Texas Online.* Austin: University of Texas and the Texas State Historical Association, June 6, 2001. Available online. URL: http://www.tsha.utexas.edu/handbook/online/articles/BB/omb1.html. Accessed July 24, 2006.

[71] *Three Decades of Mass Immigration: The Legacy of the 1965 Immigration Act.* Washington, D.C.: Center for Immigration Studies, 1995.

[72] "Chapter II: Immigration Policy." *American Immigration: An Overview.* Washington, D.C.: U.S. English, Inc., 2006.

[73] "Chapter II: Immigration Policy." *American Immigration: An Overview.* Washington, D.C.: U.S. English, Inc., 2006.

[74] "Immigration and National Security Post-Sept. 11: Updated Chronology." *Migration Information Source.* Washington, D.C.: Migration Policy Institute, 2003.

[75] "Chapter II: Immigration Policy." *American Immigration: An Overview.* Washington, D.C.: U.S. English, Inc., 2006

[76] Jonathan Weisman. "House Votes to Toughen Laws on Immigration. One Setback for Bush: No Guest-Worker Program." *Washington Post,* December 17, 2005, p. A1.

[77] "Senate Passes Comprehensive Immigration Reform, House Remains Obstacle to Enactment." Press release. Washington, D.C.: American Immigration Lawyers Association, May 26, 2006.

[78] "2006 State Legislation Related to Immigration: Enacted, Vetoed, and Pending Gubernatorial Action." Washington, D.C.: National Conference of State Legislatures, 2006.

[79] Marian L. Smith. "Overview of INS History." *A Historical Guide to the U.S. Government.* New York: Oxford University Press, 1998.

[80] "U.S. Border Patrol History." Washington, D.C.: U.S. Department of Homeland Security, Customs and Border Protection, July 15, 2003. Available online. URL: http://www.cbp.gov/xp/cgov/border_security/border_patrol/history.xml. Accessed July 24, 2006.

[81] Fred L. Koestler. "Bracero Program." *The Handbook of Texas Online.* Austin: University of Texas and the Texas State Historical Association, June 6, 2001. Available online. URL: http://www.tsha.utexas.edu/handbook/online/articles/BB/omb1.html. Accessed July 24, 2006.

[82] "Immigration and National Security Post-Sept. 11: Updated Chronology." *Migration Information Source.* Washington, D.C.: Migration Policy Institute, 2003.

[83] "Immigration and National Security Post-Sept. 11: Updated Chronology." *Migration Information Source.* Washington, D.C.: Migration Policy Institute, 2003.

[84] "Estimates, Fiscal Year 2000." *2000 Statistical Yearbook of the Immigration and Naturalization Service.* Washington, D.C.: U.S. Government Printing Office, 2002.

[85] Edward W. Fernandez. "Estimation of the Annual Emigration of U.S. Born Persons by Using Foreign Censuses and Selected Administration Data: Circa 1980." Washington, D.C.: U.S. Bureau of the Census, Population Division, January 1995.

[86] Audrey Kobayashi and Brian Ray. "Placing American Emigration to Canada in Context." *Migration Information Source.* Washington, D.C.: Migration Policy Institute, January 2005.

[87] Demetrious G. Papademetriou et al. *America's Emigrants: U.S. Retirement Migration to Mexico and Panama.* Washington, D.C.: Migration Policy Institute, 2006.

[88] Demetrious G. Papademetriou et al. *America's Emigrants: U.S. Retirement Migration to Mexico and Panama.* Washington, D.C.: Migration Policy Institute, 2006.

[89] Camille Guerin-Gonzales. *Mexican Workers and American Dreams: Immigration, Repatriation, and California Farm Labor, 1900–1939.* New Brunswick, N.J.: Rutgers University Press, 1994, pp. 97–101.

[90] Wendy Koch. "U.S. Urged to Apologize for 1930s Deportations." *USA Today,* April 5, 2006.

[91] Analilia Esparza. "Mexican Aid Effort Offers Deportees Softer Re-entry to Mexico." *Associated Press,* July 7, 2006.

[92] Lawrence Downes. "The Terrible, Horrible, Urgent National Disaster That Immigration Isn't." *New York Times,* June 20, 2006.

3

Global Perspectives

This chapter offers readers an international perspective on the impact of immigration and migration. It discusses immigration and migration in four countries: France, South Africa, Mexico, and the Philippines.

FRANCE

Introduction

France was once the country with the largest population in Europe, claiming one-fourth of Europe's population during the Middle Ages and one-fifth of the population in the 1600s. Beginning in 1697 an attempt was made to identify foreigners living in France and charge them a residency fee through implementation of a naturalization tax. The taxation effort failed, but the 1697 to 1707 tax rolls identified 8,000 foreigners, described as people who were neither by birth nor by naturalization identified as being French, living in the country.[1] Despite early efforts to track foreigners in France, between the 1600s and until after the French Revolution (1789–99) France was considered a kingdom rather than a nation; consequently, there was no clear definition of French citizenship. Additionally, during that period France had neither recognized border controls nor specific methods to identify foreigners, so people easily immigrated to France and took up residency without regularly being identified as immigrants or non-French. Following the French Revolution the country's politics and identity changed, with France now identified as a nation and a "sovereign community of citizens."[2]

Although France began officially regulating immigration in the late 1800s the French government does not recognize ethnic minority status and does not keep track of the ethnic origin of its residents. Rather, France offers just two classifications for residents, national and foreigner (*étranger*, a person born abroad without French nationality).[3] Unlike the United States, which grants citizenship to all children born in the United States even those whose parents are illegal immigrants, beginning in 1993 and through 1998 children born in France to immigrants were not granted automatic citizenship unless they were stateless. Citizenship was granted to a child born in France to immigrant parents only when the child reached adulthood (age 18 years) and formally requested it. To begin to understand the complexity of immigration and migration policies in France it is necessary to first consider the country's differentiation between foreigners and immigrants. The embassy of France in the United States explains the difference as: Foreigners "are simply people who do not have French nationality. . . . [Immigrants] are people living in France who were born abroad. . . . Immigrants who have acquired French nationality are no longer foreigners." By virtue of that, a foreigner may be born in France (children of immigrant parents) and a French person born abroad may be an immigrant to the country. Because of the way France differentiates its residents—French nationals, foreigners, and immigrants—census figures may indicate that the percentage of foreigners residing in France has declined when in fact many immigrants of foreign origin may have become naturalized and are no longer classified or counted as foreign. The French embassy explains: "Only foreigners, i.e. people permanently resident in France who state that they do not have French nationality are officially registered. Immigrants are not registered as such once they have become French: they disappear as immigrants from the general population census."[4]

Historical Background

FIRST IMMIGRANTS

Beginning in the early 1800s more immigrants moved to France than to any other country in Europe, and most of them came from Spain, Portugal, Belgium, and Poland.[5] Scholars consider 1851—the year France began keeping official population and immigration records—as the beginning of mass immigration to the country. According to that year's census information, there were 380,000 immigrants in France. The countries of origin for the largest numbers of immigrants were Spain (30,000), Italy (63,000), and Belgium (128,000).[6] Census records from 1881, 30 years later, noted that France's immigrant population had increased to 1 million people, with the top countries of origin remaining Spain (73,000), Italy (241,000), and Belgium (432,000).[7]

After France emerged as an industrial power in the late 1800s and early 1900s, immigration increased, fueled by employment needs that the native population of workers could not fulfill. Immigrants from Belgium worked in textile factories while those from Spain and Italy filled jobs in agriculture.

The first of two major waves of immigration to France occurred following World War I when immigrants were used to help rebuild the country.[8] Immigration to France went into decline after the country, like the United States, became mired in the Great Depression in the 1930s. As jobs disappeared and unemployment grew among French nationals immigrant workers became a burden on society. Much as the United States deported Mexican immigrants in response to job shortages and rising unemployment caused by the depression, so too did France. Some immigrants left France willingly after jobs dried up but others, including Polish immigrants, were forcibly removed from the country.[9]

MODERN IMMIGRATION

France began taking measures to attract immigrants when the country began to rebuild both its infrastructure and its population following World War II (1939–45). In 1946 the National Immigration Office (NIO) was established with the purpose of recruiting foreign workers. However, the NIO's recruitment efforts were unsuccessful at first and immigration continued to decline until the mid-1950s.[10] According to the 1954 census, foreigners living in France had dropped to 4 percent of the population from 6.6 percent in 1931. The NIO's immigrant worker recruitment efforts finally began to pay off in 1956, launching the second notable wave of immigration to France, which continued through 1973. By 1975 the number of foreigners living in France had increased to about 6.5 percent of the population, or roughly equal to that of 1931.[11]

Although France preferred immigrants from other European countries because they were perceived as more "culturally compatible," in the decade from 1960 to 1970 an estimated 1 million immigrants arrived in France from the Maghreb (Morocco, Algeria, Tunisia, Libya) region of Africa. Other immigrants in that period included those from Italy, who accounted for 32 percent of the immigrant population.[12]

A recession attributable to war in the Middle East and a resulting oil shortage had a negative impact on France's economy in 1973, leading to another period of high unemployment. In response to the job shortage the French government tightened its immigration policies and in 1974 officially ended work-related immigration, especially immigration by unskilled workers.[13] Although France remained a country of immigration in the 1980s and 1990s, enforcement of anti-immigration policies beginning in the late 1980s led to a steady decline in foreigners legally immigrating to France. Between 1992 and 1995 legal immigration to France dropped 40 percent. In 1992 just over 110,000 foreigners legally immigrated to France and, three years later in 1995, that number had dropped to about 68,000.[14]

Despite years of closing its doors to most immigrants, declining immigration reversed in 1997 when 102,400 legal foreign immigrants arrived in France. Many were refugees or were joining family members who had immigrated earlier for jobs.[15] The primary foreign populations living in France in 1999 included 1.7 million North Africans (immigrants from Morocco, Algeria, and Tunisia), 789,000 Portuguese, 448,000 Africans, and 443,000 Asians.[16] The total number of immigrants seeking permanent residence increased from 104,400 in 1999 to 141,000 in 2001 with 50,600 more coming for short-term stays as students or with temporary work permits. By 2003 the number of foreigners living in France jumped to 3.3 million with most from Portugal, Algeria, and Morocco.[17] Legal immigrants living in France reached about 9.8 million people or 15 percent of the population in 2005.

Why Immigrants Come to France

According to *The Challenge of French Diversity,* "Since the mid-19th century, French immigration policy has had two aims: to meet the needs of the labor market by introducing migrant workers, and to compensate French demographic deficits by favoring the permanent installation of foreign families."[18] France's participation in World War I and World War II created a need for workers to fill jobs in the country's ammunition factories and in manufacturing, mining, and agriculture so the government encouraged economic migration. Additionally, due to a low birth rate among its citizens—based on statistics France had reached zero population growth by the early 1900s—immigrants were welcomed along with their families.

After World War II France experienced a baby boom similar to that which occurred in the United States, reducing the need for immigrant families to boost the population. However, the country was also undergoing an economic boom that called for immigrants who could fill jobs. The country's postwar economic and job growth continued for nearly 30 years and immigrants, especially those willing to fill unskilled, low-paying jobs that French nationals typically refused to take, were arriving to meet the demand.

The collapse of France's African empire beginning in the 1950s led emigrants from the country's former colonies, particularly Algeria, to immigrate to France in search of jobs and political stability.[19] Refugees and asylum seekers fleeing their war-torn homelands increasingly looked toward France as a safe haven as well. In 2004 the United Nations reported that the number of refugees fleeing to the United States and Europe had fallen to its lowest level since 1988, but France was the top receiving country that year with 61,600 asylum seekers arriving. The United Nations noted, "A possible reason for the downward trend in some European countries has been 'very restrictive legislation' on asylum seekers and 'rather hostile attitudes' toward refugees."[20] Other people immigrated to France for reasons of family reunification. In 2006 family reunification accounted for about 65 percent of France's immigration, or some 113,000 immigrants annually.[21]

How France Benefits from Immigration

Throughout its history France typically depended on immigrants to build its population and provide a workforce. Little has changed over the years, but in the early 2000s rather than encouraging unskilled workers for whom there were limited employment opportunities, France began wooing highly skilled workers. To discourage low-skilled workers and attract the best and brightest, including scientists, business executives, and college professors, the government changed its immigration policies in 2006 to include a three-year work permit for educated professionals, and for foreign students who earned a master's degree at a French university, a work permit if they had a job within six months of completing their degree.[22] In the early 21st century, France also continued to benefit from immigration as a way to build its population and compensate for a birth rate that has remained below replacement levels. France's National Institute for Statistics and Economic Studies (INSEE) in Paris reported that by 2050 one of three people living in France will be 60 years old or older. The INSEE wrote: "The proportion of young people and the economically active will decrease. For every 100 inhabitants aged between 20 and 59 in 2050 will be 69 inhabitants aged at least 60, double the 2005 ratio."[23] Encouraging immigration to supply young laborers to make up the deficit in the workforce caused by the lower birthrate among French citizens and the aging and retirement of workers, known as replacement migration, was seen as one solution to the problem. The embassy of France in the United States stated: "Immigration is still in some cases put forward as the remedy for the ageing of the national population."[24]

A United Nations Population Division study on replacement migration asked the question: "Is it a solution to declining and ageing populations?" Its answer: "If retirement ages remain essentially where they are today [March 2000], increasing the size of the working-age population through international migration is the only option in the short to medium term to reduce declines in the potential support ratio."[25] A pension expert with the Paris-based Organisation for Economic Co-operation and Development (OECD) stated: "The aging workforce is the biggest economic challenge policymakers will face over the next 20 years. . . . Over the coming decades [France] will need a larger workforce to support its aging population."[26] However, the country confronts a still greater problem: high unemployment. With a 2005 unemployment rate of 10 percent overall, including about 22 percent for people under age 25, and as much as 50 percent in areas with high immigrant populations, creating jobs may be the more immediate priority. But eventually younger workers will be required to pay into the retirement system that supports the elderly and a portion of those workers may be provided by replacement immigration.[27]

Problems Associated with Immigration

SOCIAL BACKLASH

Throughout history French nationals have experienced periods of xenophobia, or the fear that the country is being overrun by foreigners. Complaints that immigrants were driving down wages and threatening the social order repeatedly have been raised as well. In 1893, after the French president was assassinated by an Italian revolutionary, a mob of French nationals attacked Italian immigrants working in France's salt evaporation ponds, killing nine and injuring hundreds. Belgian immigrants brought to France during that time to fill jobs in the coal, iron, and steel industries were taunted and referred to as vermin, and Italian and Polish immigrants were harassed for their religious beliefs.[28]

When the country's economy took a nosedive during the Great Depression in the 1930s immigrant workers were expelled from France en masse. Even during the economically thriving post–World War II era, immigrant workers were strongly encouraged to return to their homelands once their work was completed, especially those arriving from developing countries. To discourage temporary migrant workers, most of whom were men, from remaining in the country permanently the government built hostels to serve as short-term housing for them; however, many women still chose to immigrate to France to be with their husbands. Recognizing that many immigrants were remaining permanently and bringing their families into the country, in 1974 France tried to end family reunification immigration by banning it. The effort was overturned four years later by the country's high court.[29]

Fear, racism, and religious persecution toward immigrants, particularly Muslims, triggered a 1989 incident in which three Muslim girls were suspended from school for wearing *hajibs*, Islamic headscarves, to class. After thousands of Muslims marched in protest of the action, the girls' suspension was reversed by the French minister of education, and they returned to class. The controversy dominated French politics in the following years,[30] and, in 2003, the French National Assembly supported a law banning Islamic headscarves and other "conspicuous symbols" of religion, including Jewish skullcaps and large Christian crosses, in public schools.[31] Anti-immigration sentiment continued to flourish and in 1996 more than 2,000 French nationals turned out to protest against immigrants and march in memory of a French teen killed by another youth of Arab origin. Marchers carried banners with slogans that included "Protect our children," "Immigration equals insecurity," and "France for the French."[32]

While French nationals protested, immigrants also were staging protests. In 1996 a group of African and Chinese immigrants caught in the tangle of French immigration law—unable to obtain residence permits but also unable to be legally deported—protested by occupying a Paris church. Riots erupted in 2005 after two teenage boys of African origin were accidentally electrocuted while trying to hide from the French police in a neighborhood heavily populated with immigrants. Rioters, mostly the teenage children of North African Arab immigrants, injured dozens of police officers, killed at least one bystander, and torched thousands of vehicles as well as schools, hospitals, and other public buildings. The riots, described as France's "worst urban violence in a decade," were attributed to years of high unemployment, continued marginalization by French society of the immigrants, and the perception that French police were targeting immigrants for harassment. One man believed to be a North African immigrant living in the riot area said, "It's the police who are provoking us. They don't like foreigners."[33] Another wave of immigrant protests erupted in 2006 when France proposed and then passed an even more strict immigration law. Reportedly more than 11,000 protesters marched in Paris chanting, "Solidarity with immigrants." Some protesters wore stickers depicting an immigrant being thrown into a garbage can and the leader of a group of illegal immigrants called the new law "inhumane."[34]

ILLEGAL IMMIGRATION

Starting in the mid-1950s France began to experience a problem that was increasingly common in the United States as well: illegal immigration. But to assure there were enough workers to fill vacant jobs, particularly low-paying positions French citizens were often unwilling to take, France took the necessary steps to bring illegal aliens into compliance with the country's immigration laws, making them legalized workers after the fact.[35] From 1974 through 1981 there was an increase in illegal aliens, defined as foreigners living in France without a residence permit or proper papers, which the government tried to control by implementing sanctions against employers who hired illegal aliens or workers *sans papiers* (without legal documents).[36] Various acts of civil disobedience by illegal immigrants occurred in 1997, including a fight aboard an airplane transporting 77 illegal immigrants being deported to Mali, which resulted in 23 police officers being injured. The flight was one of 36 over a two-year period beginning in 1995 that were chartered to return deported illegal immigrants to Africa.[37] Despite increased deportations, in 1997 approximately 87,000 illegal immigrants were granted amnesty and made legal residents by the French government.[38]

Estimates of foreigners living illegally in France in 2005 ranged from 200,000 to 400,000. France deported 20,000 illegal aliens that year and also initiated a plan to pay others to leave and return to their homeland that was similar to Filipino repatriation policies adopted by the United States in 1935. Under the plan, illegal immigrants agreeing to leave France voluntarily would receive payment of $2,400 per adult and $600 per child or $6,000 for a family of four. However, by September 2005 just 200 illegals had accepted the offer. Responding to the government's one-time legalization program offered to families with children enrolled in French schools, in early 2006 some 14,000 illegal immigrants requested residency papers providing legal status and an additional 6,000 were expected to apply by the August 14, 2006, deadline. The French government reported that of the applicants, only about 6,000 would qualify for and be granted residency papers while an estimated 25,000 illegals were expected to be deported by the end of the year.[39] However, according to a Migration Policy Institute report, one month before the August deadline some 13,000 illegal immigrants had been deported and in September that year, one month after the deadline, 30,000 illegal immigrants had applied for residency and of those just 7,000 had been granted legal status.

Policies and Laws

EARLY GOVERNMENT REGULATIONS

The 1789 Declaration of the Rights of Man, which promoted the belief that all people are equal, became the foundation for the country's future immigration policies, notably that immigrants should assimilate into French society and not be separated or categorized by race, class, religious beliefs, or other social distinctions. The doctrine, while a noble goal, ultimately could not prevent the types of discrimination it had hoped to abolish. The country's official policy of not recognizing ethnic minorities, which continued in 2006, made it next to impossible for immigrant groups to prove discrimination based on ethnic origin and precluded counterstrategies such as affirmative action.

Government regulation of the migrant labor force began during World War I and eventually was placed under the jurisdiction of the Ministry of Labour. At that time the practice of nonintervention by the government shifted to one of intervention. Regulations included the negotiation of labor agreements with foreign governments and the introduction of an identity card for foreign workers. Additionally, three specific workforce categories were created: national civilian, colonial (workers from France's foreign colonies), and foreign.[40] The country also laid the groundwork for the establishment of official immigration policy through the integration of immigration and migration into labor policies. In 1924 numerous employers' organizations joined together and created the Société générale d'immigration. Foreign workers' access to employment in France fell under the jurisdiction of the Société. Efforts of the Société led to a law passed in 1926 that stipulated foreign workers could be employed only in the occupation for which they had come to France for one year following their arrival.[41] In response to the Great Depression a 1932 law established quotas for foreign workers, with Europeans favored over Africans. It also created enforcement orders and restricted immigration to foreign workers with authorized work identification cards.[42]

France's first law directly related to immigration not tied specifically to labor was the Decree of 1 October 1945. It was based on the country's Declaration of the Rights of Man and established equality of all immigrants with "no distinction on the basis of nationality, religious, racial, or cultural character," and integration of immigrants, who were presumed able to fully integrate socially and legally into French society. It declared France to be "officially open to immigrants and their families." Amendment and ratification of the decree one month later specified that "every foreigner residing in France for more than three months has to hold a residence permit." Other elements of the decree included permitting the government to deport immigrants believed to present a "threat to public order" and creating the National Office of Immigration.[43]

MODERN IMMIGRATION LAWS

The Central Office for Population and Migrations was established as a division of the Ministry of Social Affairs in 1966 to oversee and control immigration.[44] In 1973 the French economy took a downturn and the government tried to reverse the rising trend of immigrants remaining in the country permanently by refusing to renew immigrants' residency permits. The following year the government ceased authorizing entry of immigrant workers and officially closed its borders.[45] As the country's unemployment rate soared in 1977, returning immigrants to their homelands became a key goal of the French government. Unemployed immigrants and those who had lived in France more than five years were offered the equivalent of about €1,524 (equal to about $2,500 in 2006) as a financial incentive to leave.[46] Attempts to pay immigrants to leave voluntarily were largely unsuccessful and immigration to

France continued to increase with an average of 100,000 immigrants arriving annually.

To address the growing immigration problem various laws were adopted in the 1980s, including the "Bonnet" law, which decreed that the entry and presence of illegal immigrants in France was considered a threat to public order and that they had to be removed; the "Peyrefitte" law, which allowed the police to stop anyone suspected of being an immigrant to verify his or her identity; and the "Pasqua" law, which reduced the number of residence permits available to immigrants and granted the right to regional authorities to make the decision whether or not to escort illegal aliens back to the border.[47]

The 1990s saw existing immigration laws reinforced and new efforts directed at completely stopping immigration into France, or to achieve a goal of *immigration zéro.* Actions included imposing a penalty on people who assisted illegal aliens and additional measures to decrease legal immigration, including prohibiting foreign graduates of French universities from accepting job offers from French employers. The family reunification waiting period was increased from one year to two years, and foreign spouses who lived in France illegally prior to their marriage were denied residency permits at the time of marriage. The actions meant that immigrants who would have been granted citizenship under the previous law now remained illegal. The new law created a class of people living in France described as *inexpulsables-irrégularisables,* or immigrants who could not be deported but also were not eligible for residency permits, such as rejected asylum seekers who could not safely return to their countries but whose rights continued to be protected by international laws or the foreign parents of children born in France.

Although the French National Assembly voted in favor of a new immigration law making it easier to screen and deport illegal immigrants in 1997, a report commissioned by Prime Minister Lionel Jospin titled *L'immigration et la nationalité* (Immigration and Nationality) established the foundation for an immigration law adopted in 1998. The report noted, among other things, that the 1993 Pasqua law discouraged foreign students and young professionals from living in France and therefore "deprived the country of a source of human capital and undermined its national interests in the global competition for the brightest minds."[48] Modeled on the United States's visa provisions for highly skilled immigrants, the law created a special status for scientists and scholars as well as eased conditions for admission of certain highly skilled professionals such as computer experts. Other reforms to immigration policy included reintroduction in 1998 of the automatic right to French citizenship for children born in France to foreign parents when the child reached the age of 18 years, also similar to the U.S. policy of automatically granting citizenship to American-born children of immigrants, both legal and illegal.[49] Immigration laws passed in 2000 focused on making family reunification and citizenship simpler and fighting discrimination against immigrants living in the country by requiring that those accused of discrimination prove they are not guilty of the charge rather than making the immigrant prove he or she was discriminated against.

IMMIGRATION POLICY AFTER SEPTEMBER 11, 2001

The terrorist attacks against the United States on September 11, 2001, changed France's view of immigration from an economic and social matter to a security issue. The terrorist attacks also intensified France's battle against illegal immigration and increased suspicion toward immigrants who had been in the country long-term.[50] Immigration debates focused on "security, control, and repression." Measures taken strengthened sanctions against "border trespassers and channels of illegal immigration" and abolished residence permits for European Union citizens.[51] Immigrants rioting in Paris's suburbs in 2005 led to tightened immigration controls, including the requirement that immigrants requesting 10-year residency permits or citizenship must master the French language and prove they have integrated into French society by signing a "welcome and integration" contract, taking courses in French civics, and complying with and respecting the principles of the French Republic.[52] The government also cracked down on fraudulent marriages and began more strict screenings of foreign students.[53] A new immigration bill was passed in 2007 that would make sweeping changes to France's existing immigration policy. Changes include:

- making it easier for qualified foreigners to remain in France for three years via a "skills and talent" visa;
- making it more difficult for family members to join relatives in France by lengthening the required waiting time before immigrating from one year to 18 months, and by requiring a DNA test for children who seek to join the mother in France;
- requiring that immigrants prove they can financially support themselves and show that they are making efforts to integrate into French society;
- requiring that new immigrants take French language and cultural knowledge tests;
- removing the automatic right of immigrants living in France for 10 years to apply for long term residency.[54]

Despite widespread support for the new law by French nationals, similar to the 2006 protests by Mexican immigrants in the United States against proposed changes to U.S. immigration policy, thousands of immigrants to France gathered to demonstrate in protest against the proposed law, citing that, among other things, it promoted "selected immigration."[55]

Conclusion

The passage of eight major immigration-related reforms between 1980 and 2007 shows the influence immigration has had on key issues in France, touching on issues that range from the country's security to its culture and identity. Assimilation of immigrants and preservation of the country's national heritage are key elements of France's immigration policies. Because of France's official policy of ignoring ethnic differences while favoring the idea of a single French identity, integrating immigrants of different cultures into society has been made more difficult. France's policies are almost directly opposite to those promoted in the United States, which has traditionally embraced ethnic diversity and welcomed the cultural differences introduced by its various immigrant communities.

Admitting that many French nationals do not accept the idea that the country's identity "might be made up of contributions from abroad," in 2005 the French government launched its first effort to recognize the role immigration and immigrants have played in the country's national heritage with the establishment of the National Centre for Immigration History. At the project's official launch in 2004 Prime Minister Jean-Pierre Raffarin commented, "We must recognize the contribution made by immigration to the building of France and change perceptions of this phenomenon, for our cohesion as a nation is at stake." The museum, which opened in 2007, includes permanent exhibits related to the history of immigration in France from 1789 as well as temporary exhibits, symposiums, and a multimedia documentary resource center.[56]

SOUTH AFRICA

Introduction

Immigration policy in South Africa is closely tied to European colonization of the country. Arrival of Europeans, while slow to start, rapidly expanded with the discovery of diamonds and gold in South Africa in 1867 and 1886, respectively. Immigration of white Europeans during those early years was encouraged and immigration by black Africans was discouraged or prohibited. During the apartheid years (1948–94) the practice of segregation led to further discrimination against immigrants, specifically black Africans, Indians, Chinese, and Jews, while immigration by whites from other African countries and the United Kingdom continued to be encouraged. During apartheid the government passed more than 300 laws to assure separation of blacks from the white population and to establish a racial hierarchy with white citizens at the top and black Africans at the bottom. The official end of apartheid did not also end the segregationist policies that influenced the country's restrictive immigration laws. Xenophobia, high unemployment, and anti-immigration sentiment led to a decline in immigration to South Africa during the 1990s and fueled illegal immigration, mostly by black Africans seeking refuge from poverty and wars in neighboring countries. Updates to South Africa's policies in the early 2000s were designed to encourage immigration, especially by highly skilled workers and entrepreneurs who could benefit the country's economy. In response to the changes in policy, immigration and cross-border migration by unskilled workers increased. However, emigration and brain drain, or the loss of highly skilled and educated citizens, also increased during this time period.

Historical Background

PRECOLONIAL SETTLEMENTS

Research has shown that humans have lived in South Africa for more than 100,000 years. The oldest indigenous people in the region are the San who came to the area during the last Ice Age, about 20,000 years ago. The Khoikhoi, probably originating in Botswana, migrated into the region about 2,000 years ago. During the fifth century C.E. Bantu-speaking peoples, including the Xhosa and Zulu, arrived probably from the area around the Congo basin. By the 16th century, when the first European settlers arrived, the entire area that now constitutes South Africa had been settled.

EUROPEAN COLONIALISM

In 1488 the first European ship sailed around South Africa's Cape of Good Hope. In the 1500s some of the earliest Europeans living in the country were unwilling settlers, chiefly sailors who were stranded in South Africa following shipwrecks or after they became ill and were abandoned in the country by ship captains.[57]

The first Europeans to settle in what is now the country of South Africa were sent by the Dutch East India Company, a trading company in the Netherlands. The new Dutch settlement in South Africa's Cape Town was developed in 1652 to provide supplies for ships sailing along the trade routes between Europe and Asia. Dutch colonists continued to migrate and settle in South Africa, but immigration was low compared to the growth of immigrant populations in other European colonies at the time, such as in North

America. Dutch farmers who moved into the interior were called Trekboers, or Boers. By the end of the 1700s the number of European immigrants living in South Africa had grown to just 22,000 compared to North America, which saw its immigrant population jump from 90,000 to 700,000 between 1700 and 1780. To overcome labor shortages in their South African colonies the Dutch imported slaves from India, Madagascar, and Indonesia. According to information from the South African government, "By the mid-1700s, there were more slaves in the Cape than there were 'free burghers,'" as the European colonists were known. The slave population in the Cape had reached 36,000 by 1834, based on early statistics.[58]

Following the Fourth Anglo-Dutch War in 1797 the British claimed the area around the Cape of Good Hope from the Dutch and annexed the Cape Colony in 1805. To relieve high unemployment in England and encourage immigration to South Africa, in 1819 the British government agreed to pay its citizens to emigrate. Although an estimated 90,000 British citizens lined up to take advantage of the offer, in 1820 the government only selected 5,000 people to immigrate to its colony in South Africa's Eastern Cape.[59] With the Cape Colony under British rule the Dutch migrated deeper into South Africa's interior during the 1830s to settle in the Orange Free State and Transvaal. Beginning in the mid-1800s Jewish immigrants began arriving in South Africa, many coming from Lithuania after the 1880s.[60] A need for people to work on sugar plantations in the British-held colony of Natal led to the importation of immigrants from India as indentured laborers. By 1865 an estimated 252,000 white European immigrants were living in South Africa and an untold number of unwilling immigrants were in the country as slaves or indentured workers. To further increase the number of European citizens living in its colonies to 60 percent of the population, in 1902 the British government again tried to encourage emigration, but only about 1,200 additional British families opted to immigrate to South Africa. Also during this time, European immigrants encountered increasing resistance from indigenous populations who resented the settlers who were moving in and appropriating African lands. Despite efforts by Africans to stop Europeans from taking their land, in 1913 the British government passed the Native Lands Act, making it illegal for black Africans to purchase or rent land in South Africa outside of existing reserves, which limited African ownership to just 7 percent of the land.[61]

THE DISCOVERY OF DIAMONDS AND GOLD

Immigration changed dramatically when diamonds were discovered in a region between South Africa's Vaal and Orange rivers in 1867. According to the South African government, the discovery "drew tens of thousands of people, Black and White, to the first great industrial hub in Africa, the largest diamond deposit in the world." The British pushed out Dutch rivals in the region and claimed the diamond fields in 1871.[62] Another major mineral discovery in 1886, this time gold, in the Dutch controlled province of Transvaal, further changed immigration to South Africa. Located just two miles west of the present-day city of Johannesburg, the gold discovery was one of the world's richest. At the time Johannesburg was a small settlement, but, similar to the California gold rush in the United States in 1848, people flocked to the city. The *Economist* reported: "Word of the discovery spread quickly. Treasure-hunters swarmed. Many were miners from the diamond shafts at Kimberley, 300 miles to the south-west. Others came from further afield: blacks from elsewhere in Africa and whites from far-flung corners of the world, such as Europe, America and Australia."[63] During that time the population of Johannesburg increased to 100,000.[64]

The British opted to take the Dutch-held region by force, initiating what became known as the Boer War. The war ended in 1902, resulting in incorporation of Transvaal and Orange Free State into the British Empire. Seeking to encourage British immigration to Transvaal and Orange Free State and to disenfranchise the Dutch remaining in the area, English was established as the official language of the colonies. A British architect was hired to design mansions for wealthy English immigrants. To discourage black African migrant mineworkers from moving to the region, their wages, which were already 10 percent less than those of white workers, were further reduced.[65] When black African workers protested the reduced salaries, thousands of Chinese, willing to work for lower pay than their black counterparts, were encouraged to immigrate to the colonies. By 1904 over 60,000 Chinese immigrants were in South Africa as indentured workers.

In 1910 Transvaal, Orange Free State, Natal, and the Cape were united as the Union of South Africa under the British flag. Subsequent actions by the British government led to a rise in immigration to South Africa. According to statistics, the European immigrant population swelled to 1.3 million by 1913. Despite white control of South Africa, the growing diamond- and gold-mining industries, and an increased British presence, immigrant settlers accounted for only about 20 percent of the population by 1938, or 2.1 million people.[66]

IMMIGRATION DURING APARTHEID

During apartheid—racial segregation and inequality implemented by South Africa's white-controlled government that began in the early 20th century and continued until 1994—immigration and cross-border migration by black Africans was discouraged; however, a Global Commission on International

Migration (GCIM) study reported, "Between 1960 and 1980, skilled and semi-skilled white migrants from Zambia, Kenya and Zimbabwe were given citizenship to boost the local [white] population" of South Africa.[67] According to census data, in 1961 there were 836,000 regional migrants from other African countries living in South Africa. A Southern African Migration Project (SAMP) report noted that in the early 1970s workers employed in the mines had dropped to 400,000 but about 80 percent of them were migrants.[68] Statistics South Africa (Stats SA) reported that between 1973 and 1975 documented immigration from the United Kingdom to the country doubled. A peak in immigration occurred in 1976, with immigrants accounting for 3.7 percent of the population or 962,000 people. Another immigration peak occurred in 1982 with immigrants arriving from the United Kingdom, China, and Portugal. In 1986 the immigrant population in South Africa had increased to 1.8 million people.[69]

Despite the restrictions on Africans immigrating to South Africa during apartheid, a new type of immigrant began arriving from other African nations during the 1980s, namely, refugees. More than 300,000 Mozambicans fled to South Africa to escape the civil war in their homeland that raged from 1975 to 1994.[70]

IMMIGRATION AFTER APARTHEID

Apartheid officially ended in 1994 but its segregationist policies at first continued to influence immigration to South Africa. Post-apartheid unemployment, particularly for unskilled workers, reached levels as high as 30 percent, and xenophobia increased proportionately. According to a 2003 report: "A distinguishing characteristic of the post-Apartheid labour market, therefore, has been very high and rising rates of joblessness. Under these circumstances, immigrants are easy targets to blame for growing unemployment."[71] Due to distrust of foreigners and anti-immigrant sentiment, immigration to the country stalled beginning in 1990 and the downturn continued for about 10 years. Immigrants granted permanent residence status dropped from about 14,000 per year at the beginning of the 1990s to fewer than 4,000 annually in 2000, and in the first 10 months of 2001 only 3,053 people moved to South Africa.[72]

A new Immigration Act took effect in 2002. Although it was bogged down in anti-immigrant–based challenges to its constitutionality in the courts, South Africa's declining immigration began to shift. Asylum seekers from neighboring African countries contributed to the increase in immigration. Stats SA reported that documented immigrants jumped 61.6 percent to 10,578 in 2003 from 6,545 in 2002. According to the data, in 2003 the greatest number of immigrants came from Nigeria, followed by immigrants from the United Kingdom, Zimbabwe, Pakistan, India, and Germany.[73] Chinese also represented a growing number of immigrants in the country. As many as 200,000 mainland Chinese immigrants were living in the country in 2004, both legally and illegally.[74] Immigration from all countries, not just China, continued to increase and in 2004 the broad range of foreigners requesting to immigrate legally was described as the "Rainbow Immigration."[75] At the end of 2005 some 17,000 foreigners were waiting for permanent residence permits while South Africa's immigration experts claimed there was a backlog of more than 20,000 foreigners awaiting immigration papers. Reportedly topping the list of future immigrants were retirees and business investors from Europe and information technology and financial experts from India.[76]

Growing numbers of refugees also requested asylum in South Africa, which began formally recognizing refugees in 1993. Between 1994 and 2005 nearly 186,000 people applied for asylum in South Africa with just 26,000, most from other African nations, granted refugee status.[77] The backlog of people seeking refugee status reached more than 100,000 in 2006, according to the South African Department of Home Affairs. The delays resulted in "unlawful arrests, detention and deportation of legitimate applicants."[78]

How South Africa Benefits from Immigration

Over the years South Africa has embraced anti-immigration policies and generally supports the idea that there are few benefits in having immigrants in the country, notably unskilled black Africans from neighboring African nations. However, studies suggest otherwise. Immigrants, both skilled and unskilled, pay taxes, establish businesses, and make a positive contribution to the country's economic development. As noted in the GCIM report:

> *One area in which immigrants are having an indirect impact on the economy is the area of formal and informal businesses such as hair saloons, supermarkets, African crafts, taxis and upholstery. These businesses were established with funds from home countries, loans from friends and earnings in South Africa. . . . Immigrant owned businesses have become an important part of small, medium and micro enterprise sector. . . .* [79]

The report further noted that immigrants continue to persevere in the face of hostility from South Africans. Many plan to expand their businesses, which helps create jobs. In addition, as in the United States and other countries, immigrants often fill jobs South African nationals are unwilling to do.

Problems Associated with Immigration

ILLEGAL IMMIGRATION

Although illegal immigration from neighboring African countries by people in search of work began in the late 1800s, it was often approved by the state and at times incorporated into labor planning. Illegal immigration to South Africa from neighboring nations by black Africans in search of work increased in 1948 due to the restrictive policies of apartheid, which prohibited legal immigration of black Africans.[80] Because illegal economic migration was accepted or ignored before the early 1990s, little official data are available about the numbers of migrants and their countries of origin until the period beginning post-apartheid. The *South African Yearbook* suggested that in 1990 there were an estimated 1.2 million illegal aliens living in the country. The estimates increased annually, rising to 5 million people in the country illegally in 1994, but most scholars agreed that the figures were uncertain at best and completely wrong at worst.[81] Even after 1994 figures remain controversial. By 1996, estimates of the number of illegal aliens in the country stood as high as 11 million, but SAMP wrote, "These figures have absolutely no basis in fact," because it is nearly impossible to accurately count undocumented migrants. "The danger is that in the absence of reliable statistics, officials, politicians, and members of the general public feel free to use whatever figure they like to whip up anti-immigrant sentiment."[82] Based on South Africa's 2001 census data a more accurate estimate of illegal aliens in the country that year was 500,000.

Various factors began to affect illegal immigration to South Africa, including the end of apartheid in 1994; the country's enforcement of restrictive immigration policies; and the political instability, wars, poverty, and joblessness or low wages in neighboring countries. Xenophobia increased proportionately with the increase in illegal immigrants. Echoing the complaints about illegal immigrants heard in other countries around the world, including the United States, South Africans accused illegal aliens of taking jobs, committing crimes, depressing wages, consuming resources, spreading AIDS, and smuggling weapons and drugs. In addition to other African nations, a growing number of immigrants began entering the country illegally from Asia, eastern Europe, and especially China. A 2001 Institute for Security Studies paper estimated 100,000 Chinese were in South Africa illegally. The embassy of the People's Republic of China in Pretoria, South Africa, while admitting there were Chinese immigrants in South Africa illegally, disputed the number, saying it was too high.[83] Most Chinese nationals established legitimate businesses, but others were implicated in crimes such as false marriage scams, financial crimes, extortion, importing counterfeit products, and, like the *coyotes* in Mexico who smuggled illegal aliens into the United States, Chinese known as *snakeheads* smuggled illegal aliens into South Africa.[84]

Managing illegal immigrants became a challenge for the post-apartheid government and included offering amnesty to some and deporting others. A 1996 amnesty plan offered permanent residence status to qualified illegal aliens who had lived in the country for more than five years, had a job, did not have a criminal record, or were married to a South African. Some 150,000 illegal immigrants took advantage of the offer and applied for permanent residence status. In 1988 the government deported 44,225 illegal immigrants, most to neighboring African countries. The number of illegal aliens deported in 1995 climbed to 157,000, with 98 percent from other African nations and by 2003 South Africa had deported more than 1 million undocumented immigrants.[85]

The country's uneven handling of deportations, however, came under fire by human rights organizations and from the countries whose citizens were being removed from South Africa. A South African parliament study regarding the handling of illegal immigrants by officials and law enforcement turned up complaints of "corruption, xenophobia, incompetence and human rights abuses at the Lindela repatriation center" where illegal aliens awaiting deportation were held. The chairman of the South African Human Rights Commission said that complaints were regularly received about home affairs officials at the Lindela center. "I think we have to review the arrest, detain and deport policy as far as illegal foreigners are concerned," he said. It was agreed that greater coordination was needed between home affairs officials, police, and foreign embassies regarding uniform application of immigration laws, but no further actions to resolve problems related to the handling of illegal immigrants were reported.[86]

Policies and Laws

EARLY GOVERNMENT REGULATIONS

Under British colonialism South Africa's immigration policies were limited and the country's borders were generally open, especially to immigrants from Europe. However, from 1890 through the 1920s strict regulations were enacted that protected "the highly regulated and formalized mine contract labor system" and controlled temporary migrant workers, especially black workers from other African nations.[87] After South Africa became a union in 1910, immigration and migration policies focused on building the country but policies maintained restrictions on immigration by black Africans. South Africa's strained relations with neighboring African countries and prejudice against black Africans by white South Africans influenced the country's immigration policy. It was noted: "Serious regional tensions, as well as racial prejudices, are evident in policy-makers' attempts to create and regulate a new South African identity." The immigration-based actions taken at that time, such as excluding African emigrants from neighboring countries and strictly regulating people arriving from eastern and southern Europe "set the foundations of migration policy for the rest of the century."[88] Early laws also worked against immigrants from India, who had been brought to South Africa as indentured laborers in the 1860s during expansion of the British Empire in the region.[89]

The government implemented one of its first culturally influenced immigration restrictions in 1902 by putting in place a language requirement. Subsequent language-based immigration legislation required of all immigrants that they be able to fill out immigration forms in any European language. Reflecting the country's growing anti-Indian sentiment the languages of Indians were not accepted in the requirements, and a tax was imposed on indentured workers who did not return to India.[90] Black Africans were excluded from immigrating into South Africa and could only enter as illegal aliens or temporary contract workers beginning in 1913 and continuing until 1986. The 1930s brought about laws that further limited immigration, including excluding Jews as immigrants due to growing anti-Semitism and establishing a quota system that considered an immigrant's country of origin rather than the reasons for immigrating. A report for the GCIM stated: "The racist orientation of South African immigration policy became very evident when the government welcomed whites from neighbouring states in Southern Africa. . . . Between 1960 and 1980 skilled and semi-skilled white migrants from Zambia, Kenya and Zimbabwe were given citizenship to boost the local [white] population."[91]

AFTER APARTHEID

The end of apartheid led the government to begin considering ways to update the country's immigration and migration policies. In 1995 it passed the South African Citizenship Act, which replaced the race-based laws established in 1949 and 1970. The 1995 act stated that to achieve citizenship an immigrant must have lived in the country at least five years, have a job, have a relationship with a South African, or have dependent children born or living legally in the country. A Refugee Act that took effect in 2000 was designed to regulate the number of people seeking asylum in South Africa. The act stated that asylum seekers could not hold jobs, attend school, or open their own businesses until they were legally classified as refugees. Prior to 1993 South Africa did not recognize refugees and most lived in the country as undocumented migrants until passage of the Refugee Act.[92]

After struggling for nearly eight years to bring its immigration policies into the 21st century the South African government passed Immigration Act 13 of 2002, but implementation of the act was stalled due to "court challenges to the constitutionality of accompanying regulations." An amended law passed in 2003 that divided immigration into two categories: Direct Residence and Residence on Other Grounds. To receive a permanent residence permit under the Direct Residence category foreigners were required to have lived in the country on a work permit for five years and received an offer of permanent employment. Immigrating under the Residence on Other Grounds category required a foreigner to show proof of an offer of employment for a job no South African was qualified or available to fill. The act also allowed South African businesses to hire skilled foreign professionals, but not unskilled workers. As many as 300,000 work permits were available for skilled foreigners with one stipulation: Foreign workers were required to pay 2 percent of their taxable salary each quarter to the country's Home Affairs Department. The collected funds would be used to train native South Africans in the necessary skills to replace foreign workers.[93]

Additional amendments were made to the act the following year that included temporary residence permits, several different types of work permits, and permits specifically for retired people wishing to live only part of each year in South Africa. To be granted a Retired Persons Permit an immigrant was required to possess a pension, retirement annuity, or a retirement account with a value of at least 20,000 Rand ($2,978) or to have a net worth or assets of 12 million Rand ($1.8 million). Special business permits were also available to entrepreneurs who could prove their planned business would contribute to South Africa's economy. Further, the only foreigners permitted to immigrate were those "seriously committed to immigrating to the country permanently and to investing their assets, skills, knowledge and experience for the benefit of themselves and the people of South Africa." Due to the high unemployment rate among South African citizens unskilled and semi-skilled workers were excluded as immigrants.[94]

Emigration

DURING APARTHEID

South Africa began to experience a loss of its population during apartheid when many black South Africans fled as refugees to neighboring African nations, such as Swaziland, Botswana, and Lesotho. According to the United Nations High Commissioner for Refugees (UNHCR): "Lesotho's refugee history is closely linked to that of the apartheid South Africa. The influx of refugees started in the mid-1960s, at a time when liberation movements were banned in South Africa and their leaders imprisoned." Responding to the flight of its citizens, South African military forces raided private homes in Lesotho in 1982, allegedly to eliminate dissidents hiding in the country. The military action resulted in the deaths of 42 people, including 12 Lesotho citizens. To further stem the outward flow of South Africans to Lesotho, between 1985 and 1986 the South African government implemented an economic embargo and blockade of Lesotho, which included preventing Lesotho aircraft from flying over South Africa and stopping food and other essential goods from being imported.[95]

White South Africans were also fleeing the country and its apartheid policies. Fearing loss of its white citizens, the government enforced restrictive emigration policies that, besides making it nearly impossible for blacks to emigrate, made it almost as difficult for whites to leave. In 1973 the Canadian Broadcasting Corporation (CBC) reported: "Most emigrants [from South Africa] were forced to lie about their intentions, leaving their belongings and official papers behind. The wealthy whites that were permitted to leave the country could bring a maximum of $30,000 with them—making selling homes and businesses impractical. . . . Wages for most blacks were so low that the cost of transportation to countries like Canada was completely out of reach," which helped explain why so many black South Africans emigrated to other African countries rather than seeking refuge in European nations.[96] By 1988 when apartheid was in decline large numbers of South African emigrants were living in other countries. That year Lesotho was home to 4,000 South African refugees; there were 7,000 South Africans in Swaziland and several thousand more in Botswana.[97] A Canadian Broadcasting Corporation program reported that in 1990 "an estimated 50,000 South Africans [were] living in Canada. The majority were white, since it was difficult politically and economically for non-whites to emigrate."[98]

AFTER APARTHEID

Following the official end of apartheid, emigration from South Africa continued and picked up speed. In 1998 one of South Africa's leading policy research organizations, the Centre for Development and Enterprise (CDE), issued a report that said a review of statistics from other countries, including the United States, Canada, the United Kingdom, and Australia, suggested "as many as 400,000 to 600,000 South Africans may have emigrated since 1976, rather than the official figure of 200,000." (The total estimated population in 1995 was 45 million.) Despite some questions about the number of emigrants, according to Stats SA, in the 10 months between January and October 2001 some 10,262 people officially emigrated, but other researchers believed the number was much higher. The most recent data available from Stats SA, a 2003 study of documented migration, reported that the number of self-declared emigrants from South Africa increased from 10,890 in 2002 to 16,165 in 2003. Most emigrants, about 32 percent, listed the United Kingdom as their destination country. Other destination countries in 2003 and the approximate percentage of emigrants were Australia (14 percent), the United States (10 percent), New Zealand (6 percent), Namibia (4 percent), and Canada (2.5 percent). Although the government stopped keeping official records on its emigrants in 2004 due to changes in legislation, statistics that year indicated that about 10,000 people were leaving South Africa annually.[99]

BRAIN DRAIN

The most damaging consequence of South African emigration has been the loss of its educated, highly skilled workers. Based on South African government statistics between 1989 and 1997 "approximately 82,000 skilled people officially emigrated from South Africa to five main destination countries (the United Kingdom, the United States, Canada, Australia, and New Zealand)." However, according to the MPI, other reliable research placed the number of skilled South African emigrants during that time closer to 230,000.[100] Most of the skilled emigrants were educators, medical professionals, or those employed in industry and information technology. The International Marketing Council of South Africa reported that nearly 17,000 science and technology professionals left the country between 1994 and 2001. Commenting on the problems associated with the loss of professionals, a University of Cape Town report concluded, "The brain drain is a slow though significant erosion of the country's human resources and endowments."[101]

Among the reasons people cited for emigrating, 60 percent listed fear of crime (in 2002 the murder rate in South Africa was 10 times higher than in the United States). Other reasons were corruption, declining standards in health care and education, the AIDS epidemic (one in nine people in South Africa had HIV in 2002), and high levels of unemployment (30 to 38 percent in 2001).[102] BBC News reported that as many as 100,000 people left South Africa between 1999 and 2002, "and 70 percent of skilled South Africans still in the country say they are considering emigrating, despite government calls for them to stay and help their country."[103] Stats SA's 2003 study found that of the officially documented 16,165 emigrants that year 4,316 were classified as highly skilled professionals, semi-professionals, or technical workers. Of those 766 were health care workers, including 192 physicians and 267 nurses. Between 1994 and 2004 about 23,400 health care professionals emigrated, while about 500,000 health care jobs went unfilled. BBC News commented on the emigration of South Africa's teachers, reporting, "At any one stage, up to 5,000 South Africans are teaching in London alone."[104]

Conclusion

Although in the late 20th century and early 21st century the South African government struggled to set aside the country's apartheid-based mentality and rewrite its immigration policies, foreigners continued to be viewed with distrust, and immigration and cross-border migration by unskilled workers continued to be prohibited in the 2000s. And as the country's elite workers—teachers, doctors, nurses, engineers—emigrated to countries offering better wages and living conditions, encouraging South Africans, especially highly skilled professionals, to repatriate became critical to the government. The Come Home Campaign, launched in 2003 as a joint effort of the South African trade union Solidarity and the Company for Immigration, focused on helping expatriates return to South Africa. According to campaign officials, between 2004 and 2006 about 1,200 South Africans had returned to their homeland and an additional 3,000 were going through the repatriation process. Returning to South Africa can take from as little as six weeks to as long as five years and it can cost the repatriating person as much as 100,000 Rand ($14,888), to cover things such as airline tickets and shipping household items. Most returning South Africans were between the ages of 28 and 45 and were from the United Kingdom, the United States, Canada, Australia, New Zealand, and the Netherlands.[105]

MEXICO

Introduction

Despite the growing loss of its native population to emigration in the early 21st century, Mexico has a long history of immigration that dates back to the 1500s and Spanish colonization of the country. Over the course of history, immigrants have made their way to Mexico from most countries, including Spain, Africa, France, Germany, Korea, Poland, and China. More recently, Central American nations are seeing increased numbers of their citizens immigrating to Mexico. While some of the immigrants arrived in Mexico unwillingly, such as Africans and Koreans who came as slaves, others were economic immigrants, who came in pursuit of jobs and to earn wages higher than they found in their homelands. Some fled to Mexico seeking refuge from wars and persecution in their countries.

In the late 1800s Mexican nationals began legally immigrating to the United States to work in agriculture and other low-skilled jobs. The trend continued and grew until in the late 1900s and early 2000s the numbers of Mexican emigrants arriving in the United States, many illegally, amounted to a flood of people. On the flip side, Americans, many of them retirees, were crossing the border in the other direction to settle in Mexico. Most expatriates were looking for a better climate and lower cost of living. The porous nature of the border between Mexico and the United States led to problems between the two countries by the mid-2000s as more and more immigrants from Mexico and Central America, many illegal, used Mexico as a passageway into the United States. Increasing illegal drug and human smuggling across the border from Mexico into the United States further aggravated problems between the two countries. In response to the growing problems of immigration to and emigration from Mexico, the government made modifications to its immigration policies, which had been in place and unchanged since 1917.

Historical Background

FIRST PEOPLES

The earliest evidence of humans living in Mexico is of hunter-gatherers and dates to about 20,000 years ago. These early Mesoamericans eventually founded numerous separate civilizations in Mexico including the Olmec (fl. ca. 1200–300 B.C.E.); Teotihuacán, Monte Albán, and Maya (fl. ca. 1000 B.C.E.–1521 C.E.); and finally the Mexica-Aztec (fl. ca. 1200–1521). At the time the Mexica-Aztec rose to prominence in about 1400, Mexico had a population of nearly 24 million people.

EUROPEAN AND ASIAN COLONIZATION

Spanish colonialism and immigration to Mexico began in 1521 and continued for 300 years through the early 1800s. Large numbers of Africans immigrated to Mexico with the Spanish beginning in the 16th century. Because the Spanish colonists preferred to use Mexican Indians for slave labor, Africans traveled to Mexico first as servants to the Spanish. The use of Indians as slaves was abolished in 1542 by the Spanish government and, to compensate for the shortage of laborers, the Spanish began importing African slaves. By 1553 more than 20,000 Africans were in Mexico as slaves. Between 1595 and 1622 more than 50,000 Africans arrived in Mexico aboard slave ships. An estimated 110,525 African slaves had been sent to Mexico by

1639. According to early census figures and church records, in 1803 one city in Mexico listed 12,500 African and mulatto (mixed race European and African) residents compared to 11,000 Spanish and 9,500 native Mexican Indians.[106]

Following its war for independence from Spain in 1823 Mexico established the United Mexican States, which included most of the lands in North America formerly held by Spain. To establish communities and build the population in its remote and sparsely populated northern territories Mexico offered land grants to families living in America willing to immigrate. Although requirements to receive Mexico's land grants included converting to the Catholic faith and becoming a citizen of Mexico, thousands of Americans chose to emigrate and claim the land being offered by Mexico, including territories that eventually became the states of Texas, New Mexico, Arizona, Colorado, Nevada, Utah, and California.

The French also established a presence in Mexico. A group of French colonists arrived in 1831 and established a settlement at Coatzacoalcos. The settlement failed, but the colonists relocated and established colonies in Veracruz, Mexico City, Nautla, and Jicaltepec. Following a military invasion of Mexico by France in 1838 the Mexican government deported many of the French immigrants. Another invasion by France occurred in 1863 but the occupation was brief, ending in 1867 when Mexico's army, supported by the United States, ousted the French invaders.

During the mid-1800s German immigrants developed the city of Mazatlán into a trading port,[107] and Jews began arriving in Mexico in 1531 after they were deported from Spain. An invitation by the Mexican government in 1884 was extended to a group of Jewish bankers to open bank offices in Mexico, which further encouraged Jews to settle in the country.[108]

In 1905 more than 1,000 immigrants from Korea, believing they were sailing to Hawaii to work on the sugar plantations, were instead diverted to Mexico and were sold by a Japanese slave trader to work on cactus plantations and in cactus processing plants. Although the Korean slaves were freed four years later most chose to remain in Mexico due to the ongoing occupation of their homeland by Japan.[109]

During World War I (1914–18) immigrants arrived in Mexico from Germany, Yugoslavia, Poland, and other European nations. People fleeing religious persecution in Russia and Lebanon also immigrated to Mexico in the late 1800s and early 1900s. Information from the National Archives notes that in 1929 some 3,000 immigrants from Lebanon were living in Mexico.[110] At the beginning of the 20th century Chinese immigrants began arriving in Mexico, either lured by the promise of jobs and high wages or to escape anti-Chinese policies in the United States. By 1920 nearly 10,000 Chinese lived in Mexicali, a town on the U.S.-Mexico border in Mexico's state of Baja California. While its Chinese population was notably smaller than in U.S. cities such as San Francisco, Mexicali eventually became more culturally Chinese than Mexican and a section of the city became known as *Chinseca* (Chinatown). World War II triggered the arrival of another group of immigrants from central and eastern Europe as well as more Chinese fleeing the Japanese and communism.[111]

Modern Immigration

Beginning in the 20th century increasing numbers of immigrants were arriving in Mexico from Central American countries to the south, especially Guatemala, Honduras, and El Salvador. In the early to mid-1900s the majority of Central Americans—an estimated 45,000 to 75,000 annually—came as temporary migrants seeking seasonal work on Mexico's coffee plantations or in planting and harvesting local produce such as sugar cane and bananas. After 1970, civil wars, earthquakes, hurricanes, few employment opportunities, and other problems in their homelands forced many Central Americans to emigrate in search of refuge. The United Nations High Commissioner for Refugees reported that in the three-year period of 1981–83 during the height of the civil war in Guatemala, more than 200,000 of that country's citizens sought asylum in Mexico.[112] Beginning in the late 1980s through the late 1990s, emigrants from Guatemala began arriving in Mexico in search of employment rather than solely for political asylum. In 1992 more than 87,000 Guatemalans entered Mexico legally as migrant workers and an estimated 250,000 arrived illegally. At the end of their country's civil war in 1996 thousands of Guatemalan refugees living in Mexico began returning to their homeland and by 2000 nearly 43,000 had repatriated.

Despite the presence of immigrants in Mexico, their numbers have remained small compared to the country's overall population as well as to the immigrant populations in other countries, including the United States. Mexico's 2000 census listed approximately 493,000 foreign-born residents among its population of 100 million people, including about 340,000 Americans, 27,600 Guatemalans, and 5,400 El Salvadorans. Residents listed with foreign ancestry included 400,000 Arabs, most of them from Lebanon; 150,000 Argentines; 20,000 Koreans; 50,000 Jews; and 9 million people with European ancestry, mostly Spanish. According to 2006 statistics Mexico's population had grown to 105 million people, but of those only .5 percent were foreign born, compared to the United States, which reported that 13 percent of its population of 299 million was foreign born.

Why Immigrants Come to Mexico

Central Americans typically immigrated to Mexico for refuge or work (even though Mexico's average pay was as little as $6 per day in the late-1990s, it was estimated to be at least 50 percent more than in Guatemala). Americans who immigrate to Mexico often cite the lower cost of living as a reason for moving south of the border. A 2004 article published in *Hispanic Vista* stated that many U.S. emigrants living in Mexico were retirees enticed by an improved standard of living "based on the higher purchasing power of their retirement benefits. A monthly income of $2,000 allows a retired couple twice the standard of living in Mexico, with domestic help, as is available to them in the U.S." In addition, discounts are offered on everything from prescription drugs to groceries at thousands of locations throughout Mexico on the basis of a special card issued by Mexico's Institute for Elderly Adults.[113]

How Mexico Benefits from Immigration

As Mexico's citizens emigrate to the United States in search of better-paying jobs and employment opportunities, migrant workers from Central America have stepped in to do work that would otherwise be left undone, such as harvesting crops on Mexican farms. Americans, especially retirees, who immigrate to Mexico create a demand for goods and services that in turn creates jobs and helps boost the economies of the communities in which they settle. According to one study, retirees in Mexico "consistently mentioned hiring local people to build homes, cook and clean, tend gardens, and provide care to spouses or other family members who could not care for themselves." Further, Americans donate to and help support local public libraries, scholarship funds for local students, and orphanages, or they serve as volunteers who help staff various community organizations and facilities as well as nongovernmental organizations in the different communities where they settle.[114]

Problems Associated with Immigration

Despite the benefits immigrants bring to Mexico, one downside of American immigrants living in Mexico that has been noted is the rising cost of real estate and the increasing cost of living their presence causes. Demand for housing in Mexico's cities that attract American immigrants often pushes locals out of the housing market. An American living in one Mexican community said, "There were whole neighborhoods where it was all Mexican families, and now there's one Mexican family left on the block." Some communities that have become overdeveloped and overpriced due to the influx of American immigrants have seen not only the Mexican residents move away but also many of the American immigrants who had first settled in the areas.[115]

ILLEGAL IMMIGRATION

Just as the United States has experienced growing numbers of illegal immigrants entering by way of its southern border with Mexico, illegal immigration to Mexico has increased as immigrants enter by way of its southern border with Guatemala. However, unlike the United States, which is the final destination of most illegal immigrants, Mexico has become a transit country for Central Americans and illegal immigrants from other countries. Rather than remaining in Mexico, many Central American migrants join the stream of Mexican emigrants making their way into the United States in search of better employment opportunities and improved living conditions. They do so unless they are caught by Mexican law enforcement officials and are detained or deported.[116]

The number of immigrants illegally crossing the border into Mexico from Guatemala rose 25 percent in 2002 from the previous year, with at least 212,000 illegal immigrants cared for in shelters that provide a refuge to migrants in the southern border state of Chiapas.[117] Records indicate that in 2003 Mexico deported 147,000 illegal immigrants, 90 percent of whom were from Guatemala, Honduras, and Nicaragua. According to Mexico's National Institute of Migration, in 2004 more than almost 430,000 transitory immigrants were caught entering the country illegally with 211,000 deported and 215,000 detained.[118] Guatemalans accounted for nearly 43 percent of Mexico's recorded undocumented immigrants in 2004, followed by Hondurans (about 34 percent) and El Salvadorans (about 18 percent). The remainder came from Nicaragua and other countries, including Cuba, Ecuador, China, and Somalia.

ILLEGAL DRUG TRAFFICKING

The link between illegal immigration and illegal drug trafficking has become almost indisputable and the crime-related problems for law enforcement officials and private citizens living on both sides of the Mexico-U.S. border are steadily increasing. A 1997 editorial predicted the future of illegal immigration and illegal drug smuggling between Mexico and the United States: "It would appear that the illegal immigration problem is also tied to the drug trafficking problem. The trips of literally hundreds of so called 'mules,' illegal aliens carrying drugs and attempting to enter the United States are reportedly facilitated each week by the Mexican drug cartels."[119] Additionally, evidence suggests that Mexican drug dealers spend more than $500 million annually to bribe corrupt Mexican police and military members as well as U.S. and Mexican customs officials willing to ignore the illicit activities and thus assuring easy passage of illegal aliens and illegal drugs across the border.[120]

The problems with illegal drug trafficking have continued to increase. In 2005 Nuevo Laredo, Mexico, near the Texas border, experienced "more than 100 unsolved killings in the last year, downtown crossfires, brazen assassinations [a new police chief on his first day of work in June and a city councilman on Aug. 5], sending in [Mexican] federal troops to replace local police officers who were thought to be in league with criminal gangs and the kidnappings of at least 43 Americans in the last 12 months."[121] The 2006 arrest of the head of one of Mexico's top drug gangs based in Tijuana, whose family drug cartel had served as the model for the drug cartel portrayed in the 2000 movie *Traffic,* did little to slow down the illegal drug flow from Mexico. That year a 2,400-foot-long smuggling tunnel was found along the U.S.-Mexico border that linked a warehouse in Tijuana, Mexico, to one in San Diego, California. It was one of 35 such smuggling tunnels discovered that link the United States and Mexico, enabling the undetected illegal passage of people and drugs between the two countries.[122]

As violence at the border related to smuggling illegal drugs and illegal immigration escalated, in July 2006 the U.S. House Subcommittee on International Terrorism and Non-proliferation convened the first of several hearings to discuss border security. Subcommittee chairman Rep. Ed Royce (R-Calif.) told congressional leaders in attendance, "Drug cartels, smuggling rings and gangs operating on both the Mexico and U.S. sides [of the border] are increasingly well-equipped and more brazen than ever before in attacking federal, state, and local law enforcement officials." Rep. Ted Poe (R-Tex.) added, "My opinion is that we should expect no help from Mexico on this issue. The Mexican government policy is to promote entry into the United States, not stop it."[123]

Following pressure from the United States to control the illegal drug trade in Mexico, the Mexican government agreed to review its drug law, which decriminalized the possession of small amounts of drugs and allowed people charged with possessing illegal drugs to claim they are addicts and the drugs are for personal use to support their habit.[124] In addition, the Mexican government agreed to suspend trials of suspected drug traffickers wanted in the United States so they could be extradited for prosecution in American courts.[125]

Policies and Laws

EARLY GOVERNMENT REGULATIONS

The Constitution of the United Mexican States adopted in 1917 included numerous articles related to immigration policies. Article 27 stated that "only Mexicans by birth or naturalization and Mexican companies" could acquire and own land, and foreign citizens were prohibited from owning land "within 100 km of the borders or 50 km of the sea." Article 32 gave Mexicans priority over foreigners for all employment and prohibited foreigners, immigrants, and naturalized citizens of Mexico from serving as "military officers, Mexican-flagged ship and airline crew, or chiefs of seaports and airports." Other jobs that noncitizens, foreign-born residents, and naturalized citizens could not hold included serving as members of the clergy, firefighters, police officers, judges, town council members, and other local-level government positions. Foreign-born people in Mexico are also strictly forbidden from participating in any political activities or public demonstrations.[126]

MODERN IMMIGRATION LAWS

While key immigration-related elements set forth in the 1917 constitution remained in effect in 2006, a law regulating immigration in Mexico—the General Law of Population—was enacted in 1974, reformulated in 1999, and reformulated again in 2005. The law clearly defines Mexico's three types of immigrant status as well as other immigration-related matters such as penalties against illegal aliens and those who assist them. The three types of immigrant recognized by Mexico are nonimmigrants, immigrants, and immigrated persons. A nonimmigrant is a foreigner who enters the country for a short-term visit, including tourists, people entering the country in-transit to another country, visitors such as people entering to attend business meetings or to conduct market studies, students, and refugees. An immigrant is a foreigner entering the country to establish permanent residency and includes retirees, professionals such as teachers, technicians entering to train Mexican workers, relatives and family members of other immigrants or permanent residents, and artists and sportsmen. An immigrated person is someone who has been in Mexico for five years and has requested a Declaration as an Immigrated Person from the government, allowing them to remain in the country permanently without additional document renewals or extensions.[127]

At its most basic level the law attempts to assure that all foreigners are in Mexico legally, have no criminal record, are financially self-supporting and will not become a burden on society, will provide both economic and social benefits to the country, and will contribute to the overall well-being of Mexico. According to the requirements of *rentista* visas, which are issued to people entering Mexico and not planning to seek employment, the immigrant must have proven independent income from investments and/or pensions of 400 times Mexico's daily minimum wage (in 2006 that amount was 19,468 pesos or in U.S. dollars about $1,000 per month) for an individual, plus an additional 200 days minimum wage (9,734 pesos) for dependent family members. The law also requires that all foreign visitors be registered with immigration authorities. Penalties are harsh for foreigners and others who violate the law, including being fined, imprisoned, or deported. Fines, imprisonment, or deportation are also enacted against foreigners caught entering the country with false documents or remaining in the country as visa overstayers. Those caught in the country illegally are considered felons and may be sentenced up to two years in prison and fined up to 5,000 pesos (in 2006, approximately $450). Any Mexican citizen who aids an illegal alien is also considered a criminal and will be treated accordingly with fines and imprisonment. Foreigners who have been deported and are caught trying to reenter the country without proper authorization may be sentenced to up to 10 years in prison. Also, any private individual may make a citizen's arrest of undesirable (illegal) aliens caught in the country.[128]

In the 1999 reforms, the law restricting elected government officials to native-born Mexicans was changed to allow candidates for office to be native-born but to have one foreign-born parent. The change opened the door for President Vicente Fox, whose mother was from Spain, to be elected to office in 2000. However, beginning in 2003 the government was actively encouraging cities to ban non-native Mexicans from a variety of jobs through its "model city statutes."[129]

As early as 2004 some Mexican officials were beginning to acknowledge that the country lacked a realistic and workable immigration policy. Immigration laws that required arrest and deportation of foreigners in the country without proper documentation clashed with basic constitutional guarantees that state in article 11: "Everyone has the right to enter and leave the Republic, to travel through its territory and to change his residence without necessity of a letter of security, passport, safe-conduct or any other similar requirement."[130] Noting the contradictions between Mexico's immigration laws and constitutional rights one commentary stated: "While police try to send the migrants back, officials from other branches of Mexico's government patrol the border to help advise the migrants of their human rights as they pass through the country."[131] The Mexican government took steps to resolve some of the problems in 2006 when the Senate approved a bill for a new immigration law to update the country's policies, notably laws related to illegal immigration. Proposed changes included elimination of the prison sentence for illegal aliens caught in the country and doubling the prison sentence to 12 years for people caught smuggling immigrants across the border.[132]

IMMIGRATION POLICY AFTER SEPTEMBER 11, 2001

Following the September 11, 2001, terrorist attacks on the United States, Mexico increased law enforcement on its southern border with Guatemala in response to increased concerns in the United States about ease of access illegal immigrants had to the country by way of Mexico.

Under pressure from the United States, Mexico beefed up law enforcement at its borders, including establishment of highway checkpoints and deployment of military forces. But Mexico's southern border consists of dense jungle rather than open desert like its northern border with the United States, making it difficult to effectively stop the growing tide of illegal immigrants from South and Central America. Mexican officials reported that between 2002 and 2006 deportations and detentions of illegal immigrants in the country increased 74 percent, but the number of illegal immigrants arriving in the country, most of them on their way to America, continued to grow.[133]

STANDOFF WITH THE UNITED STATES

In response to the public outcry over an estimated 12 million Mexicans living illegally in the United States, in 2005 the U.S. government began rigorously enforcing existing immigration laws, including a 1986 law that allowed fines of up to $11,000 against companies that knowingly hired illegal aliens. Diplomatic relations between Mexico and the United States deteriorated at the end of 2005 when the U.S. House of Representatives passed a bill that would make illegal immigration a felony, require detention of illegal immigrants, add church and social groups to a list of agencies that by statute are prohibited from aiding illegal aliens, and that contained a proposal to build fences along 700 miles of the Mexico-U.S. border. President Vicente Fox reacted harshly. The president of Mexico publicly condemned the U.S. government's proposed action as "shameful." He further criticized the United States, saying the bill was "a troubling reflection of America's willingness to tolerate 'xenophobic groups that impose the law at will.'"[134] Opinion in the United States described Mexico's criticisms as "The old blame game—in which Mexico attributed illegal migration to the voracious American demand for labor and accused lawmakers of xenophobia . . ." rather than recognizing "how little Mexico has done to try to keep its people home."[135]

Evidence of a breakdown in diplomacy between the two countries continued when the Mexican Foreign Ministry leveled complaints against the U.S. ambassador to Mexico after the ambassador criticized the Mexican government for its failure to control illegal drug-related violence on the border and then temporarily closed the American consulate in Nuevo Laredo, Mexico, a city particularly hard hit by drug violence.[136] Additional problems between the two countries arose in December 2005 when U.S. Border Patrol agents shot and killed a Mexican man trying to enter the United States illegally to take a job picking fruit in California. The Mexican government called the shooting "a racist violation of human rights." American officials claimed the victim was a *pollero,* namely, someone who smuggled other illegal immigrants across the border, and that he had been arrested and deported at least 12 times trying to illegally enter the United States. The Border Patrol further claimed the man pelted the agents with rocks and was shot as he tried to escape.[137]

Tensions increased in 2006 when the U.S. government lodged complaints against the Mexican government for its failure to control illegal drug trafficking. The government cited an incident outside El Paso, Texas, in which a group of men dressed as Mexican soldiers came to the aid of drug smugglers, helping them escape from American law enforcement officers. The U.S. government demanded the Mexican government investigate the incident. In response, Mexican officials claimed that the soldiers helping the drug traffickers were actually Americans in disguise, and they also demanded an explanation about delays in the investigation into the December shooting death by U.S. Border Patrol agents of a Mexican citizen illegally crossing the border into the United States.[138]

During a meeting in April 2006, the presidents of both countries agreed to continue working together to reach a solution of the illegal immigration problem. However, Mexico's president Fox continued to inject a policy position on immigration reform in calling for Washington to enact a guest-worker program for Mexican migrants seeking employment in the United States. Despite U.S. president Bush's support of Fox's guest-worker proposal, other American leaders rejected the plan. In May members of the California legislature boycotted President Fox's speech to a joint session of the state government while others who attended wore buttons stating *No más* (No more) in protest against Fox's efforts to influence and liberalize America's immigration laws.[139] Mexico's attitude toward U.S. immigration policies softened somewhat in 2006 when the U.S. Senate passed an immigration bill that was markedly different from the earlier bill passed by the House. The Senate bill tightened controls on the border but also created a guest-worker program and offered citizenship to most illegal aliens who met specific criteria. President Fox, during a visit to the United States, stated that his country's government could accept tighter security on the Mexico-U.S. border as long as the United States made it possible for Mexican citizens to migrate legally. Commenting on the Senate bill, President Fox thanked U.S. president George W. Bush. The two leaders agreed to "work together to secure the border and build economic prosperity in both countries," according to a White House spokesperson.[140]

Emigration and Depopulation

EARLY EMIGRATION

The beginnings of Mexico's depopulation due to emigration can be traced to shortly after the end of the Mexican-American War when Mexicans began immigrating to the United States in search of work in 1850. Between 1850 and 1880 an estimated 55,000 Mexican emigrants arrived in the United States to fill jobs on cattle ranches in Texas and in the fruit orchards of California. When the United States began construction of a transcontinental railroad, additional Mexican immigrants arrived to take jobs as railway workers. Between 1880 and 1890 it was estimated that 60 percent of the crews working the railroads in the western United States were Mexican immigrants. During the Mexican Revolution (1910–20) the country's citizens emigrated in search of refuge as well as jobs. An estimated 53,000 Mexicans immigrated to the United States each year between 1910 and 1917.[141] Besides working on the railroad and in agriculture, Mexican immigrants arriving in the United States at that time found work in the steel industry and as painters, upholsterers, plumbers, and more. However, complaints by the migrants that their U.S. employers were taking advantage of them led the Mexican government in 1920 to require a contract for its citizens migrating to the United States for work that was signed by an immigration official before they were permitted to leave the country.[142] To assure the rights of Mexican workers were protected the contracts had to establish the emigrant's salary, work schedule, place of employment, and other conditions.

MODERN EMIGRATION

Since those first emigrants, large numbers of Mexican citizens have continued to leave Mexico in search of jobs and the higher salaries available in the United States. The result of the mass exodus has been a lack of workers to fill jobs in Mexico. Especially hard hit are rural communities across Mexico, which have been emptied of their populations. By 2001 more than 3,300 residents of Casa Blanca, a small city located 250 miles northwest of Mexico City in the state of Zacatecas, had immigrated to the United States in search of work, most of them settling in Tulsa, Oklahoma. A Casa Blanca teacher commented that in 1989 the school had 500 students enrolled but that in 2001 the number of students had dropped to 100. With just 2,500 residents remaining in Casa Blanca, empty houses lined the streets and some referred to the small community as a ghost town. The town of El Cargadero, also in the state of Zacatecas, lost many of its citizens but, nevertheless, businesses in the area paid such low wages, as little as $4 per day, that those remaining who could work refused to take the available jobs. Overall an estimated 30,000 people annually were leaving the state of Zacatecas to go to America. The state of Zacatecas was not unique. Officials in Michoacán, a state in central Mexico, reported that 50,000 of its citizens were migrating annually to the United States for economic reasons.[143]

The North American Free Trade Agreement (NAFTA), implemented in 1994 among the United States, Mexico, and Canada, helped create more than 2 million jobs in Mexico and led to higher wages than those traditionally paid; still, the trend of depopulation due to emigration as Mexicans moved north for jobs continued. The U.S.-operated factories known as *maquiladoras* provided Mexican workers steady employment, but at wages far below those paid to workers in the United States. The average wages workers in most *maquiladoras* earned were $55 for a 45-hour workweek.[144] According to a 2006 report in *High Country News*, "Mexican factory workers earn several times what they made before NAFTA but they can still make more washing windows in Los Angeles than on the assembly line in a Tijuana *maquiladora*." NAFTA also harmed Mexico's agricultural industries by forcing Mexican farmers to compete with large U.S. farming conglomerates. Unable to compete with government-subsidized U.S. farms and forced to sell their crops at reduced prices Mexican farmers could not pay high salaries, which led more citizens to emigrate for work in the United States. Noting the lack of people to fill jobs picking tomatoes in greenhouses on a farm in rural Francisco Villa, Sonora, the farm's owner said, "Nobody wants to work. . . . I don't blame them. The wages are very low." A day's earnings for workers who did show up to pick tomatoes were 90 pesos (about $8.50 U.S.). The workers who did not arrive to pick tomatoes were "probably 500 miles north, in Phoenix or Tucson, earning $10 an hour landscaping rich people's yards or hanging drywall in new homes."[145]

The Benefits of Emigration: Remittances

Despite the loss of its labor force, the Mexican government embraced the practice of emigration, and reaped the benefits of its citizens migrating both legally and illegally to the United States for jobs. Mexican migration for work was described as "a multibillion-dollar venture for Mexico."[146] The "multibillion dollars" received by Mexico came in the form of remittances: the money migrant workers sent to family members left behind in Mexico. Migrant workers' relatives spend the money for food, clothing, and medicine. In addition, migrants also pool their money and aid cash-poor or corrupt local governments by supporting public works projects.

Based on estimates, remittances amounted to approximately $6.3 billion annually in 2001 and they comprised Mexico's third-largest source of income with only oil and tourism producing more revenue.[147] By 2004 emigration and the remittances migrant workers in the United States sent back to their homeland were described as "Mexico's principal economic program." That year remittances jumped to $16.6 billion, up 23 percent from 2003.[148]

The incoming flow of cash proved such a boon to the economy that the Mexican government launched a program to match the remittances called "3 × 1" to help fund public works projects. In 2005 the government program paid $60 million to match the $20 million invested in communities by Mexican expatriates to support various projects, including paving roads, buying computers for schools, and repairing public facilities such as churches.[149] In 2006 remittances from the United States had increased to $20 billion annually or 3 percent of Mexico's gross domestic product, according to the Inter-American Development Bank. Additionally, remittances had surpassed oil revenues as a revenue source.

Conclusion

Despite the Mexican government's stated intentions to reform its immigration laws, in 2006 most of the debate about immigration remained focused on the importance of influencing proposed immigration reform in the United States, including creation of a guest-worker program to allow Mexicans to migrate freely across the border for jobs in America. Also, the possibility that remittances could ultimately dry up as a source of income for the country due to more migrant workers taking their families with them to live in America led the Mexican congress to adopt a resolution in 2006 that stated: "A large number of Mexicans do not find in their own country an economic and social environment that facilitates their full development and well-being." Based on that statement, the government proposed a variety of incentives to encourage its citizens to return home, including tax breaks for migrants who build homes in Mexico, a medical insurance program, and a plan that would enable repatriating immigrants to be paid pensions earned on jobs in the United States. Other proposals included reforms to the Labor and Social Development Ministries that would encourage migrant workers to return to Mexico.[150]

THE PHILIPPINES

Introduction

The Republic of the Philippines is an archipelago of more than 7,000 islands scattered between the South China Sea and the Philippine Sea east of Vietnam. Beginning with colonization by the Spanish, the island nation has experienced immigration on a limited level. The island nation is more familiar with emigration, with the export of its citizens to other countries as a labor force. The Overseas Foreign Workers (OFW) program began in the 1970s as a method to manage the Philippines's high unemployment rate and to produce income for the country through payment of remittances by its

OFWs. In the 21st century the OFW program is thriving, but it is a double-edged sword as the Philippines loses not only low-skilled workers but also the best of its highly skilled workers such as medical professionals and teachers. The consequences of brain drain that the government must now address include a lack of adequate health care for Filipinos. In addition, the Philippines has seen an influx of new immigrants arriving from China and South Korea, many of whom come into the country illegally. The country is also looking for strategies to encourage its OFWs who have become permanent emigrants to repatriate.

Historical Background

FIRST IMMIGRANTS

Research suggests that about 30,000 years ago people known as Negritos migrated to the Philippine Islands from Borneo, Sumatra, and Malaya. Immigrants from what is now Indonesia and Malaysia reached the Philippines by sea in two groups, the first in about 3000 B.C.E. and the second in about 1000 B.C.E. They were followed by the arrival of immigrants from Malaya in 200 B.C.E., and immigrants from China began arriving in the Philippines as traders in about 1000 C.E. Eventually many of the Chinese traders chose to remain in the Philippines as permanent settlers.

Arab and Malay Muslims began arriving in the Philippines in the late 14th century, coming first as traders and then later remaining to establish sultanates (communities) primarily on the island of Mindanao and on other southern islands but also in the southern section of the island of Luzon. Also during that period Japanese immigrants established a trading post on the northern coast of Luzon. Malayan immigrants continued to settle in the Philippines through the 16th century.

The first Europeans—Spanish explorers—reached the Philippines in 1521 and claimed the islands for Spain. A subsequent Spanish expedition reached the Philippines in 1542 from Mexico, which was also a Spanish colony, known as New Spain. At that time the Spanish named the islands Las Islas Felipinas in honor of Philip II of Spain.[151] In 1564 official Spanish overlordship of the northern Philippine Islands occurred following the arrival of another expedition from Mexico. From 1565 to 1821 the Philippines were officially ruled by the viceroy of New Spain. After 1821 it was administered directly from Spain. The first Spanish settlement, now the town of San Miguel, was established in 1565 on the island of Cebu by five Augustinian friars (a Roman Catholic monastic order) and a troop of Spanish soldiers. The city of Manila on the island of Luzon, now the nation's capital, was declared a Spanish city in 1571. Most of the early colonists in the Philippines arrived from New Spain rather than Spain, including 300 immigrants who came in 1567 and 200 who came in 1570. While no specific numbers are available, it is believed that by the time Spanish rule of the Philippines ended in 1898 thousands of Spaniards had settled in the island nation.

From the late 1500s until 1603 Chinese immigrated to the Philippines as settlers, as business owners, and as laborers for Spanish colonists. The number of Chinese in the Philippines continued to grow and, in time, the Spanish felt threatened by their presence; the Chinese were subject to discrimination and periodic deportations.

The Dutch also made an appearance in the Philippines, first as hostile invaders who battled the Spanish settlers in the 1600s and much later as immigrants. According to the Philippine embassy in the Netherlands, the earliest reported immigration to the Philippines by the Dutch was in 1897 and, by 1948, enough Dutch citizens were living in the Philippines to establish an embassy there.[152]

Spain controlled the Philippines until the end of the Spanish-American War (February–December 1898) at which time the United States bought the Philippines from Spain for $20 million.[153] In 1900, two years after losing the Philippines to the United States, about 900,000 Spanish-speaking residents remained in the Philippines, but their numbers were on the decline. As the Spanish population decreased, other immigrant populations increased, with many migrating to the Philippines as missionaries, notably the Dutch and Chinese, or with the U.S. military. According to the 1903 census, the Philippines had a population of approximately 7.6 million people including 42,000 Chinese, 14,000 Caucasians (Spaniards and American military members), and 500 African Americans (also members of the U.S. military). Based on the 1941 census the Philippines had a population of 17 million, including 117,000 Chinese, 30,000 Japanese, and more than 9,000 Americans.[154]

MODERN IMMIGRATION

Beginning in the mid-20th century the island nation saw an increase in immigrants arriving from China and South Korea, many of whom immigrated to the Philippines to escape the rise of communism and the loss of basic freedoms in their homelands.[155] Later emigration from those countries came in response to the 1998 Asian financial crisis, an economic downturn that resulted in devaluation of the impacted countries' currencies, business bankruptcies, and job losses. Particularly hard hit by the financial crisis were Indonesia, South Korea, and Thailand, while it had less impact on the economy of the Philippines.

Following improvement in diplomatic relations between the Philippines and China, Chinese immigration to the Philippines increased. Although

Filipino officials hoped to attract foreign investors from China to help boost their economy, most immigrants from China beginning in the 1980s were not the big investors the Philippine government wanted. Rather, the new immigrants "were mainly relatives of the earlier immigrants who made it to the Philippines. . . . Aside from kinship ties, friendship, school and village ties started to entice more and more immigrants from China."[156] According to statistics, by 2006 the Chinese constituted one of the largest ethnic minority groups in the Philippines, with a population of 1.5 million or about 2 percent of the country's population of 76.5 million. Besides the Chinese, South Koreans were immigrating to the Philippines in growing numbers. In 2004 some 370,000 South Koreans visited the Philippines as temporary migrants and that number was expected to increase to 500,000 in 2005. An estimated 46,000 South Koreans reportedly planned to immigrate to the Philippines and set up permanent residences that year. Of the Korean immigrants, most were businessmen, students, or missionaries.[157]

Why Immigrants Come to the Philippines

Despite an unemployment rate of between 8.7 and 10.3 percent in 2005[158] that drove Filipinos to other countries in search of work, many people who immigrate to the Philippines do so in search of employment opportunities. Korean immigrants saw the "potentials for growth and development. And they are willing to invest their time, money, and effort for the opportunity to get a piece of the 'golden egg' that the Philippines can provide," stated one report.[159] Other immigrants, such as the Chinese, move to the Philippines to join family members who immigrated earlier and to escape political turmoil in their homelands.

Problems Associated with Immigration

ILLEGAL IMMIGRATION

Filipino officials estimated that between 1996 and 1999 at least 120,000 Chinese had entered the country illegally. Others arrived legally but remained in the country illegally as visa overstayers. The increase in the number of Chinese nationals who arrived as tourists, but remained in the country illegally, became known as a "silent migration."[160] Responding to the rising number of illegal Chinese aliens living and doing business in the country and to concerns that an increasing number of Chinese immigrants were involved in drug trafficking, human trafficking, money laundering, computer and technology crimes, and arms dealing, the Philippine Bureau of Immigration and Deportation began conducting sting operations in areas where undocumented Chinese nationals were known to operate businesses. During one two-day sting in December 2005, 144 Chinese were arrested and charged with being in the country without legal residence permits and with operating unlicensed retail businesses.[161] According to a report about Chinese organized crime by the Federal Research Division of the U.S. Library of Congress, the Philippines "legal system is ill equipped to enforce international law or to protect against transnational crime. Loopholes in the system continue to frustrate the efforts of Philippine police to prosecute non-indigenous insurgent groups such as Chinese syndicates."[162] The nation also served as a transit country similar to Mexico with immigrants using it as a gateway to other countries. Chinese women living in mainland China illegally entered the Philippines and used the country as a route to reconnect with their husbands living in Hong Kong, which retained its own legal system and immigration policy even after it was returned to China in 1997. According to a 1998 report, women in China "are reportedly buying false Philippine passports for $20,000 to $50,000 in order to speed up reunions with husbands in Hong Kong." With forged Philippine passports in hand the women traveled from China to the Philippines as tourists, then, while posing as Filipinos, they traveled as tourists to Hong Kong. After reuniting with their spouses they applied for dependent visas using their legal Chinese identification.[163]

Policies and Laws

Policies and laws regarding immigration in the Philippines are two-sided. Like all countries that accept immigrants, the Philippines has policies designed to control immigration into the country by foreigners. Unlike other countries that encourage labor migration but have very limited programs to support their workers abroad, such as Mexico, the Philippines heavily regulates and controls emigration of its citizens as temporary migrant workers.

IMMIGRATION POLICIES

Immigration policies in the Philippines are based on the country's Immigration Act of 1940, also known as Commonwealth Act No. 613. The act established the Bureau of Immigration and defined two categories of immigrants: foreign nationals planning to remain permanently in the Philippines (immigrants), and foreign nationals planning to be in the country for a specific and temporary period of time such as tourists and business people (nonimmigrants). For the purpose of issuing visas, immigrants are further classified as quota and nonquota immigrants. The act states: "The Philippines allows the admission of quota immigrants not exceeding fifty (50) annually of any nationality whose country has diplomatic relations with the Philippines or grants the same immigration privilege to Filipino citizens." Nonquota immigrants include native-born citizens of the Philippines who have been naturalized in a foreign country but are returning to the Philippines for permanent residence, and spouses or the unmarried children under 21 years old of a Philippine citizen. Foreigners excluded from immigrating include people who are deemed "idiots or insane" who have a "loathsome or dangerous contagious disease or epilepsy," who have been convicted of a crime, are polygamists, are over age 15 years and illiterate, and anyone who may become a public burden such as "paupers, vagrants, and beggars." The act also regulates the deportation of aliens, including foreigners who enter the country illegally, and foreigners found guilty of a crime and are sentenced to more than one year in jail, who violate drug laws, or who become impoverished and dependent on public aid. A special visa is available to foreign retirees wishing to live in the Philippines. To qualify for a Special Retiree Resident visa the applicant must be 35 years old or older and must hold a six-month term deposit in a financial institution valued at $75,000 if under 49 years old and $50,000 if 50 years old or older.[164]

Since the act's adoption in 1940, numerous changes have been implemented. The Alien Registration Act of 1950 established mandatory registration of all foreign nationals working in the Philippines and their dependents as well as all foreigners planning to stay for 30 days or more. At the time of registration the immigrant was fingerprinted and issued an identification card. Enforcement of the act over the years became lax, but in 2005 the Bureau of Immigration announced that it was "resuming compulsory registration of foreign national workers and their dependents." To reduce the use of forged documents a microchip-based identification card replaced the paper-based Alien Certificate of Registration cards.[165]

In the 1990s the government introduced measures to address the country's growing population of illegal aliens, estimated at 100,000 in 1995. The Alien Social Integration Act passed in 1995 granted legal resident status to qualified illegal aliens. Described as an amnesty program, it also served as a vehicle for the government to raise money. The act allowed illegal aliens who had entered the country before 1992 to pay a $10,000 fee in exchange for permanent residence status. It was believed that 40 percent of the illegal aliens in the country would legalize their status, netting the government an estimated $39 million in fees. Of the first group of illegal aliens applying for legal status most were from China and Taiwan.[166]

The government introduced the Immigration and Naturalization Act in 2002 to update the country's longstanding immigration policies, but in 2004 no action had been taken and the bill was being held in committee. The following year the *Manila Times* published a plea that the country's president, "certify the Immigration Reform Act of 2005 as urgent," and reiterated that it was important to "move Philippine immigration policy closer to the challenges of the 21st century."[167]

EMIGRATION POLICIES

In the 1970s the country began actively exporting its citizen workforce, known as overseas foreign workers (OFWs), as a source of income. To effectively promote and manage its OFWs the government established a system to regulate and control the labor emigration process. Passage in 1974 of the Labor Code of the Philippines established the foundation for the country's overseas employment programs.[168] The migrant labor policy is two-sided with both public and private elements. The public Philippine Overseas Employment Administration (POEA) created in 1982 processes OFWs' contracts and predeployment payments; licenses, regulates, and monitors private employee recruitment agencies; and manages all aspects of emigrating laborers as they prepare to go abroad for work. Private Philippine-based agencies are licensed by the POEA to recruit Filipino laborers for employers in other countries.[169]

In 1995 the government passed the Migrant Workers and Overseas Filipinos Act, which instituted policies regulating overseas employment and established standards for the protection and welfare of migrant workers and their families as well as other overseas Filipinos who might need help. The act also established close monitoring of the labor policies of countries receiving Filipino workers and required that Filipino workers register with the Philippine embassy in the country where they were employed.[170] Another government agency, the Overseas Workers Welfare Administration (OWWA), picks up where the POEA leaves off by providing support and assistance to labor migrants and their families while the worker is overseas.[171] The OWWA accepts and responds to complaints of mistreatment and other problems encountered by OFWs. In 1994 the OWWA received more than 10,000 complaints from OFWs about employer abuses that ranged from physical mistreatment to rape. Responses from the government range from arranging for Kuwaiti airlines to fly home free of charge Filipina maids in Kuwait who complained of employer abuse to refusing to send domestic workers to Hong Kong following repeated reports of employer abuse there.[172] Emigrants who encounter legal problems while living and working abroad are helped and supported by the Office of the Undersecretary of Migrant Workers Affairs. In the 30 years since its original plan to promote economic migration the government's related policies have remained constant. The Philippines' national Economic Development Plan stated in 2001, "Overseas employment is a 'legitimate option for the country's workforce,'" and it outlined a four-point strategy for promoting the employment of Filipino's abroad.[173]

Economic Migration

Several forces drive economic migration from the Philippines, including poverty, high unemployment, low wages, and government policies that encourage Filipinos to take jobs in other countries. Data indicated that in 2001 (the most recent available) an estimated 40 percent of the population in the Philippines lived below the poverty level.[174] In October 2005 the Philippine Bureau of Labor and Employment Statistics reported an average unemployment rate of 8.7 percent to 10.3 percent. Of those workers with jobs, 21 percent were underemployed, working at jobs for which they were overqualified. The Philippine National Wages and Productivity Commission reported that in 2006 the monthly minimum wage in the Philippines, depending on the type of job, ranged from $68 to $210, which meant average annual earnings for most workers were about $816 to $2,520. However, it was noted that not all employers in the country honored the minimum wage and many paid lower salaries.[175]

While many Filipinos emigrate to work at unskilled jobs, including as laborers in factories, construction, and domestic help such as maids, others leave for highly skilled or professional positions, including nurses, doctors, physical therapists, and lawyers. Official estimates in 2004 listed "at least 240,000 foreign maids—the absolute majority are Filipinas" working in Hong Kong,[176] and in 2006 there were some 300,000 Filipino nurses working overseas.[177]

In the early 1900s economic emigration for most Filipinos meant a trip to the United States with the top destination being Hawaii. The first group of Filipino migrant workers arrived in the U.S. Territory of Hawaii in 1906 to work on sugar cane and pineapple plantations. Estimates placed the number of Filipino workers immigrating to Hawaii between 1906 and 1934 at about 120,000. Other research indicated that 150,000 Filipino workers arrived in the United States between 1907 and 1930. Following World War II and through the 1960s as many as 12,000 Filipinos immigrated to Hawaii as workers, members of the U.S. military, and as war brides. Beginning in the mid-1960s the United States, Canada, Australia, New Zealand, and many European nations changed their immigration policies, opening the door to emigrants from the Philippines.[178]

Economic migration from the Philippines began in earnest in the early 1970s and, by 1975, Filipinos who emigrated for temporary employment totaled 36,035. That number grew steadily each year and reached more than

930,000 in 2004. In total by 2004 some 3.6 million Filipinos had left as temporary labor emigrants who planned to return to the Philippines at the end of their job contracts and more than 3 million had immigrated permanently to other countries. Another 1.3 million Filipinos were believed to be illegal immigrants in the countries where they were living and working, primarily the United States and Malaysia. A Migration Policy Institute report noted, "As of December 2004, an estimated 8.1 million Filipinos—nearly 10 percent of the country's 85 million people—were working and/or residing in close to 200 countries and territories."[179]

In addition to the United States, top destination countries for Filipinos emigrating for employment included Hong Kong, Singapore, Italy, and Japan. But Filipinos were also migrating for work in countries that were not traditional immigrant-receiving nations such as Germany, Lebanon, and Iraq. A 2005 survey found that 33 percent of Filipinos polled agreed with the statement, "If it were only possible, I would migrate to another country and live there." Additionally, 60 percent of the children who had a parent working overseas said they also planned to immigrate to other countries for work when they were old enough. And unlike Mexico's migrant workers who typically are men, migrant workers leaving the Philippines are increasingly women.[180] In Hong Kong, for example, 90 percent of the OFWs from the Philippines in 2005 were women.

BENEFITS OF ECONOMIC MIGRATION

The goals of the Philippines government when it began exporting its labor force included decreasing the country's high unemployment and using income from remittances paid by its migrant laborers to pay off the country's growing international debt. In 2001 the government proposed deploying 1 million workers overseas annually and expected to reach its target in 2005.[181] According to government census statistics, by September 2005 an estimated 1.33 million Filipinos were working overseas. Remittances paid by foreign workers, which can be as much as 70 percent to 85 percent of their monthly earnings depending on the country where they are working and the contract arrangements with the overseas employer, reached $7.6 billion in 2003. The *Asia Times* reported remittances collected by the government were "almost 100 times the figures of foreign direct investments."[182] The Philippines received $8.5 billion in remittances in 2004 from its OFWs and that amount reached $10.8 billion in 2005.[183] A 2004 study reported that 17 percent of Filipino households received remittance money from a family member temporarily working abroad, which accounted for 25 percent of the total money households spent. It added that if remittances paid by family members who had emigrated permanently were also considered the dollar amounts would be much higher.[184]

PROBLEMS ASSOCIATED WITH ECONOMIC MIGRATION

Due to the outflow of workers the country has experienced a depleted labor force and OFW families have suffered from the problems associated with family separations. The downside of economic migration on families was noted in 1998 when *Migration News* reported that "an estimated 30 percent of Filipino children—some 8 million—live in households where at least one parent has gone overseas."[185] Commenting on brain drain and loss of the country's health care workers, in 2006 the *Korea Times* wrote: "Mass emigration—apart from the various personal problems related to separation of families—also has negative economic and social effects. In the case of the Philippines, the health system is one of the main 'victims.'"[186]

BRAIN DRAIN

While a shortage of unskilled jobs in the Philippines has forced some workers abroad, low pay has pushed highly skilled workers such as nurses and doctors to seek foreign employment, leaving similar positions in the Philippines unfilled. A 2002 study by the University of Illinois reported that the salary for registered nurses in the Philippines was between $2,000 and $2,400 per year compared to a median yearly income of $48,090 for registered nurses in the United States. In 2005, the reported salary for nurses in the Philippines remained about $2,280 annually while the median annual income for U.S. nurses jumped to $54,670. Annual salaries for doctors in the Philippines ranged from $2,724 to $3,708 in 2006 compared to U.S. doctors who earned from $156,000 to more than $321,000.[187] Enticed by the promise of higher wages nurses could earn overseas, an estimated 80 percent of Filipino doctors had left their profession and become registered nurses in 2006.[188]

The result was a shortage of nurses and deteriorating health care in the Philippines. Of the approximately 1,600 private hospitals in the Philippines in 2006 only 700 remained open due to a shortage of doctors and nurses. Jamie Galvez Tan, a professor at the University of the Philippines and the country's former health secretary, stated, "At some hospitals on the southern island of Mindanao, there is one nurse for 55 patients. The ideal ratio is one nurse for four patients." It was further noted that at Philippine General Hospital in Manila, a government-run health care facility, the ratio was one nurse for 26 patients.[189]

FILIPINO EMIGRANTS IN THE UNITED STATES

U.S. policies have not always eased the path for immigrants from the Philippines. The first Filipino immigrants arrived in the United States in the 1600s and 1700s as escaped slaves fleeing Spanish ships on the way to Mexico and established fishing businesses in an area around New Orleans, Louisiana. Although the Philippines became a U.S. territory in 1901 the status of Filipinos in America remained vague. The U.S. Immigration Act of 1924 classified Filipinos as nationals rather than alien immigrants and they traveled with U.S. passports; however, they were ineligible for U.S. citizenship. Passage of the Tydings-McDuffie Act in 1934 established the groundwork for the Philippines to become independent and took away the status as nationals from Filipinos. It reclassified Filipinos as aliens, limited the number of Filipinos who could immigrate to America to 50 people per year, and led to passage of the Filipino Repatriation Act one year later, which paid Filipinos to return to their homeland and not return to the United States. In 1941, while the Philippines were still a commonwealth of the United States, World War II was underway and more than 200,000 Filipinos were drafted into the U.S. military. Despite actively serving in the U.S. military throughout World War II, Filipinos were denied the benefits earned by other U.S. men and women who served in the military when the U.S. government passed the First Supplemental Surplus Appropriation Rescission Act in 1946. Under terms of the act, the Philippine army received $200 million "on the basis that service in the Commonwealth Army should not be deemed to have been service in the Armed Forces of the United States." The Second Supplemental Surplus Appropriation Rescission Act, also passed in 1946, stated that Filipinos who served as scouts with the U.S. military from 1941 to 1946 with approval from the Philippine government were not considered to have served with the U.S. military. The Immigration Act of 1990 finally offered Filipinos, many who had been living in America for years but denied citizenship due to the 1945 Rescission Act, the opportunity to become U.S. citizens.[190]

Government attitudes changed toward Filipinos when the United States experienced a shortage of medical personnel, particularly nurses, and the government began actively recruiting Filipino nurses. In 2005 the government allowed 50,000 new green cards to be available to immigrant nurses, many of which could be granted to Filipino nurses.[191] The government proposed in 2006 to remove any limitations on the number of nurses wishing to immigrate to the United States.[192]

Opening the door to immigrating nurses did little to help other Filipinos wishing to immigrate to the United States, many hoping to reunite with family already in America. U.S. immigration policy limits the number of visas issued worldwide each year to 226,000 for people immigrating to reunite with family members living in the United States and to 140,000 for people immigrating for employment. Additionally, limits are set for each country, further reducing the number of visas available and increasing the wait time to years to receive a visa. According to the *Philippine News*, in

2006 the "priority date for adult unmarried children of Filipino/U.S. citizens being approved for this month is October 1, 1991. . . . Therefore, those being approved have waited for almost 15 years," for a visa to enter the United States.[193]

Conclusion

Recognizing the threat to the health care system caused by the exodus of the country's highly trained medical personnel, in 2006 the Philippine government began considering measures to prevent doctors from emigrating. The Philippines health secretary Francisco Duque said, "We're focusing on keeping doctors here and legislation is the only way to do that. We want to plug the hole."[194]

Acknowledging the contributions and efforts of the country's OFWs, each year the government also celebrates Migrant Workers Day and presents 20 migrant workers the Baygong Bayani (modern-day hero) award. The award honors outstanding OFWs "for their significant efforts in fostering goodwill, enhancing and promoting the image of the Filipinos as competent, responsible, and dignified workers, as well as their contributions to the socio-economic development of their respective communities and the country as a whole."[195]

In an attempt to reduce Filipino temporary labor migrants from becoming permanent immigrants, the government enacted changes to its emigration policy in 1995 to include encouraging the return of OFWs and helping them reintegrate into the local economy. Services provided by the government meant to encourage OFWs to maintain their ties to the Philippines included supporting schools abroad in communities with large numbers of Filipino migrants, providing counseling to OFWs that emphasizes Filipino values, and allowing OFWs to vote in national elections on the condition that the voting migrant return to the Philippines within two years of the election. In addition, returning migrants receive privileges such as tax-free shopping for one year, reduced-rate loans for starting a business, and eligibility for subsidized educational scholarships.[196] In 2003 the government adopted the Citizenship Retention and Reacquisition Act, which allowed native-born Filipinos who had lost their Philippine citizenship by becoming naturalized citizens in another country to reacquire their Filipino citizenship. The act also has helped make it easier for Filipino-American retirees to return to the Philippines because it enables them to secure Philippines citizenship while maintaining their American citizenship.

To increase homeland ties and encourage Filipino-Americans to invest in the Philippines real estate market and boost the country's construction industry, in 2006 the government launched a marketing program through several of its consulates in the United States offering to sell expats luxury condominiums and villas in some of the islands' resort areas. Among the key targets of the program are older Filipino-Americans who may want to live in their homeland after they retire. But the program was not limited to wealthy Filipino expats who could afford the $175,000 to $215,000 price tag on the condos and villas. Several participating developers were offering Filipinos the chance to buy homes with small down payments and monthly payments as low as $200.[197]

---

[1] Peter Sahlins. *Unnaturally French: Foreign Citizens in the Old Regime and After.* Ithaca, N.Y.: Cornell University Press, 2004.

[2] Peter Sahlins. *Unnaturally French: Foreign Citizens in the Old Regime and After.* Ithaca, N.Y.: Cornell University Press, 2004.

[3] Tony McNeill. "Immigration in Postwar France," Lectures 1–3, February 1998. Available online. URL: www.unc.edu/depts/europe/conferences/Veil2000/articles/immigration-in-postwar-france.pdf. Accessed July 24, 2006.

[4] Emmanuel Peignard. *Immigration in France.* Embassy of France in the United States, July 2001.

[5] *Overview of France's Immigration History.* Washington, D.C: Center of Concern, August 4, 2006.

[6] Tony McNeill. "Immigration in Postwar France," Lectures 1–3, February 1998. Available online. URL: www.unc.edu/depts/europe/conferences/Veil2000/articles/immigration-in-postwar-france.pdf. Accessed July 24, 2006.

[7] Neija Hamadaoui. "The Nation Shows Its Gratitude to Immigrants." *Label France* 57 (January–March 2005).

[8] Emmanuel Peignard. *Immigration in France.* Embassy of France in the United States, July 2001.

[9] Tony McNeill. "Immigration in Postwar France," Lectures 1–3, February 1998. Available online. URL: www.unc.edu/depts/europe/conferences/Veil2000/articles/immigration-in-postwar-france.pdf. Accessed July 24, 2006.

[10] Emmanuel Peignard. *Immigration in France.* Embassy of France in the United States, July 2001.

[11] Neija Hamadaoui. "The Nation Shows Its Gratitude to Immigrants." *Label France* 57 (January–March 2005).

[12] Emmanuel Peignard. *Immigration in France.* Embassy of France in the United States, July 2001.

[13] Tony McNeill. "Immigration in Postwar France," Lectures 1–3, February 1998. Available online. URL: www.unc.edu/depts/europe/conferences/Veil2000/articles/immigration-in-postwar-france.pdf. Accessed July 24, 2006.

[14] "France Amends Immigration Law." *Migration News* 4, no. 2 (April 1997).

[15] Kimberly Hamilton. "The Challenge of French Diversity." *Migration Information Source.* Washington, D.C.: Migration Policy Institute, November 2004.

[16] Neija Hamadaoui. "The Nation Shows Its Gratitude to Immigrants." *Label France* 57 (January–March 2005).

[17] Reynald Blion, Catherine Wihtol de Wenden, and Nedjma Meknache. "France." *EU and U.S. Approaches to the Management of Immigration.* Brussels: Migration Policy Group, 2003.

[18] Kimberly Hamilton and Patrick Simon. "The Challenge of French Diversity." *Migration Information Source.* Washington, D.C.: Migration Policy Institute, 2004.

[19] *Indepth: France Riots. Understanding the Violence.* CBC News Online, November 14, 2005. Available online. URL: http://www.cbc.ca/news/background/paris_riots/. Accessed July 24, 2006.

[20] *France, Not U.S., Is Now Destination of Choice for Refugees.* NewsMax.com Wires, March 1, 2005. Available online. URL: http://www.newsmax.com/archives/articles/2005/3/1/102024.shtml. Accessed July 27, 2006.

[21] Kara Murphy. "France's New Law: Control Immigration Flows, Court the Highly Skilled." *Migration Information Source.* Washington, D.C.: Migration Policy Institute, November 1, 2006.

[22] Katrin Bennhold. "France to Favor Skilled Immigration." *International Herald Tribune,* February 9, 2006.

[23] Isabelle Robert-Bobeé. *Population Trends in France—Looking Ahead to 2050—An Increasing and Ageing Population.* Paris: Institut National dela Statistique et des E'tudes, 2006.

[24] Emmanuel Peignard. *Immigration in France.* Embassy of France in the United States, July 2001.

[25] "France." *Replacement Migration: Is It a Solution to Declining and Ageing Populations?* New York: United Nations Department of Economic and Social Affairs, Population Division, 2000.

[26] "Global Aging: It's Not Just Europe—China and Other Emerging-Market Economies Are Aging Fast, Too. There Are Solutions, but It's Time to Act." *Business Week,* January 31, 2005.

[27] "Global Aging: It's Not Just Europe—China and Other Emerging-Market Economies Are Aging Fast, Too. There Are Solutions, but It's Time to Act." *Business Week,* January 31, 2005.

[28] Tony McNeill. "Immigration in Postwar France," Lectures 1–3, February 1998. Available online. URL: www.unc.edu/depts/europe/conferences/Veil2000/articles/immigration-in-postwar-france.pdf. Accessed July 24, 2006.

[29] Tony McNeill. "Immigration in Postwar France," Lectures 1–3, February 1998. Available online. URL: www.unc.edu/depts/europe/conferences/Veil2000/articles/immigration-in-postwar-france.pdf. Accessed July 24, 2006.

[30] Tony McNeill. "Immigration in Postwar France," Lectures 1–3, February 1998. Available online. URL: www.unc.edu/depts/europe/conferences/Veil2000/articles/immigration-in-postwar-france.pdf. Accessed July 24, 2006.

[31] *French Report Backs Veil Ban.* CNN.com. December 11, 2003. Available online. URL http://www.cnn.cmo/2003/WORLD/europe/12/11/france.religion.reut. Accessed April 20, 2007.

[32] "France: African Immigrants." *Migration News* 3, no. 4 (October 1996).

[33] Craig S. Smith. "Angry Immigrants Embroil France in Wider Riots." *New York Times*, November 5, 2005.

[34] Jean-Marie Godard. "France: Thousands Protest French Immigration Bill." *Associated Press*, May 15, 2006.

[35] Tony McNeill. "Immigration in Postwar France," Lectures 1–3, February 1998. Available online. URL: www.unc.edu/depts/europe/conferences/Veil2000/articles/immigration-in-postwar-france.pdf. Accessed July 24, 2006.

[36] Reynald Blion, Catherine Wihtol de Wenden, and Nedjma Meknache. "France." *EU and U.S. Approaches to the Management of Immigration*. Brussels: Migration Policy Group, 2003.

[37] "France Amends Immigration Law." *Migration News* 4, no. 2 (April 1997).

[38] "French Immigration Bill." *Migration News* 4, no. 4 (December 1997).

[39] "France, Germany, Benelux." *Migration News* 13, no. 3 (December 2006).

[40] Vincent Viet. "Immigrant France. The Development of a Policy, 1914–1997." *Actes de l'histoire de l'immigration*, January 22, 1999.

[41] Vincent Viet. "Immigrant France. The Development of a Policy, 1914–1997." *Actes de l'histoire de l'immigration*, January 22, 1999.

[42] Vincent Viet. "Immigrant France. The Development of a Policy, 1914–1997." *Actes de l'histoire de l'immigration*, January 22, 1999.

[43] Reynald Blion, Catherine Wihtol de Wenden, and Nedjma Meknache. "France." *EU and U.S. Approaches to the Management of Immigration*. Brussels: Migration Policy Group, 2003.

[44] Vincent Viet. "Immigrant France. The Development of a Policy, 1914–1997." *Actes de l'histoire de l'immigration*, January 22, 1999.

[45] Antonella C. Attardo. "Immigration Law and Policy: France." *Legislationline*. Warsaw, Poland: Office for Democratic Institutions and Human Rights, 2006. Available online. URL: http://www.legislationonline.org/?tid=131&jid=19&less=false. Accessed August 1, 2006.

[46] Reynald Blion, Catherine Wihtol de Wenden, and Nedjma Meknache. "France." *EU and U.S. Approaches to the Management of Immigration*. Brussels: Migration Policy Group, 2003.

[47] Reynald Blion, Catherine Wihtol de Wenden, and Nedjma Meknache. "France." *EU and U.S. Approaches to the Management of Immigration*. Brussels: Migration Policy Group, 2003.

[48] Virginie Guiraudon. "Immigration Policy in France." *U.S.-France Analysis*. Washington, D.C.: The Brookings Institution, 2002.

[49] Virginie Guiraudon. "Immigration Policy in France." *U.S.-France Analysis*. Washington, D.C.: The Brookings Institution, 2002.

[50] Reynald Blion, Catherine Wihtol de Wenden, and Nedjma Meknache. "France." *EU and U.S. Approaches to the Management of Immigration*. Brussels: Migration Policy Group, 2003.

[51] Reynald Blion, Catherine Wihtol de Wenden, and Nedjma Meknache. "France." *EU and U.S. Approaches to the Management of Immigration.* Brussels,: Migration Policy Group, 2003.

[52] Kara Murphy. "France's New Law: Control Immigration Flows, Court the Highly Skilled." *Backgrounder.* Washington, D.C.: Migration Policy Institute, November 2004.

[53] "World Briefing—Europe: France: Immigration Rules Tightened." *New York Times,* November 30, 2005.

[54] "Five Facts about France's New Immigration Law." *Basque News and Information Channel,* May 2, 2006. Available online. URL: http://www.google.com/search?client=safari&rls=en&q=%22Five+facts+about+france's+new+immigration+law%22&ie=UTF-8&oe=UTF-8. Accessed August 2, 2006.

[55] Jean-Marie Godard. "France: Thousands Protest French Immigration Bill." *Associated Press,* May 15, 2006.

[56] Neija Hamadaoui. "The Nation Shows Its Gratitude to Immigrants." *Label France,* 57 (January–March 2005).

[57] "History." *South Africa Yearbook, 2004/05.* South African Government Information, November 30, 2005.

[58] "History." *South Africa Yearbook, 2004/05.* South African Government Information, November 30, 2005.

[59] *Settlers. 1820–1899: Expanding Cape Colony.* South Africa Cultures, Batho Portal. Available online. URL: http://www.sacultures.org.za/pebble.asp?relid=4092&t=168&translated=false&Culture=English. Accessed August 21, 2006.

[60] Jay Sand. "The Jews of Africa." *South Africa History.* Available online. URL: http://www.mindspring.com/~jaypsand/sa2.htm. Accessed August 15, 2006.

[61] Claude Lützelschwab. "Colonial Settler Economies in Africa." *Settler Economies in World History,* session 97, 14th International Economic History Congress, Helsinki, Finland: August 21–25, 2006.

[62] "History." *South Africa Yearbook, 2004/05.* South African Government Information, November 30, 2005.

[63] "Johannesburg—Historical Background. *The Economist Cities Guide,* 2006. Available online. URL: http://www.economist.com/cities/findStory.cfm?CITY_ID=JOH&FOLDER=Facts-History. Accessed April 23, 2007.

[64] "Johannesburg—Historical Background. *The Economist Cities Guide,* 2006. Available online. URL: http://www.economist.com/cities/findStory.cfm?CITY_ID=JOH&FOLDER=Facts-History. Accessed April 23, 2007.

[65] "Johannesburg—Historical Background. *The Economist Cities Guide,* 2006. Available online. URL: http://www.economist.com/cities/findStory.cfm?CITY_ID=JOH&FOLDER=Facts-History. Accessed April 23, 2007.

[66] Claude Lützelschwab. "Colonial Settler Economies in Africa." *Settler Economies in World History.* Session 97, 14th International Economic History Congress, Helsinki, Finland: August 21–25, 2006.

[67] Brij Maharaj. "Immigration to Post-Apartheid South Africa." *Global Migration Perspectives,* no. 1. Geneva: Global Commission on International Migration, June 2004.

[68] Jonathan Crush. "South Africa: New Nation, New Migration Policy?" *Migration Information Source.* Washington, D.C.: Migration Policy Institute, June 2003.

[69] *Documented Migration,* 2003, Report No. 03-51-03. Pretoria: Statistics South Africa, 2005.

[70] Jonathan Crush. "South Africa: New Nation, New Migration Policy?" *Migration Information Source.* Washington, D.C.: Migration Policy Institute, June 2003.

[71] Dorrit Posel. "Have Migration Patterns in Post-Apartheid South Africa Changed?" Paper prepared for the Conference on African Migration in Comparative Perspective, Johannesburg, South Africa, June 4–7, 2003.

[72] "South Africa Hit by 'Brain-Drain.'" *BBC News,* July 24, 2002. Available online. URL: http://www.news.bbc.co.uk/1/hi/world/africa/21492997.stm. Accessed August 21, 2006.

[73] *Documented Migration, 2003,* Report No. 03-51-03. Pretoria: Statistics South Africa, 2005.

[74] Janet Wilhelm. "From China With Love." *Mail & Guardian* (South Africa), January 6, 2006.

[75] *Rainbow Immigration.* International Marketing Council of South Africa, November 5, 2004.

[76] "Thousands Wait as Immigration Battles Backlog." *South Africa.* South African Migration Project, December 12, 2005.

[77] "Africa: Development, Migrants." *Migration News* 13, 1 (January 2006).

[78] Gcinumzi Ntlakana. Statement on the Refugee Backlog Project presented at the Court Classique Hotel, Arcadia, Pretoria, April 20, 2006. Available online. URL: http://home-affairs.pwv.gov.za/speeches.asp?id=157. Accessed August 21, 2006.

[79] Brij. Maharaj. "Immigration to Post-Apartheid South Africa." *Global Migration Perspectives,* 1. Geneva: Global Commission on International Migration, June 2004.

[80] Jonathan Crush. "South Africa: New Nation, New Migration Policy?" *Migration Information Source.* Washington, D.C.: Migration Policy Institute, June 2003.

[81] Brij Maharaj. "Immigration to Post-Apartheid South Africa." *Global Migration Perspectives,* 1. Geneva: Global Commission on International Migration, June 2004.

[82] Jonathan Crush. "A Bad Neighbor Policy?: Migrant Labour and the New South Africa." *Southern Africa Report* 12, no. 1 (November 1996), p. 3.

[83] Janet Wilhelm. "From China with Love." *Mail & Guardian* (South Africa), January 6, 2006.

[84] Janet Wilhelm. "From China with Love." *Mail & Guardian* (South Africa), January 6, 2006.

[85] Brij Maharaj. "Immigration to Post-Apartheid South Africa." *Global Migration Perspectives,* 1. Geneva: Global Commission on International Migration, June 2004.

[86] "Illegal Immigrants Present Easy Pickings." *Business Day* (Johannesburg, South Africa), October 12, 2004.

[87] Jonathan Crush. "South Africa: New Nation, New Migration Policy?" *Migration Information Source.* Washington, D.C.: Migration Policy Institute, June 2003.

[88] Audie Klotz. "International Relations and Migration in Southern Africa." *African Security Review* 6, 3 (1997).

[89] Audie Klotz. "International Relations and Migration in Southern Africa." *African Security Review* 6, 3 (1997).

[90] Audie Klotz. "International Relations and Migration in Southern Africa." *African Security Review* 6, 3 (1997).

[91] Brij Maharaj. "Immigration to Post-Apartheid South Africa." *Global Migration Perspectives,* 1. Geneva: Global Commission on International Migration, June 2004.

[92] Jonathan Crush. *South Africa: New Nation, New Migration Policy?* Washington, D.C.: Migration Policy Institute, June 2003.

[93] "Permanent Residence in South Africa." South African Consulate General in New York, May 9, 2005.

[94] "Permanent Residence in South Africa." South African Consulate General in New York, May 9, 2005.

[95] Delphine Marie. "Lesotho Marks the End of an Era for Apartheid's Refugees." *UNHCR News,* August 26, 2006.

[96] Cheryl Freedman. *South Africans Find a Home in Canada.* Canadian Broadcasting Corporation radio news program, November 19, 1973. Available online. URL: http://archives.cbc.ca/idc-1-71-703-4121/conflict_war/apartheid.clip5. Accessed on August 20, 2006.

[97] Delphine Marie. "Lesotho Marks the End of an Era for Apartheid's Refugees." *UNHCR News,* August 26. 2006.

[98] Cheryl Freedman. *South Africans Find a Home in Canada.* Canadian Broadcasting Corporation radio news program, November 19, 1973. Available online. URL: http://archives.cbc.ca/idc-1-71-703-4121/conflict_war/apartheid.clip5. Accessed on August 20, 2006.

[99] *Documented Migration, 2003,* Report No. 03-51-03. Pretoria: Statistics South Africa, 2005.

[100] Jonathan Crush. "South Africa: New Nation, New Migration Policy?" *Migration Information Source.* Washington, D.C.: Migration Policy Institute, June 2003.

[101] J. B. Meyer, et al. *Emigration and Immigration: The South African Figures.* Cape Town, South Africa: University of Cape Town, Development Policy Research Unit, 2000.

[102] "South Africa Hit by 'Brain-Drain.'" *BBC News,* July 24, 2002. Available online. URL: http://www.news.bbc.co.uk/1/hi/world/africa/21492997.stm. Accessed August 21, 2006.

[103] "South Africa Hit by 'Brain-Drain.'" *BBC News,* July 24, 2002. Available online. URL: http://www.news.bbc.co.uk/1/hi/world/africa/21492997.stm. Accessed August 21, 2006.

[104] Kader Asmal. "South Africa's Brain Drain Dilemma." *BBC News,* April 19, 2004. Available online. URL: http://news.bbc.co.uk/1/hi/world/africa/3629657.stm. Accessed August 21, 2006.

[105] "South Africans Are Coming Home." *Independent Online* (South Africa), August 17, 2006. Available online. URL: http://www.int.iol.co.za/index.php?set_id=1&click_id=13&art_id=qw1155818882460B263. Accessed August 17, 2006.

[106] Bobby Vaughn. "Blacks in Mexico—A Brief Overview." *Mexico Connect Magazine,* 2006. Available online. URL: http://www.mexconnect.com/mex_feature/ethnic/bv/brief.htm. Accessed August 20, 2006.

[107] "History of Mazatlán." *Discovery Mazatlán,* 2006. Available online. URL: http://www.discoverymazatlan.com/History. Accessed August 20, 2006.

[108] Shep Lenchek. "Jews in Mexico, a Struggle for Survival." *Mexico Connect Magazine,* 2000. Available online. URL: http://www.mexconnect.com/mex_/travel/slenchek/sljews inmexico1.html. Accessed August 20, 2006.

[109] Ryu Jin. "'Henequen' Recall 100 Years of Sorrow." *Korean Times,* September 9, 2005.

[110] Martha Diaz de Kuri and Lurdes Macluf. *From Lebanon to Mexico: Chronicle of an Emigrant People,* 1995. Available online. URL: http://www.caza-zgharta.com/demogra phy/mexico1.htm. Accessed August 23, 2006.

[111] Joe Cummings. "Sweet & Sour Times on the Border: A Review of Chinese Immigration to Mexico." *Mexico Connect Magazine,* 2006. Available online. URL: http://www.mexconnect.com/mex_/travel/jcummings/jcchina.html. Accessed August 20, 2006.

[112] Manuel Ángel Castillo. "Mexico: Caught between the United States and Central America." *Migration Information Source.* Washington, D.C.: Migration Policy Institute, April 2006.

[113] Sal Osio. "Americans in Mexico." *HispanicVista,* November 8, 2004.

[114] Demetrious G. Papademetriou, et al. *America's Emigrants: U.S. Retirement Migration to Mexico and Panama.* Washington, D.C.: Migration Policy Institute, 2006.

[115] Demetrious G. Papademetriou, et al. *America's Emigrants: U.S. Retirement Migration to Mexico and Panama.* Washington, D.C.: Migration Policy Institute, 2006.

[116] Manuel Ángel Castillo. "Mexico: Caught between the United States and Central America." *Migration Information Source.* Washington, D.C.: Migration Policy Institute, April 2006.

[117] "Central-American Migration to Mexico Increased 25 Percent This Year, Says NGO." *News Mexico, Travel Guide.* San Francisco: Global Exchange, November 15, 2002.

[118] "Mexico's Immigration Problem: The Kamikazes of Poverty." *The Economist,* January 29, 2004.

[119] C. L. Staten. "The Mexico/USA Border: A Gathering Storm." *EmergencyNet News,* May 28, 1997. Available online. URL: http://www.emergencynet.com/mexusa97.htm. Accessed August 18, 2006.

[120] C. L. Staten. "The Mexico/USA Border: A Gathering Storm." *EmergencyNet News,* May 28, 1997. Available online. URL: http://www.emergencynet.com/mexusa97.htm. Accessed August 18, 2006.

[121] Ralph Blumenthal and Ginger Thompson. "Texas Town Is Unnerved by Violence in Mexico." *New York Times,* August 11, 2005, p. A18.

[122] "Drug Haul in Secret Border Tunnel." *BBC News,* January 27, 2006

[123] Sara A. Carter. "Smuggling, Drug-Running, Violence Defines Mexican Border Testimony." *Inland Valley Daily Bulletin* (Ontario, California), July 6, 2006.

[124] James C. McKinley, Jr. and John Broder. "Under U.S. Pressure, Mexico President Seeks Review of Drug Law." *New York Times,* May 4, 2006, p. A11.

[125] Ginger Thompson and Clifford Krauss. "Mexico Pledges to Extradite Drug Traffickers to the U.S." *New York Times,* March 29, 2006, p. A13.

[126] *The 1917 Constitution of Mexico.* Available online. URL: http://www.ilstu.edu/class// hist263/docs/1917const.html. Accessed August 19, 2006.

[127] "General Law of Population." *Mexicanlaws.com Newsletter,* June 2006. Available online. URL: http://www.mexicolaws.com/newsletter_june_2006.htm. Accessed August 19, 2006.

[128] "General Law of Population." *Mexicanlaws.com Newsletter,* June 2006. Available online. URL: http://www.mexicolaws.com/newsletter_june_2006.htm. Accessed August 19, 2006.

[129] Mark Stevenson. "Mexico Works to Bar Non-Natives from Jobs." *Associated Press,* May 21, 2006.

[130] *The 1917 Constitution of Mexico.* Available online. URL: http://www.ilstu.edu/class// hist263/docs/1917const.html. Accessed August 19, 2006.

[131] "Mexico's Immigration Problem: The Kamikazes of Poverty." *The Economist,* January 29, 2004.

[132] Kelly Simmons and Ana Vinas. "Changes to Laws in U.S. and Mexico Affect Immigration." *frontera Norte/Sur,* November 1, 1996.

[133] Ginger Thompson. "Mexico Worries about Its Own Southern Border." *New York Times,* June 18, 2006, p. 1.

[134] Ginger Thompson. "Mexican Leader Condemns U.S. for Migrant Bill Passed by House." *New York Times,* December 20, 2005, p. A6.

[135] Ginger Thompson. "Some in Mexico See Border Wall as Opportunity." *New York Times,* May 25, 2006, p. A1.

[136] James C. McKinley, Jr. "Bush's Ambassador to Mexico Is Sometimes Undiplomatic." *New York Times,* August 20, 2005, p. A4.

[137] James C. McKinley, Jr. "A Border Killing Inflames Mexican Anger at U.S. Policy." *New York Times,* January 14, 2006, p. A3.

[138] James C. McKinley, Jr. "U.S. and Mexico Trade Complaints over Border Security Issues." *New York Times,* January 27, 2006, p. A9.

[139] John M. Broder. "In California, Fox of Mexico Is Embraced and Snubbed." *New York Times,* May 26, 2006, p. A19.

[140] Ginger Thompson. "Mexican President Thanks Bush for Support on Changes in Immigration." *New York Times,* May 27, 2006, p. A19.

[141] *First Migrant Workers.* El Paso, Tex.: Sin Fronteras Organizing Project, December 1999. Available online. URL: http://farmworkers.org/immigrat.html. Accessed August 15, 2006.

[142] *First Migrant Workers.* El Paso, Tex.: Sin Fronteras Organizing Project, December 1999. Available online. URL: http://farmworkers.org/immigrat.html. Accessed August 15, 2006.

[143] Ginger Thompson. "Migrant Exodus Bleeds Mexico's Heartland." *New York Times,* July 17, 2001.

[144] Jeff Faux. "How NAFTA Failed Mexico: Immigration Is Not a Development Policy." *The American Prospect* 14, 7 (July 3, 2003).

[145] Michael Marizco. "Abandonment. Plenty of Jobs, Not Enough Pay: Economic Forces Push Mexican Workers North." *High Country News,* May 15, 2006, p. 4.

[146] Ginger Thompson. "Migrant Exodus Bleeds Mexico's Heartland." *New York Times,* July 17, 2001.

[147] Ginger Thompson. "Migrant Exodus Bleeds Mexico's Heartland." *New York Times,* July 17, 2001.

[148] Allan Wall. "Mexico's Safety Valve." *Spokesmanreview.com,* August 16, 2004. Available online. URL: http://www.spokesmanreview.com/breaking/story/asp?ID=2682. Accessed July 27, 2006.

[149] "Mexico: HTAs, Fertility, Labor." *Migration News* 13, no. 4 (October 2006).

[150] Michael Lettieri. *The Immigration Bomb Explodes.* Press release, March 29, 2006, Council on Hemispheric Affairs.

[151] "Philippine History." *Pinas.* Available online. URL: http://pinas.dlsu.edu.ph/history/history.html. Accessed August 23, 2006.

[152] *Brief History of the Philippine-Netherlands Relations.* The Hague, Netherlands: The Philippine Embassy, 2004.

[153] "Philippine History." *Pinas.* Available online. URL: http://pinas.dlsu.edu.ph/history/history.html. Accessed August 23, 2006.

[154] "Philippine History." *Pinas.* Available online. URL: http://pinas.dlsu.edu.ph/history/history.html. Accessed August 23, 2006.

[155] Raul Palabrica. "Puzzling Inward Migration in the Philippines." *Philippine Daily Inquirer,* August 11, 2002.

[156] See Ang Teresita. "Influx of New Chinese Immigrants to the Philippines: Problems and Challenges." Lecture, Fifth ISSCO Conference, Copenhagen, Denmark, May 10–13, 2004, p.

[157] Ronald Meinardus. "The 'Korean Wave' in the Philippines." *Korean Times,* December 15, 2005.

[158] "Philippines." *The World Fact Book.* Washington, D.C.: Central Intelligence Agency, September 7, 2006.

[159] Raul Palabrica. "Puzzling Inward Migration in the Philippines." *Philippine Daily Inquirer,* August 11, 2002.

[160] Raul Palabrica. "Puzzling Inward Migration in the Philippines." *Philippine Daily Inquirer,* August 11, 2002 p.

[161] "FM Spokesman Says 144 Chinese Arrested in Philippines Released." *People's Daily Online* (China), December 21, 2005. Available online. URL: http://english.people.com.cn/200512/21/eng20051221_229676.html. Accessed September 7, 2006.

[162] Glenn E. Curtis et al. *Transnational Activities of Chinese Crime Organizations.* Washington, D.C.: Library of Congress, Federal Research Division, April 2003.

[163] "China and Hong Kong." *Migration News* 5, no. 4 (March 1998).

[164] *Commonwealth Act No. 613.* Philippine Bureau of Immigration. Available online. URL: http://www.immigration.gov.ph/immigration_laws.php. Accessed September 6, 2006.

[165] "Philippines—ACR Slated for Enforcement by March 31, 2005." *Immigration Headlines,* Fragomen Global Immigration Services, February 16, 2005.

[166] "Philippines Approves New Migrant Worker Act." *Migration News* 2, no. 3 (July 1995).

[167] "Rewrite the 1940 Immigration Law." *Manila Times* (Philippines), May 21, 2005, p.

[168] Maruja M. B. Asis. "The Philippines Culture of Migration." *Migration Information Source.* Washington, D.C.: Migration Policy Institute, January 2006.

[169] Maruja M. B. Asis. "The Philippines Culture of Migration." *Migration Information Source.* Washington, D.C.: Migration Policy Institute, January 2006.

[170] Maruja M. B. Asis. "The Philippines Culture of Migration." *Migration Information Source.* Washington, D.C.: Migration Policy Institute, January 2006.

[171] Kevin O'Neil. "Labor Export as Government Policy: The Case of the Philippines." *Migration Information Source.* Washington, D.C.: Migration Policy Institute, January 1, 2004.

[172] "Philippines Approves New Migrant Worker Act." *Migration News* 2, no. 3 (July 1995).

[173] Kevin O'Neil. "Labor Export as Government Policy: The Case of the Philippines." *Migration Information Source.* Washington, D.C.: Migration Policy Institute, January 1, 2004.

[174] "Philippines." *The World Fact Book.* Washington, D.C.: Central Intelligence Agency, September 7, 2006.

[175] *Statistics.* Philippine National Wages and Productivity Commission. Available online. URL: http://www.nwpc.dole.gov.ph/pages/statistics/stat_comparative.html. Accessed September 7, 2006.

[176] Pepe Escobar. "Will the Last One Leaving Please Turn Off the Lights." *Asia Times* (Hong Kong), October 6, 2004.

[177] Ronald Meinardus. "Migration, Population and the Globalization of Labor." *Korean Times,* July 3, 2006.

[178] Maruja M. B. Asis. "The Philippines Culture of Migration." *Migration Information Source.* Washington, D.C.: Migration Policy Institute, January 2006.

[179] Maruja M. B. Asis. "The Philippines Culture of Migration." *Migration Information Source.* Washington, D.C.: Migration Policy Institute, January 2006.

[180] Maruja M. B. Asis. "The Philippines Culture of Migration." *Migration Information Source.* Washington, D.C.: Migration Policy Institute, January 2006.

[181] Maruja M. B. Asis. "The Philippines Culture of Migration." *Migration Information Source.* Washington, D.C.: Migration Policy Institute, January 2006.

[182] Pepe Escobar. "Will the Last One Leaving Please Turn Off the Lights." *Asia Times* (Hong Kong), October 6, 2004.

[183] Maruja M. B. Asis. "The Philippines Culture of Migration." *Migration Information Source.* Washington, D.C.: Migration Policy Institute, January 2006.

[184] Kevin O'Neil. "Labor Export as Government Policy: The Case of the Philippines." *Migration Information Source.* Washington, D.C.: Migration Policy Institute, January 1, 2004.

[185] "Philippines: Emigration Stable." *Migration News* 5, no. 4 (November 1998).

[186] Ronald Meinardus. "Migration, Population and the Globalization of Labor." *Korean Times*, July 3, 2006.

[187] *Immigration of Doctors and Nurses Two-Edged.* Press release, University of Illinois Extension, Urbana-Champaign, May 30, 2006.

[188] Celia W. Dugger. "U.S. Plan to Lure Nurses May Hurt Poor Nations." *New York Times*, May 24, 2006.

[189] George Nishiyama. "Philippines Health Care Paralyzed by Nurses Exodus." *Reuters*, February 28, 2006.

[190] Gwen Yeo et al. "Filipino American Elders through the Decades of the 1900s." *Cohort Analysis as a Tool in Ethnogeriatrics: Historical Profiles of Elders from Eight Ethnic Populations in the United States.* Stanford, Calif.: Stanford Geriatric Education Center, Stanford University School of Medicine, 1999.

[191] Alfredo G. Rosario. "U.S. Reopens Market for Nurses, Therapists." *Manila Times* (Philippines), May 21, 2005.

[192] *Immigration of Doctors and Nurses Two-Edged.* Press release, University of Illinois Extension, Urbana-Champaign, May 30, 2006.

[193] Glenn Rose. "Immigrant Visas Subject to Annual Limits." *PhilippineNews.com*, August 30, 2006. Available online. URL: http://www.philippinenews.com/news/view_article.html?article_id=0272870a415e16867b837ae6b1de7c0a. Accessed September 7, 2006.

[194] George Nishiyama. "Philippines Health Care Paralyzed by Nurses Exodus." *Reuters*, February 28, 2006.

[195] *PGMA Presents Bagong Bayani Awards to Outstanding OFWs.* Press release, Government of the Republic of the Philippines, December 2, 2005.

[196] Kevin O'Neil. "Labor Export as Government Policy: The Case of the Philippines." *Migration Information Source.* Washington, D.C.: Migration Policy Institute, January 1, 2004.

[197] Kemba Dunham. "Philippine Effort to Lure Expatriate Real-Estate Investment from U.S. May Serve as Test Case." *Wall Street Journal*, June 5, 2006, p. A2.

PART II

Primary Sources

4

United States Documents

This chapter provides a selection of primary sources specific to immigration in the United States. It is divided into three categories: Important legislation passed by the U.S. government that notably impacted immigration; presidential speeches and writings related to immigration; and papers, speeches, or reports by scholars that present varying insights into immigration. Documents are organized and listed in chronological order within each section. All documents are reproduced in full unless identified as excerpted.

I. FEDERAL LEGISLATIVE DOCUMENTS

Due to space limitations, most of the documents included in this section are historical rather than contemporary. Several key modern immigration laws have been excluded, including the **Immigration and Nationality Act of 1952.** Known as the McCarran-Walter Act, which consolidated all previous U.S. immigration acts, laws, and statutes, revised the annual quotas system, and eliminated race as a reason to ban. Also excluded were three later acts that revised the McCarran-Walter Act: the **Immigration and Naturalization Act of 1965,** known as the Hart-Cellar Immigration Bill, eliminated annual quotas based on race, religion, or nation of origin, replacing them with quotas based on each immigrant's skills and profession; the **Immigration Act of 1990,** which increased the total allowed annual immigrants to 700,000 with a decrease to 675,000 beginning in 1995, established a lottery system for issuing visas, and removed AIDS from the list of diseases that make immigrants ineligible to enter the United States; and the **Legal Immigration and Family Equity (LIFE) Act of 2000,** which benefited people in the United States illegally, specifically those who arrived without legal documentation or those who remained as visa overstayers. The acts are available online at the following Web sites: (Walter-McCarran Act) Documents of American History, http://tucnak.fsv.cuni.cz/~calda/Documents/1950s/

McCarran_52/html; (Hart-Cellar Bill) U.S. Historical Documents, http://www.historicaldocuments.com/ImmigrationActof1965.html; (Act of 1990) Library of Congress, http://thomas.loc.gov/cgi-bin/query/z?c101:S.358.ENR:; and (LIFE Act) U.S. Department of Justice, http://www.usdoj.gov/eoir/vll/legislation/LIFEactsum.html.

The Immigration Act of 1790 (March 26, 1790) (excerpt)

This act was the country's first law that focused on immigrants and specified who could become naturalized citizens of the United States. The act limited naturalization to "free white persons." Although the government began allowing the naturalization of immigrants from some Asian countries in the 1940s, the racial requirements set forth in this act remained in effect until 1952.

> That any alien, being a free white person, who shall have resided within the limits and under the jurisdiction of the United States for the term of two years, may be admitted to become a citizen thereof, on application to any common law court of record, in any one of the States wherein he shall have resided for the term of one year at least, and making proof to the satisfaction of such court, that he is a person of good character, and taking the oath or affirmation prescribed by law, to support the Constitution of the United States, which oath or affirmation such court shall administer; and the clerk of such court shall record such application, and the proceedings thereon; and thereupon such person shall be considered as a citizen of the United States. And the children of such persons so naturalized, dwelling within the United States, being under the age of twenty-one years at the time of such naturalization, shall also be considered as citizens of the United States. And the children of citizens of the United States, that may be born beyond sea, or out of the limits of the United States, shall be considered as natural born citizens: *Provided,* that the right of citizenship shall not descend to persons whose fathers have never been resident in the United States: . . .

Source: U.S. Historical Documents. Available online. URL: http://www.historicaldocuments.com/ImmigrationActof1790.htm. Accessed November 14, 2006.

Alien and Sedition Acts (1798)

As the United States prepared for war with France in 1798 the government, fearful that aliens living in the country would be loyal to the French or would criticize federal policies, passed this act to tighten restrictions on foreign-born

Americans, including increasing the residency requirements for citizenship to 14 years from five, and permitting the arrest, imprisonment, and deportation of aliens considered dangerous to the country during wartime. The acts also made it a crime for American citizens to speak, write, or publish anything deemed false, malicious, or scandalous against the U.S. government.

FIFTH CONGRESS OF THE UNITED STATES:

At the Second Session,

Begun and held at the city of Philadelphia, in the state of Pennsylvania, on Monday, the thirteenth of November, one thousand seven hundred and ninety-seven.

An Act Concerning Aliens.

SECTION 1. Be it enacted by the Senate and the House of Representatives of the United States of America in Congress assembled, That it shall be lawful for the President of the United States at any time during the continuance of this act, to order all such aliens as he shall judge dangerous to the peace and safety of the United States, or shall have reasonable grounds to suspect are concerned in any treasonable or secret machinations against the government thereof, to depart out of the territory of the United Slates, within such time as shall be expressed in such order, which order shall be served on such alien by delivering him a copy thereof, or leaving the same at his usual abode, and returned to the office of the Secretary of State, by the marshal or other person to whom the same shall be directed. And in case any alien, so ordered to depart, shall be found at large within the United States after the time limited in such order for his departure, and not having obtained a license from the President to reside therein, or having obtained such license shall not have conformed thereto, every such alien shall, on conviction thereof, be imprisoned for a term not exceeding three years, and shall never after be admitted to become a citizen of the United States. Provided always, and be it further enacted, that if any alien so ordered to depart shall prove to the satisfaction of the President, by evidence to be taken before such person or persons as the President shall direct, who are for that purpose hereby authorized to administer oaths, that no injury or danger to the United Slates will arise from suffering such alien to reside therein, the President may grant a license to such alien to remain within the United States for such time as he shall judge proper, and at such place as he may designate. And the President may also require of such alien to enter into a bond to the United States, in such penal sum as he may direct, with one or more sufficient sureties to the satisfaction of the person authorized by the President to take the same, conditioned for the good behavior of such alien during his residence in the United States, and not violating his license, which license the President may revoke, whenever he shall think proper.

SEC. 2. And be it further enacted, That it shall be lawful for the President of the United States, whenever he may deem it necessary for the public safety, to order to be removed out of the territory thereof, any alien who may or shall be in prison in pursuance of this act; and to cause to be arrested and sent out of the United States such of those aliens as shall have been ordered to depart therefrom and shall not have obtained a license as aforesaid, in all cases where, in the opinion of the President, the public safety requires a speedy removal. And if any alien so removed or sent out of the United Slates by the President shall voluntarily return thereto, unless by permission of the President of the United States, such alien on conviction thereof, shall be imprisoned so long as, in the opinion of the President, the public safety may require.

SEC. 3. And be it further enacted, That every master or commander of any ship or vessel which shall come into any port of the United States after the first day of July next, shall immediately on his arrival make report in writing to the collector or other chief officer of the customs of such port, of all aliens, if any, on board his vessel, specifying their names, age, the place of nativity, the country from which they shall have come, the nation to which they belong and owe allegiance, their occupation and a description of their persons, as far as he shall be informed thereof, and on failure, every such master and commander shall forfeit and pay three hundred dollars, for the payment whereof on default of such master or commander, such vessel shall also be holden, and may by such collector or other officer of the customs be detained. And it shall be the duty of such collector or other officer of the customs, forthwith to transmit to the office of the department of state true copies of all such returns.

SEC. 4. And be it further enacted, That the circuit and district courts of the United States, shall respectively have cognizance of all crimes and offences against this act. And all marshals and other officers of the United States are required to execute all precepts and orders of the President of the United States issued in pursuance or by virtue of this act.

SEC. 5. And be it further enacted, That it shall be lawful for any alien who may be ordered to be removed from the United States, by virtue of this act, to take with him such part of his goods, chattels, or other property, as he may find convenient; and all property left in the United States by any alien, who may be removed, as aforesaid, shall be, and remain subject to his order and disposal, in the same manner as if this act had not been passed.

SEC. 6. And be it further enacted, That this act shall continue and be in force for and during the term of two years from the passing thereof.

Jonathan Dayton, Speaker of the House of Representatives.
TH. Jefferson, Vice President of the United States and President of the Senate.
I Certify that this Act did originate in the Senate.
Attest, Sam. A. Otis, Secretary
APPROVED, June 25, 1798.
John Adams
President of the United States.

An Act Respecting Alien Enemies

SECTION 1. Be it enacted by the Senate and House of Representatives of the United States of America in Congress assembled, That whenever there shall be a declared war between the United States and any foreign nation or government, or any invasion or predatory incursion shall be perpetrated, attempted, or threatened against the territory of the United States, by any foreign nation or government, and the President of the United States shall make public proclamation of the event, all natives, citizens, denizens, or subjects of the hostile nation or government, being males of the age of fourteen years and upwards, who shall be within the United States, and not actually naturalized, shall be liable to be apprehended, restrained, secured and removed, as alien enemies. And the President of the United States shall be, and he is hereby authorized, in any event, as aforesaid, by his proclamation thereof, or other public act, to direct the conduct to be observed, on the part of the United States, towards the aliens who shall become liable, as aforesaid; the manner and degree of the restraint to which they shall be subject, and in what cases, and upon what security their residence shall be permitted, and to provide for the removal of those, who, not being permitted to reside within the United States, shall refuse or neglect to depart therefrom; and to establish any other regulations which shall be found necessary in the premises and for the public safety: Provided, that aliens resident within the United States, who shall become liable as enemies, in the manner aforesaid, and who shall not be chargeable with actual hostility, or other crime against the public safety, shall be allowed, for the recovery, disposal, and removal of their goods and effects, and for their departure, the full time which is, or shall be stipulated by any treaty, where any shall have been between the United States, and the hostile nation or government, of which they shall be natives, citizens, denizens or subjects: and where no such treaty shall have xisted, the President of the United States may ascertain and declare such reasonable time as may be consistent with the public safety, and according to the dictates of humanity and national hospitality.

SEC. 2. And be it further enacted, That after any proclamation shall be made as aforesaid, it shall be the duty of the several courts of the United States, and of each state, having criminal jurisdiction, and of the several judges and justices of the courts of the United States, and they shall be, and are hereby respectively, authorized upon complaint, against any alien or alien enemies, as aforesaid, who shall be resident and at large within such jurisdiction or district, to the danger of the public peace or safety, and contrary to the tenor or intent of such proclamation, or other regulations which the President of the United States shall and may establish in the premises, to cause such alien or aliens to be duly apprehended and convened before such court, judge or justice; and after a full examination and hearing on such complaint and sufficient cause therefor appearing, shall and may order such alien or aliens to be removed out of the territory of the United States, or to give sureties of their good behaviour, or to be otherwise restrained, conformably to the proclamation or regulations which shall and may be established as aforesaid, and may imprison, or otherwise secure such alien or aliens, until the order which shall and may be made, as aforesaid, shall be performed.

SEC. 3. And be it further enacted, That it shall be the duty of the marshal of the district in which any alien enemy shall be apprehended, who by the President of the United States, or by order of any court, judge or justice, as aforesaid, shall be required to depart, and to be removed, as aforesaid, to provide therefor, and to execute such order, by himself or his deputy, or other discreet person or persons to be employed by him, by causing a removal of such alien out of the territory of the United States; and for such removal the marshal shall have the warrant of the President of the United States, or of the court, judge or justice ordering the same, as the case may be.

APPROVED, July 6, 1798.

FIFTH CONGRESS OF THE UNITED STATES:

At the Second Session,

Begun and held at the city of Philadelphia, in the state of Pennsylvania, on Monday, the thirteenth of November, one thousand seven hundred and ninety-seven.

An Act in Addition to the Act, Entitled "An Act for the Punishment of Certain Crimes Against the United States."

SECTION 1. Be it enacted by the Senate and House of Representatives of the United States of America, in Congress assembled, That if any persons shall unlawfully combine or conspire together, with intent to oppose any measure or measures of the government of the United States, which are or shall be directed by proper authority, or to impede the operation of any law of the United States, or to intimidate or prevent any person holding a place or office in or under the government of the United States, from undertaking, performing or executing his trust or duty, and if any person or persons, with intent as aforesaid, shall counsel, advise or attempt to procure any insurrection, riot, unlawful assembly, or combination, whether such conspiracy, threatening, counsel, advice, or attempt shall have the proposed effect or not, he or they shall be deemed guilty of a high misdemeanor, and on conviction, before any court of the United States having jurisdiction thereof, shall be punished by a fine not exceeding five thousand dollars, and by imprisonment during a term not less than six months nor exceeding five years; and further, at the discretion of the court may be holden to find sureties for his good behaviour in such sum, and for such time, as the said court may direct.

SEC. 2. And be it farther enacted, That if any person shall write, print, utter or publish, or shall cause or procure to be written, printed, uttered or published, or shall knowingly and willingly assist or aid in writing, printing, uttering or publishing any false, scandalous and malicious writing or writings against the government of the United States, or either house of the Congress of the United States, or the President of the United States, with intent to defame the said government, or either house of the said Congress, or the said President, or to bring them, or either of them, into contempt or disrepute; or to excite against them, or either or any of them, the hatred of the good people of the United States, or to stir up sedition within the United States, or to excite any unlawful combinations therein, for opposing or resisting any law of the United States, or any act of the President of the United States, done in pursuance of any such law, or of the powers in him vested by the constitution of the United States, or to resist, oppose, or defeat any such law or act, or to aid, encourage or abet any hostile designs of any foreign nation against the United States, their people or government, then such person, being thereof convicted before any court of the United States having jurisdiction thereof, shall be punished by a fine not exceeding two thousand dollars, and by imprisonment not exceeding two years.

SEC. 3. And be it further enacted and declared, That if any person shall be prosecuted under this act, for the writing or publishing any libel aforesaid, it shall be lawful for the defendant, upon the trial of the cause, to give in evidence in his defence, the truth of the matter contained in publication charged as a libel. And the jury who shall try the cause, shall have a right to determine the law and the fact, under the direction of the court, as in other cases.

SEC. 4. And be it further enacted, That this act shall continue and be in force until the third day of March, one thousand eight hundred and one, and no longer: Provided, that the expiration of the act shall not prevent or defeat a prosecution and punishment of any offence against the law, during the time it shall be in force.

Jonathan Dayton, Speaker of the House of Representatives.
Theodore Sedgwick, President of the Senate pro tempore.
I Certify that this Act did originate in the Senate.
Attest, Sam. A. Otis, Secretary
APPROVED, July 14, 1798
John Adams
President of the United States.

Source: U.S. Historical Documents. Available online. URL: http://www.historicaldocuments.com/AlienandSedition%20Acts.htm. Accessed November 14, 2006.

The Indian Removal Act (May 28, 1830)

By the early 19th century the United States's population was rapidly growing and expanding into lands occupied by Native American tribes in the country's lower South. To acquire the lands for European settlers and other white Americans the government negotiated treaties with the southern Indians to trade land in the East for land in the West. Native American attempts to resist the land takeover or to assimilate into white communities failed. To force Native Americans living east of the Mississippi River to relocate to lands in the West President Andrew Jackson pushed the Indian Removal Act through both houses of Congress in 1830. The act resulted in the forced migration of thousands of Native Americans in what would become known as the Trail of Tears.

An Act to provide for an exchange of lands with the Indians residing in any of the states or territories, and for their removal west of the river Mississippi.

Be it enacted by the Senate and House of Representatives of the United States of America, in Congress assembled, That it shall and may be lawful for the President of the United States to cause so much of any territory belonging to the United States, west of the river Mississippi, not included in any state or organized territory, and to which the Indian title has been extinguished, as he may judge necessary, to be divided into a suitable number of districts, for the reception of such tribes or nations of Indians as may choose to exchange the lands where they now reside, and remove there; and to cause each of said districts to be so described by natural or artificial marks, as to be easily distinguished from every other.

And be it further enacted, That it shall and may be lawful for the President to exchange any or all of such districts, so to be laid off and described, with any tribe or nation of Indians now residing within the limits of any of the states or territories, and with which the United States have existing treaties, for the whole or any part or portion of the territory claimed and occupied by such tribe or nation, within the bounds of any one or more of the states or territories, where the land claimed and occupied by the Indians, is owned by the United States, or the United States are bound to the state within which it lies to extinguish the Indian claim thereto.

And be it further enacted, That in the making of any such exchange or exchanges, it shall and may be lawful for the President solemnly to assure the tribe or nation with which the exchange is made, that the United States will forever secure and guaranty to them, and their heirs or successors, the country so exchanged with them; and if they prefer it, that the United States will cause a patent or grant to be made and executed to them for the same: *Provided always,* That such lands shall revert to the United States, if the Indians become extinct, or abandon the same.

And be it further enacted, That if, upon any of the lands now occupied by the Indians, and to be exchanged for, there should be such improvements as add value to the land claimed by any individual or individuals of such tribes or nations, it shall and may be lawful for the President to cause such value to be ascertained by appraisement or otherwise, and to cause such ascertained value to be paid to the person or persons rightfully claiming such improvements. And upon the payment of such valuation, the improvements so valued and paid for, shall pass to the United States, and possession shall not afterwards be permitted to any of the same tribe.

And be it further enacted, That upon the making of any such exchange as is contemplated by this act, it shall and may be lawful for the President to cause such aid and assistance to be furnished to the emigrants as may be necessary and proper to enable them to remove to, and settle in, the country for which they may have exchanged; and also, to give them such aid and assistance as may be necessary for their support and subsistence for the first year after their removal.

And be it further enacted, That it shall and may be lawful for the President to cause such tribe or nation to be protected, at their new residence, against all interruption or disturbance from any other tribe or nation of Indians, or from any other person or persons whatever.

And be it further enacted, That it shall and may be lawful for the President to have the same superintendence and care over any tribe or nation in the country to which they may remove, as contemplated by this act, that he is now authorized to have over them at their present places of residence: *Provided,* That nothing in this act contained shall be construed as authorizing or directing the violation of any existing treaty between the United States and any of the Indian tribes.

And be it further enacted, That for the purpose of giving effect to the Provisions of this act, the sum of five hundred thousand dollars is hereby appropriated, to be paid out of any money in the treasury, not otherwise appropriated.

Source: U.S. Historical Documents. Available online. URL: http://www.historicaldocuments.com/IndianRemovalAct.htm. Accessed November 14, 2006.

Homestead Act (May 20, 1862)

To encourage Americans to migrate and settle sparsely populated U.S. territories in the West, the government passed this act. Under terms of the act, any adult citizen or immigrant planning to acquire citizenship could claim 160 acres of federal land. To achieve ownership of the property, the claimant was required to pay a small registration fee, live on the property five years, build a house on the property, and plant crops on the land. A short cut to ownership was also available. It required that the person claiming the land live on the property for just six months and pay the government $1.25 per acre.

CHAP. LXXV. An Act to secure Homesteads to actual Settlers on the Public Domain.

Be it enacted by the Senate and House of Representatives of the United States of America in Congress assembled, That any person who is the head of a family, or who has arrived at the age of twenty-one years, and is a citizen of the United States, or who shall have filed his declaration of intention to become such, as required by the naturalization laws of the United States, and who has never borne arms against the United States Government or given aid and comfort to its enemies, shall, from and after the first January, eighteen hundred and. sixty-three, be entitled to enter one quarter section or a less quantity of unappropriated public lands, upon which said person may have filed a preemption claim, or which may, at the time the application is made, be subject to preemption at one dollar and twenty-five cents, or less, per acre; or eighty acres or less of such unappropriated lands, at two dollars and fifty cents per acre, to be located in a body, in conformity to the legal subdivisions of the public lands, and after the same shall have been surveyed: Provided, That any person owning and residing on land may, under the provisions of this act, enter other land lying contiguous to his or her said land, which shall not, with the land so already owned and occupied, exceed in the aggregate one hundred and sixty acres.

SEC. 2. And be it further enacted, That the person applying for the benefit of this act shall, upon application to the register of the land office in which he or she is about to make such entry, make affidavit before the said register or receiver that he or she is the head of a family, or is twenty-one years or more of age, or shall have performed service in the army or navy of the United States, and that he has never borne arms against the Government of the United States or given aid and comfort to its enemies, and that such application is made for his or her exclusive use and benefit, and that said entry is made for the purpose of actual settlement and cultivation, and not either directly or indirectly for the use or benefit of any other person or persons whomsoever; and upon filing the said affidavit with the register or receiver, and on payment of ten dollars, he or she shall thereupon be permitted to enter the quantity of land specified: Provided, however, That no certificate shall be given or patent issued therefor until the expiration of five years from the date of such entry; and if, at the expiration of such time, or at any time within two years thereafter, the person making such entry; or, if he be dead, his widow; or in case of her death, his heirs or devisee; or in case of a widow making such entry, her heirs or devisee, in case of her death; shall prove by two credible witnesses that he, she, or they have resided upon or cultivated the same for the term of five years immediately succeeding the time of filing the affidavit aforesaid, and shall make affidavit that no part of said land has been alienated, and that he has borne due allegiance to the Government of the United States; then, in such case, he, she, or they, if at that time a citizen of the United States, shall be entitled to a patent, as in other cases provided for by law: And provided, further, That in case of the death of both father and mother, leaving an Infant child, or children, under twenty-one years of age, the right and fee shall ensure to the benefit of said infant child or children; and the executor, administrator, or guardian may, at any time within two years after the death of the surviving parent, and in accordance with the laws of the State in which such children for the time being have their domicil, sell said land for the benefit of said infants, but for no other purpose; and the purchaser shall acquire the absolute title by the purchase, and be entitled to a patent from the United States, on payment of the office fees and sum of money herein specified.

SEC. 3. And be it further enacted, That the register of the land office shall note all such applications on the tract books and plats of, his office, and keep a register of all such entries, and make return thereof to the General Land Office, together with the proof upon which they have been founded.

SEC. 4. And be it further enacted, That no lands acquired under the provisions of this act shall in any event become liable to the satisfaction of any debt or debts contracted prior to the issuing of the patent therefor.

SEC. 5. And be it further enacted, That if, at any time after the filing of the affidavit, as required in the second section of this act, and before the expiration of the five years aforesaid, it shall be proven, after due notice to the settler, to the satisfaction of the register of the land office, that the person having filed such affidavit shall have actually changed his or her residence, or abandoned the said land for more than six months at any time, then and in that event the land so entered shall revert to the government.

SEC. 6. And be it further enacted, That no individual shall be permitted to acquire title to more than one quarter section under the provisions of this act; and that the Commissioner of the General Land Office is hereby required to prepare and issue such rules and regulations, consistent with this act, as shall be necessary and proper to carry its provisions into effect; and that the registers and receivers of the several land offices shall be entitled to receive the same compensation for any lands entered under the provisions of this act that they are now entitled to receive when the same quantity of land is entered with money, one half to be paid by the person making the application at the time of so doing, and the other half on the issue of the certificate by the person to whom it may be issued; but this shall not be construed to enlarge the maximum of compensation now prescribed by law for any register or receiver: Provided, That nothing contained in this act shall be so construed as to impair or interfere in any manner whatever with existing preemption rights: And provided, further, That all persons who may have filed their applications for a preemption right prior to the passage of this act, shall be entitled to all privileges of this act: Provided, further, That no person who has served, or may hereafter serve, for a period of not less than fourteen days in the army or navy of the United States, either regular or volunteer, under the laws thereof, during the existence of an actual war, domestic or foreign, shall be deprived of the benefits of this act on account of not having attained the age of twenty-one years.

SEC. 7. And be it further enacted, That the fifth section of the act entitled "An act in addition to an act more effectually to provide for the punishment of certain crimes against the United States, and for other purposes," approved the third of March, in the year eighteen hundred and fifty-seven, shall extend to all oaths, affirmations, and affidavits, required or authorized by this act.

SEC. 8. And be it further enacted, That nothing in this act shall be construed as to prevent any person who has availed him or herself of the benefits of the first section of this act, from paying the minimum price, or the price to which the same may have graduated, for the quantity of land so entered at any time before the expiration of the five years, and obtaining a patent therefor from the government, as in other cases provided by law, on making proof of settlement and cultivation as provided by existing laws granting preemption rights.

APPROVED, May 20, 1862.

Source: U.S. Historical Documents. Available online. URL: http://www.historicaldocuments.com/HomesteadAct .htm. Accessed November 14, 2006.

Chinese Exclusion Act (May 6, 1882)

The Chinese Exclusion Act was the first immigration law passed by the U.S. government that targeted a specific ethnic group and codified racism into federal law. The act denied citizenship to Chinese immigrants already in the country and prohibited further immigration into the country by Chinese. Passage of the act led to creation of the first group of illegal aliens: Chinese who entered the country outside of the law.

Forty-Seventh Congress. Session I. 1882
Chapter 126. An act to execute certain treaty stipulations relating to Chinese.

Preamble. Whereas, in the opinion of the Government of the United States the coming of Chinese laborers to this country endangers the good order of certain localities within the territory thereof:

Therefore,

Be it enacted by the Senate and House of Representatives of the United States of America in Congress assembled, That from and after the expiration of ninety days next after the passage of this act, and until the expiration of ten years next after the passage of this act, the coming of Chinese laborers to the United States be, and the same is hereby, suspended; and during such suspension it shall not be lawful for any Chinese laborer to come, or, having so come after the expiration of said ninety days, to remain within the United States.

SEC. 2. That the master of any vessel who shall knowingly bring within the United States on such vessel, and land or permit to be landed, a Chinese laborer, from any foreign port of place, shall be deemed guilty of a misdemeanor, and on conviction thereof shall be punished by a fine of not more than five hundred dollars for each and every such Chinese laborer so brought, and may be also imprisoned for a term not exceeding one year.

SEC. 3. That the two foregoing sections shall not apply to Chinese laborers who were in the United States on the seventeenth day of November, eighteen hundred and eighty, or who shall have come into the same before the expiration of ninety days next after the passage of this act, and who shall produce to such master before going on board such vessel, and shall produce to the collector of the port in the United States at which such vessel shall arrive, the evidence hereinafter in this act required of his being one of the laborers in this section mentioned; nor shall the two foregoing sections apply to the case of any master whose vessel, being bound to a port not within the United States by reason of being in distress or in stress of weather, or touching at any port of the United States on its voyage to any foreign port of place: Provided, That all Chinese laborers brought on such vessel shall depart with the vessel on leaving port.

SEC. 4. That for the purpose of properly indentifying Chinese laborers who were in the United States on the seventeenth day of November, eighteen hundred and eighty, or who shall have come into the same before the expiration of ninety days next after the passage of this act, and in order to furnish them with the proper evidence of their right to go from and come to the United States of their free will and accord, as provided by the treaty between the United States and China dated November seventeenth, eighteen hundred and eighty, the collector of customs of the district from which any such Chinese laborer shall depart from the United States shall, in person or by deputy, go on board each vessel having on board any such Chinese laborer and cleared or about to sail from his district for a foreign port, and on such vessel make a list of all such Chinese laborers, which shall be entered in registry-books to be kept for that purpose, in which shall be stated the name, age, occupation, last place of residence, physical marks or peculiarities, and all facts necessary for the indentification of each of such Chinese laborers, which books shall be safely kept in the custom-house; and every such Chinese laborer so departing from the United States shall be entitled to, and shall receive, free of any charge or cost upon application therefor, from the collector or his deputy, at the time such list is taken, a certificate, signed by the collector or his deputy and attested by his seal of office, in such form as the Secretary of the Treasury shall prescribe, which certificate shall contain a statement of the name, age, occupation, last place of residence, personal description, and fact of identification of the Chinese laborer to whom the certificate is issued, corresponding with the said list and registry in all particulars. In case any Chinese laborer after having received such certificate shall leave such vessel before her departure he shall deliver his certificate to the master of the vessel, and if such Chinese laborer shall fail to return to such vessel before her departure from port the certificate shall be delivered by the master to the collector of customs for cancellation. The certificate herein provided for shall entitle the Chinese laborer to whom the same is issued to return to and re-enter the United States upon producing and delivering the same to the collector of customs of the district at which such Chinese laborer shall seek to re-enter; and upon delivery of such certificate by such Chinese laborer to the collector of customs at the time of re-entry in the United States, said collector shall cause the same to be filed in the custom house and duly canceled.

SEC. 5. That any Chinese laborer mentioned in section four of this act being in the United States, and desiring to depart from the United States by land, shall have the right to demand and receive, free of charge or cost, a certificate of identification similar to that provided for in section four of this act to be issued to such Chinese laborers as may desire to leave the United States by water; and it is hereby made the duty of the collector of customs of the district next adjoining the foreign country to which said Chinese laborer desires to go to issue such certificate, free of charge or cost, upon application by such Chinese laborer, and to enter the same upon registry-books to be kept by him for the purpose, as provided for in section four of this act.

SEC. 6. That in order to the faithful execution of articles one and two of the treaty in this act before mentioned, every Chinese person other than a laborer who may be entitled by said treaty and this act to come within the

United States, and who shall be about to come to the United States, shall be identified as so entitled by the Chinese Government in each case, such identity to be evidenced by a certificate issued under the authority of said government, which certificate shall be in the English language or (if not in the English language) accompanied by a translation into English, stating such right to come, and which certificate shall state the name, title, or official rank, if any, the age, height, and all physical peculiarities, former and present occupation or profession, and place of residence in China of the person to whom the certificate is issued and that such person is entitled conformably to the treaty in this act mentioned to come within the United States. Such certificate shall be prima-facie evidence of the fact set forth therein, and shall be produced to the collector of customs, or his deputy, of the port in the district in the United States at which the person named therein shall arrive.

SEC. 7. That any person who shall knowingly and falsely alter or substitute any name for the name written in such certificate or forge any such certificate, or knowingly utter any forged or fraudulent certificate, or falsely personate any person named in any such certificate, shall be deemed guilty of a misdemeanor; and upon conviction thereof shall be fined in a sum not exceeding one thousand dollars, and imprisoned in a penitentiary for a term of not more than five years.

SEC. 8. That the master of any vessel arriving in the United States from any foreign port or place shall, at the same time he delivers a manifest of the cargo, and if there be no cargo, then at the time of making a report of the entry of vessel pursuant to the law, in addition to the other matter required to be reported, and before landing, or permitting to land, any Chinese passengers, deliver and report to the collector of customs of the district in which such vessels shall have arrived a separate list of all Chinese passengers taken on board his vessel at any foreign port or place, and all such passengers on board the vessel at that time. Such list shall show the names of such passengers (and if accredited officers of the Chinese Government traveling on the business of that government, or their servants, with a note of such facts), and the name and other particulars, as shown by their respective certificates; and such list shall be sworn to by the master in the manner required by law in relation to the manifest of the cargo. Any willful refusal or neglect of any such master to comply with the provisions of this section shall incur the same penalties and forfeiture as are provided for a refusal or neglect to report and deliver a manifest of cargo.

SEC. 9. That before any Chinese passengers are landed from any such vessel, the collector, or his deputy, shall proceed to examine such passengers, comparing the certificates with the list and with the passengers; and no passenger shall be allowed to land in the United States from such vessel in violation of law.

SEC. 10. That every vessel whose master shall knowingly violate any of the provisions of this act shall be deemed forfeited to the United States, and shall be liable to seizure and condemnation on any district of the United States into which such vessel may enter or in which she may be found.

SEC. 11. That any person who shall knowingly bring into or cause to be brought into the United States by land, or who shall knowingly aid or abet the same, or aid or abet the landing in the United States from any vessel of any Chinese person not lawfully entitled to enter the United States, shall be deemed guilty of a misdemeanor, and shall, on conviction thereof, be fined in a sum not exceeding one thousand dollars, and imprisoned for a term not exceeding one year.

SEC. 12. That no Chinese person shall be permitted to enter the United States by land without producing to the proper officer of customs the certificate in this act required of Chinese persons seeking to land from a vessel. And any Chinese person found unlawfully within the United States shall be caused to be removed therefrom to the country from whence he came, by direction of the United States, after being brought before some justice, judge, or commissioner of a court of the United States and found to be one not lawfully entitled to be or remain in the United States.

SEC. 13. That this act shall not apply to diplomatic and other officers of the Chinese Government traveling upon the business of that government, whose credentials shall be taken as equivalent to the certificate in this act mentioned, and shall exempt them and their body and household servants from the provisions of this act as to other Chinese persons.

SEC. 14. That hereafter no State court or court of the United States shall admit Chinese to citizenship; and all laws in conflict with this act are hereby repealed.

SEC. 15. That the words "Chinese laborers", whenever used in this act, shall be construed to mean both skilled and unskilled laborers and Chinese employed in mining.

Approved, May 6, 1882.

Source: Mount Holyoke College. Available online. URL: http://www.mtholyoke.edu/acad/intrel/chinex.htm. Accessed November 14, 2006.

The Immigration Act of 1924 (May 26, 1924) (excerpt)

Also known as the Johnson-Reed Act, this law established an annual permanent immigrant quota system. It reduced the temporary quotas set in 1921 from 358,000 to 164,000 annual immigrants and reduced the yearly immigration limit from 3 percent to 2 percent for each foreign-born group living in the country based on the 1890 census. The act's quota system favored immigrants from northern Europe and banned immigrants ineligible for citizenship. Additionally, before coming to the United States immigrants were required to obtain a visa from the American consul in their country of origin, which allowed the U.S. government to pre-screen immigrants. Because the new quotas did not differentiate between immigrants and refugees many Jews fleeing Nazi Germany in the 1930s were barred from immigrating to the United States.

SIXTY EIGHTH CONGRESS. SESS.I. Ch. 185, 190. 1924.

[...]Be it enacted by the Senate and House of Representatives of the United States of America in Congress assembled, That this Act may be cited as the "Immigration Act of 1924"

Sec. 2. (a) A consular officer upon the application of any immigrant (as defined in section 3) may (under the conditions hereinafter prescribed and subject to the limitations prescribed in this Act or regulations made thereunder as to the number of immigration visas which may be issued by such officer) issue to such immigrant an immigration visa which shall consist of one copy of the application provided for in section 7, visaed by such consular officer. Such visa shall specify (1) the nationality of the immigrant; (2) whether he is a quota immigrant (as defined in section 5) or a non-quota immigrant (as defined in section 4); (3) the date on which the validity of the immigration visa shall expire; and such additional information necessary to the proper enforcement of the immigration laws and the naturalization laws as may be by regulations prescribed.

(b) The immigrant shall furnish two copies of his photograph to the consular officer. One copy shall be permanently attached by the consular officer to the immigration visa and the other copy shall be disposed of as may be by regulations prescribed.

(c) The validity of an immigration visa shall expire at the end of such period, specified in the immigration visa, not exceeding four months, as shall be by regulations prescribed. In the case of an immigrant arriving in the United States by water, or arriving by water in foreign contiguous territory on a continuous voyage to the United States, if the vessel, before the expiration of the validity of his immigration visa, departed from the last port outside the United States and outside foreign contiguous territory at which the immigrant embarked, and if the immigrant proceeds on a continuous voyage to the United States, then, regardless of the time of his arrival in the United States, the validity of his immigration visa shall not be considered to have expired.

(d) If an immigrant is required by any law, or regulations or orders made pursuant to law, to secure the visa of his passport by a consular officer before being permitted to enter the United States, such immigrant shall not be required to secure any other visa of his passport than the immigration visa issued under this Act, but a record of the number and date of his immigration visa shall be noted on his passport without charge therefor. This subdivision shall not apply to an immigrant who is relieved, under subdivision (b) of section 13, from obtaining an immigration visa.

(e) The manifest or list of passengers required by the immigration laws shall contain a place for entering thereon the date, place of issuance, and number of the immigration vsa of each immigrant. The immigrant shall surrender his immigration visa to the immigration officer at the port of inspection, who shall at the time of inspection indorse on the immigration visa the date, the port of entry, and the name of the vessel, if any, on which the immigrant arrived. The immigration visa shall be transmitted forthwith by the immigration officer in charge at the port of inspection to the Department of Labor under regulations prescribed by the Secretary of Labor.

(f) No immigration visa shall be issued to an immigrant if it appears to the consular officer, from statements in the application, or in the papers submitted therewith, that the immigrant is inadmissible to the United States under the immigration laws, nor shall such immigration visa be issued if the application fails to comply with the provisions of this Act, nor shall such immigration visa be issued if the consular officer knows or has reason to believe that the immigrant is inadmissible to the United States under the immigration laws.

(g) Nothing in this Act shall be construed to entitle an immigrant, to whom an immigration visa has been issued, to enter the United States, if, upon arrival in the United States, he is found to be inadmissible to the United States under the immigration laws. The substance of this subdivision shall be printed conspicuously upon every immigration visa.

(h) A fee of $9 shall be charged for the issuance of each immigration visa, which shall be covered into the Treasury as miscellaneous receipts.

DEFINITION OF "IMMIGRANT."

Sec. 3. When used in this Act the term "immigrant" means an alien departing from any place outside the United States destined for the United States, except (1) a government official, his family, attendants, servants, and employees, (2) an alien visiting the United States temporarily as a tourist or temporarily for business or pleasure, (3) an alien in continuous transit through the United States, (4) an alien lawfully admitted to the United States who later goes in transit from one part of the United States to another through foreign contiguous territory, (5) a bona fide alien seaman serving as such on a vessel arriving at a port of the United States and seeking to enter temporarily the United States solely in the pursuit of his calling as a seaman, and (6) an alien entitled to enter the United States solely to carry on trade under and in pursuance of the provisions of a present existing treaty of commerce and navigation.

NON-QUOTA IMMIGRANTS.

Sec. 4. When used in this Act the term "non-quota immigrant" means-

(a) An immigrant who is the unmarried child under 18 years of age, or the wife, of a citizen of the United States who resides therein at the time of the filing of a petition under section 9;

(b) An immigrant previously lawfully admitted to the United States, who is returning from a temporary visit abroad;

(c) An immigrant who was born in the Dominion of Canada, Newfoundland, the Republic of Mexico, the Republic of Cuba, the Republic of Haiti, the Dominican Republic, the Canal Zone, or an independent country of Central or South America, and his wife, and his unmarried children under 18 years of age, if accompanying or following to join him;

(d) An immigrant who continuously for at least two years immediately preceding the time of his application for admission to the United States has been, and who seeks to enter the United States solely for the purpose of, carrying on the vocation of minister of any religious denomination, or professor of a college, academy, seminary, or university; and his wife, and his unmarried children under 18 years of age, if accompanying or following to join him; or

(e) An immigrant who is a bona fide student at least 15 years of age and who seeks to enter the United States solely for the purpose of study at an accredited school, college, academy, seminary, or university, particularly designated by him and approved by, the Secretary of labor, which shall have agreed to report to the Secretary of Labor the termination of attendance of each immigrant student, and if any such institution of learning fails to make such reports promptly the approval shall be withdrawn.

* *** *

EXCLUSION FROM UNITED STATES.

Sec. 13. (a) No immigrant shall be admitted to the United States unless he (1) has an unexpired immigration visa or was born subsequent to the issuance of the immigration visa of the accompanying parent, (2) is of the nationality specified in the visa in the immigration visa, (3) is a non-quota immigrant if specified in the visa in the immigration visa as such, and (4) is otherwise admissible under the immigration laws.

(b) In such classes of cases and under such conditions as may be by regulations prescribed immigrants who have been legally admitted to the United States and who depart therefrom temporarily may be admitted to the United States without being required to obtain an immigration visa.

(c) No alien ineligible to citizenship shall be admitted to the United States unless such alien (1) is admissible as a non-quota immigrant under the provisions of subdivision (b), (d), or (e) of section 4, or (2) is the wife, or the unmarried child under 18 years of age, of an immigrant admissible under such subdivision (d), and is accompanying or following to join him, or (3) is not an immigrant as defined in section 3.

(d) The Secretary of Labor may admit to the United States any otherwise admissible immigrant not admissible under clause (2) or (3) of subdivision (a) of this section, if satisfied that such inadmissibility was not known to, and could not have been ascertained by the exercise of reasonable diligence by, such immigrant prior to the departure of the vessel from the last port outside the United States and outside foreign contiguous territory or, in the case of an immigrant coming from foreign contiguous territory, prior to the application of the immigrant for admission.

(e) No quota immigrant shall be admitted under subdivision (d) if the entire number of immigration visas which may be issued to quota immigrants of the same nationality for the fiscal year already been issued. If such entire number of immigration visas has not been issued, then the Secretary of State, upon the admission of a quota immigrant under subdivision (d), shall reduce by one the number of immigration visas which may be issued to quota immigrants of the same nationality during the fiscal year in which such immigrant is admitted; but if the Secretary of State finds that it will not be practicable to make such reduction before the end of such fiscal year, then such immigrant shall not be admitted.

(f) Nothing in this section shall authorize the remission or refunding of a fine, liability to which has accrued under section 16.

DEPORTATION.

Sec. 14. Any alien who at any time after entering the United States is found to have been at the time of entry not entitled under this Act to enter the United States, or to have remained therein for a longer time than permitted under this Act or regulations made thereunder, shall be taken into custody and deported in the same manner as provided for in sections 19 and 20 of the Immigration Act of 1917: Provided, That the Secretary of Labor may, under such conditions and restrictions as to support and care as he may deem necessary, permit permanently to remain in the United States, any alien child who, when under sixteen years of age was heretofore temporarily admitted to the United States and who is now within the United States and either of whose parents is a citizen of the United States.

MAINTENANCE OF EXEMPT STATUS.

Sec. 15. The admission to the United States of an alien excepted from the class of immigrants by clause (2), (3), (4), (5), or (6) of section 3, or declared to be a non-quota immigrant by subdivision (e) of section 4, shall be for such time as may be by regulations prescribed, and under such conditions as may be by regulations prescribed (including, when deemed necessary for the classes mentioned in clauses (2), (3), (4), or (6) of section 3, the giving of bond with sufficient surety, in such sum and containing such conditions as may be by regulations prescribed) to insure that, at the expiration of such time or upon failure to maintain the status under which he was admitted, he will depart from the United States.

* *** *

GENERAL DEFINITIONS.

Sec. 28. As used in this Act–

(a) The term "United States," when used in a geographical sense, means the States, the Territories of Alaska and Hawaii, the District of Columbia, Porto Rico, and the Virgin Islands; and the term "continental United States" means the States and the District of Columbia;

(b) The term "alien" includes any individual not a native-born or naturalized citizen of the United States, but this definition shall not be held to include Indians of the United States not taxed, nor citizens of the islands under the jurisdiction of the United States;

(c) The term "ineligible to citizenship," when used in reference to any individual, includes an individual who is debarred from becoming a citizen of the United States under section 2169 of the Revised Statutes, or under section 14 of the Act entitled "An Act to execute certain treaty stipulations relating to Chinese," approved May 6, 1882, or under section 1996, 1997, or 1998 of the Revised Statutes, as amended, or under section 2 of the Act entitled "An Act to authorize the President to increase temporarily the Military Establishment of the United States," approved May 18, 1917, as amended, or under law amendatory of, supplementary to, or in substitution for, any of such sections;

(d) The term "immigration visa" means an immigration visa issued by a consular officer under the provisions of this Act;

(e) The term "consular officer" means any consular or diplomatic officer of the United States designated, under regulations prescribed under this Act, for the purpose of issuing immigration visas under this Act. In case of the Canal Zone and the insular possessions of the United States the term "consular officer" (except as used in section 24) means an officer designated by the President, or by his authority, for the purpose of issuing immigration visas under this Act;

(f) The term "Immigration Act of 1917" means the Act of February 5, 1917, entitled "An Act to regulate the immigration of aliens to, and the residence of aliens in, the United States";

(g) The term "immigration laws" includes such Act, this Act, and all laws, conventions, and treaties of the United States relating to the immigration, exclusion, or expulsion of aliens;

(h) The term "person" includes individals, partnerships, corporations, and associations;

(i) The term "Commissioner General" means the Commissioner General of Immigration;

(j) The term "application for admission" has reference to the application for admission to the United States and not to the application for the issuance of the immigration visa;

(k) The term "permit" means a permit issued under section 10;

(l) The term "unmarried," when used in reference to any as of any time, means an individual who at such time is not married, whether or not previously married;

(m) The terms "child," "father," and "mother," do not include child or parent by adoption unless the adoption took place before January 1, 1924;

(n) The terms "wife" and "husband" do not include a wife or husband by reason of a proxy or picture marriage.

Source: U.S. Historical Documents. Available online. URL: http://www.historicaldocuments.com/ImmigrationActof1924.htm. Accessed November 14, 2006.

USA PATRIOT Act (October 26, 2001) (excerpts)

President George W. Bush signed this bill into law following the September 11, 2001, terrorist attacks on the United States. The 132-page document grants federal officials far-reaching authority to control activities from tracking and gathering communications and regulating U.S. financial institutions to prevent money laundering to strengthening border crossings to prevent alien terrorists from entering the country. Some of the provisions in the act directly target immigration and immigrants.

The Uniting and Strengthening America by Providing Appropriate Tools Required to Intercept and Obstruct Terrorism Act of 2001 (USA PATRIOT Act)

Title IV – Protecting the Border

Subtitle A – Protecting the Northern Border

Section 402 authorizes a tripling of the number of Border Patrol personnel, Customs personnel, and immigration inspectors along the Northern Border and an additional $50 million each for Customs and INS to improve monitoring technology along the Northern Border.

Section 403 grants INS and State Department personnel access to the FBI's NCIC-III and the Wanted Persons File for the purpose of checking the criminal history of a visa applicant. INS and State would have access only to extracts from the actual databases, and would have to submit the visa applicant's fingerprints in order to get the full criminal history. This section also instructs the Attorney General and the Secretary of State to develop and certify within two years of enactment a technology standard that can be used to verify the identity of visa applicants and that can be used as the basis of an integrated system that will verify identity at ports of entry and share information with other law enforcement agencies.

Section 404 removes the existing restrictions on overtime pay for INS personnel.

Section 405 requires the Attorney General to report to Congress on the feasibility of expanding the FBI's Integrated Automated Fingerprint Identification System (IAFIS) to include visa applicants and visa holders wanted in connection with a criminal investigation, so they may be denied a visa or identified upon entry into or exit from the United States.

Subtitle B – Enhanced Immigration Provisions

Section 411 broadens the grounds for excluding terrorists and aliens with ties to terrorist organizations. It authorizes the exclusion of the spouses and children of aliens who have committed acts linking them to terrorist organizations within the past five years and makes inadmissible any alien determined by the Attorney General and the Secretary of State to have been associated with a terrorist organization and who intends to commit terrorist acts while in the United States. (Such aliens already are excludable under current law, since they are entering with the intent to engage in "unlawful activity.")

Section 412 directs the Attorney General to detain any alien certified to be engaged in terrorist activities. It authorizes the Attorney General to certify any alien as a terrorist where there are reasonable grounds to believe that he is affiliated with a designated terrorist organization or engaged in terrorist activities. It requires the Attorney General to place such aliens in removal proceedings, charge them with a criminal offense or release them within seven days of taking them into custody. It authorizes the Attorney General to detain certified terrorists for additional periods of up to six months if their removal is unlikely in the near future and if the alien's release will threaten national security or public safety. It limits judicial review of such detention to habeus corpus proceedings. Finally, it requires the Attorney General to report to Congress every six months on the number of certified aliens, the grounds for certification, their nationalities, the length of their detention, and the disposition of their cases.

Section 413 authorizes the Secretary of State to share information in State's visa-lookout database and, under certain circumstances, information on individual aliens with foreign governments in order to combat terrorism and trafficking in controlled substances, persons, or weapons.

Section 414 expresses the Sense of Congress regarding the need to expedite implementation of the integrated entry and exit data system enacted in Section 110 of the Illegal Immigration Reform and Immigrant Responsibility

Act (IIRAIRA) of 1996. It requests that the Attorney General fully implement this system at airports, seaports, and land border ports "with all deliberate speed and as expeditiously as practicable." It directs the Attorney General to focus on the use of biometric technology and the development of tamper-resistant, machine-readable documents during the development stage of the entry and exit system. It requires that the resulting system be interfaced with law enforcement databases used by federal agencies to identify and detain individuals who pose a threat to U.S. security. Finally, it requires the Office of Homeland Security to report to Congress within 12 months on "the information that is needed from any United States agency to effectively screen visa applicants and applicants for admission to the United States to identify" terrorists and other dangerous aliens.

Section 415 directs the Office of Homeland Security to participate in the development of the entry and exit system.

Section 416 directs the Attorney General to implement fully and to expand the foreign student tracking system enacted in the 1996 IIRAIRA. It requires the student database to include information on the date and port of entry and it authorizes the Attorney General to permit flight schools, language training schools, and vocational schools to participate in the expanded program.

Section 417 requires the Secretary of State annually to audit the implementation of the requirement that visa waiver countries issue machine-readable passports to their citizens. It advances the deadline by which countries must issue machine-readable passports in order to participate in the visa waiver program from 2007 to 2003, and it authorizes the Secretary of State to waive this requirement for countries that are "making progress toward" issuing machine-readable passports and have taken appropriate measures to protect against misuse of current passports.

Section 418 directs the Secretary of State to determine whether consular shopping—the practice of traveling to a third country to apply for a visa to the United States, in order to avoid tighter security practices in the Consulate in one's home country—is a problem and to address it if it is.

Subtitle C – Preservation of Immigration Benefits for Victims of Terrorism

Section 421 authorizes the Attorney General to grant special immigrant status (a category of legal permanent residence) to any alien for whom a petition for family- or employment-based legal permanent residence was filed and revoked because the petitioner, applicant, or alien beneficiary was killed or lost his or her job as a result of terrorist activities. It also authorizes special immigrant status for any alien who is the grandparent of a child, both of whose parents died as a result of terrorist activity, if either parent was a citizen, national, or lawful permanent resident of the United States on September 10, 2001.

Section 422 automatically extends by up to one year the authorized period of stay for nonimmigrants who were disabled by the terrorist attacks, along with their spouses and children. It extends the authorized period of stay for nonimmigrants who were prevented from entering the United States because of the terrorist attacks and permits FY 2001 diversity lottery winners who were prevented from entering the United States by the terrorist attacks to enter during the first six months of FY 2002, but to be counted against the quotas for FY 2001. It also grants legal permanent residence to the spouse and children of any FY 2001 diversity lottery winner who died as a result of the terrorist attacks. Finally, it extends the grant of parole for any parolee who was out of the country and unable to return before his or her parole expired on or after September 11, 2001, and it extends for 30 days any period for voluntary departure that expired between September 11 and October 11, 2001.

Section 423 permits aliens who entered the country as the spouses or minor children of U.S. citizens to retain immediate relative status, even though the citizen-sponsor died as a result of the terrorist attacks. It permits the spouses, children, and unmarried adult sons and daughters of lawful permanent residents, for whom immigration petitions have been filed, to retain their status as valid petitioners, even though the resident-alien petitioner died as a result of the terrorist attacks. It permits those spouses, children, and unmarried adult sons and daughters of lawful permanent residents for whom no petition was filed to file a petition on their own behalf for lawful permanent residence. It allows any alien who is the spouse or child of an alien killed in the terrorist attacks and who had applied for adjustment of status to lawful permanent residence to have the application adjudicated as if the death had not occurred. Finally, it waives the public charge grounds for inadmissibility for all aliens granted benefits under this section.

Section 424 authorizes any alien whose 21st birthday occurred in September 2001 to be considered a minor child for an additional 90 days for purposes of adjudicating a petition or application for immigration benefits, and any alien whose 21st birthday occurs after September 2001 to be considered a minor child for an additional 45 days for purposes of adjudicating a petition or application for immigration benefits.

Section 425 authorizes the Attorney General to provide "temporary administrative relief" to any alien who was here legally on September 10, is the relative of an individual who died or was disabled by the terrorist attacks, and is not otherwise entitled to relief under this subtitle.

Section 426 requires the Attorney General to establish standards of evidence for proving that any death, disability, or loss of employment due to physical damage to a business is the result of the terrorist attacks, for purposes of applying for the benefits under this subtitle.

Section 427 prohibits any benefits under this subtitle from being granted to terrorists or their family members.

Source: Center for Immigration Studies. Available online. URL: http://www.cis.org/articles/2001/back1501.html. Accessed November 24, 2006.

II. PRESIDENTIAL SPEECHES AND WRITINGS

Thomas Jefferson: "Notes on the State of Virginia," Query 8, 1787 (excerpt)

In this writing, Thomas Jefferson discussed the problems associated with excessive immigration based on the principles set forth in the U.S. Declaration of Independence.

. . . But are there no inconveniences to be thrown into the scale against the advantage expected from a multiplication of numbers by the importation of foreigners? It is for the happiness of those united in society to harmonize as much as possible in matters which they must of necessity transact together. Civil government being the sole object of forming societies, its administration must be conducted by common consent. Every species of government has its specific principles. Ours perhaps are more peculiar than those of any other in the universe. It is a composition of the freest principles of the English constitution, with others derived from natural right and natural reason. To these nothing can be more opposed than the maxims of absolute monarchies. Yet, from such, we are to expect the greatest number of emigrants. They will bring with them the principles of the governments they leave, imbibed in their early youth; or, if able to throw them off, it will be in exchange for an unbounded licentiousness, passing, as is usual, from one extreme to another. It would be a miracle were they to stop precisely at the point of temperate liberty. These principles, with their language, they will transmit to their children. In proportion to their numbers, they will share with us the legislation. They will infuse into it their spirit, warp and bias its direction, and render it a heterogeneous, incoherent, distracted mass. I may appeal to experience, during the present contest, for a verification of these conjectures. But, if they be not certain in event, are they not possible, are they not probable? Is it not safer to wait with patience 27 years and three months longer, for the attainment of any degree of population desired, or expected? May not our government be more homogeneous, more peaceable, more durable? Suppose 20 millions of republican Americans thrown all of a sudden into France, what would be the condition of that kingdom? If it would be more turbulent, less happy, less strong, we may believe that the addition of half a million of foreigners to our present numbers would produce a similar effect here. If they come of themselves, they are entitled to all the rights of citizenship: but I doubt the expediency of inviting them by extraordinary encouragements. . . .

Source: Vindicating the Founders: Race, Sex, Class, and Justice in the Origins of America, by Thomas G. West. Available online. URL: http://www.vindicatingthefounders.com/library/index.asp?document=37. Accessed November 24, 2006.

Andrew Jackson: "Second Annual Message to Congress," December 6, 1830 (excerpts)

In this message to Congress, President Jackson discussed the passage of the Indian Removal Act and the reaction of the various Native American tribes to the new act. The speech also thanked the government for taking actions that would separate the civilized white settlers from the savage hunters.

Fellow Citizens of the Senate and House of Representatives:

The pleasure I have in congratulating you upon your return to your constitutional duties is much heightened by the satisfaction which the condition of our beloved country at this period justly inspires. The beneficent Author of All Good has granted to us during the present year health, peace, and plenty, and numerous causes for joy in the wonderful success which attends the progress of our free institutions.

With a population unparalleled in its increase, and possessing a character which combines the hardihood of enterprise with the considerateness of wisdom, we see in every section of our happy country a steady improvement in the means of social intercourse, and correspondent effects upon the genius and laws of our extended Republic.

The apparent exceptions to the harmony of the prospect are to be referred rather to inevitable diversities in the various interests which enter into the composition of so extensive a whole than any want of attachment to the Union—interests whose collisions serve only in the end to foster the spirit of conciliation and patriotism so essential to the preservation of that Union which I most devoutly hope is destined to prove imperishable.

* *** *

It gives me pleasure to announce to Congress that the benevolent policy of the Government, steadily pursued for nearly 30 years, in relation to the removal of the Indians beyond the white settlements is approaching to a happy consummation. Two important tribes have accepted the provision made for their removal at the last session of Congress, and it is believed that their example will induce the remaining tribes also to seek the same obvious advantages.

The consequences of a speedy removal will be important to the United States, to individual States, and to the Indians themselves. The pecuniary advantages which it promises to the Government are the least of its recommendations. It puts an end to all possible danger of collision between the authorities of the General and State Governments on account of the Indians. It will place a dense and civilized population in large tracts of country now occupied by a few savage hunters. By opening the whole territory between Tennessee on the north and Louisiana on the south to the settlement of the whites it will incalculably strengthen the SW frontier and render the adjacent States strong enough to repel future invasions without remote aid. It will relieve the whole State of Mississippi and the western part of Alabama of Indian occupancy, and enable those States to advance rapidly in population, wealth, and power. It will separate the Indians from immediate contact with settlements of whites; free them from the power of the States; enable them to pursue happiness in their own way and under their own rude institutions; will retard the progress of decay, which is lessening their numbers, and perhaps cause them gradually, under the protection of the Government and through the influence of good counsels, to cast off their savage habits and become an interesting, civilized, and Christian community. These consequences, some of them so certain and the rest so probable, make the complete execution of the plan sanctioned by Congress at their last session an object of much solicitude.

Toward the aborigines of the country no one can indulge a more friendly feeling than myself, or would go further in attempting to reclaim them from their wandering habits and make them a happy, prosperous people. I have endeavored to impress upon them my own solemn convictions of the duties and powers of the General Government in relation to the State authorities. For the justice of the laws passed by the States within the scope of their reserved powers they are not responsible to this Government. As individuals we may entertain and express our opinions of their acts, but as a Government we have as little right to control them as we have to prescribe laws for other nations.

With a full understanding of the subject, the Choctaw and the Chickasaw tribes have with great unanimity determined to avail themselves of the liberal offers presented by the act of Congress, and have agreed to remove beyond the Mississippi River. Treaties have been made with them, which in due season will be submitted for consideration. In negotiating these treaties they were made to understand their true condition, and they have preferred maintaining their independence in the Western forests to submitting to the laws of the States in which they now reside. These treaties, being probably the last which will ever be made with them, are characterized by great liberality on the part of the Government. They give the Indians a liberal sum in consideration of their removal, and comfortable subsistence on their arrival at their new homes. If it be their real interest to maintain a separate existence, they will there be at liberty to do so without the inconveniences and vexations to which they would unavoidably have been subject in Alabama and Mississippi.

Humanity has often wept over the fate of the aborigines of this country, and Philanthropy has been long busily employed in devising means to avert it, but its progress has never for a moment been arrested, and one by one have many powerful tribes disappeared from the earth. To follow to the tomb the last of his race and to tread on the graves of extinct nations excite melancholy reflections. But true philanthropy reconciles the mind to these vicissitudes as it does to the extinction of one generation to make room for another. In the monuments and fortifications of an unknown people, spread over the extensive regions of the West, we behold the memorials of a once powerful race, which was exterminated or has disappeared to make room for the existing savage tribes. Nor is there any thing in this which, upon a comprehensive view of the general interests of the human race, is to be regretted. Philanthropy could not wish to see this continent restored to the condition in which it was found by our forefathers. What good man would prefer a country covered with forests and ranged by a few thousand savages to our extensive Republic, studded with cities, towns, and prosperous farms, embellished with all the improvements which art can devise or industry execute, occupied by more than 12,000,000 happy people, and filled with all the blessings of liberty, civilization, and religion?

The present policy of the Government is but a continuation of the same progressive change by a milder process. The tribes which occupied the countries now constituting the Eastern States were annihilated or have melted away to make room for the whites. The waves of population and civilization are rolling to the westward, and we now propose to acquire the countries occupied by the red men of the South and West by a fair exchange, and, at the expense of the United States, to send them to a land where their existence may be prolonged and perhaps made perpetual.

Doubtless it will be painful to leave the graves of their fathers; but what do they more than our ancestors did or than our children are now doing? To better their condition in an unknown land our forefathers left all that was dear in earthly objects. Our children by thousands yearly leave the land of their birth to seek new homes in distant regions. Does Humanity weep at these painful separations from every thing, animate and inanimate, with which the young heart has become entwined? Far from it. It is rather a source of joy that our country affords scope where our young population may range unconstrained in body or in mind, developing the power and faculties of man in their highest perfection.

These remove hundreds and almost thousands of miles at their own expense, purchase the lands they occupy, and support themselves at their new homes from the moment of their arrival. Can it be cruel in this Government when, by events which it can not control, the Indian is made discontented in his ancient home to purchase his lands, to give him a new and extensive territory, to pay the expense of his removal, and support him a year in his new abode? How many thousands of our own people would gladly embrace the opportunity of removing to the West on such conditions! If the offers made to the Indians were extended to them, they would be hailed with gratitude and joy.

And is it supposed that the wandering savage has a stronger attachment to his home than the settled, civilized Christian? Is it more afflicting to him to leave the graves of his fathers than it is to our brothers and children? Rightly considered, the policy of the General Government toward the red man is not only liberal, but generous. He is unwilling to submit to the laws of the States and mingle with their population. To save him from this alternative, or perhaps utter annihilation, the General Government kindly offers him a new home, and proposes to pay the whole expense of his removal and settlement.

In the consummation of a policy originating at an early period, and steadily pursued by every Administration within the present century—so just to the States and so generous to the Indians—the Executive feels it has a right to expect the cooperation of Congress and of all good and disinterested men. The States, moreover, have a right to demand it. It was substantially a part of the compact which made them members of our Confederacy. With Georgia there is an express contract; with the new States an implied one of equal obligation. Why, in authorizing Ohio, Indiana, Illinois, Missouri, Mississippi, and Alabama to form constitutions and become separate States, did Congress include within their limits extensive tracts of Indian lands, and, in some instances, powerful Indian tribes? Was it not understood by both parties that the power of the States was to be coextensive with their limits, and that with all convenient dispatch the General Government should extinguish the Indian title and remove every obstruction to the complete jurisdiction of the State governments over the soil? Probably not one of those States would have accepted a separate existence—certainly it would never have been granted by Congress—had it been understood that they were to be confined for ever to those small portions of their nominal territory the Indian title to which had at the time been extinguished.

It is, therefore, a duty which this Government owes to the new States to extinguish as soon as possible the Indian title to all lands which Congress themselves have included within their limits. When this is done the duties of the General Government in relation to the States and the Indians within their limits are at an end. The Indians may leave the State or not, as they choose. The purchase of their lands does not alter in the least their personal relations with the State government. No act of the General Government has ever been deemed necessary to give the States jurisdiction over the persons of the Indians. That they possess by virtue of their sovereign power within their own limits in as full a manner before as after the purchase of the Indian lands; nor can this Government add to or diminish it.

May we not hope, therefore, that all good citizens, and none more zealously than those who think the Indians oppressed by subjection to the laws of the States, will unite in attempting to open the eyes of those children of the forest to their true condition, and by a speedy removal to relieve them from all the evils, real or imaginary, present or prospective, with which they may be supposed to be threatened.

* *** *

Source: Miller Center of Public Affairs, Scripps Library and Multimedia Archives, University of Virginia. Available online. URL: http://millercenter.virginia.edu/scripps/diglibrary/prezspeeches/jackson/aj_1830_1206.html. Accessed November 24, 2006.

Abraham Lincoln: Electric Cord Speech, Chicago, Illinois, July 10, 1858 (excerpts)

In this speech, President Lincoln discusses the ethnic diversity of the United States attributable to immigration and states his opinion that citizenship is based on the principles established by the Declaration of Independence, not on ethnic or religious identity.

... Now, it happens that we meet together once every year, sometime about the 4th of July, for some reason or other. These 4th of July gatherings I suppose have their uses. If you will indulge me, I will state what I suppose to be some of them.

We are now a mighty nation, we are thirty—or about thirty millions of people, and we own and inhabit about one-fifteenth part of the dry land of the whole earth. We run our memory back over the pages of history for about eighty-two years and we discover that we were then a very small people in point of numbers, vastly inferior to what we are now, with a vastly less extent of country,—with vastly less of everything we deem desirable among men,—we look upon the change as exceedingly advantageous to us and to our posterity, and we fix upon something that happened away back, as in some way or other being connected with this rise of prosperity. We find a race of men living in that day whom we claim as our fathers and grandfathers; they were iron men, they fought for the principle that they were contending for; and we understood that by what they then did it has followed that the degree of prosperity that we now enjoy has come to us. We hold this annual celebration to remind ourselves of all the good done in this process of time of how it was done and who did it, and how we are historically connected with it; and we go from these meetings in better humor with ourselves—we feel more attached the one to the other, and more firmly bound to the country we inhabit. In every way we are better men in the age, and race, and country in which we live for these celebrations. But after we have done all this we have not yet reached the whole. There is something else connected with it. We have besides these men—descended by blood from our ancestors—among us perhaps half our people who are not descendants at all of these men, they are men who have come from Europe—German, Irish, French and Scandinavian—men that have come from Europe themselves, or whose ancestors have come hither and settled here, finding themselves our equals in all things. If they look back through this history to trace their connection with those days by blood, they find they have none, they cannot carry themselves back into that glorious epoch and make themselves feel that they are part of us, but when they look through that old Declaration of Independence they find that those old men say that "We hold these truths to be self-evident, that all men are created equal," and then they feel that that moral sentiment taught in that day evidences their relation to those men, that it is the father of all moral principle in them, and that they have a right to claim it as though they were blood of the blood, and flesh of the flesh of the men who wrote that Declaration, (loud and long continued applause) and so they are. That is the electric cord in that Declaration that links the hearts of patriotic and liberty-loving men together, that will link those patriotic hearts as long as the love of freedom exists in the minds of men throughout the world.

Source: Vindicating the Founders: Race, Sex, Class, and Justice in the Origins of America, by Thomas G. West. Available online. URL: http://www.vindicatingthefounders.com/library/index.asp?document=47. Accessed November 24, 2006.

William J. Clinton: Remarks by President on Signing Budget and Immigration Bill, September 30, 1996

President Bill Clinton issued these comments following his signing of H.R. 3610. In addition to financing for antidrug programs, and investigating and prosecuting terrorists, the bill included immigration reform legislation to fight illegal immigration.

STATEMENT OF THE PRESIDENT

I have signed into law tonight H.R. 3610, a fiscal 1997 omnibus appropriations and immigration reform bill.

This bill is good for America, and I am pleased that my Administration could fashion it with Congress on a bipartisan basis. It moves us further toward our goal of a balanced budget while protecting our values and priorities—educating our children, providing a clean environment, fighting crime, protecting our families from drugs, and combating terrorism.

The bill restores substantial sums for education and training, fully paid for in my balanced budget plan and furthering my agenda of life-long education to help Americans acquire the skills they need to get good jobs in the new global economy.

It provides the funds through which Head Start can serve an additional 50,000 disadvantaged young children; fulfills my request for the Goals 2000 education reform program to help states raise their academic standards; increases funding for the Safe and Drug-Free Schools program, helping states educate children to reduce violence and drug abuse; and fulfills my request for the largest Pell Grant college scholarship awards in history, expanding the number of middle- and low-income students who receive aid by 126,000—to 3.8 million.

For the environment, the bill provides funds to support the Environmental Protection Agency's early implementation of two major new environmental laws that I signed this summer—the Safe Drinking Water Act, and the Pesticide and Food Safety Law. At the same time, the bill does not contain any of the riders that would have been harmful to the environment.

For law enforcement, the bill ensures that my program to put 100,000 more police on the streets of America's communities by the year 2000 proceeds on schedule; with this bill, we will have provided funding for 64,000 of the 100,000 that I called for at the start of my Administration. The bill also increases funds for Justice Department law enforcement programs, for the FBI's crime-fighting efforts, and for new Federal prisons.

As I had urged, the bill also extends the Brady Bill to ensure that those who commit domestic violence cannot purchase guns, rejecting efforts to weaken that proposal.

I am pleased that the bill provides $1.4 billion in funding to address my requests for anti-drug programs. It doubles funding for Drug Courts; increases funds for drug interdiction efforts by the Defense, Transportation, and Treasury departments; and provides the resources to expand the Drug Enforcement Administration's domestic efforts along the Southwest border and elsewhere.

For counter-terrorism, the bill funds my request for over $1.1 billion to fight terrorism and to improve aviation security and safety. It enables the Justice and Treasury Departments to better investigate and prosecute terrorist acts, and it provides funds to implement the recommendations of Vice President Gore's Commission on Aviation Safety and Security and the Federal Aviation Administration's recent 90-day safety review. These funds will enable us to hire 300 more aviation security personnel, deploy new explosive detection teams, and buy high-technology bomb detection equipment to screen luggage.

This bill also includes landmark immigration reform legislation that reinforces the efforts we have made over the last three years to combat illegal immigration. It strengthens the rule of law by cracking down on illegal immigration at the border, in the workplace, and in the criminal justice system—without punishing those living in the United States legally, or allowing children to be kept out of schools and sent into the streets.

The bill also provides needed resources to respond to fires in the western part of the nation and to the devastation brought by Hurricanes Fran and Hortense.

I am disappointed that one of my priorities a ban on physician "gag rules"—was not included in the bill. Several States have passed similar legislation to ensure that doctors have the freedom to inform their patients of the full range of medical treatment options, and Congress should have reached agreement on this measure.

Nevertheless, this bill is good for America, and I am pleased to sign it.

Source: Clinton Presidential Center, Online Library Archives. Available online. URL: http://click.historicaldocuments.com/www.clintonpresidentialcenter.org/legacy3.htm?dt=presidential+speeches. Accessed November 24, 2006.

George W. Bush: State of the Union Address, January 20, 2004 (excerpts)

When President Bush delivered his 2004 State of the Union Address, one of the top concerns for the American public was controlling illegal immigration and tightening security at the U.S. borders. Among the suggestions President Bush offered in this speech relating to immigration included opposing amnesty for aliens in the country illegally and implementing a guest-worker program for temporary migrant workers.

Mr. Speaker, Vice President Cheney, members of Congress, distinguished guests, and fellow citizens: America this evening is a nation called to great responsibilities. And we are rising to meet them.

As we gather tonight, hundreds of thousands of American servicemen and women are deployed across the world in the war on terror. By bringing hope to the oppressed, and delivering justice to the violent, they are making America more secure.

Each day, law enforcement personnel and intelligence officers are tracking terrorist threats; analysts are examining airline passenger lists; the men and women of our new Homeland Security Department are patrolling our coasts and borders. And their vigilance is protecting America.

Americans are proving once again to be the hardest working people in the world. The American economy is growing stronger. The tax relief you passed is working.

* *** *

Our greatest responsibility is the active defense of the American people. Twenty-eight months have passed since September 11th, 2001 over two years without an attack on American soil. And it is tempting to believe that the danger is behind us. That hope is understandable, comforting and false. The killing has continued in Bali, Jakarta, Casablanca, Riyadh, Mombasa, Jerusalem, Istanbul, and Baghdad. The terrorists continue to plot against America and the civilized world. And by our will and courage, this danger will be defeated.

Inside the United States, where the war began, we must continue to give our homeland security and law enforcement personnel every tool they need to defend us. And one of those essential tools is the Patriot Act, which allows federal law enforcement to better share information, to track terrorists, to disrupt their cells, and to seize their assets. For years, we have used similar provisions to catch embezzlers and drug traffickers. If these methods are good for hunting criminals, they are even more important for hunting terrorists.

Key provisions of the Patriot Act are set to expire next year. The terrorist threat will not expire on that schedule. Our law enforcement needs this vital legislation to protect our citizens. You need to renew the Patriot Act.

America is on the offensive against the terrorists who started this war. Last March, Khalid Shaikh Mohammed, a mastermind of September the 11th, awoke to find himself in the custody of U.S. and Pakistani authorities. Last August the 11th brought the capture of the terrorist Hambali, who was a key player in the attack in Indonesia that killed over 200 people. We're tracking al Qaeda around the world, and nearly two-thirds of their known leaders have now been captured or killed. Thousands of very skilled and determined military personnel are on the manhunt, going after the remaining killers who hide in cities and caves, and one by one, we will bring these terrorists to justice.

* *** *

Tonight, I also ask you to reform our immigration laws so they reflect our values and benefit our economy. I propose a new temporary worker program to match willing foreign workers with willing employers when no Americans can be found to fill the job. This reform will be good for our economy because employers will find needed workers in an honest and orderly system. A temporary worker program will help protect our homeland, allowing Border Patrol and law enforcement to focus on true threats to our national security.

I oppose amnesty, because it would encourage further illegal immigration, and unfairly reward those who break our laws. My temporary worker program will preserve the citizenship path for those who respect the law, while bringing millions of hardworking men and women out from the shadows of American life.

Source: U.S. Historical Documents. Available online. URL: http://www.historicaldocuments.com/StateoftheUnionAddress2004.htm. Accessed November 14, 2006.

III. SCHOLARLY PAPERS AND SPEECHES

Benjamin Franklin: "Information to Those Who Would Remove to America," September 1782

In this paper, Benjamin Franklin expresses the various virtues necessary for European immigrants to succeed in America and attempts to dispel some of the beliefs many held about what awaited them once they arrived, such as the wealth of Americans, the abundance of employment opportunities, and the availability of free land.

Many persons in Europe, having directly or by letters, expressed to the writer of this, who is well acquainted with North America, their desire of transporting and establishing themselves in that country; but who appear to have formed, through ignorance, mistaken ideas and expectations of what is to be obtained there; he thinks it may be useful, and prevent inconvenient, expensive, and fruitless removals and voyages of improper persons, if he gives some clearer and truer notions of that part of the world, than appear to have hitherto prevailed.

He finds it is imagined by numbers, that the inhabitants of North America are rich, capable of rewarding, and disposed to reward, all sorts of ingenuity; that they are at the same time ignorant of all the sciences, and, consequently, that strangers, possessing talents in the belles-lettres, fine Arts, etc., must be highly esteemed, and so well paid, as to become easily rich themselves; that there are also abundance of profitable offices to be disposed of, which the natives are not qualified to fill; and that, having few persons of family among them, strangers of birth must be greatly respected, and of course easily obtain the best of those offices, which will make all their fortunes; that the governments too, to encourage emigrations from Europe, not only pay the expense of personal transportation, but give lands gratis to strangers, with Negroes to work for them, utensils of husbandry, and stocks of cattle. These are all wild imaginations; and those who go to America with expectations founded upon them will surely find themselves disappointed. The truth is, that though there are in that country few people so miserable as the poor of Europe, there are also very few that in Europe would be called rich; it is rather a general happy mediocrity that prevails. There are few great proprietors of the soil, and few tenants; most people cultivate their own lands, or follow some handicraft or merchandise; very few rich enough to live idly upon their rents or incomes, or to pay the high prices given in Europe for paintings, statues, architecture, and the other works of art, that are more curious than useful. Hence the natural geniuses, that have arisen in America with such talents, have uniformly quitted that country for Europe, where they can be more suitably rewarded. It is true, that letters and mathematical knowledge are in esteem there, but they are at the same time more common than is apprehended; there being already existing nine colleges or universities, viz. four in New England, and one in each of the Provinces of New York, New Jersey, Pennsylvania, Maryland, and Virginia, all furnished with learned professors; besides a number of smaller academies; these educate many of their youth in the languages, and those sciences that qualify men for the professions of divinity, law, or physick. Strangers indeed are by no means excluded from exercising those professions; and the quick increase of inhabitants everywhere gives them a chance of employ, which they have in common with the natives. Of civil offices, or employments, there are few; no superfluous ones, as in Europe; and it is a rule established in some of the states, that no office should be so profitable as to make it desirable. The 36th Article of the Constitution of Pennsylvania, runs expressly in these words; "As every freeman, to preserve his independence, (if he has not a sufficient estate) ought to have some profession, calling, trade, or farm, whereby he may honestly subsist, there can be no necessity for, nor use in, establishing offices of profit; the usual effects of which are dependence and servility, unbecoming freemen, in the possessors and expectants; faction, contention, corruption, and disorder among the people. Wherefore, whenever an office, through increase of fees or otherwise, becomes so profitable, as to occasion many to apply for it, the profits ought to be lessened by the legislature."

These ideas prevailing more or less in all the United States, it cannot be worth any man's while, who has a means of living at home, to expatriate himself, in hopes of obtaining a profitable civil office in America; and, as to military offices, they are at an end with the war, the armies being disbanded. Much less is it advisable for a person to go thither, who has no other quality to recommend him but his birth. In Europe it has indeed its value; but it is a commodity that cannot be carried to a worse market than that of America, where people do not inquire concerning a stranger, *What is he?* but, *What can he do?* If he has any useful art, he is welcome; and if he exercises it, and behaves well, he will be respected by all that know him; but a mere man of quality, who, on that account, wants to live upon the public, by some office or salary, will be despised and disregarded. The husbandman is in honor there, and even the mechanic, because their employments are useful. The people have a saying, that God Almighty is himself a mechanic, the greatest in the universe; and he is respected and admired more for the variety, ingenuity, and utility of his handiworks, than for the antiquity of his family. They are pleased with the observation of a Negro, and frequently mention it, that *Boccarorra* (meaning the white men) *make de black man workee, make de horse workee, make de ox workee, make ebery ting workee; only de hog. He, de hog, no workee; he eat, he drink, he walk about, he go to sleep when he please, he libb like a gentleman.* According to these opinions of the Americans, one of them would think himself more obliged to a genealogist, who could prove for him that his ancestors and relations for ten generations had been ploughmen, smiths, carpenters, turners, weavers, tanners, or even shoemakers, and consequently that they were useful members of society; than if he could only prove that they were gentlemen, doing nothing of value, but living idly on the labor of others, mere *fruges consumere nati* [footnote: "born / Merely to eat up the corn.—Watts"], and otherwise *good for nothing,* till by their death their estates, like the carcass of the Negro's gentleman-hog, come to be *cut up.*

With regard to encouragements for strangers from government, they are really only what are derived from good laws and liberty. Strangers are welcome, because there is room enough for them all, and therefore the old inhabitants are not jealous of them; the laws protect them sufficiently, so that they have no need of the patronage of great men; and every one will enjoy securely the profits of his industry. But, if he does not bring a fortune with him, he must work and be industrious to live. One or two years' residence gives him all the rights of a citizen; but the government does not at present, whatever it may have done in former times, hire people to become settlers, by paying their passages, giving land, Negroes, utensils, stock, or any other kind of emolument whatsoever. In short, America is the land of labor, and by no means what the English call *Lubberland,* and the French *Pays de Cocagne,* where the streets are said to be paved with half-peck loaves, the houses tiled with pancakes, and where the fowls fly about ready roasted, crying, *Come eat me!*

Who then are the kind of persons to whom an emigration to America may be advantageous? And what are the advantages they may reasonably expect?

Land being cheap in that country, from the vast forests still void of inhabitants, and not likely to be occupied in an age to come, insomuch that the propriety of an hundred acres of fertile soil full of wood may be obtained near the frontiers, in many places, for eight or ten guineas, hearty young laboring men, who understand the husbandry of corn and cattle, which is nearly the same in that country as in Europe, may easily establish themselves there. A little money saved of the good wages they receive there, while they work for others, enables them to buy the land and begin their plantation, in which they are assisted by the good will of their neighbors, and some credit. Multitudes of poor people from England, Ireland, Scotland, and Germany, have by this means in a few years become wealthy farmers, who, in their own countries, where all the lands are fully occupied, and the wages of labor low, could never have emerged from the poor condition wherein they were born.

From the salubrity of the air, the healthiness of the climate, the plenty of good provisions, and the encouragement to early marriages by the certainty of subsistence in cultivating the earth, the increase of inhabitants by natural generation is very rapid in America, and becomes still more so by the accession of strangers; hence there is a continual demand for more artisans of all the necessary and useful kinds, to supply those cultivators of the earth with houses, and with furniture and utensils of the grosser sorts, which cannot so well be brought from Europe. Tolerably good workmen in any of those mechanic arts are sure to find employ, and to be well paid for their work, there being no restraints preventing strangers from exercising any art they understand, nor any permission necessary. If they are poor, they begin first as servants or journeymen; and if they are sober, industrious, and frugal, they soon become masters, establish themselves in business, marry, raise families, and become respectable citizens . . .

The almost general mediocrity of fortune that prevails in America obliging its people to follow some business for subsistence, those vices, that arise usually from idleness, are in a great measure prevented. Industry and constant employment are great preservatives of the morals and virtue of a nation. Hence bad examples to youth are more rare in America, which must be a comfortable consideration to parents. To this may be truly added, that serious religion, under its various denominations, is not only tolerated, but respected and practiced. Atheism is unknown there; infidelity rare and secret; so that persons may live to a great age in that country, without having their piety shocked by meeting with either an atheist or an infidel. And the Divine Being seems to have manifested his approbation of the mutual forbearance and kindness with which the different sects treat each other, by the remarkable prosperity with which He has been pleased to favor the whole country.

Source: Vindicating the Founders: Race, Sex, Class, and Justice in the Origins of America, by Thomas G. West. Available online. URL: http://www.vindicatingthefounders.com/library/index.asp?document=40. Accessed November 24, 2006.

Philip Martin: "The Battle over Unauthorized Immigration to the United States," April 11, 2006

Philip Martin, a professor in the Department of Agriculture and Economic Resources at the University of California-Davis, discusses the impact of illegal immigration on the U.S. labor force. He also writes about some of the measures proposed by the U.S. government in 2006 to manage illegal immigration.

The rising number of unauthorized foreign-born people in the United States—which approached 12 million in 2005, one-third of all foreign-born U.S. residents—has prompted massive public debate, huge public demonstrations, and recent congressional action.

In December, the U.S. House of Representatives approved an enforcement-only bill that would authorize building a 700-mile wall on the border between Mexico and the United States. Now, the U.S. Senate is considering a bill that increases enforcement efforts, launches new guest worker programs, and allows some of the unauthorized foreign-born to eventually become legal immigrants and naturalized U.S. citizens. But compromise has come to a standstill, at least for now. On Friday, April 7, the Senate adjourned for a two-week recess without passing a bipartisan compromise bill. The debate will resume in late April.

These proposed reforms come at a time when parts of the U.S. economy are highly dependent on the labor of the unauthorized, and the governments of the migrants' countries of origin want to preserve the availability of U.S. jobs and remittances. Largely unskilled Latino migrants have spread to a new range of U.S. industries and areas, from Midwestern meatpacking to construction and food preparation. About 10 percent of the labor forces of Mexico as well as some Central American and Caribbean countries are now employed in the United States, and remittances are a major source of foreign exchange.

Immigration reforms in 2006 will determine whether the United States continues to absorb between 500,000 and 1 million Latin American workers a year—and whether new immigrant workers will be unauthorized, legal guest workers, or foreign-born on the path to American citizenship.

Unauthorized Immigrants Make Up Almost 5 Percent of the U.S. Labor Force

There were 37 million foreign-born U.S. residents in 2005—including 11.5 million naturalized U.S. citizens, between 11.5 million and 12 million unauthorized immigrants, and 10.5 million legal immigrants. Demographer Jeff Passel of the Pew Hispanic Center estimates that the number of the unauthorized foreign-born in the United States rose by 400,000 in 2005. Some 850,000 unauthorized foreign-born people entered the United States in 2005, but others left, became legal, or died.

About 56 percent of the total number of unauthorized immigrants are Mexican, and 22 percent are from elsewhere in Latin America. Most of the unauthorized are recent arrivals: Two-thirds were in the United States less than 10 years, and 40 percent were in the United States less than five years. Passel estimates that 1.8 million unauthorized foreign-born people arrived in the 1980s, 5.0 million in the 1990s, and 4.4 million between 2000 and 2005.

Using Current Population Survey data, Passel also estimates that 7.2 million unauthorized foreign-born people were in the U.S. labor force in March 2005—almost 5 percent of all U.S. workers. Unauthorized immigrants made up 24 percent of hired farm workers, 17 percent of cleaners, 14 percent of construction workers, and 12 percent of food preparation workers. Within construction, an estimated 36 percent of insulation installers and 29 percent of drywallers were unauthorized. However, the vast majority of workers in these professions are still U.S.-born.

Competing Bills and Competing Solutions

The House Bill: Mandates for Verification and a 700-Mile Wall

The U.S. House bill—named the Border Protection, Antiterrorism, and Illegal Immigration Control Act (H.R. 4437)—has as its centerpiece an expansion of the Basic Pilot employee verification program. According to this provision, all U.S. employers would have to submit the Social Security and immigration numbers of newly hired workers within three days to government agencies by telephone or computer. If the workers' data did not match those in government records, employers would notify these workers to correct the data within 30 days or be on notice that the workers were likely unauthorized, which could subject the employer to fines.

The bill would give U.S. employers two years to meet the three-day verification requirement and six years to verify current employees. Fines for employers who violate the law would rise up to $25,000, and "illegal presence" in the United States would become a felony, which could make it hard for currently unauthorized workers to become legal guest workers and immigrants. The House bill also introduces penalties on those who support or shield illegal migrants—a provision that critics say could mean up to five years in prison for those people (such as employees of social service agencies and churches) that help the unauthorized foreign-born.

One of the House bill's most controversial provisions authorizes (at a cost of $2 billion) adding 700 miles of fencing to the current 106 miles of fence along the Mexico-U.S. border. While the House vote to build more fencing (approved 260-159) was stronger than its vote for the overall bill, the reaction of Mexico and other Latin American governments has been strongly negative. Mexican Foreign Secretary Luis Ernesto Derbez, who asked Central American nations to join in opposition to additional fencing, said: "Mexico is not going to bear, it is not going to permit, and it will not allow a stupid thing like this wall."

President Bush has called for "comprehensive immigration reform" that includes more enforcement to prevent illegal entries as well as a new guest worker program to deal with the unauthorized foreign-born already here. But the House bill does not include a new guest worker program. As Rep.

Tom Tancredo, R-Colo., leader of a House immigration reform caucus with 90 members, put it: "Our borders must be secured and our laws must be enforced before any guest worker plan can go into effect."

The Senate Bills: Exploring Options for Legalization and Guest Workers

The Senate is currently grappling with immigration reform, and all of the major bills being considered by that body include beefed-up enforcement measures—such as hiring more U.S. Border Patrol agents and expanding the employee verification system—that parallel those in the House bill. But most senators have also accepted Bush's comprehensive immigration reform approach—specifically, that unauthorized foreign-born people in the United States with jobs should have a path open to them to earn legal immigrant status after six years and U.S. citizenship after 11 years.

However, Republican senators are divided. Some of these senators advocate enforcement and a guest worker program, meaning that unauthorized foreign-born people with U.S. jobs could work an additional six years as legal guest workers but would then have to return to their countries of origin. Other G.O.P. senators join most Democrats in preferring that unauthorized foreign-born residents in the United States be able to convert to immigrant status.

The Senate debated immigration reform in both March and early April, but did not approve a bill. There appeared to be majority support in the Senate for a comprehensive bill that would step up enforcement and offer "earned legalization" to those who have been in the United States for at least five years. But the vote to approve this compromise, which would have divided the unauthorized foreign-born into three groups based on how long they had been in the country, failed on a 38-60 vote on April 7. An alternative enforcement-only bill failed on a 36-62 vote.

A Nation at a Crossroads about Unauthorized Immigration

Three lessons emerge from the current debate. First, there is no enthusiasm among U.S. policymakers for repeating the approach to unauthorized migration embodied in the Immigration Reform and Control Act of 1986 (IRCA), which involved legalization first and enforcement later. The act allowed 2.7 million foreign-born people to become immigrants and eventually citizens, but ineffective enforcement meant the entry and employment of unauthorized workers continued. Both the House bill and the Senate bills have stronger enforcement provisions than IRCA.

Second, there are fundamental disagreements about how to deal with the unauthorized foreign-born already in the United States. The House's enforcement-only approach aims to drastically reduce illegal entries and employment. Combined with other recent federal legislation (for instance, making it more difficult for states to issue drivers' licenses to the unauthorized foreign-born), the goal of this approach is to reduce the number of unauthorized foreign-born residents by attrition and then deal at a future date with the reduced numbers who remain. By contrast, a majority of senators seem willing to allow some unauthorized foreign-born people who have built lives in the United States to become immigrants and eventually citizens.

Third, immigration reform comes when the United States is at a crossroads in its dealings with Latin American countries that are the source of 80 percent of the unauthorized foreign-born in the United States. Trade agreements such as the North American Free Trade Agreement (NAFTA), the Central American Free Trade Agreement (CAFTA), and the Doha round of the World Trade Organization's trade talks have all aimed to encourage countries now sending migrants to the United States to instead send more goods and fewer migrants.

However, freer trade tends to produce a migration hump—a temporary surge of more emigration as protected local industries are exposed to competition while the investment that creates jobs takes time to have its migration-retarding effects. The migration hump from NAFTA and other accords is still ongoing, and U.S. policymakers appear to have grown tired of waiting for the reduction in immigration these accords should eventually bring.

Americans, immigrants, and migrant-sending countries are closely watching the congressional debate over immigration reform. There is general agreement that more must be done to reduce unauthorized migration, but disagreement over whether the solution lies more in border fences or workplace enforcement. Similarly, there is agreement that unauthorized foreign-born parents with U.S.-born children are not likely to be deported, but disagreement on whether they should nonetheless be encouraged to return on their own or offered a path to immigrant status. The stakes are high, affecting the lives of millions of immigrants and Americans as well as potential migrants.

Source: The Population Reference Bureau. Available online. URL: http://www.prb.org/Template.cfm?section=PRB&template=/ContentManagement/ContentDisplay.cfm&ContentID=13774. Accessed July 24, 2006.

Mark Krikorian: "Visa Overstays: Can We Bar the Terrorist Door?" May 11, 2006 (excerpts)

In his statement presented to the U.S. House of Representatives Committee on International Relations, Subcommittee on Oversight and Investigations, Mark Krikorian, executive director of the Center for Immigration Studies, discusses the importance of border security, but he points out that a greater threat to national security may be visa overstayers.

Much of the discussion on the intersection of immigration and terrorism has focused on securing our porous land borders. And border enforcement is indeed an important tool in protecting our homeland.

* *** *

But as important as border control is for security, it is not sufficient. It must be supplemented with a tightly run immigration system inside the country as well. This includes addressing problems like the lack of worksite enforcement, the staggering prevalence of fraud in the processing of immigration benefits, and the absurd visa lottery.

* *** *

But perhaps most important is the issue of visa overstays. (Strictly speaking, it is not the visa itself, issued by the State Department, which expires and turns the foreign visitor into an illegal alien, but rather the length of stay granted the alien by the immigration inspector at the airport or land crossing.) Estimates are that as many as 40 percent of illegal aliens are overstayers, who entered the country legally but did not leave when their time ran out, representing perhaps 4 million or more people.

And, in fact, the majority of those terrorists who were illegal aliens when they committed their crimes were overstayers. Of the 12 al Qaeda operatives who were illegal aliens in the United States when they took part in terrorism between 1993 and 2001 (out of the 48 examined in the Center for Immigration Studies report, *The Open Door*), seven were visa overstayers. These include two conspirators in the first World Trade Center attack, Mohammed Salameh and Eyad Ismoil. Other terrorist overstayers were Lafi Khalil, who was involved in the New York subway bomb plot, and four of the 9/11 terrorists: Zacarias Moussaoui, Satam al Suqami, Nawaf al Hamzi, and Hani Hanjour. . . . Given the prevalence of overstays among terrorists in the United States, it's an important security goal to limit this phenomenon as much as possible. This can be done in two ways: keeping likely overstays from being issued visas in the first place, and detecting overstays once they do happen.

Section 214(b) of the Immigration and Nationality Act states that "every alien shall be presumed to be an immigrant until he establishes to the satisfaction of the consular officer . . . that he is entitled to nonimmigrant status." Individuals who appear likely to overstay their temporary visa are called "intending immigrants"—that is, they will try to settle permanently in the United States. Consular officers are not to issue "nonimmigrant" (i.e., temporary) visas unless the applicant can demonstrate that he has a residence abroad to which he is likely to return (with some exceptions), that the visit to the United States will be temporary, and that the applicant has enough money to finance the visit and return trip. Officers are trained to look for evidence of strong ties to the applicant's home country, such as family, a good job, property, and other things that would increase the likelihood that an applicant will return, and to be skeptical of applicants who fit the profile of a probable overstayer. The criteria vary from country to country, but these individuals are generally young, unemployed or earning a low income, and unmarried. Section 214(b) is by far the most common reason for applications to be refused.

This is specifically relevant to terrorism because ordinary intending immigrants and terrorists often have similar characteristics—youth, no families of their own, no consistent career, no property or other deep attachments in their home countries. In other words, stricter standards for the issuance of visas to prevent ordinary overstays could be a powerful tool to reduce the terrorist threat as well.

* *** *

Therefore, stricter adherence to the expectations of the statute, a stronger prevailing attitude of skepticism among consular officers, and greater understanding of the need to invoke Section 214(b), the keystone of nonimmigrant visa law, could be a highly effective tool against terrorism. With some four million overstayer illegal aliens, strict adherence to 214(b) could also have a significant impact on efforts to reduce illegal immigration.

Screening visa applicants for intending immigrants has security benefits because "intending terrorists" have similar characteristics. But if the terrorist gets in anyway, there's also a significant likelihood that he'll actually overstay, because of the time involved in organizing and preparing for any significant terrorist attack. And this is why detecting and removing overstays is important not merely for ordinary immigration control but also for security reasons.

The first task is to know whether a foreign visitor actually left before his length of stay expired. We have no real way of knowing this now, given the complete breakdown of the comically inadequate, paper-based system of tracking the departure of foreign visitors via the I-94 form. And without knowing which foreign visitors have left, we have no way of knowing who has remained illegally.

The potential for true departure tracking exists in US-VISIT, the new biometric screening system for foreign visitors, which the Department of Homeland Security began implementing in 2004. The system records the entry of foreign visitors, authenticates their identity, and screens them against security databases. It has been fully implemented at air and sea ports, but in only a very limited way at land ports. If the program is allowed to proceed as planned, the exit recording system will eventually require visitors to "check out" as they leave. By matching the recorded entries against the exits, DHS would be able to determine which visitors have overstayed their visas and become illegal aliens. In addition to providing ICE with enforcement leads as soon as an alien overstays, it is expected that the act of recording entries and exits, together with increased enforcement activity and the imposition of penalties for visa violations, will help dampen the temptation to overstay.

* *** *

If and when the exit-recording function of US-VISIT is ever fully implemented, then aliens identified as overstayers should be added to the FBI's National Crime Information Center (NCIC) database. In that way, if they are ever arrested for a crime or pulled over for a traffic stop, they could be held by local police and then turned over to DHS's Bureau of Immigration and Customs Enforcement (ICE). This could become a key component of interior enforcement. Although no hard figures exist, with perhaps 4 million visa overstayers living in the United States, there is no question that tens of thousands of them are arrested or pulled over in traffic stops each year. Traffic stops and arrests are a significant opportunity to apprehend those in the country illegally and we should take full advantage of it.

* *** *

Any serious effort to foil terrorist attacks on the United States must have as a centerpiece the prevention and removal of overstays as part of a broader effort to restore credibility to our immigration-control system. The means to do this are available to us, but much work remains, both in policy changes and implementation of earlier policies. The only responsible course of action is to do all we can, quickly, to bar the door to future terrorist overstayers.

Source: Center for Immigration Studies. Available online. URL: http://www.cis.org/articles/2006/msktestimony051106.html. Accessed November 24, 2006.

5

International Documents

This chapter provides a selection of immigration-related documents and speeches from the four countries highlighted in chapter 3 of this book: France, South Africa, Mexico, and the Philippines. Documents are organized and listed in chronological order within each section. All documents are reproduced in full unless identified as excerpted.

FRANCE

Declaration of Human and Civic Rights of 26 August 1789

This Declaration established the foundation for all of France's future immigration laws, including the Decree of 1 October 1945, which reinforced the country's principles of equality for all immigrants regardless of race, religion, or culture, and integration of all immigrants into French society.

> The representatives of the French People, formed into a National Assembly, considering ignorance, forgetfulness or contempt of the rights of man to be the only causes of public misfortunes and the corruption of Governments, have resolved to set forth, in a solemn Declaration, the natural, unalienable and sacred rights of man, to the end that this Declaration, constantly present to all members of the body politic, may remind them unceasingly of their rights and their duties; to the end that the acts of the legislative power and those of the executive power, since they may be continually compared with the aim of every political institution, may thereby be the more respected; to the end that the demands of the citizens, founded henceforth on simple and incontestable principles, may always be directed toward the maintenance of the Constitution and the happiness of all. In consequence whereof, the National Assembly recognises and declares, in the presence

and under the auspices of the Supreme Being, the following Rights of Man and of the Citizen.

Article First Men are born and remain free and equal in rights. Social distinctions may be based only on considerations of the common good.

Article 2 The aim of every political association is the preservation of the natural and imprescriptible rights of Man. These rights are Liberty, Property, Safety and Resistance to Oppression.

Article 3 The principle of any Sovereignty lies primarily in the Nation. No corporate body, no individual may exercise any authority that does not expressly emanate from it.

Article 4 Liberty consists in being able to do anything that does not harm others: thus, the exercise of the natural rights of every man has no bounds other than those that ensure to the other members of society the enjoyment of these same rights. These bounds may be determined only by Law.

Article 5 The Law has the right to forbid only those actions that are injurious to society. Nothing that is not forbidden by Law may be hindered, and no one may be compelled to do what the Law does not ordain.

Article 6 The Law is the expression of the general will. All citizens have the right to take part, personally or through their representatives, in its making. It must be the same for all, whether it protects or punishes. All citizens, being equal in its eyes, shall be equally eligible to all high offices, public positions and employments, according to their ability, and without other distinction than that of their virtues and talents.

Article 7 No man may be accused, arrested or detained except in the cases determined by the Law, and following the procedure that it has prescribed. Those who solicit, expedite, carry out, or cause to be carried out arbitrary orders must be punished; but any citizen summoned or apprehended by virtue of the Law, must give instant obedience; resistance makes him guilty.

Article 8 The Law must prescribe only the punishments that are strictly and evidently necessary; and no one may be punished except by virtue of a Law drawn up and promulgated before the offense is committed, and legally applied.

Article 9 As every man is presumed innocent until he has been declared guilty, if it should be considered necessary to arrest him, any undue harshness that is not required to secure his person must be severely curbed by Law.

Article 10 No one may be disturbed on account of his opinions, even religious ones, as long as the manifestation of such opinions does not interfere with the established Law and Order.

Article 11 The free communication of ideas and of opinions is one of the most precious rights of man. Any citizen may therefore speak, write and publish freely, except what is tantamount to the abuse of this liberty in the cases determined by Law.

Article 12 To guarantee the Rights of Man and of the Citizen a public force is necessary; this force is therefore established for the benefit of all, and not for the particular use of those to whom it is entrusted.

Article 13 For the maintenance of the public force, and for administrative expenses, a general tax is indispensable; it must be equally distributed among all citizens, in proportion to their ability to pay.

Article 14 All citizens have the right to ascertain, by themselves, or through their representatives, the need for a public tax, to consent to it freely, to watch over its use, and to determine its proportion, basis, collection and duration.

Article 15 Society has the right to ask a public official for an accounting of his administration.

Article 16 Any society in which no provision is made for guaranteeing rights or for the separation of powers, has no Constitution.

Article 17 Since the right to Property is inviolable and sacred, no one may be deprived thereof, unless public necessity, legally ascertained, obviously requires it, and just and prior indemnity has been paid.

Source: Conseil Constitutionnel. Available online. URL: http://www.conseil-constitutionnel.fr/langues/anglais/essential.htm. Accessed November 25, 2006.

Immigration Bill 2006

Despite protests by thousands of immigrants, the French government overwhelmingly passed an immigration bill in June 2006 and adopted it in July that tightened immigration for unskilled workers and allowed only highly skilled immigrants from outside the European Union to obtain renewable "skills and talents" residency permits. The bill is scheduled to take effect in early 2007.

Following is a summary of the bill's key components as published by the Migration Policy Institute.

Recruiting skilled workers

The new law authorizes the government to identify particular professions and geographic zones of France that are "characterized by recruitment difficulties." For those identified employers, the government plans to facilitate the recruitment of immigrant workers with needed skills or qualifications. However, this means employers who are not on the government-selected list may have more difficulty (or may face longer waiting periods) obtaining residence permits for migrant workers they wish to employ.

Under the new law, foreigners who possess skill sets of interest to French employers in the designated areas will be granted "skills and talents" visas, valid for three years. . . . Eligible candidates must be able to demonstrate that they will contribute to the economic or intellectual and cultural development of both France and their country of origin.

The government will only issue this visa to qualified immigrants from a developing country if the sending country has signed a "co-development" agreement with France or if the immigrants in question agree to return to their country of origin within six years.

Facilitating foreign students' stay

In addition to high-skilled workers, foreign students seeking to stay on in France after they complete their studies will also benefit from the new law by being given greater opportunities to do so.

The new law will require foreign students to receive approval to study in France from their country of origin. Once in France, foreign students who receive a master's or higher degree will be allowed to pursue a "first professional experience" that contributes to the economic development of both France and the student's country of origin. The student will be granted a six-month renewable visa to look for and take up work in France.

Tightening the rules on family reunification

The government's objective in modifying family reunification policy is three-fold: to ensure that immigrants respect French values, to promote their integration into French society, and to fight forced or polygamous marriages.

The new law better defines conditions for family reunification. Accordingly, a family member of an immigrant who does not respect the basic principles of family life in France (recognition of the secular state, equality between a man and a woman, and monogamy) will not be allowed to enter France. Furthermore, an immigrant must now wait 18 months, instead of 12, to apply to bring a family member to France.

In an effort to prevent immigrant families from becoming dependent on France's welfare system, the law also requires immigrants to prove they can independently support all family members who seek to come to France. Specifically, they must earn at least the French minimum wage and not be reliant on assistance from the French state. Access to government assistance is also limited to European Union citizens. Those who reside in France longer than three months without working or studying must be able to support themselves without relying on social or medical benefits from the French government.

Another modification to the family reunification policy is that spouses of French citizens must wait three years (instead of two) before applying for a 10-year residence permit. Four years of marriage are required for the spouse of a French citizen to apply for French citizenship. Finally, an immigrant found to be practicing polygamy can have his or her visa revoked.

Limiting access to residence and citizenship

[It was argued] the country's previous (1998) law "rewarded" immigrants who broke the law by offering them legal status after being residents for 10 years. The new law changes this by simplifying the procedure whereby the government can directly deport unauthorized migrants who are refused the right to stay in France.

Key exceptions were made for some illegal immigrants [regarding] the deportation of immigrant families with school-aged children. In order to avoid deportation, these immigrants had to meet several criteria, including having a child enrolled in the French school system and demonstrating a "real will" to integrate. Illegally resident immigrants who disturb the "public order" would also be vulnerable to deportation.

Access to both citizenship and legal residence is dependent on the newly defined requirements of integration. A law explicitly states the integration responsibilities of immigrants. Specifically, immigrants must sign a "welcome and integration" contract and take French language and civic[s] courses. Before applying for permanent residence, immigrants must accordingly prove that they are "well-integrated" into French society. . . . Integration in this regard means that the immigrant respects and complies with the principles of the French Republic and has a sufficient knowledge of the French language.

Source: The Migration Policy Institute *Backgrounder*. Available online. URL: http://www.migrationpolicy.org/pubs/Backgrounder2_France.php. Accessed June 7, 2007. A French-language version of the complete document is available online. URL: http://www.assemblee-nationale.fr/12/projets/pl2986.asp. Accessed November 25, 2006.

SOUTH AFRICA

Immigration Act 2002 (excerpts)

This act outlines the objectives and structures of South Africa's immigration policies, specifically referencing Section 2 of Act 13 of 2002. Topics include explanations of immigrant categories, types of businesses immigrants may establish, refugees, issuing immigration permits, and related fees.

The Republic of South Africa can accommodate only a certain number of immigrants. South Africa has a vast reserve of unskilled and semi-skilled workers who are entitled to employment opportunities and to an economically viable lifestyle. For this reason no one in the unskilled and the semi-skilled categories will be accepted as an immigrant worker in South Africa. Because of the considerable need for the creation of job opportunities for South African workers as well as for their training and development, South Africa cannot afford to grant permits for immigration to persons who are not seriously committed to immigrating to the country permanently and to investing their assets, skills, knowledge and experience for the benefit of themselves and the people of South Africa.

Objectives and Structures of Immigration Control

The objectives and functions of immigration control are as follows (with special reference to Section 2 of the Immigration Act, 2002 (Act 13 of 2002):

Section 2(1)

In the administration of this Act, the Department shall pursue the following objectives:

- facilitating and simplifying the issuance of permanent and temporary residence to those who are entitled to them, and concentrating resources and efforts in enforcing this Act at community level and discouraging illegal foreigners;

- facilitating foreign investments, tourism and industries in the Republic which are reliant on international exchanges of people and personnel
- enabling exceptionally skilled or qualified people to sojourn in the Republic
- administering the prescribed fees, fines and other payments it exacts or receives in such a fashion as to defray the overall cost of its operation.

Section 2(2)

In order to achieve the objectives set out in subsection (1), the Department shall monitor and exact compliance from any person or entity exercising responsibilities or bearing duties or obligations in terms of this Act. . . .

IMMIGRATION CATEGORIES are divided into 2 major categories. Section 26 and Section 27.

Section 26 - Direct Residence

which subject to Section 25 of the Immigration Act (2002), the Department shall issue permanent residence permits to four categories of foreigners who are dealt with in Section 26(a-d)

26(a) refers to a foreigner

- who has been in SA on a work permit for 5 years
- who has received a permanent offer of employment
- whose employer's chartered accountant submitted a certification that the post exists and is intended to be filled by such foreigner
- in respect of whom the Dept. of Labor certified that the terms and conditions of the person's employment are not inferior to those applicable to South African citizens/permanent residents in the same field.

Should a foreigner meet the above requirements, his/her spouse and children under the age of 21 years will likewise qualify for permanent residence in the RSA in terms of Section 27 (g)

26(b) refers to a spouse of a SA citizen/permanent resident provided that:

- a good faith relationship exists
- a permanent residence permit shall lapse if, within 3 years after the date of application, the relationship no longer exists, except in the case of death.

26(c) refers to a child of a citizen or permanent residence under the age of 21 provided that:

- a permit shall lapse if the child does not submit an application to the Department within 2 years of his/her 21st birthday for confirmation of his/her residential status.

26(d) refers to a child of a citizen above the age of 21.

Section 27: Residence on Other Grounds

The Department may issue a permanent residence permit to foreigners of good character who qualify for permanent residence status in terms of one of the categories in Section 27 (a-g) of the Act.

The above applications may be submitted at any regional office of DHA. Except for persons mentioned in Sections 27 (a) and (c), who must submit their applications at a regional office in the province where they are employed or where the business is established/invested into.

Section 27(a) Refers to a foreigner;

- who is able to submit an offer of employment
- whose employer's chartered accountant submitted a certification that the post exists, the position and related job description was advertised in the prescribed manner and that no qualified SA citizen or resident was available to fill the position
- in respect of whom the Department of Labor certified that the terms and conditions of such officer, including salary and benefits, are not inferior to those prevailing in relevant market segment for citizens/ residents, taking into account the applicable collective bargaining agreements and other applicable standards, if any
- whose application falls within the yearly limits of available permits prescribed from time to time for each sector of industry, trade and commerce, following consultation with the Department of Trade & Industry, Labor and Education.

Should a foreigner meet the above requirements, his/her spouse and children under the age of 21 years will likewise qualify for permanent residence status in the RSA, in terms of section 27(g).

Section 27(b) refers to a foreigner who has demonstrated to the Department's satisfaction, his/her possessing extraordinary skills or qualifications.

Should a foreigner meet the above requirements, his/her immediate family members will likewise qualify to apply for permanent residence in the RSA in terms of Section 27(g).

Section 27(c) refers to a foreigner who:

- intends to establish a business in the RSA; or
- already holds a business permit to conduct a business in RSA; or
- intends to invest in an existing business in the RSA

All three of which must invest or have already invested the prescribed financial contribution which shall be part of is part of the (intended) book value of the business, as certified by the chartered accountant. The Department may waive or reduce the specific capitalization requirements for business which shall from time to time be published, if such a step will be in national interest, or if when the Department of Trade & Industry makes a request to this effect.

The business to be established must be in line with one of the following sectors:

- Information and communication technology
- Clothing and textiles
- Chemicals and biotechnology
- Agro processing
- Metals and minerals
- Automotives and transport

Once permanent residence status has been acquired under this section of the Act, the person concerned has to renew the certification of the chartered accountant two years after permanent residence status has been granted, and again three years later. Failure to do so shall result in the permanent residence permit to lapse.

Should a foreigner meet these requirements, his/her spouse and children under the age of 21 will likewise qualify for permanent residence in terms of section 27(g).

Section 27(d) refers to refugees as referred to in section 27(c) of the Refugees Act, 1998 (Act 130 of 1998). Should a refugee meet these requirements, his/her spouse and children under the age of 21 will also qualify to permanent residence in the RSA in terms of Section 27(g).

Section 27(e) refers to foreigners who intend to retire in the RSA (no specific age limit) provided that a chartered accountant certifies that the person concerned has:

- the right to a pension or
- an irrevocable annuity or
- a retirement account
- any of which will give a person a minimum prescribed amount for the rest of his/her life or that person has a minimum prescribed networth of R15M or $25,000.00 monthly income.

Should a foreigner meet these requirements, his/her spouse and children under the age of 21 will likewise qualify for permanent residence in the RSA in terms of Section 27(g).

Should a retired person wish to work in the RSA, he/she must submit a contract of employment and proof that a South African citizen/resident is not available for the occupation applied for.

Should a refugee meet these requirements, his/her spouse and children under the age of 21 will also qualify for permanent residence in the RSA in terms of Section 27(g).

Section 27 (e) refers to a foreigner who has provided a certification by a chartered accountant that he/she has a prescribed minimum networth of R20M and has paid a prescribed fee of R100,000.00 to the Department.

Should a person meet the above requirement, his/her spouse and children under the age of 21 will also qualify to apply for permanent residence in the RSA in terms of Section 27(g).

Section 27(g) refers to a relative or a citizen/resident within the first step of kinship (parents, children and spouses). Specific regulations to be considered are regulations 2, 33(8), 33(20) 33 (21) and 33 (22).

Interview

A personal interview is required for all applicants, 21 years and above. Interviews will be conducted by this office or by other South African Missions in North America depending on applicant's point of residence. If a personal interview is not feasible for the reason that applicant's point of residence is of great distance from/to the respective South African Mission, a telephonic interview will be considered. Interviews will be arranged by the respective Missions provided that all requirements have been duly complied with by the applicant.

Immigration Fees

US$1,155.00: Administrative fee in respect of a formal application for an immigration permit per individual or per family. The fee is non-refundable irrespective of whether the application is approved or not. This is payable upon submission of the formal immigration application.

US$ 88.00: Administrative fee for an application for extension of validity of an immigration permit

All fees are non-refundable and must be paid in cash, money order or certified bank check payable to the South African Consulate General-New York.

Processing Time

Formal Applications: 12–18 months

Issuance and Validity of an Immigration Permit

Immigration permits are issued by the Regional Offices of the Department of Home Affairs in South Africa. These permits are forwarded to this office for onward transmission to applicants. The validity period of an immigration permit is six months. If the person is unable to arrive in the Republic within this period, an application for extension must be submitted to this office prior to the expiration date. Extensions are granted for a maximum period of six months and require a fee of US$88.00.

Withdrawal of an Immigration Permit

The Minister may withdraw an immigration permit by notice in writing and will order the holder of such permit to leave the Republic within the period indicated in the notice on the basis of the following:

- the application contains false information;
- the holder fails to comply with a condition imposed under Section 25(3);
- the holder, within a period of three (3) years from date of issue of such permit, engages in an occupation other than the occupation stated in the permit, without the consent of the Minister;
- the holder obtained the permit on the basis of a marriage entered into less than two (2) years prior to the date of the issue of the permit

and such marriage is judicially annulled or terminated within two years subsequent to the said date;

- the holder did not enter the Republic for the purpose of permanent residence therein, and upon the expiration of the period mentioned in said notice, the permit shall become null and void.

Source: South African Consulate General in New York. Available online. URL: http://www.southafrica-newyork.net/homeaffairs/immigration.htm. Accessed November 25, 2006.

Mr. Gcinumzi Ntlakana, Acting Deputy Director-General, National Immigration Branch: Statement on the Refugee Backlog Project, April 20, 2006

In his statement Mr. Ntlakana discusses the problems South Africa has encountered due to the large number of refugees entering the country for asylum. He also outlines measures being taken to resolve the problems.

1. BACKGROUND

The phenomenal increase in the number of asylum seekers in the past twelve years is directly linked to the achievement of a peaceful transition in South Africa. Since the eradication of apartheid, South Africa has become a safe haven for thousands of individuals from all over the world that are forced to flee their own communities or countries because of persecution or a well-founded fear of persecution.

Before 1994, there was neither policy or legislation governing refugees in South Africa as it was only regarded a refugee-producing country. But with the advent of democracy in 1994, South Africa did not only see the liberation of the oppressed masses from an apartheid system, but it also became a safe haven for displaced and persecuted people.

The dawn of the new era meant South Africa's acceptance back into the international community of nations. In 1996, ending its years of international isolation and status as a refugee-producing country, South Africa signed the United Nation 1951 Convention and the 1967 Protocol relating to the status of Refugees. These instruments, including the Expanded Organisation of African Unity (OAU) Convention on Refugees, were incorporated into the South African Refugees Act. This law became effective in 2000 and continues to be the country's primary piece of legislation governing asylum seekers and refugees in the country.

This new dispensation and bloodless transition to a democratic order, created a climate of HOPE for most people in the war-torn countries across the world. The increased movement of people to the south with the HOPE for a better life has put pressure on our system leaving gaps in allowing some applicants who would not normally qualify to slip and achieve refugee status while also refusing some valid claims.

Newly arrived asylum seekers are registered and issued with a temporary residence permit in terms of Section 22 of the Refugees Act. Section 22 permit allows the holder to sojourn in the Republic while his or her claim is under consideration by the Refugee Status Determination Officers who are based at Refugee Reception Offices. These permits are renewed every thirty days at any Refugee Reception Office in the country. . . . Part of the rights extended to refugees is to apply and obtain an identity and travel documents issued by the South African government. The identity document has a thirteen digit number which is required in terms of the South African Identification Act for identification purposes to access services from any organization or institution like, financial institutions, license department, social, welfare and population development department etc.

Those whose claims have been rejected as unfounded are afforded an opportunity to lodge appeals as prescribed in the Refugees Act and the Refugee Appeal Board. . . . On the other hand, there are those whose claims are said to be manifestly unfounded, fraudulent, and abusive. These are automatically forwarded by the Refugee Status Determination Officers to the Standing Committee for Refugee Affairs who have legislative obligation to review such cases when forwarded to them.

The influx of asylum seekers, lack of capacity and inadequate availability of resources to facilitate the registration of asylum seekers has created a backlog of applications that runs over 100,000. These have resulted in some instances to unlawful arrests, detention and deportation of legitimate applicants. As a result of all these challenges, the Ministry of Home Affairs established a Departmental Steering Committee to come up with practical sustainable solutions that will ensure that all asylum applications—dating back to 1998—are immediately dealt with.

2. PLAN TO REDUCE BACKLOG

The challenges required the Department to establish a steering committee that will fast track the processing of backlog applications. Temporary offices in four provinces (Gauteng - Crown Mines, KwaZulu-Natal - eThekwini, Western Cape - Cape Town and Eastern Cape - Port Elizabeth) have also been set up to expedite the processing of these applications dating received between 1998 after the promulgation of the Refugee Act 130 of

1998 and July 2005. As at Tuesday 4 April, the refugee backlog stood at 103,410 cases. . . .

2.2 Awareness Programme to Change Behavioural Attitudes Toward Refugees/Asylum Seekers

Coupled with the refugee backlog challenge is the negative public perception toward refugee and asylum seekers who are seen to be taking away jobs from South Africans. In worst cases, refugees or displaced people are generally considered to be criminals/crooks and these wrong perception[s] have necessitated a parallel awareness raising campaign that will aim, among others, to:

- To encourage and promote Refugee Activism among South African communities toward Refugees or asylum seekers
- To position DHA as a Caring, Compassionate and Responsive organ of state in dealing with Refugee issues
- To integrate all worthy immigration programmes and initiatives under a common campaign
- To educate refugees about their rights and responsibilities
- To work closely with other law enforcement agencies in clean-up operations to discourage illegal immigration in South Africa.

3. POSITIONING SOUTH AFRICAN GOVERNMENT ON ISSUES OF DISPLACED PEOPLE WITHIN THE UNITED NATIONS CONTEXT

South Africa is chairing the G77 (a group of 132 developing countries) for 2006 at the United Nations level, and with illegal migration increasingly becoming a global trend, there is a particular challenge in dealing with variety of issues of development and migration, all of which relate to national interests and priorities.

Migration and development, is among the critical issues that form the key themes of the UN's agenda for 2006. The G77 coordination mechanism in South Africa is currently hard at work monitoring migration development and interacting with counterparts around G77 and migration issues. The outcome of this exercise will form part of a High-Level Dialogue on Migration that will be held from 14 to 15 September 2006, where ministers are to participate at plenary sessions, panel and roundtable discussions during the 61st Session of the UN General Assembly. . . .

Source: South African Ministry of Home Affairs. Available online. URL: http://home-affairs.pwv.gov.za/speeches.asp?id=157. Accessed November 17, 2006.

MEXICO

Constitution of Mexico 1917 (excerpts)

In 2006 this document, and the country's immigration-related policies it contained, remained in effect. Items specific to foreigners in the country include Chapter I, Article 11, which grants all persons the right to enter and leave the country; Article 16, which allows for citizen's arrests; and Article 27, which prohibits ownership of land by foreigners. Articles in Chapter II define Mexican citizenship and naturalization of foreigners, employment of foreigners, and banning foreigners from military service. Chapter III defines foreigners.

Chapter I

Individual Guarantees

Article 1. Every person in the United Mexican States shall enjoy the guarantees granted by this Constitution, which cannot be restricted or suspended except in such cases and under such conditions as are herein provided

Article 2. Slavery is forbidden in the United Mexican States. Slaves who enter national territory from abroad shall, by this act alone, recover their freedom and enjoy the protection afforded by the laws.

Article 3.(1) The education imparted by the Federal State shall be designed to develop harmoniously all the faculties of the human being and shall foster in him at the same time a love of country and a consciousness of international solidarity, in independence and justice. . . .

Article 4. No person can be prevented from engaging in the profession, industrial or commercial pursuit, or occupation of his choice, provided it is lawful. The exercise of this liberty shall only be forbidden by judicial order when the rights of third parties are infringed, or by administrative order, issued in the manner provided by law, when the rights of society are violated. No one may be deprived of the fruits of his labor except by judicial decision. The law in each state shall determine the professions which may be practiced only with a degree, and set forth the requirements for obtaining it and the authorities empowered to issue it. . . .

Article 11. Everyone has the right to enter and leave the Republic, to travel through its territory and to change his residence without necessity of a letter of security, passport, safe-conduct or any other similar requirement. The exercise of this right shall be subordinated to the powers of the judiciary, in cases of civil or criminal liability, and to those of the administrative authorities insofar as concerns the limitations imposed by the laws regarding emigration, immigration and public health of the country, or in regard to undesirable aliens resident in the country. . . .

Article 16. No one shall be molested in his person, family, domicile, papers, or possessions except by virtue of a written order of the competent authority stating the legal grounds and justification for the action taken. No order of arrest or detention shall be issued against any person other than by the competent judicial authority, and unless same is preceded by a charge, accusation, or complaint for a credible party or by other evidence indicating the probable guilt of the accused; in cases of *flagrante delicto,* any person may arrest the offender and his accomplices, turning them over without delay to the nearest authorities. Only in urgent cases instituted by the public attorney without previous complaint or indictment and when there is no judicial authority available, may the administrative authorities, on their strictest accountability, order the detention of an accused person, turning him over immediately to the judicial authorities. Every search warrant, which can be issued only by judicial authority and which must be in writing, shall specify the place to be searched, the person or persons to be arrested, and the objects sought, the proceedings to be limited thereto; at the conclusion of which a detailed statement shall be drawn up in the presence of two witnesses proposed by the occupant of the place searched, or by the official making the search in his absence or should he refuse to do so.

Administrative officials may enter private homes for the sole purpose of ascertaining whether the sanitary and police regulations have been complied with; and may demand to be shown the books and documents required to prove compliance with fiscal rulings, in which latter cases they must abide by the provisions of the respective laws and be subject to the formalities prescribed for cases of search. . . .

Article 27. Ownership of the lands and waters within the boundaries of the national territory is vested originally in the Nation, which has had, and has, the right to transmit title thereof to private persons, thereby constituting private property. . . . Legal capacity to acquire ownership of lands and waters of the Nation shall be governed by the following provisions:

I Only Mexicans by birth or naturalization and Mexican companies have the right to acquire ownership of lands, waters, and their appurtenances, or to obtain concessions for the exploitation of mines or of waters. The State may grant the same right to foreigners, provided they agree before the Ministry of Foreign Relations to consider themselves as nationals in respect to such property, and bind themselves not to invoke the protection of their governments in matters relating thereto; under penalty, in case of noncompliance with this agreement, of forfeiture of the property acquired to the Nation. Under no circumstances may foreigners acquire direct ownership of lands or waters within a zone of one hundred kilometers along the frontiers and of fifty kilometers along the shores of the country. . . .

Chapter II

Mexicans

Article 30. Mexican nationality is acquired by birth or by naturalization:

A Mexicans by birth are:

I Those born in the territory of the Republic, regardless of the nationality of their parents:

II Those born in a foreign country of Mexican parents; of a Mexican father and a foreign mother; or of a Mexican mother and an unknown father;

III Those born on Mexican vessels or airships, either war or merchant vessels.

B Mexicans by naturalization are:

I Foreigners who obtain letters of naturalization from the Secretariat of Foreign Relations;

II A foreign woman who marries a Mexican man and has or establishes her domicile within the national territory.

Article 31. The obligations of Mexicans are:

I To see that their children or wards, under fifteen years of age, attend public or private schools to obtain primary, elementary and military education during the time prescribed by the Law on Public Education in each State.

II To be present on the days and hours designated by the Ayuntamiento of the place in which they reside, to receive civic and military instruction which will equip them for the exercise of their rights as citizens, give them skill in the handling of arms, and acquaint them with military discipline.

III To enlist and serve in the National Guard, according to the respective organic law, to secure and defend the independence, the territory, the honor, the rights and interests of the homeland, as well as domestic tranquility and order.

IV To contribute to the public expenditures of the Federation, and the State and Municipality in which they reside, in the proportional and equitable manner provided by law.

Article 32. (14)Mexicans shall have priority over foreigners under equality of circumstances for all classes of concessions and for all employment, positions, or commissions of the Government in which the status of citizenship is not indispensable. In time of peace no foreigner can serve in the Army nor in the police or public security forces.

In order to belong to the National Navy or the Air Force, and to discharge any office or commission, it is required to be a Mexican by birth. This same status is indispensable for captains, pilots, masters, engineers, mechanics, and in general, for all personnel of the crew of any vessel or airship protected by the Mexican merchant flag or insignia. It is also necessary to be Mexican by birth to discharge the position of captain of the port and all services of pratique and airport commandant, as well as all functions of customs agent in the Republic.

Chapter III

Foreigners

Article 33. Foreigners are those who do not possess the qualifications set forth in Article 30. They are entitled to the guarantees granted by Chapter I, Title I, of the present Constitution; but the Federal Executive shall have the exclusive power to compel any foreigner whose remaining he may deem inexpedient to abandon the national territory immediately and without the necessity of previous legal action.

Foreigners may not in any way participate in the political affairs of the country.

Article 37.

A Mexican nationality is lost:

I By the voluntary acquisition of a foreign nationality;

II By accepting or using titles of nobility which imply submission to a foreign state;

III By residing, if a Mexican by naturalization, for five consecutive years in the country of origin;

IV By passing in any public instrument, when Mexican by naturalization, as a foreigner, or by obtaining and using a foreign passport;

B Mexican citizenship is lost:

I By accepting or using titles of nobility which imply submission to a foreign government;

II By rendering voluntary services to a foreign government without permission of the Federal Congress or of its Permanent Committee;

III By accepting or using foreign decorations without permission of the Federal Congress or of its Permanent Committee;

IV By accepting titles or functions from the government of another country without previous permission of the Federal Congress or its Permanent Committee, excepting literary, scientific, or humanitarian titles which may be freely accepted;

V By aiding a foreigner or a foreign country, against the Nation, in any diplomatic claim or before an international tribunal;

VI In other cases which the laws may specify.

Source: Illinois State University. Available online. URL: http://www.ilstu.edu/class/hist263/docs/1917const.html #TitleI. Accessed November 25, 2006.

General Law of Population (translated excerpts)

This law, adopted in 1947 to encourage population growth, is the foundation of all Mexican immigration legislation. The law was revised in 1974 to recognize the impact of the country's rapidly expanding population—which grew from 20 million in 1940 to 48 million in 1970. It defines categories of immigrants, specifies foreigners who may enter and their allowable activities while in the country, and establishes the National Immigration Institute of Mexico as the federal department that oversees immigration-related matters. Capitulates 4 and 5 of the law establish policies related to emigration and repatriation of Mexican nationals.

CAPITULATE I

OBJECT AND ATTRIBUTIONS

The dispositions of this Law are of public order and general observance in the Republic. Its object is to regulate the phenomena that affect the population as far as volume, structures, dynamics and distribution in the national territory, with the purpose of obtaining the benefits of economic and social development.

CAPITULATE II

MIGRATION

Article 7: [regarding] the subjects of migratory order, the Secretary of the Interior [is charged]:

To organize and to coordinate the different migratory services;

To watch the entrance and exit of national[s] and foreigners, and to review the documentation of such;

To apply this Law and its Regulations and the other faculties that confer this Law and its Regulations as well as other legal or prescribed dispositions to him.

Article 11: International transit of people by ports, airports and borders will only be able to occur at the places designated for it and within established schedules, with the intervention of the migratory authorities.

Article 13: Nationals and foreigners who enter or leave the country [must abide by] the requirements hereby demanded and applicable by the Law, its Regulations and other dispositions.

Article 15: Mexicans who enter the country will verify their nationality, will [undergo a] medical examination when it is considered necessary, and will provide the statistical intelligence data that are required. In the case of [the entering national] having a contagious [disease], authorities of Migration will expedite [procedures] for the national to be taken care of in a place that the sanitary authorities determine.

Article 16: The Service of Migration has the priority, with the exception of the one of health, to inspect the entrance or exit of people, national or foreign, [through] the coasts, ports, borders and airports of the Republic.

Article 22: No passenger or crew member of marine transport will be able to disembark before the authorities of Migration carry out the corresponding inspection.

Article 23: The foreign crew of aerial, terrestrial or marine transport will only be able to remain in national territory the authorized time.

Article 24: The pilots of air transports, ship captains and drivers of motor transport will have to present/display to the authorities of Migration for inspection at the time of entrance or exit the necessary list of passengers and crew as well as all data for their identification.

Article 26: Foreigners in transit who disembark with authorization of the Service of Migration in some home port, but remain [in the Republic] without legal authorization after the departure of the ship or airship in which they arrived will have to appear immediately to the Office of Migration. In this case, the office will take appropriate measures for the immediate exit [of said foreigner].

CAPITULATE III

IMMIGRATION

Article 32: The Secretary of the Interior will fix the number of foreigners who will be allowed in the country, [based upon previous] corresponding demographic studies, named activities [or purposes for entering], zones of residence and possible contributions to national progress.

Article 33: In accordance with Article 32, preferred permission [to enter the country] will be granted to scientists, technicians or foreigners dedicated to the investigation or education of covered disciplines that are not sufficiently covered by Mexican [nationals].

Article 35: Foreigners who undergo political persecutions or those that flee from their country of origin will be admitted provisionally by the authorities of Migration while the Secretary of the Interior [reviews] each case in the most expeditious way.

Article 36: The Secretary of the Interior will take measures necessary to facilitate the assimilation in Mexico of foreign investigators [or educators of covered disciplines], scientists and technicians.

Article 37: The Secretary of the Interior will be able to deny entrance to the country by any foreigner for the following reasons:

International reciprocity does not exist

It [upsets] the national demographic balance

They do not [fit within stated] quotas in Article 32

It is considered harmful for the economic interests of the nationals

They have [broken] national laws or have [criminal records] abroad

They have [broken] this Law

They are mentally or physically unhealthy in the opinion of the sanitary authority.

Article 38: It is the [role] of the Secretary of the Interior to suspend or prohibit the admission of foreigners if it is determined to be in the national interest.

Article 39: The Secretary of the Interior will be able to authorize legal permanent residence to foreigners married to Mexican nationals or whom have children born in the country. If the marriage is dissolved, the foreign spouse may have [his/her] migratory status canceled and be required to leave the country, [unless] the Secretary of the Interior authorizes a new migratory status.

Article 40: Mexican nationals who have lost their citizenship will have to fulfill the [requirements] established by the Law for foreigners to enter or continue to reside in the country.

Article 41: Foreigners will be able to enter the country legally either as: Nonimmigrant or Immigrant.

Article 42: Nonimmigrant is the foreigner who, with permission of the Secretary of the Interior, enters the country temporarily with any of the following characteristics:

Tourist. [A person entering the country for] recreational; health; artistic, cultural or sports activities, not for financial gain, for a maximum period of six months.

Transmigrant. [A person entering the country] in transit to another country will be able to remain in national territory for thirty days.

Visitor. [A person entering the country] in order to dedicate himself to the exercise of some activity, [whether or not for financial gain], with authorization may remain in the country for one year.

Minister. In order to practice the ministry with the aims of the religious association to which [he/she] belongs, permission will be granted to remain one year with up to four temporary renewals with multiple entrances and exits.

Refugee. [A person who enters the country] in order to protect [his/her] life, security or freedom when they have been threatened by generalized violence, foreign aggression, internal conflicts, massive violation of human rights or other circumstances that have seriously disturbed the public order in their country of origin that has forced them to flee to another country. The refugee will lose migratory [status] to remain legally in the country if [he/she] breaks national law.

Student. [A person who enters the country] in order to begin, finish or perfect studies in official institutions or educational establishments. They may remain in the country only for the period of time studies last and that is necessary to obtain a final scholastic document.

Distinguished Visitor. In special cases courtesy permissions [to enter and reside in the country for up to six months] will be granted to investigators, scientists, or humanists of international prestige, journalists or other prominent people.

Local Visitor. Foreigners [visiting the country's] seaports or border cities for a period not to exceed three days.

Provisional Visitor. Foreigners who arrive at seaports or airports but whose documentation may lack some secondary requirements may be authorized to remain in the country for up to 30 days.

Correspondent. Professional journalists who enter the country temporarily to cover a special event.

Article 44: Immigrant is the foreigner who legally enters the country to establish permanent residence.

Article 48: The characteristics of an Immigrant are:

Renista. Person [who enters the country for permanent residence] and plans to live on [personal] resources [that include income from] capital in certificates, titles and treasury bills or other [generated] from national institutes outside of the country. The Secretary of the Interior also will be able to authorize renistas to serve as professors, scientific or technical scientists and investigators when it is considered to be beneficial to the country.

Investors. Person [who enters the country] in order to invest capital in industry, commerce and services in accordance with national laws, and that contribute to the economic and social development of the country.

Office of Trust. Person [who enters the country] in order to assume the position of unique administrator or other positions in companies or institutions established in the Republic.

Scientist. Person [who enters the country] in order to direct or make scientific research, to spread scientific knowledge, to prepare investigations or educational works, when these activities are made in the interest of national development.

Technician. Person [who enters the country] in order to perform technical or specialized functions that cannot be performed, in the opinion of the Secretary of the Interior, by residents in the country.

Relatives. Person [who enters the country] to live as an economic dependent of a spouse or a blood relative, immigrant, or Mexican [national].

Artists and Sportsmen. Person [who enters the county] in order to [pursue] artistic activities or sports, whenever the Secretary of the Interior determines the activities are beneficial for the country.

Assimilated. Person [who enters the country] in order to perform any allowed or honest activity and who has or has had a Mexican spouse or son and who is not included in other categories in the terms of the established Regulations.

Article 53: Immigrants with legal residence in the country [for a period of] five years, who have observed this Law and its Regulations and whose activities have been positive and honest for the community will be able to acquire the migratory quality of immigrant.

CAPITULATE IV

EMIGRATION

Article 77: Mexicans who leave the country in order to reside abroad are emigrants and foreigners.

CAPITULATE V

REPATRIATION

Article 81: Mexicans who return to the country to reside after at least two years abroad are considered repatriated national emigrants.

Article 82: The Secretary of the Interior will [encourage] repatriation of Mexicans and will promote their establishment in places where they can be useful [based on] their knowledge and capacity.

Source: Migración Internacional. An English version of the document is available online. URL: http://translate.google.com/translate?hl=en&sl=es&u=http://www.migracioninternacional.com/docum/leypob.html&sa=X&oi=translate&resnum=1&ct=result&prev=/search%3Fq%3Dley%2Bgeneral%2Bde%2Bpoblacion%26 hl%3Den%26lr%3D%26client%3Dsafari%26rls%3Den. Accessed November 25, 2006.

PHILIPPINES

Immigration Act of 1940 (August 26, 1940) (excerpts)

Also known as Commonwealth Act No. 613, this document remained in effect in 2006 and is the foundation of all Philippine immigration laws. It lists two categories of immigrants and establishes immigrant quotas based on the diplomatic ties the Philippines has with sending countries.

BUREAU OF IMMIGRATION

IMMIGRANT INSPECTORS

Sec. 5. (a) The position of Immigrant Inspector is created, appointments to which shall be made upon the recommendation of the Commissioner of Immigration in accordance with the Civil Service Laws.

(b) Whenever he shall deem it necessary, the Commissioner of Immigration may appoint, with the consent of the proper Department Head, any qualified employee of the Government to serve as Acting Immigrant Inspector. Acting Immigrant Inspectors shall have the same powers and authority as Immigrant Inspectors.

Sec. 6. *Powers of Immigration Officer.* - The examination of aliens concerning their right to enter or remain in the Philippines shall be performed by Immigrant Inspectors with the advice of medical authorities in appropriate cases. Immigrant Inspectors are authorized to exclude any alien not properly documented as required by this Act, admit any alien complying with the applicable provisions of the immigration laws and to enforce the immigration laws and regulations prescribed thereunder.... Immigrant Inspectors shall have the power to arrest, without warrant, any alien who in their presence or view is entering or is still in the course of entering the Philippines in violation of immigration laws or regulations prescribed thereunder.

DOCUMENTATION OF NONIMMIGRANTS

Sec. 10. *Presentation of unexpired passport.* - Nonimmigrants must present for admission into the Philippines unexpired passports or official documents in the nature of passports issued by the governments of the countries to which they owe allegiance or other travel documents showing their origin and identity as prescribed by regulations, and valid passport visas granted by diplomatic or consular officers, except that such documents shall not be required of the following aliens:

(a) A child qualifying as a nonimmigrant, born subsequent to the issuance of the passport visa of an accompanying parent, the visa not having expired; and

(b) A seaman qualifying as such under Section 9 (c) of this Act.

IMMIGRANTS

Sec. 13. Under the conditions set forth in this Act, there may be admitted into the Philippines immigrants, termed *"quota immigrants"* not in excess of fifty (50) of any one nationality or without nationality for any one calendar year, except that the following immigrants, termed *"non-quota immigrants,"* may be admitted without regard to such numerical limitations.

(a) The wife or the husband or the unmarried child under twenty-one years of age of a Philippine citizen, if accompanying or following to join such citizen;

(b) A child of alien parents born during the temporary visit abroad of the mother, the mother having been previously lawfully admitted into the Philippines for permanent residence, if the child is accompanying or coming to join a parent and applies for admission within five years from the date of its birth;

(c) A child born subsequent to the issuance of the immigration visa of the accompanying parent, the visa not having expired;

(d) A woman who was a citizen of the Philippines and who lost her citizenship because of her marriage to an alien or by reason of the loss of Philippine citizenship by her husband, and her unmarried child under twenty-one years of age, if accompanying or following to join her;

(e) A person previously lawfully admitted into the Philippines for permanent residence, who is returning from a temporary visit abroad to an unrelinquished residence in the Philippines;

(g) A natural-born citizen of the Philippines, who has been naturalized in a foreign country, and is returning to the Philippines for permanent residence, including his spouse and minor unmarried children, shall be considered a non-quota immigrant for purposes of entering the Philippines.

DOCUMENTATION OF IMMIGRANTS

Sec. 15. *Presentation of unexpired passport; in the case of the children.* -Immigrants must present for admission into the Philippines unexpired passports or official documents in the nature of passports issued by the governments of the countries to which they owe allegiance or other travel documents showing their origin and identity as prescribed by regulations, and valid immigration visas issued by consular officers, except that children born subsequent to the issuance of the immigration visa or a reentry permit in case of children born abroad during the temporary visit abroad of their mothers. . . . No child shall, however, be exempt from these documentary requirements unless the alleged mother shall have proved her state of pregnancy before the consular officers in the case of children born subsequent to the issuance of a valid immigration visa, or before the immigration authority prior to her departure from the Philippines in the case of children born abroad of mothers with valid reentry permits: *Provided, however,* That in the latter case should the mother become pregnant after her departure from the Philippines the fact of her pregnancy shall be proved before the consul officers who shall issue the appropriate certification for presentation to the immigration authorities upon her return to the Philippines.

IMMIGRATION VISAS FOR QUOTA IMMIGRANTS

Sec. 18. An immigration visa shall not be issued by a consular officer to an immigrant whose admission into the Philippines is subject to the numerical limitations imposed by Section Thirteen of this Act until the consular officer shall have received from the Commissioner of Immigration the allotment of a quota number to be placed upon the visa for the immigrant.

Sec. 19. *Preference in allotment of quota numbers.* - In allotting quota numbers, the Commissioner of immigration shall accord preference to immigrants who are the fathers and mothers of Philippine citizens who are twenty-one years of age or over, and the wives, husbands, and unmarried children under of twenty-one years of age, of aliens lawfully admitted into the Philippines for permanent residence and residing therein. Such preference shall be accorded only upon petition made therefor under regulations prescribed by the Commissioner.

IMMIGRATION VISAS FOR NON-QUOTA IMMIGRANTS

Sec. 20. *In case of prearranged employment.* - (a) A passport visa for a non-immigrant referred to in Section Nine (g) of this Act who is coming to pre-arranged employment shall not be issued by a consular officer until the consular officer shall have received authorization for the issuance of the visa. . . . The petition shall state fully the nature of the labor or service for which the nonimmigrant is desired, the probable length of time for which he is to be engaged, the wages and other compensation which he is to receive, the reasons why a person in the Philippines cannot be engaged to perform the labor or service for which the nonimmigrant is desired and why the nonimmigrant's admission would be beneficial to the public interest.

Sec. 21. Non-quota immigration visas may be issued by the consular officers to other immigrants claiming non-quota status upon the receipt of satisfactory proof that they are entitled to such status.

REENTRY PERMITS

Sec. 22. *Filing of application; issuance of permit.* - Any lawful resident alien about to depart temporarily from the Philippines who desires a reentry permit may apply to the Commissioner of Immigration for such permit. If the Commissioner finds that the applicant has been lawfully admitted into the Philippines for permanent residence, he shall issue the permit which shall be valid for a period not exceeding one year except that upon application for extension and good cause therefor being shown by the applicant, it may be extended by the Commissioner for additional periods not exceeding one year each. . . .

EMIGRATION CLEARANCE CERTIFICATE

Sec. 22-A. *Issuance of certificate.* Any alien about to depart from the Philippines temporarily or for permanent residence abroad shall, before leaving the country, apply to the Commissioner of Immigration for a clearance certificate. If the Commissioner finds that the applicant has no pending obligation with the Government, its instrumentalities, agencies and subdivisions, and that there is no pending, criminal, civil or administrative action which, by law requires his presence, in the Philippines, the Commissioner shall issue the certificate upon surrender of the alien or all other certificates previously issued to him by the Bureau of Immigration showing his admission and/or residence in the Philippines.

DETENTION OF ARRIVING ALIENS

Sec. 25. *Period of detention of aliens.* - For the purpose of determining whether aliens arriving in the Philippines belong to any of the classes excluded by the immigration laws, the Period examining immigration officers may order such aliens detained on board the vessel bringing them or in such other place as the officers may designate, such detention to be for a sufficient length of time to enable the officers to determine whether they belong to an excluded class and their removal to such other place to be at the expense of the vessel bringing them.

MEDICAL EXAMINATION OF ARRIVING ALIENS

Sec. 28. *Designation of examining team.* - The physical and mental examination of arriving aliens shall be made by medical officers of the Government designated under order of the President to make such examinations, who shall certify for the information of the immigration officers and the boards of special inquiry any and all physical and mental defects or disease observed after an examination by them of such aliens. Should such medical officers be not available, private physicians may be employed for examining arriving aliens, the necessary expenses therefor to be chargeable against the appropriation provided for the Bureau of Immigration.

EXCLUDED CLASSES

Sec. 29. (a) The following classes of aliens shall be excluded from entry into the Philippines:

(1) Idiots or insane persons and persons who have been insane;

(2) Persons afflicted with a loathsome or dangerous contagious disease, or epilepsy:

(3) Persons who have been convicted of a crime involving moral turpitude;

(4) Prostitutes, or procurers, or persons coming for any immoral purposes;

(5) Persons likely to become, public charge;

(6) Paupers, vagrants, and beggars;

(7) Persons who practice polygamy or who believe in or advocate the practice of polygamy;

(8) Persons who believe in or advocate the overthrow by force and violence of the Government of the Philippines, or of constituted lawful authority, or who disbelieve in or are opposed to organized government, or who advocate the assault or assassination of public officials because of their office, or who advocate or teach principles, theories, or ideas contrary to the Constitution of the Philippines or advocate or teach the unlawful destruction of property, or who are members of or affiliated with any organization entertaining or teaching such doctrines;

(9) Persons over fifteen years of age, physically capable of reading, who cannot read printed matter in ordinary use in any language selected by the alien, but this provision shall not apply to the grandfather, grandmother, father, mother, wife, husband or child of a Philippine citizen or of an alien lawfully resident in the Philippines;

(10) Persons who are members of a family accompanying an excluded alien, unless in the opinion of the Commissioner of Immigration no hardship would result from their admission;

(11) Persons accompanying an excluded person who is helpless from mental or physical disability or infancy, when the protection or guardianship of such accompanying person or persons is required by the excluded person . . . ;

(12) Children under fifteen years of age, unaccompanied by or not coming to a parent, except that any such children may be admitted in the discretion of the Commissioner of Immigration, if otherwise admissible;

(13) Stowaways, except that any stowaway may be admitted in the discretion of the Commissioner of Immigration, if otherwise admissible;

(14) Persons coming to perform unskilled manual labor in pursuance of a promise or offer of employment, express or implied, but this provision shall not apply to persons bearing passport visas authorized by Section Twenty of this Act;

(15) Persons who have been excluded or deported from the Philippines, but this provision may be waived in the discretion of the Commissioner of Immigration. . . .

(16) Persons who have been removed from the Philippines at the expense of the Government of the Philippines, as indigent aliens . . . ; and

(b) Notwithstanding the provisions of this Section, the Commissioner of Immigration, in his discretion, may permit to enter any alien properly documented, who is subject to exclusion under this section, but who is:

(1) An alien lawfully resident in the Philippines who is returning from a temporary visit abroad;

(2) An alien applying for temporary admission.

IMMIGRANT HEAD TAX

Sec. 31. A tax of twenty-five pesos shall be collected for every alien over sixteen years of age admitted into the Philippines for a stay exceeding sixty days. The tax shall be paid to the Immigration Officer. . . .

DEPORTATION OF ALIENS

Sec. 37. (a) The following aliens shall be arrested upon the warrant of the Commissioner of Immigration or of any other officer designated by him for the purpose and deported upon the warrant of the Commissioner of Immigration after a determination by the Board of Commissioners of the existence of the ground for deportation as charged against the alien:

(1) Any alien who enters the Philippines by means of false and misleading statements or without inspection and admission by the immigration authorities at a designated port of entry or at any place other than at a designated port of entry;

(2) Any alien who enters the Philippines who was not lawfully admissible at the time of entry;

(3) Any alien who is convicted in the Philippines and sentenced for a term of one year or more for a crime involving moral turpitude committed within five years after his entry to the Philippines, or who, at any time after such entry, is so convicted and sentenced more than once;

(4) Any alien who is convicted and sentenced for a violation of the law governing prohibited drugs;

(5) Any alien who practices prostitution or is an inmate of a house of prostitution or is connected with the management of a house of prostitution, or is a procurer;

(6) Any alien who becomes a public charge within five years after entry from causes not affirmatively shown to have arisen subsequent to entry;

(7) Any alien who remains in the Philippines in violation of any limitation or condition under which he was admitted as a nonimmigrant;

(8) Any alien who believes in, advises, advocates or teaches the overthrow by force and violence of the Government of the Philippines, or of constituted law and authority, or who disbelieves in or is opposed to organized government or who advises, advocates, or teaches the assault or assassination of public officials because of their office, or who advises, advocates, or teaches the unlawful destruction of property, or who is a member of or affiliated with any organization entertaining, advocating or teaching such doctrines, or who in any manner whatsoever lends assistance, financial or otherwise, to the dissemination of such doctrines;

(11) Any alien who engages in profiteering, hoarding, or black-marketing, independent of any criminal action which may be brought against him;

(13) Any alien who defrauds his creditor by absconding or alienating properties to prevent them from being attached or executed;

REMOVAL OF INDIGENT ALIENS

Sec. 43. The Commissioner of Immigration shall have the authority to remove either to their native country, or to the country from whence they come, or to the country of which they are citizens or subjects, at any time after entry, at the expense of any appropriation available, such aliens as fall into distress or need public aid from causes arising subsequent to their entry and are desirous of being so removed, but any person thus removed shall forever be ineligible for readmission except, upon the authorization of the Board of Commissioners obtained previous to embarkation for the Philippines.

Source: Chan Robles Virtual Law Library. Available online. URL: http://www.chanrobles.com/commonwealthactno613.htm. Accessed November 25, 2006.

Labor Code of the Philippines (1974) (excerpts)

Passage of this bill, known as Presidential Decree No. 442, established the foundation for the Philippines's overseas employment program and further encouraged economic migration by Filipinos.

GENERAL PROVISIONS

Art. 3. Declaration of basic policy. The State shall afford protection to labor, promote full employment, ensure equal work opportunities regardless of sex, race or creed and regulate the relations between workers and employers. The State shall assure the rights of workers to self-organization, collective bargaining, security of tenure, and just and humane conditions of work.

Art. 4. Construction in favor of labor. All doubts in the implementation and interpretation of the provisions of this Code, including its implementing rules and regulations, shall be resolved in favor of labor.

Art. 5. Rules and regulations. The Department of Labor and other government agencies charged with the administration and enforcement of this Code or any of its parts shall promulgate the necessary implementing rules and regulations. Such rules and regulations shall become effective fifteen (15) days after announcement of their adoption in newspapers of general circulation. . . .

Source: Republic of the Philippines Department of Labor and Employment. Available online. URL: http://www.dole.gov.ph/laborcode/. Accessed November 25, 2006.

Migrant Workers and Overseas Filipinos Act (June 7, 1995)

This act, also known as Republic Act No. 8042, further regulated the country's overseas workers by implementing additional policies designed to protect and promote the welfare of "migrant workers, their families, and overseas Filipinos in distress and for other purposes."

Sec. 2. Declaration of Policies.

(a) In the pursuit of an independent foreign policy and while considering national sovereignty, territorial integrity, national interest and the right to self-determination paramount in its relations with other states, the State shall, at all times, uphold the dignity of its citizens whether in country or overseas, in general, and Filipino migrant workers, in particular.

(b) The State shall afford full protection to labor, local and overseas, organized and unorganized, and promote full employment and equality of employment opportunities for all. Towards this end, the State shall provide adequate and timely social, economic and legal services to Filipino migrant workers.

(c) While recognizing the significant contribution of Filipino migrant workers to the national economy through their foreign exchange remittances, the State does not promote overseas employment as a means to sustain economic growth and achieve national development. The existence of the overseas employment program rests solely on the assurance that the dignity and fundamental human rights and freedoms of the Filipino citizen shall not, at any time, be compromised or violated. The State, therefore, shall continuously create local employment opportunities and promote the equitable distribution of wealth and the benefits of development.

(d) The State affirms the fundamental equality before the law of women and men and the significant role of women in nation-building. Recognizing the contribution of overseas migrant women workers and their particular vulnerabilities, the State shall apply gender sensitive criteria in the formulation and implementation of policies and programs affecting migrant workers and the composition of bodies tasked for the welfare of migrant workers.

(e) Free access to the courts and quasi-judicial bodies and adequate legal assistance shall not be denied to any person by reason of poverty. In this regard, it is imperative that an effective mechanism be instituted to ensure that the rights and interest of distressed overseas Filipinos, in general, and Filipino migrant workers, in particular, documented or undocumented, are adequately protected and safeguarded.

(f) The right of Filipino migrant workers and all overseas Filipinos to participate in the democratic decision-making processes of the State and to be represented in institutions relevant to overseas employment is recognized and guaranteed.

(g) The State recognizes that the ultimate protection to all migrant workers is the possession of skills. Pursuant to this and as soon as practicable, the government shall deploy and/or allow the deployment only of skilled Filipino workers.

(h) Non-governmental organizations, duly recognized as legitimate, are partners of the State in the protection of Filipino migrant workers and in the promotion of their welfare. The State shall cooperate with them in a spirit of trust and mutual respect.

(i) Government fees and other administrative costs of recruitment, introduction, placement and assistance to migrant workers shall be rendered free without prejudice to the provision of Sec. 36 hereof.

Nonetheless, the deployment of Filipino overseas workers, whether land-based or sea-based, by local service contractors and manning agencies employing them shall be encouraged. Appropriate incentives may be extended to them. . . .

I. DEPLOYMENT

Sec. 4. *Deployment of Migrant Workers.* - The State shall deploy overseas Filipino workers only in countries where the rights of Filipino migrant workers are protected. The government recognizes any of the following as a guarantee on the part of the receiving country for the protection and the rights of overseas Filipino workers:

(a) It has existing labor and social laws protecting the rights of migrant workers;

(b) It is a signatory to multilateral conventions, declarations or resolutions relating to the protection of migrant workers;

(c) It has concluded a bilateral agreement or arrangement with the government protecting the rights of overseas Filipino workers; and

(d) It is taking positive, concrete measures to protect the rights of migrant workers.

Sec. 5. *Termination or Ban on Deployment.* - Notwithstanding the provisions of Sec. 4 hereof, the government, in pursuit of the national interest or when public welfare so requires, may, at any time, terminate or impose a ban on the deployment of migrant workers.

II. ILLEGAL RECRUITMENT

Sec. 6. *Definition.* - For purposes of this Act, illegal recruitment shall mean any act of canvassing, enlisting, contracting, transporting, utilizing, hiring, or procuring workers and includes referring, contract services, promising or advertising for employment abroad, whether for profit or not, when undertaken by a non-licensee or non-holder of authority . . . any such non-licensee or non-holder who, in any manner, offers or promises for a fee employment abroad to two or more persons shall be deemed so engaged. It shall likewise include the following acts, whether committed by any person, whether a non-licensee, non-holder, licensee or holder of authority:

(a) To charge or accept directly or indirectly any amount greater than that specified in the schedule of allowable fees prescribed by the Secretary of Labor and Employment, or to make a worker pay any amount greater than that actually received by him as a loan or advance;

(b) To furnish or publish any false notice or information or document in relation to recruitment or employment;

(c) To give any false notice, testimony, information or document or commit any act of misrepresentation for the purpose of securing a license or authority under the Labor Code;

(d) To induce or attempt to induce a worker already employed to quit his employment in order to offer him another unless the transfer is designed to liberate a worker from oppressive terms and conditions of employment;

(e) To influence or attempt to influence any person or entity not to employ any worker who has not applied for employment through his agency;

(f) To engage in the recruitment or placement of workers in jobs harmful to public health or morality or to the dignity of the Republic of the Philippines;

(g) To obstruct or attempt to obstruct inspection by the Secretary of Labor and Employment or by his duly authorized representative;

(h) To fail to submit reports on the status of employment, placement vacancies, remittance of foreign exchange earnings, separation from jobs, departures and such other matters or information as may be required by the Secretary of Labor and Employment;

(i) To substitute or alter to the prejudice of the worker, employment contracts approved and verified by the Department of Labor and Employment from the time of actual signing thereof by the parties up to and including the period of the expiration of the same without the approval of the Department of Labor and Employment;

(j) For an officer or agent of a recruitment or placement agency to become an officer or member of the Board of any corporation engaged in travel agency or to be engaged directly or indirectly in the management of a travel agency;

(k) To withhold or deny travel documents from applicant workers before departure for monetary or financial considerations other than those authorized under the Labor Code and its implementing rules and regulations;

(l) Failure to actually deploy without valid reason as determined by the Department of Labor and Employment; and

(m) Failure to reimburse expenses incurred by the worker in connection with his documentation and processing for purposes of deployment, in cases where the deployment does not actually take place without the worker's fault. Illegal recruitment when committed by a syndicate or in large scale shall be considered an offense involving economic sabotage.

Illegal recruitment is deemed committed by a syndicate if carried out by a group of three (3) or more persons conspiring or confederating with one another. It is deemed committed in large scale if committed against three (3) or more persons individually or as a group. . . .

Sec. 7. *Penalties.* -

(a) Any person found guilty of illegal recruitment shall suffer the penalty of imprisonment of not less than six (6) years and one (1) day but not more than twelve (12) years and a fine of not less than Two hundred thousand pesos (P200,000.00) nor more than Five hundred thousand pesos (P500,000.00).

(b) The penalty of life imprisonment and a fine of not less than Five hundred thousand pesos (P500,000.00) nor more than One million pesos (P1,000,000.00) shall be imposed if illegal recruitment constitutes economic sabotage as defined herein.

Sec. 8. *Prohibition on Officials and Employees.* - It shall be unlawful for any official or employee of the Department of Labor and Employment, the Philippine Overseas Employment Administration (POEA), or the Overseas Workers Welfare Administration (OWWA), or the Department of Foreign Affairs, or other government agencies involved in the implementation of this Act, or their relatives within the fourth civil degree of consanguinity or affinity, to engage, directly or indirectly in the business of recruiting migrant workers as defined in this Act. The penalties provided in the immediate preceding paragraph shall be imposed upon them.

Such liabilities shall continue during the entire period or duration of the employment contract and shall not be affected by any substitution, amendment or modification made locally or in a foreign country of the said contract.

* *** *

Sec. 13. *Free Legal Assistance; Preferential Entitlement Under the Witness Protection Program.* - A mechanism for free legal assistance for victims of illegal recruitment shall be established within the Department of Labor and Employment including its regional offices. Such mechanism must include coordination and cooperation with the Department of Justice, the Integrated Bar of the Philippines, and other non-governmental organizations and volunteer groups.

III. SERVICES

Sec. 14. *Travel Advisory/Information Dissemination.* - To give utmost priority to the establishment of programs and services to prevent illegal recruitment, fraud and exploitation or abuse of Filipino migrant workers, all embassies and consular offices, through the Philippine Overseas Employment Administration (POEA), shall issue travel advisories or disseminate information on labor and employment conditions, migration realities and other facts; and adherence of particular countries to international standards on human and workers' rights which will adequately prepare individuals into making informed and intelligent decisions about overseas employment. Such advisory or information shall be published in a newspaper of general circulation at least three (3) times in every quarter.

Sec. 15. *Repatriation of Workers; Emergency Repatriation Fund.* - The repatriation of the worker and the transport of his personal belongings shall be the primary responsibility of the agency which recruited or deployed the worker overseas. All costs attendant to repatriation shall be borne by or charged to the agency concerned and/or its principal. Likewise, the repatriation of remains and transport of the personal belongings of a deceased worker and all costs attendant thereto shall be borne by the principal and/or the local agency. However, in cases where the termination of employment in due solely to the fault of the worker, the principal/employer or agency shall not in any manner be responsible for the repatriation of the former and/or his belongings.

The Overseas Workers Welfare Administration (OWWA), in coordination with appropriate international agencies, shall undertake the repatriation of workers in cases of war, epidemic, disaster or calamities, natural or man-made, and other similar events without prejudice to reimbursement by the responsible principal or agency. However, in cases where the principal or recruitment agency cannot be identified, all costs attendant to repatriation shall be borne by the OWWA....

Sec. 16. *Mandatory Repatriation of Underage Migrant Workers.* - Upon discovery or being informed of the presence of migrant workers whose actual ages fall below the minimum age requirement for overseas deployment, the responsible officers in the foreign service shall without delay repatriate said workers and advise the Department of Foreign Affairs through the fastest means of communication available of such discovery and other relevant information.

* *** *

Sec. 18. *Functions of the Re-placement and Monitoring Center.* - The Center shall provide the following services:

(a) Develop livelihood programs and projects for returning Filipino migrant workers in coordination with the private sector;

(b) Coordinate with appropriate private and government agencies in the promotion, development, re-placement and the full utilization of their potentials;

(c) Institute, in cooperation with other government agencies concerned, a computer-based information system on skilled Filipino migrant workers which shall be accessible to all local recruitment agencies and employers, both public and private;

(d) Provide a periodic study and assessment of job opportunities for returning Filipino migrant workers; and

(e) Develop and implement other appropriate programs to promote the welfare of returning Filipino migrant workers.

Sec. 19. *Establishment of a Migrant Workers and other Overseas Filipinos Resource Center.* - Within the premises and under the administrative jurisdiction of the Philippine Embassy in countries where there are large concentrations of Filipino migrant workers, there shall be established a Migrant Workers and Other Overseas Filipinos Resource Center with the following services:

(a) Counselling and legal services;

(b) Welfare assistance including the procurement of medical and hospitalization services;

(c) Information, advisory and programs to promote social integration such as post-arrival orientation, settlement and community networking services and activities for social interaction;

(d) Institute a scheme of registration of undocumented workers to bring them within the purview of this Act. For this purpose, the Center is enjoined to compel existing undocumented workers to registered [sic] with it within six (6) months from the effectivity of this Act, under pain of having his/her passport cancelled;

(e) Human resource development, such as training and skills upgrading;

(f) Gender sensitive program and activities to assist particular needs of women migrant workers;

(g) Orientation program for returning worker and other migrants; and

(h) Monitoring of daily situations, circumstances and activities affecting migrant workers and other overseas Filipinos.

Sec. 20. *Establishment of a Shared Government Information System for Migration.* - An inter-agency committee composed of the Department of Foreign Affairs and its attached agency, the Commission on Filipinos Overseas, the Department of Labor and Employment, the Philippine Overseas Employment Administration, the Overseas Workers Welfare Administration, the Department of Tourism, the Department of Justice, the Bureau of Immigration, the National Bureau of Investigation, and the National Statistics Office shall be established to implement a shared government information system for migration. . . . The inter-agency committee shall convene to identify existing databases which shall be declassified and shared among member agencies. These shared databases shall initially include, but not be limited to, the following information:

(a) Masterlists of Filipino migrant workers/overseas Filipinos classified according to occupation/job category, civil status, by country/state of destination including visa classification;

(b) Inventory of pending legal cases involving Filipino migrant workers and other Filipino nationals, including those serving prison terms;

(c) Masterlist of departing/arriving Filipinos;

(d) Statistical profile on Filipino migrant workers/overseas Filipinos/ tourists;

(e) Blacklisted foreigners/undesirable aliens;

(f) Basic data on legal systems, immigration policies, marriage laws and civil and criminal codes in receiving countries particularly those with large numbers of Filipinos;

(g) List of labor and other human rights instruments where receiving countries are signatories;

(h) A tracking system of past and present gender disaggregated cases involving male and female migrant workers; and

(i) Listing of overseas posts which may render assistance to overseas Filipinos, in general, and migrant workers, in particular.

Sec. 21. *Migrant Workers Loan Guarantee Fund.* - In order to further prevent unscrupulous illegal recruiters from taking advantage of workers seeking employment abroad, the OWWA, in coordination with government financial institutions, shall institute financing schemes that will expand the grant of pre-departure loan and family assistance loan. For this purpose, a Migrant Workers Loan Guarantee Fund is hereby created and the revolving amount of One hundred million pesos (P100,000,000.00) from the OWWA is set aside as a guarantee fund in favor of participating government financial institutions.

Sec. 22. *Rights and Enforcement Mechanism Under International and Regional Human Rights Systems.* - The Department of Foreign Affairs is mandated to undertake the necessary initiative such as promotions, acceptance or adherence of countries receiving Filipino workers to multilateral convention, declaration or resolutions pertaining to the protection of migrant workers' rights. The Department of Foreign Affairs is also mandated to make an assessment of rights and avenues of redress under international and regional human rights systems that are available to Filipino migrant workers who are victims of abuse and violation and, as far as practicable and through the Legal Assistant for Migrant Workers Affairs created under this Act, pursue the same on behalf of the victim if it is legally impossible to file individual complaints. If a complaints machinery is available under international or regional systems, the Department of Foreign Affairs shall fully apprise the Filipino migrant workers of the existence and effectiveness of such legal options.

IV. GOVERNMENT AGENCIES

Sec. 23. *Role of Government Agencies.* - The following government agencies shall perform the following to promote the welfare and protect the rights of migrant workers and, as far as appiicable, all overseas Filipinos:

(b.1) *Philippine Overseas Employment Administration* - Subject to deregulation and phase-out as provided under Sec.s 29 and 30 herein, the Administration shall regulate private sector participation in the recruitment and overseas placement of workers by setting up a licensing and registration system. It shall also formulate and implement, in coordination with appropriate entities concerned, when necessary, a system for promoting and monitoring the overseas employment of Filipino workers taking into consideration their welfare and the domestic manpower requirements.

(b.2) *Overseas Workers Welfare Administration* - The Welfare officer or in his absence, the coordinating officer shall provide the Filipino migrant worker and his family all the assistance they may need in the enforcement of contractual obligations by agencies or entities and/or by their principals. In the performance of this function, he shall make representation and may call on the agencies or entities concerned to conferences or conciliation meetings for the purpose of settling the complaints or problems brought to his attention.

V. THE LEGAL ASSISTANT FOR MIGRANT WORKERS AFFAIRS

Sec. 24. *Legal Assistant for Migrant Workers Affairs.* - There is hereby created the position of Legal Assistant for Migrant Workers Affairs under the Department of Foreign Affairs who shall be primarily responsible for the provision and overall coordination of all legal assistance services to be provided to Filipino migrant workers as well as overseas Filipinos in distress.

Sec. 25. *Legal Assistance Fund.* - There is hereby established a legal assistance fund for migrant workers, hereinafter referred to as the Legal Assistance Fund, in the amount of One hundred million pesos (P100,000,000.00) to be constituted from the following sources:

Fifty million pesos (P50,000,000.00) from the Contingency Fund of the President;

Thirty million pesos (P30,000,000.00) from the Presidential Social Fund; and

Twenty million pesos (P20,000,000.00) from the Welfare Fund for Overseas Workers established under Letter of Instruction No. 537, as amended by Presidential Decrees Nos. 1694 and 1809.

Sec. 26. *Uses of the Legal Assistance Fund.* - The Legal Assistance Fund created under the preceding Sec. shall be used exclusively to provide legal services to migrant workers and overseas Filipinos in distress in accordance with the guidelines, criteria and procedures promulgated in accordance with Sec. 24(a) hereof. The expenditures to be charged against the Fund shall include the fees for the foreign lawyers to be hired by the Legal Assistant for Migrant Workers Affairs to represent migrant workers facing charges abroad, bail bonds to secure the temporary release of workers under detention, court fees and charges and other litigation expenses. . . .

VIII. PROFESSIONAL AND OTHER HIGHLY-SKILLED FILIPINOS ABROAD

Sec. 31. *Incentives to Professionals and Other Highly-Skilled Filipinos Abroad.* - Pursuant to the objective of encouraging professionals and other highly-skilled Filipinos abroad especially in the field of science and technology to participate in, and contribute to national development, the government shall provide proper and adequate incentives and programs so as to secure their services in priority development areas of the public and private sectors.

IX. MISCELLANEOUS PROVISIONS

Sec. 37. *The Congressional Migrant Workers Scholarship Fund.* - There is hereby created a Congressional Migrant Workers Scholarship Fund which shall benefit deserving migrant workers and/or their immediate descendants below twenty-one (21) years of age who intend to pursue courses or training primarily in the field of science and technology. The initial seed fund of Two hundred million pesos (P200,000,000.00) shall be constituted from the following sources:

(a) Fifty million pesos (P50,000,000.00) from the unexpended Countrywide Development Fund for 1995 in equal sharing by all Members of Congress; and

(b) The remaining One hundred fifty million pesos (P150,000,000.00) shall be funded from the proceeds of Lotto draws.

Sec. 39. *Migrant Workers Day.* - The day of signing by the President of this Act shall be designated as the Migrant Workers Day and shall henceforth be commemorated as such annually.

Approved: June 7, 1995

Source: Chan Robles Virtual Law Library. Available online. URL: http://www.chanrobles.com/republicactno8042.htm. Accessed November 25, 2006.

PART III

Research Tools

6

How to Research Immigration and Migration

GETTING STARTED

To research a topic as broad and constantly changing as immigration and migration it is important to first decide what aspect of the subject will be discussed in your paper or presentation. Because the movement of people has been critical to the spreading of populations and the expansion of civilizations, as well as having an impact in all sending and receiving nations, immigration has been monitored, studied, and regulated worldwide for hundreds of years. Since the September 11, 2001, terrorist attacks on the United States, immigration has taken on new significance as nations analyze and update their immigration policies to restrict terrorists who may enter countries as immigrants. Countries, scholars, and governmental and private organizations have researched and published documents, studies, newspaper and journal articles, books and other data about immigration. The result is a vast amount of information covering all areas of the subject available in print and on the Internet. Sorting through the volumes of information is the primary challenge when researching this subject. To speed the process and avoid becoming overwhelmed by a research project about immigration and migration, first take some time to consider the following:

- What area of immigration and migration will be researched? If a student researcher is uncertain about what area to focus on, it may be helpful to do some preliminary research by reading articles in encyclopedias that will provide a general overview of the subject.
- What period of history will the research cover? Because migration dates back to the dawn of history, narrowing down the time frame is critical.

Generally, key events in history have also had an impact on immigration and are helpful when trying to tighten the focus of a research project. Periods of war such as World War I (1914–18), World War II (1939–45), the Vietnam War (1959–75), the war in Iraq (2003–); and other periods of political instability such as apartheid in South Africa (1948–90) and the overthrow of Cuba's government by Fidel Castro (1959) are examples of historical events that have directly impacted immigration and migration. The events of 9/11 had a profound impact on immigration not only in the United States but also worldwide.

- What specific aspect of immigration and migration will be covered? Since there are numerous types of immigration, from prehistoric hunter-gatherer societies to 20th-century refugees, it is helpful to decide in advance what form of immigration will be researched. For example, if the focus is on the broader topic of economic migration in the 21st century, then that topic can be narrowed to Mexicans illegally entering the United States for employment. If the focus is on the broader topic of refugees, then that topic can be narrowed to a specific country and time period, such as black Africans from Mozambique seeking asylum in South Africa during the civil war in their homeland.

The above examples are limited, but they may be helpful for students beginning to research immigration and migration.

COLLECTING INFORMATION

Once the student researcher has narrowed the focus of his or her project on immigration, it is time to decide how much and what types of information are needed. An oral report to the class will require less research and different data from that needed for a lengthy written paper on the topic. Other things that will help determine the types of information gathered include the specific area and time period of immigration being considered. If the area of immigration to be discussed deals with events in the past, such as Irish refugees immigrating to America following Ireland's potato famine (1845–49), historical information will be needed; however, if the topic is more current, such as changing immigration policy in the United States post-9/11, current sources will be needed. Creating a timeline may help determine the best sources of information:

- The Internet will provide information about immediate events;
- Newspapers, weekly news magazines, and the Internet are resources for information about events within the past weeks or months;

- Scholarly journals, magazines, newspaper archives, and reports by related professional organizations can provide information about events that occurred more than several months or longer in the past;
- Encyclopedias, history and other printed books, and similar reference resources can provide information about historical events.

Typically, current immigration-related topics require research that focuses on recent activities while historical topics will require research from the time period specific to the event. For example, a student researching the 2006 protests by Mexican immigrants in the United States will find information in print newspapers and news magazines or in new sources on the Internet. However, a student researching emigration from South Africa during apartheid will need to turn to encyclopedias, scholarly journals, and print books. When researching immigration it is important to remember, regardless of the time period—contemporary or historical—there are different perspectives for specific events. For example, information about Mexican protesters marching in the United States in 2006 is presented from various perspectives, including that of the protesters and their supporters as well as from people who strongly opposed the protests. Information about South African emigration during apartheid is presented from the perspective of South Africa's government, from the perspective of the emigrants, and from the perspective of countries receiving the emigrants.

When gathering information, researchers should remember that many encyclopedias, scholarly journals, newspaper archives, and print books are now available on the Internet. Schools and public libraries also often have online databases available to help student researches such as InfoTrac, Ebscohost, ProquestSIRS, and Opposing Viewpoints.

United States

Students researching immigration in the United States may find valuable information from various U.S. government sources, most available online, including:

- U.S. Border Patrol, http://www.borderpatrol.com. This site contain information about the history of the Border Patrol and current activities of the organization on both the U.S.-Mexico and U.S.-Canada borders.
- The U.S. Census Bureau, http://www.census.gov. This site provides historical statistics about foreigners in the United States as well as foreign-born population profiles and other immigrant-related information.

- U.S. Citizenship and Immigration Services, http://www.uscis.gov. This site includes information about U.S. immigration laws and policies, educational resources, immigration forms, and more.
- U.S. Customs and Border Protection, http://www.cbp.gov. Information available on this site includes fact sheets with information about border security and illegal immigration.
- The U.S. Department of Homeland Security, http://www.dhs.gov. This site provides links to numerous immigration-related government sites, including the Office of Immigration Statistics, the Yearbook of Immigration Statistics, and fact sheets on immigration.
- The National Conference of State Legislators, http://www.ncls.org. Information about state-level activities related to immigration is available on this site.

Researchers searching for information about immigration policies in countries outside of the United States can generally find related documents on the Internet or by contacting the specific country's embassy in the United States.

France

- Embassy of France in the United States, http://www.ambafrance-us.org.
- National Institute for Statistics and Economic Studies, http://www.insee.fr/en/home/home_page.asp. This site includes statistical information and census data about foreigners and immigrant populations in France.

South Africa

- South African Consulate General in New York, http://www.southafrica-newyork.net/. The visa and passports link on this site provides information about South Africa's immigration policies and laws.
- South Africa Government Communication and Information System, http://www.gcis.gov.za. Available on this site is the South African Yearbook, which is searchable online and includes a variety of statistical data related to immigration and migration to the country, and emigration from the country.
- Statistics South Africa, http://www.statssa.gov.za. This government-sponsored site also provides census and statistical data about the country's population, including immigrants, emigrants, refugees, and asylum seekers.

Mexico

- Embassy of Mexico in the United States of America, http://portal.sre.gob.mx/usa. This site focuses on information about the country, including immigration issues. It provides access to various news articles and press releases such as "Mexico and the Migration Phenomenon" and "Law Enforcement and Border Security."
- National Immigration Institute of Mexico, http://www.consulmexny.org/eng/visas_immigration.htm. This is the primary resource for information about immigration in Mexico.

The Philippines

- Embassy of the Republic of the Philippines in Washington, D.C., http://www.philippineembassy-usa.org. This site provides access to press releases, news reports, and updates about immigration- and emigrant-related topics.
- Philippine Bureau of Immigration, http://www.immigration.gov.ph. This is the primary resource for information about immigration to the Philippines. It also provides links to other government sites.

EVALUATING THE RESEARCH

Before sitting down to write the paper or prepare the presentation it is important for student researchers to take time to carefully review the documents and the sources he or she has gathered. While this can often be a challenging task, given the amount of information available about immigration and migration, it is critical to assure the accuracy, reliability, dependability, and trustworthiness of each resource.

Sources

Things to keep in mind when evaluating a document's source should include the person or organization that prepared the material. If the document is produced by a specific country's government, consider other policies at the time that may have influenced the writing or data, such as apartheid in South Africa, or employment and economic conditions in the United States during the Great Depression (1929–41). Documents or material provided by private organizations should also be considered from the perspective of the group's agenda. Questions to be considered include whether the organization is a not-for-profit that provides a broad range of unbiased information; whether the organization is financially supported by other groups or individuals focused on one side of the immigration debate, either pro-immigration or anti-immigration; consider for whom the information is intended. Is it directed at a general audience such as newspaper or magazine articles and does it present a narrow point of view designed to appeal to readers of the publication or does it provide a balanced portrayal of the topic, telling both sides of the story? Or, is the target audience academics or people who may be experts in the field, such as readers of scholarly journals? The information contained in scholarly publications and other academic documents, such as spellings of names, dates, and locations of events, is generally more reliable than information published in the mass media, which may contain inaccuracies due to the rush to meet publication deadlines.

Since almost anyone with a computer and some know-how can create a Web log or post data on the Internet, information gathered using Internet search engines needs special attention to assure it is reliable and accurate. For each document downloaded from the Internet ask the following questions:

- Who is the author? To find out if the author is qualified to write on the subject, look for his or her credentials, which are often posted with the document and check for other related books, articles, or studies the author has published.
- What are the author's sources? In most cases, the sources used to write the article are cited at the end of the document. Review those sources for reliability.
- Why did the author write the document? Was the purpose to sway readers to his or her point of view or is the document intended as an objective presentation of the information; are political or social agendas or unstated biases evident in the work?
- Who sponsored the work? Is the author's article or document officially endorsed by a legitimate organization or institution such as a government agency or a university or is the document on the author's personal page and not reviewed or endorsed by an organization or institution?
- How current is the information? Many Web sites include a "last updated" date. Also check the page to see if it notes how the information listed was gathered and compiled.

If any uncertainty remains after answering the above questions, information gathered from Web sites should be verified with more reliable sources, either print or online.

Publication Dates

When reviewing information, especially for events that are current news, articles should be organized according to the date of publication to assure the final documents used are the most accurate and up to date. Because immigration, especially illegal immigration, has generated so much controversy in recent years, information regarding the topic changes almost as quickly as it is published. For example, it was reported in December 2005 that the U.S. House had passed a measure to toughen immigration laws that included building a fence along the U.S.-Mexico border. In May 2006 it was reported the U.S. Senate had passed a measure that created a guest-worker program and enabled some illegal aliens to achieve legal status. However, at the end of 2006 neither measure had been implemented. The only action related to immigration passed by the federal government was a bill signed into law in October 2006 that authorized construction of a 700-mile-long fence on the U.S.-Mexico border as suggested in the original House bill. The possibility of errors in the mass media as publications rush to be first with the story also makes it wise to compare several news reports on specific topics to seek out discrepancies.

When reviewing sources for historical immigration events, publication dates may provide insight into the writer's perspective or analysis of the topic. For example, information about Arab and Muslim immigrants in the United States before the September 2001 terrorist attacks was dramatically different from the information written after 9/11. Before 9/11 the U.S. Census Bureau estimated 1.2 million people claiming Arab ancestry were living in the United States, but other studies reported that the number was too low. Debates continued about the actual size of the U.S. Muslim population. Post-9/11 Muslim and Arab immigrants, whether Muslim or not and mostly young men, were singled out for detention without any distinction made between those being held for immigration violations and those suspected as terrorists. In addition, the U.S. Justice Department established a program that required male immigrants from 24 Arab and Muslim nations to register with local immigration offices.

Language Style

The style, or tone, in which a document is written can reflect the author's perspective. Questions to consider when evaluating the style of a document about immigration and migration are: How was the document meant to be used, such as in an instructional setting or to promote the writer's or organization's point of view on the topic; does the tone promote open conversation or encourage controversy? Is the document critical or supportive of immigration and migration and how does the document make you feel when you read it, threatened by immigrants or secure with their presence?

Government documents, scholarly writings, and studies or reports by private organizations about immigration often have a writing style different from newspaper editorials and magazine articles written by journalists who may be promoting their publication's point of view or perspective in an attempt to sway readers to their way of thinking. Language style in scholarly articles about immigration and migration will usually be more formal than newspaper or magazine articles, which often use more casual language.

Integrity

Reviewing documents for reliability and dependability, that is, their integrity, can help eliminate materials that provide information about immigration that may be biased or prejudiced and thus interfere with a researcher's ability to make objective or impartial judgments about the topic. Depending on the social and economic circumstances in countries at different times in history, immigrants have either been embraced and welcomed or shunned and expelled. That fact also has impacted the available information during different times in history. For example, information disseminated by organizations like the Minutemen (a civilian group that claims to deter illegal immigration but that others call racist) often promotes the idea that Mexican immigrants in the United States cause overpopulation; increase illegal drug and gang crimes; strain the country's social resources such as schools, hospitals, and welfare organizations; take jobs from American workers; and result in lower wages being paid to every working person. Much of the information provided by groups like the Minutemen and the Federation for American Immigration Reform (an immigration reduction organization) is designed to stir emotions, and influence how people feel about immigrants, and that information often leads to xenophobia. Based on available statistics reported by the American Immigration Lawyers Association, rather than taking jobs from Americans, immigrants are often self-employed or establish small businesses that create new jobs. Additionally, the idea that immigrants strain the country's social infrastructure also has been contradicted by statistics that report the collective annual earnings of immigrants amount to $240 billion, immigrants pay $90 billion in taxes annually, and they collect $5 billion in welfare.

Legitimate organizations may be biased or prejudiced in their reporting as well. The Heritage Foundation, a Washington, D.C.–based conservative think tank that publishes information about U.S. economic, defense, and foreign policies, in 2006 issued a report warning that a guest-worker program included in the Senate's proposed immigration bill would inundate the country with as many as 193 million new legal immigrants by 2026. Other reports noted that the data was unrealistic given that the number cited was larger than the entire populations of Mexico and Central America combined.

USING THE INTERNET

The popularity of doing research on the Internet is undeniable. The following Web sites can help ease the search and provide access to information that is more likely to be reliable.

Search Engines

- Answers.com. This site searches for information from authoritative rather than popular sites. Among the resources it accesses are the Columbia University Press and Merriam-Webster. Also offered is a reference browse section that includes searching texts such as the *Reader's Guide to American History* and *Encyclopedia Britannnica.*
- Clusty.com. This site was named one of the 50 coolest Web sites of 2005 by *Time* magazine. It groups search results from several search engines then sorts them by topic. Among the news sources it accesses are Reuters, CNN, the *Washington Post,* the *New York Times,* and BBC News.
- LII.org. The Librarian's Index to the Internet provides well-organized access to reliable, trustworthy Internet resources. Each site offered is reviewed several times before it is included as a resource.
- Questia.com. This online library has one of the world's large collections of complete books and journal articles as well as newspaper and magazine articles that can be searched by word, phrase, topic, author, or title.

Organizations and Publications

- Center for Immigration Studies, http://www.cis.org. This organization describes itself as "an independent, non-partisan, non-profit research organization. . . . Only think tank devoted exclusively to research and policy analysis of the economic, social, demographic, fiscal, and other impacts of immigration on the United States." Its stated mission is "pro-immigrant, low immigration." Topics covered on the site include statistics, immigration history, legal and illegal immigration, refugees and asylum seekers, and guest workers.

- Immigration History Research Center, http://www.ihrc.umn.edu/research/. This Web site is sponsored and maintained by the University of Minnesota. In provides information about immigration and migration-related books, periodicals, and archived collections as well as links to other sites with resources for migration studies.
- Migration Policy Institute, http://www.migrationpolicy.org. This organization describes itself as "an independent, nonpartisan, nonprofit think tank dedicated to the movement of people worldwide." Options on the site include studies, reports, and research about U.S. immigration, European migration, immigrant integration, and refugee protection. Also available is access to *Migration Information Source,* which provides a global analysis by authorities in the subject of international migration trends and other tools, data, and facts about population movements.
- Migration News, http://www.migration.ucdavis.edu/mn/index.php. This free online publication is supported by the German Marshall Fund of the United States and the University of California-Berkeley Center for German and European Studies. It provides reviews and analysis of key international immigration and integration developments quarterly by region: North America, Europe, Asia, and Other.

7

Facts and Figures

GENERAL

1.1 Movement of Indo-European Tribes Triggered by the Hypothesized Flooding of the Black Sea, ca. 5600 B.C.E.

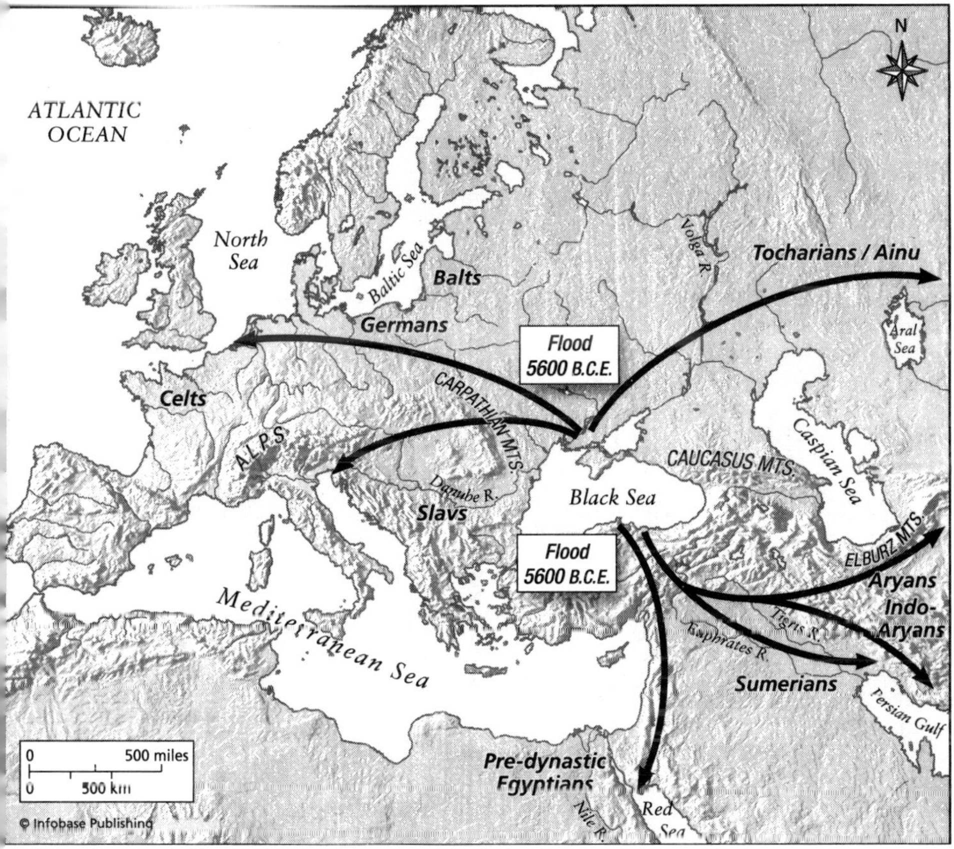

Source: Iowa State University C. Ford, Ph.D.

1.2 Peoples and Kingdoms in the Early Ninth Century

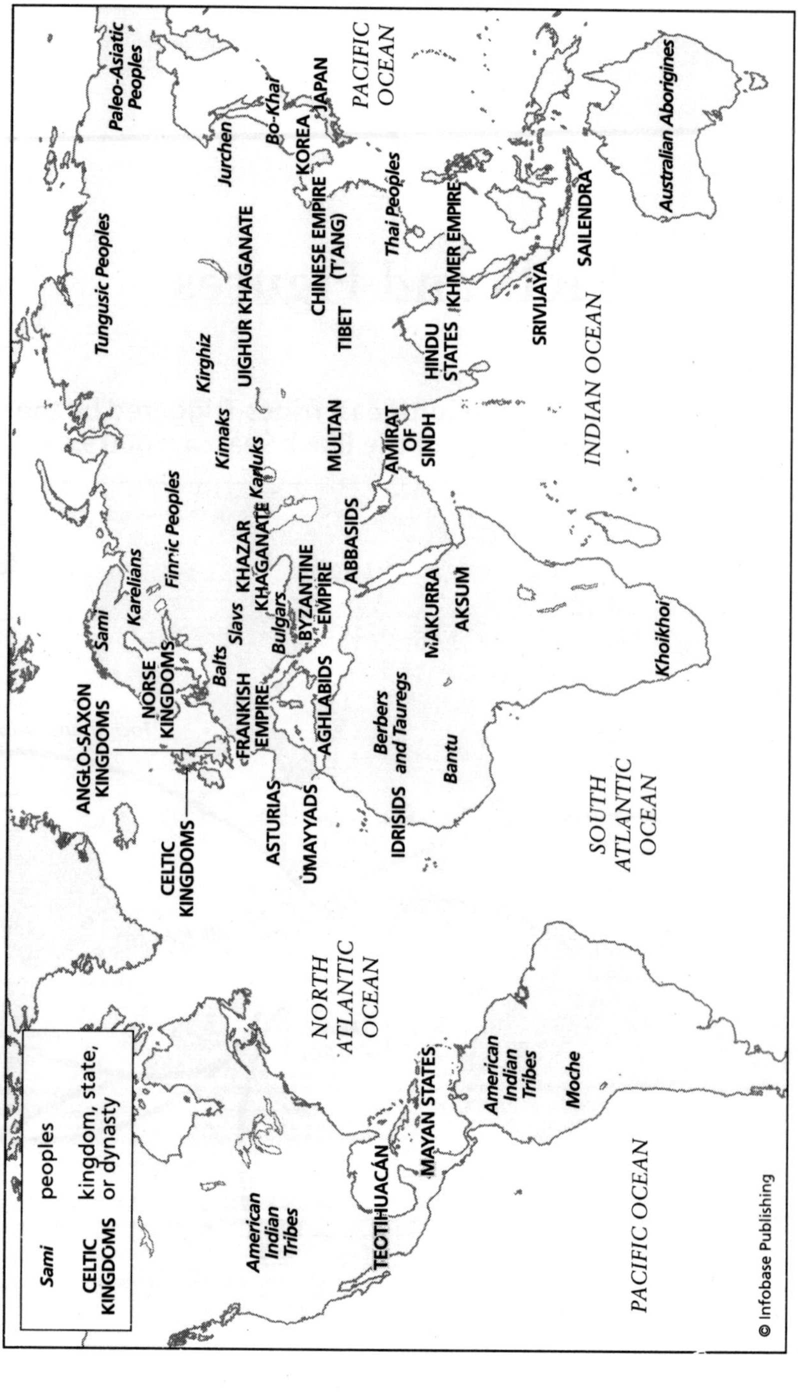

1.3 International Migrants Living in the Primary Immigrant-Receiving Destination Countries and Regions, 1910–2000

Thousands

	1910			1930			1960			2000		
	POPULATION	MIGRANTS	SHARE	POPULATION	MIGRANTS	SHARE	POPULATION	MIGRANTS	SHARE	POPULATION	MIGRANTS	SHARE
Australia	4,455	787	17.7	6,630	356	5.4	10,276	1,701	16.6	19,153	4,705	24.6
Canada	7,207	1,587	22.0	10,377	2,308	22.2	17,909	2,766	15.4	30,769	5,826	18.9
New Zealand	1,008	306	30.3	1,534	77	5.0	2,372	334	14.1	3,784	850	22.5
United States	91,972	13,516	14.7	122,775	14,204	11.6	186,158	9,735	5.2	285,003	34,988	12.3
Sub-total traditional countries of immigration	104,642	16,196	15.5	141,316	16,945	12.0	216,715	14,537	6.7	338,709	46,369	13.7
Argentina	7,885	2,358	29.9	10,922	2,828	25.9	20,616	2,615	12.7	37,074	1,419	3.8
Uruguay	1,080	181	16.8	..	..	..	2,538	192	7.6	3,342	89	2.6
Western Europe	143,099	3,348	2.3	158,583	4,233	2.7	151,902	7,002	4.6	183,502	18,836	10.3
Total	256,706	22,083	8.6	310,821	24,006	7.7	391,771	24,346	6.2	562,627	66,713	11.9

Source: United Nations World Economic and Social Survey 2004

UNITED STATES

2.1 Immigration to and Emigration from the United States by Decade from 1901–1990

PERIOD	IMMIGRANTS TO THE U.S. (THOUSANDS)	EMIGRANTS FROM THE U.S. (THOUSANDS)	NET IMMIGRATION (THOUSANDS)	RATIO: EMIGRATION/ IMMIGRATION
Total, 1901–90	**37,869**	**11,882**	**25,987**	**.31**
1981–90	7,338	1,600	5,738	.22
1971–80	4,493	1,176	3,317	.26
1961–70	3,322	900	2,422	.27
1951–60	2,515	425	2,090	.17
1941–50	1,035	281	754	.27
1931–40	528	649	-121	1.23
1921–30	4,107	1,685	2,422	.41
1911–20	5,736	2,157	3,579	.38
1901–10	8,795	3,008	5,787	.34

Source: U.S. 1995 Statistical Yearbook

2.2 Illegal Aliens in the United States, 2005, and Methods of Entry

MODES OF ENTRY FOR THE UNAUTHORIZED MIGRANT POPULATION		
Entered Legally with Inspection	Non-Immigrant Visa Overstayers	4 to 5.5 Million
	Border Crossing Card Violators	250,000 to 500,000
	Sub-total Legal Entries	*4.5 to 6 Million*
Entered Illegally without Inspection	Evaded the Immigration Inspectors and Border Patrol	6 to 7 million
Estimated Total Unauthorized Population in 2006		11.5 to 12 Million

Source: Pew Hispanic Center Estimates based on the March 2005 Current Population Survey and Department of Homeland Security reports.

2.3 Estimated Number of Illegal Aliens in the United States Workforce in 2005 and Positions Held

POSITION HELD	NUMBER OF ILLEGAL ALIENS EMPLOYED
Cooks	436,000
Construction Workers	400,000
Maids and Housekeeping	342,000
Landscape and Grounds Workers	299,000
Carpenters	277,000
Janitors and Building Cleaners	262,000
Agricultural Workers	247,000
Painters, Construction, Maintenance	167,000
Cashiers	158,000
Drivers, Sales Workers, Truck Drivers	151,000
Total Employed, estimate	**2.74 million**

Source: Pew Hispanic Center and U.S. Department of Labor Statistics

2.4 Locations of Proposed Fences Along U.S./Mexico Border and the Number of Illegal Alien Apprehensions and Deaths at those Locations, 2006 Estimates

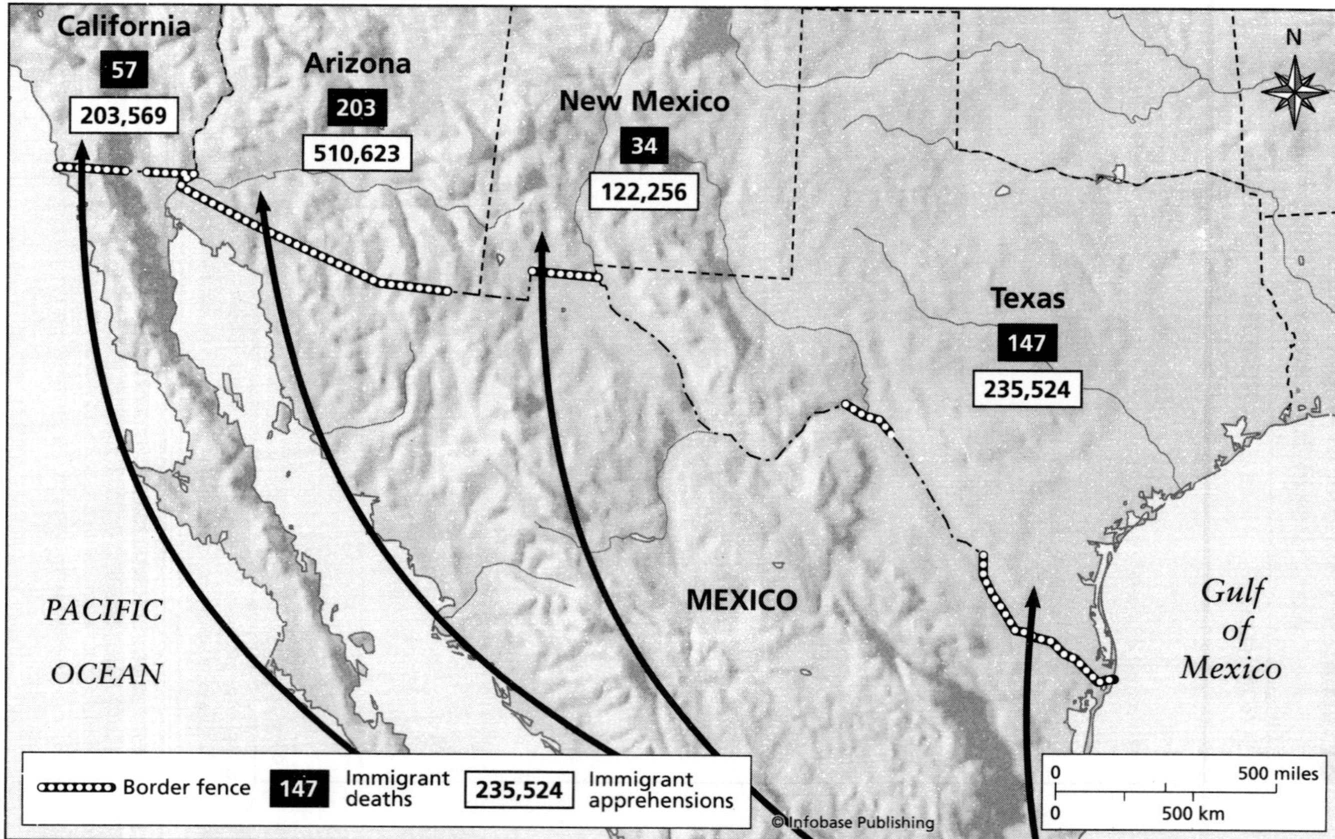

Source: High Country News, wwww.hcn.com

GLOBAL PERSPECTIVES

3.1 Migrants Entering France According to Reason for Immigration, 2004

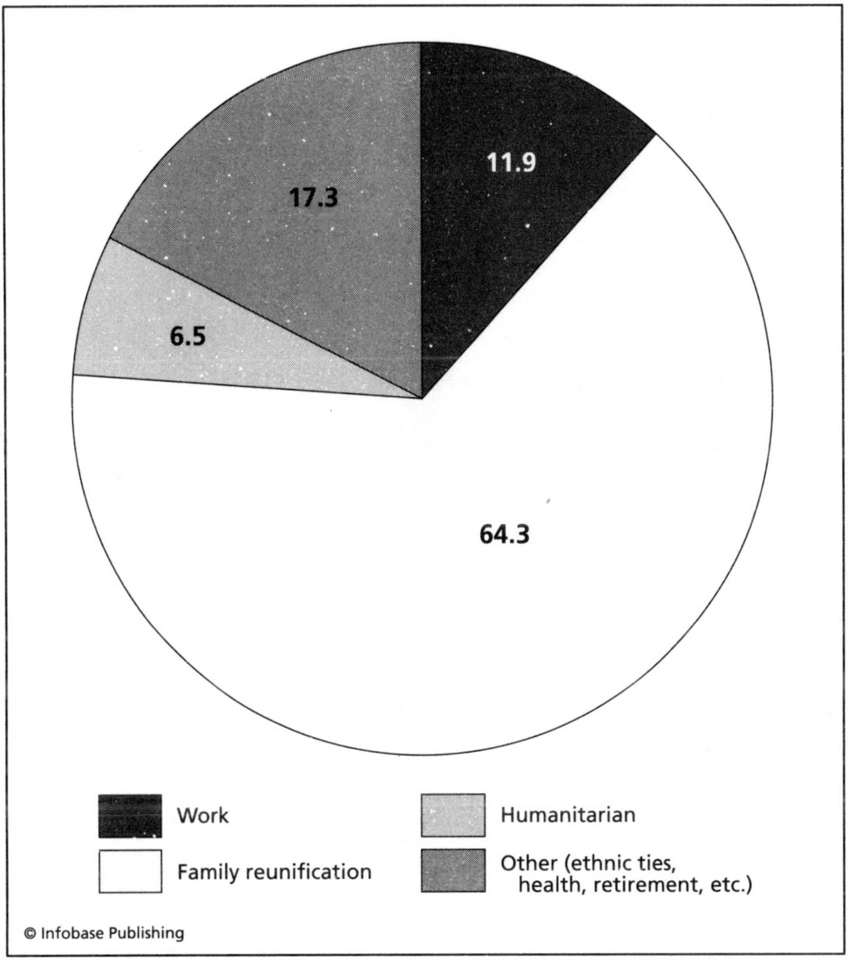

Source: OECD 2006, International Migration Outlook, Migration Information Source

3.2 Population of France in 1999 by Nationality and Place of Birth (in thousands)

NATIONALITY	PLACE OF BIRTH		TOTAL	%
	BORN IN FRANCE	BORN ABROAD		
French by birth	51,340	1,560	52,900	90.4
French by acquisition	800	1,580	2,360	4.0
Foreigners	510	2,750	3,260	5.6
Total population	52,650	5,870	58,520	100.0
Of which				
Foreigners by nationality or origin	1,310	4,310	5,620	9.6
Foreign born			4,310	7.4

Source: INSEE, Census 1999, and Migration Information Source

3.3 South Africa, 1899–1910

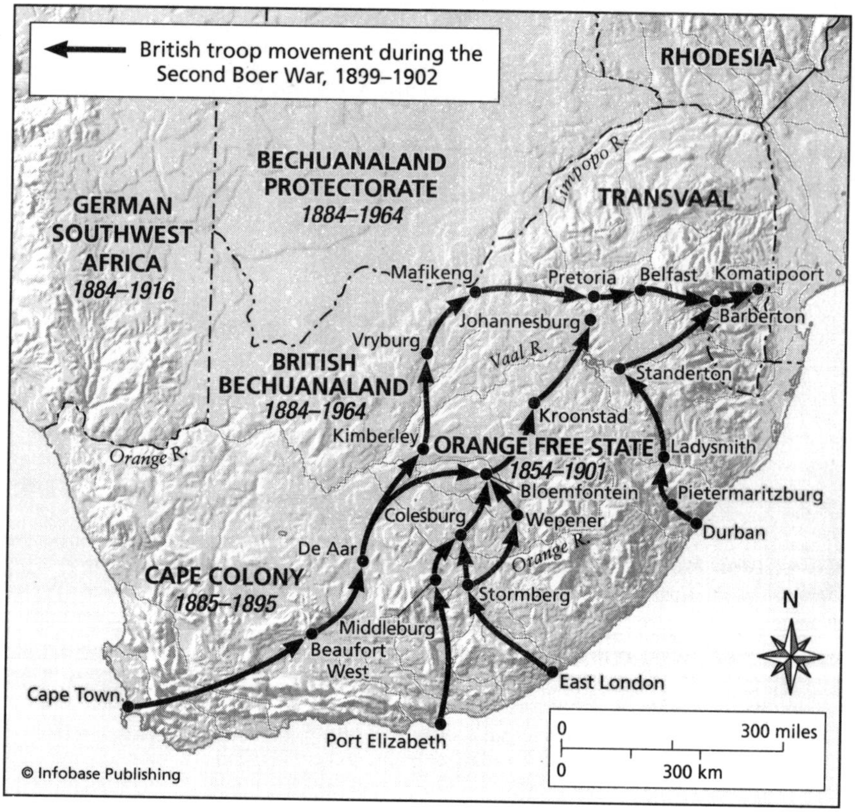

3.4 Self-Declared Emigration from South Africa in 2003 by Occupation

OCCUPATION	NUMBER OF EMIGRANTS
Engineers and Related Technologists/ Technicians, Architects	700
Natural Sciences (Computer, Chemical, Agricultural, Food Sciences, etc.)	593
Medical, Dental, Health Services (Physicians, Nurses, Dentists, Pharmacists)	766
Education Professions (Teachers, Administrators, Support Staff)	666
Humanities (Lawyers, Religious, Personnel and Management)	1,198
Accountants and Economic Related	736
Executive, Managerial, Administrative	1,729
Clerical and Sales	1,895
Arts, Sports, Entertainment	393
Farming, Forestry, Nursery Related Professions	34
Production-Related Professions (Mining and Quarry Workers, Semi-skilled and Unskilled Laborers)	73
Other Unspecified Occupations	1,713
Total Employed Self-Declared Emigrants	**10,496**

Source: Statistics South Africa, Documented Migration 2003

3.5 Remittances Received by Developing Countries Paid by Migrant Workers, 2004

COUNTRY	TOTAL REMITTANCES, IN US$ BILLIONS
India	$21.7
China	$21.3
Mexico	$18.1
Philippines	$11.6
Morocco	$4.2
Serbia	$4.1
Pakistan	$3.9
Egypt	$3.3
Colombia	$3.2
Nigeria	$2.8

Source: Global Economic Prospects, 2006, World Bank, Washington, D.C.

3.6 Number of Overseas Foreign Workers (OFWs) Deployed by the Philippines Annually, 1975–2004

YEAR	LAND-BASED	SEA-BASED	TOTAL
1975	12,501	23,534	36,035
1976	19,221	28,614	47,835
1977	36,676	33,699	70,375
1978	50,961	37,280	88,241
1979	92,519	44,818	137,337
1980	157,394	57,196	214,590
1981	210,936	55,307	266,243
1982	250,115	64,169	314,284
1983	380,263	53,594	434,207
1984	300,378	50,604	350,982
1985	320,494	52,290	372,784
1986	323,517	54,697	378,214
1987	382,229	67,042	449,271
1988	385,117	85,913	471,030
1989	355,346	103,280	458,626
1990	334,883	111,212	446,095
1991	489,260	125,759	615,019
1992	549,655	136,806	686,461
1993	550,872	145,758	696,030
1994	564,031	154,376	718,407
1995	488,173	165,401	653,574
1996	484,653	175,469	660,122
1997	559,227	188,469	747,696
1998	638,343	193,300	831,643
1999	640,331	196,689	837,020
2000	643,304	198,324	841,628
2001	662,648	204,951	867,599
2002	682,315	209,593	891,908
2003	651,938	216,031	867,969
2004	704,586	229,002	933,588

Note: Figures for 1975 to 1983 refer to number of contracts processed; figures for 1984 to 2004 refer to number of workers deployed abroad.

Source: Migration Information Source

8

Key Players A to Z

DANIEL K. AKAKA (1924–) U.S. senator from Hawaii (1990–). In 2006 he proposed an amendment to U.S. immigration laws that would grant the children of Filipino World War II veterans special immigrant status for the purpose of family reunification. At the time of presenting his proposal he stated, "Making this small change to our nation's immigration policy would go a long way toward making our immigration laws more just, ..."

ALANA BAILEY (UNKNOWN BIRTHDATE) Chief executive officer of AfriForum and manager of South Africa's Come Home Campaign. Initiated in 2003, the privately run campaign's goal is reducing emigration from South Africa and encouraging repatriation of South Africans who have immigrated to other countries.

LUCÍA DEL CARMEN BERMÚDEZ (UNKNOWN BIRTHDATE) Coordinator of the Mexican government's migration protection agency, Grupo Beta. It was established in 1990 to protect migrants from attacks by Mexican police, local farmers, smugglers, and gangs while crossing Mexico's borders, both the southern border with Guatemala and the northern border with the United States. The organization has been described as Mexico's counterpart to the U.S. Border Patrol.

TONY BLAIR (1953–) Prime minister of the United Kingdom (1997–2006). Responding to British sentiment that illegal immigration was out of control, in 2004 he promised a "top-to-bottom review" of the United Kingdom's immigration policy. Plans called for prohibiting access to public housing for unemployed illegal aliens and restricting access to government welfare benefits for illegal aliens. Other immigration-related issues in which he became embroiled during his time in office include the 2006 controversy over Muslim women wearing veils in public. Immigration officials were given permission to request of Muslim women that they remove their veils so their identity could be verified. At the time Blair described the veils as a "mark of separation," and he noted that they made some "outside the community feel uncomfortable."

WILLIAM BRADFORD (1590–1657) One of the signers of the Mayflower Compact, a leader of the Pilgrim settlers, and governor of Plymouth Colony. His handwritten journals followed the lives of the immigrants who settled at Plymouth.

GEORGE W. BUSH (1946–) 43rd president of the United States, sworn into office on January 20, 2001, and reelected for a second term and sworn in on January 20, 2005. Responding to concerns about the growing number of illegal aliens in the United States, following his re-election in 2005 he began urging U.S. legislators to reform the country's immigration laws. His requests included securing the country's borders, implementing a guest-worker program, and providing a way for illegal aliens already in the country who meet specific criteria to become citizens. In 2006 he signed a bill, the Secure Fence Act, authorizing construction of a fence along 700 miles of the U.S.-Mexico border. He also increased the number of Border Patrol agents from 9,000 to more than 12,000 and deployed the National Guard to assist the Border Patrol.

JACQUES CARTIER (1491–1557) French explorer who attempted to find a way through or around North America to East Asia. He eventually made his way up the St. Lawrence River to reach what is now Quebec, Canada. His discoveries helped make it possible for immigrants from France to settle in North America.

CÉSAR CHÁVEZ (1927–1993) Cofounder of the National Farm Workers Association, which later became the United Farm Workers (UFW). Working as an activist he urged Mexican Americans to register to vote and he fought for workers rights. His efforts led to strikes in 1966 by agricultural workers in California and Texas demanding higher wages. UFW members, led by Chávez, marched through the Imperial Valley and Coachella Valley in Southern California to the border of Mexico to protest growers' use of illegal aliens as temporary replacement workers during the 1966 strike. Other UFW strikes and boycotts directed by Chávez included those in the 1970s against lettuce and grape growers by migrant workers demanding higher wages, and in the 1980s protesting the use of toxic pesticides on grape fields.

JEAN-PIERRE CHEVÈNEMENT (1939–) French politician (minister of defense 1988–91, minister of interior 1997–2000, candidate for president 2002). The Chevènement Law of 1998 clarified the terms and conditions under which people could claim refugee status in France and made it easier for immigrants to enter France temporarily for cultural and scientific exchanges.

WILLIAM J. CLINTON (1946–) 42nd president of the United States (1993–2001). In his 1995 State of the Union address he said, "We are a nation of immigrants. But we are also a nation of laws. It is wrong and ultimately self-defeating for a nation of immigrants to permit the kind of abuse of our immigration laws we have seen in recent years, and we must do more to stop it." Immigration-related proposals and actions he took while in office included the Immigration Enforcement Improvements Act of 1995, which aimed to secure the country's borders, speed deportation of illegal aliens, and actively enforce existing laws prohibiting employment of illegal aliens; and signing the LIFE (Legal Immigration and Family Equity) Act in 2000, which, among other things, created a new visa category for the spouses and children of foreign legal permanent residents in the country and provided an opportunity for undocumented illegal aliens who had applied for amnesty under the 1986 Immigration and Reform and Control Act to receive green cards.

FRANCISCO FERNÁNDEZ DE CÓRDOBA (?–1517) Spanish explorer. He was one of the first Europeans to reach Mexico. He arrived in Yucatán in 1517 by way of Cuba in search of slaves. He was killed there that year in a battle with the Mexican Mayas. However, his discoveries paved the way for other explorers and the eventual immigration of Spanish colonists to Mexico.

JONATHAN CRUSH (UNKNOWN BIRTHDATE) Researcher and director of the Southern African Migration Project (SAMP). His areas of specialization include South African immigration policy, international migration, and transnationalism. In addition to publishing numerous scholarly articles about immigration and migration in South Africa, he is editor of SAMP's Migration Policy Series. SAMP is described as an "international network of organizations founded in 1996 to promote awareness of migration-development linkages" in the Southern African Development Community. The organization "provides policy advice and expertise, offers training in migration policy and management, and conducts public education campaigns on migration-related issues." Areas of study include brain drain, xenophobia, and migration development.

FREDERIK WILLEM DE KLERK (1938–) 10th president of South Africa and the final state president during apartheid (1989–94). He shared the 1993 Nobel Peace Prize with Nelson Mandela for his part in ending apartheid. The apartheid years dramatically impacted immigration to and emigration from South Africa.

LUIS ERNESTO DERBEZ (1947–) Mexico's secretary of foreign affairs. In 2006 he became embroiled in a diplomatic battle over U.S. complaints that Mexican soldiers helped drug smugglers crossing the U.S.-Mexico border escape American law enforcement officers. He alleged the soldiers were actually Americans in disguise. He also demanded an investigation into the 2005 death of a Mexican migrant worker who was illegally crossing the U.S.-Mexico border and shot by U.S. Border Patrol agents.

LOU DOBBS (1945–) CNN news anchor, editorial writer, and host of the syndicated radio program *Lou Dobbs Tonight.* He is an outspoken critic of illegal immigration, is opposed to amnesty for illegal aliens, and supports active enforcement of border security. Although his critics have accused him of xenophobia and anti-Hispanic racism, he strongly denies the charges. He uses his nightly CNN television program as a platform to campaign for a crackdown on illegal immigration and illegal drug trafficking, especially on the U.S.-Mexico border.

FRANCISCO T. DUQUE III (1957–) Health secretary of the Philippines (2005–). Recognizing the problems for the Philippines's health care system caused by the increasing emigration of its doctors and nurses, he began pushing for government legislation to "plug the hole" and keep medical personnel from leaving the country for higher paying jobs in the United States and elsewhere.

JOSEPH EJERCITO ESTRADA (1937–) 13th president of the Philippines (1998–2001). Shortly after taking office and several years before the September 11, 2001, terrorist attacks on the United States, he asked the Philippine Congress to update the country's immigration and deportation laws to combat international terrorism. At that time, Filipino immigration officials also began to more closely scrutinize immigrants entering the country who were suspected of being foreign terrorists.

GERÓNIMO GUTIÉRREZ FERNANDEZ (UNKNOWN BIRTHDATE) Mexico's undersecretary for North American affairs. In his position he has worked on legal and illegal immigration into and from Mexico. Speaking before a congressional panel convened by the Mexican government in 2006 on the topic, "Mexico in the Face of the Migratory Phenomenon," he agreed that Mexico had tougher immigration laws than those the United States was considering. He also agreed that Mexico needed to review its immigration laws, including correcting its treatment of migrants in the country. In another interview he stated that Mexico does not support undocumented migration and is committed to fighting human smuggling and trafficking.

VICENTE FOX (1942–) 62nd president of Mexico (2000–06). During his time in office he actively pressed the U.S. government to implement reforms such as creating guest-worker programs that would allow more Mexican nationals to work legally in the United States. He also adamantly opposed construction of a fence along the U.S.-Mexico border, which U.S. president George Bush approved in 2006, and he accused U.S. immigration policy of being too focused on border security and failing to recognize the contributions Mexican migrant workers make to the U.S. economy. On his own side of the border, he was pressured by the U.S. government to deal with illegal aliens entering Mexico from Central America and ultimately entering America illegally. He was also pushed by the U.S. government to deal with Mexico's growing illegal drug traffickers. Before leaving office, he was working with the Mexican Congress to update the country's immigration law.

DONNA GABACCIA (1949–) Professor of immigration history and director of the Immigration History Research Center at the University of Minnesota. She specializes in U.S. immigration history, comparative world migrations, and international Italian migration. She is author of numerous books and articles on immigrant life in the United States and Italian migration around the world. She is an editor of the recent special issue, "Gender and Migration," of the *International Migration Review* and coeditor with Vicki Ruiz of *American Dreaming, Global Realities: Re-thinking U.S. Immigration History.*

NICK GRIFFIN (1959–) Chairman of the British National Party (BNP). He proposes paying nonwhites to leave Britain and the European Union and return to their country of ethnic origin. The BNP emphasizes dismantling multiculturalism in the country, which it believes has a negative impact on both British and immigrant cultures.

JUAN JOSE GUTIERREZ (UNKNOWN BIRTHDATE) National director of Latino Movement USA. He is an outspoken promoter of rights for illegal immigrants and is a key organizer of immigrant marches and protests, including the March 2006 protest march in Los Angeles that attracted an estimated 2 million immigrants and the May 2006 "Day Without Immigrants" national boycott of U.S. businesses by migrant workers, designed to prove the value of immigrants to the U.S. economy. Prior to becoming director of Latino Movement USA he was director of the One Stop Immigration and Education Center, based in Los Angeles. The center encouraged immigrants to take advantage of amnesty, offered instruction in English and civics, and held neighborhood meetings with politicians, among other activities.

CHUNG-WHA HONG (1966?–) Executive director, New York Immigration Coalition (NYIC). The NYIC is a nonprofit organization that advocates for more than 200 New York groups and agencies that work with immigrants, refugees, and asylum seekers. In 2006 the NYIC helped organize thousands of immigrants in New York to march in protest against Congress's proposed immigration restrictions. The organization also is working to organize New York's dozens of ethnic communities into one political force.

ANDREW JACKSON (1767–1845) Seventh president of the United States (1829–37). He was an active proponent of the removal of Native Americans from their lands in the Southeast to lands in the mostly unsettled West, thereby clearing the way for white settlers to occupy lands in the rapidly expanding United States. In 1830 he pushed through Congress legislation known as the Indian Removal Act. His action led to the forced migration of thousands of Native Americans to the West in what became known as the Trail of Tears.

LYNDON B. JOHNSON (1908–1973) 36th president of the United States (1963–69). Johnson signed while in office the Immigration and Nationality Act Amendments of 1965, also known as the Hart-Celler Act. The act abolished nation-of-origin quotas for immigration that had been in effect since 1924, and increased the annual total number of immigrants allowed to enter the country from Eastern Hemisphere countries to 170,000 and from Western Hemisphere countries to 120,000. Visas were also made available to immigrants on a first-come, first-serve basis. At the time of the signing he described the bill as "not revolutionary. . . . It does not affect the lives of millions. It will not reshape the structure of our daily lives or add importantly to either our wealth or our power." However, since its adoption the act has had a major impact on immigration to the country, and it has helped transform the social, cultural, and economic landscape of American society through increased immigration, both legal and illegal.

EDWARD KENNEDY (1932–) United States senator (1962–). He was a supporter of the 1965 Hart-Cellar Act, which, among other things, abolished nation-of-origin quotas on immigration. Still fighting for immigration reform in 2006 he said, "Our immigration system is broken, and enforcement alone will not fix it." Also in 2006 he supported legislation that would strengthen security at the borders, create an "amnesty" program for undocumented workers who met specific criteria, and implement a temporary worker program. In addition, he vocally condemned legislative proposals that would forcibly deport millions of illegal aliens from the country.

CHRISTOPHER KUI (1959?–) Executive director of Asian Americans for Equality (AAFE). As director of the AAFE he works actively for the rights of Asian Americans and to give a voice to Asian immigrants. The AAFE evolved from a group of New York Chinatown residents, students, and professionals who protested a 1974 incident in New York City in which the builders of a high-rise development known as the Confucius Plaza refused to hire Chinese workers. The AAFE also has staged protests against raids on illegal sweatshops and in opposition to harassment of garment workers and undocumented immigrants.

JEAN-MARIE LE PEN (1928–) Candidate for president of France in the 1974, 1988, 1995, 2002, and 2007 elections. He founded the Front National Party in 1972 and in both 1984 and 1999 won a seat in the European Parliament. The European Court of Justice removed him from the parliamentary position in 2003 after he assaulted another candidate. He strongly opposes globalization and supports ending all immigration into France. Some critics have described him as a symbol of French xenophobia.

MIGUEL LÓPEZ DE LEGAZPI (1502–1572) Spanish conquistador who established the first permanent European settlement in the Philippines (1565). The settlement led to further immigration and eventual occupation of the islands by the Spanish for almost 350 years. New immigrants who arrived included Mexican laborers brought from New Spain, as Mexico was known at the time.

EMMA LOZANO (UNKNOWN BIRTHDATE) Immigrants rights activist and president and founder of Chicago, Illinois–based Pueblo Sin Fronteras. Some have described her as the "face of the immigration movement" in the United States. Founded in 1987, Pueblo Sin Fronteras's stated goal is making people in the United States aware that the immigration debate is "about real, human families, and their struggle to stay together." In 2006 the organization supported the immigration reform bill proposed by Senators John McCain and Edward Kennedy. It also campaigns for legal immigrants to apply for U.S. citizenship, register to vote, and demand legalization of illegal aliens in the country.

GASSAMA MADY (UNKNOWN BIRTHDATE) President of an association for the defense of illegal immigrants in France. He was among thousands of people who marched in 2006 in protest against France's new immigration law. He described the law as "inhuman" and vowed to continue fighting until the legislation was overturned.

NELSON MANDELA, (1918–) 11th president of South Africa (1994–99). He was an active and vocal opponent of apartheid—the practice of racial segregation—and leader of the African National Conference. In 2006 he received the Ambassador of Conscience Award, presented by Amnesty International for leadership in promoting and protecting human rights. He also received the Nobel Peace Prize in 1993.

FERDINAND MARCOS (1917–1989) 10th president of the Philippines (1965–86). The Labor Code of the Philippines was passed during his tenure (1974), which implemented the policies that created the country's overseas employment programs. Organized labor migration that began then continued in 2006 with the country dependent on the remittances sent by its overseas foreign workers for relief from its economic problems and high unemployment.

BRUNSON MCKINLEY (1943–) Elected director general of the International Organization for Migration (IOM) in 1998 and reelected to a second term in 2003. He served as the first American ambassador to Haiti and in 1990 began specializing in migration issues. IOM is described as the "leading inter-governmental organization in the field of migration and works closely with governmental, intergovernmental and non-governmental partners," including 118 member states and 20 observer states with offices in more than 100 countries. The IOM's stated goal is promoting humane and orderly migration of people by providing services and advice to both governments and migrants.

VISCOUNT ALFRED MILNER (1854–1925) British high commissioner of southern Africa and governor of Cape Colony (appointed 1897). During his service in South Africa he actively promoted immigration to the country by British nationals and proclaimed English the official language of the colonies, requiring that it be taught in all schools. Despite opposition, he imported indentured Chinese laborers to the country who were willing to work for lower wages than black Africans. In 1906 he was censured by the British House of Commons for violating the Chinese labor ordinance when he did not forbid flogging Chinese migrant workers who broke the law rather than putting them in prison.

JEFF DAVIS MILTON (1861–1947) The son of the fifth governor of Florida and a former Texas Ranger, Jeff Davis Milton became known as the "first Border Patrolman." In 1904 he was appointed mounted Chinese inspector, a position under the direction of the U.S. Immigration Service, to prevent Chinese immigrants trying to avoid the U.S. Chinese exclusion law from entering the United States at the U.S.-Mexico border. In 1919 he was assigned to help guard a boatload of Russian immigrants deemed radicals who were being deported to Russia by the U.S. government.

EDUARDO MEDINA-MORA (1957–) Mexico's secretary of public safety. In 2006 he helped write a law that would decriminalize possession of small amounts of illegal drugs in an effort to crack down on drug dealing. The law drew criticism from the U.S. government, which claimed it would increase illegal drug trafficking (often tied to illegal immigration), at the U.S.-Mexico border.

CECILIA MUNOZ (1962–) Activist, lobbyist, politician, and senior immigration policy analyst at the National Council of La Raza (NCLR). The NCLR is described as the "largest Hispanic civil rights and advocacy organization in the United States." Its mission is to improve opportunities for Hispanic Americans in five key areas: civil rights and immigration, assets and investments, employment and economics, education, and health.

KATHLEEN NEWLAND (UNKNOWN BIRTHDATE) Cofounder and codirector of the Migration Policy Institute (MPI). Her work focuses on the management of refugees and migration, international humanitarianism, and migration and development. Before joining MPI she served as a consultant to the United Nations High Commissioner for Refugees, and worked as a researcher for the Washington, D.C.–based Worldwatch Institute where she analyzed migration, population, refugee, and women's issues.

DEMETRIOUS PAPADEMETRIOU (1947?–) Cofounder and codirector of the Migration Policy Institute (MPI). Prior to joining the MPI he was the head immigration official with the U.S. Department of Labor. In addition to having published more than 200 books, research reports, and articles about immigration and migration, he serves as an adviser on immigration to government and political officials in 20 countries. The MPI is a Washington, D.C.–based nonpartisan think tank that attempts to present both positive and negative aspects of international migration.

OSCAR PAREDES (1961?–) Ecuadorian labor leader, founder and executive director of the Latin American Workers' Project. The project, established in 1997, assists new immigrants by opening job centers, holding immigration-law workshops, teaching English as a second language, and holding literacy classes. In addition, the project helps empower low-wage migrant workers and day laborers to organize their efforts to achieve better wages, improved working conditions, and civil rights.

CHARLES PASQUA (1927–) Interior minister of France (1986–88, 1993–95). During his terms in office he pushed through anti-immigration legislation, including the 1986 Pasqua Law, which reduced the number of immigrants allowed residency permits and granted regional authorities and police the right to decide whether or not to forcibly deport illegal aliens caught in the country. The 1991 Pasqua Law further limited access to French territory by illegal aliens and limited the number of other immigrants allowed to enter and live in the country. In 1994 he instructed French police to increase identity checks of foreigners and foreign-looking French nationals.

JUAN PONCE DE LEÓN (1460?–1521) Spanish explorer who discovered Florida. Although his attempts to establish a colony there failed, his exploration opened the door for the arrival of future immigrants from Spain.

FIDEL V. RAMOS (1928–) 12th president of the Philippines (1992–98). While in office he signed the Migrant Workers and Overseas Act (1995), which implemented stricter monitoring of the immigration policies of destination countries to ensure that Filipino migrant workers would be adequately protected. It also tightened regulations for labor recruitment and required that Filipino overseas foreign workers register with Philippines embassies in destination countries.

ERNST GEORG RAVENSTEIN (1834–1913) German-born geographer who worked at the Royal Geographical Society in London. In 1885 he published a paper titled "The Laws of Migration" in the *Journal of the Statistical Society* that presented his findings on the patterns of human movements in Great Britain. His migration theory postulated that most migrants travel only short distances, long-distance migrants generally prefer to go to large cities that offer commerce and industry, each stream of migration produces a counter stream, women are more likely to be internal migrants while men are more likely to be international migrants, most migration is from agricultural areas to cities, and economics is the primary reason people migrate.

CARDINAL JEAN-PIERRE RICARD (1944–) Archbishop of Bordeaux, France, and president of the French bishops' conference. He was among French religious leaders in 2006 who signed a letter addressed to French prime minister Dominique de Villepin that stated France needed immigration laws but affirmed that the new law the government had passed was overly severe, would encourage discrimination, and would destabilize immigrant families.

NICOLAS SARKOZY (1955–) Interior minister of France. He authored France's new immigration law, passed in 2006, which, among other things, gave the government authority to selectively choose which foreigners could live and work in the country, and required that immigrants learn the French language. The law made it possible for France to prohibit admission of low-skilled, poorly educated immigrants in favor of highly skilled professional workers and abolished the right of illegal immigrants who have lived in the country for 10 years to receive residency papers. He was elected president of France in 2007.

CAPTAIN JOHN SMITH (1580–1631) English adventurer and one of the founders of Jamestown, Virginia. The settlement, the first permanent English colony in North America, was established in 1607. Although most of the original settlers died within the first year of arriving in North America, more English immigrants began arriving in Jamestown in 1609.

SAMUEL A. STOUFFER (1900–1960) 43rd president of the American Sociological Association (1953). His migration theory, "Intervening Opportunities: A Theory Relating Distance and Mobility," was published in 1940 in volume 5 of the *American Sociological Review.* The theory suggested that migration between two places depends upon the number of intervening opportunities between a migrant's location of origin and the planned destination, that is, people will migrate from one place to another based on the real or perceived opportunities available at the destination. It further determined that the number of people migrating is directly proportional to the number of opportunities at the destination and is inversely proportional to the number of intervening opportunities between the place of origin and destination.

HERMAN STUMP (1837–1917) U.S. superintendent of immigration from 1893 to 1895 and commissioner-general of immigration from 1895 to 1897. In 1889 he was elected to Congress, and he served in the House of Representatives until 1893. While serving in Congress he served on the immigration committee that drafted the Immigration Act of 1891, which created the U.S. Immigration Service. President Grover Cleveland appointed him to serve as superintendent of the Office of Immigration in 1892. Congress moved the Office of Immigration from under the Treasury Department and created the Bureau of Immigration in 1895 at which time he became commissioner of immigration.

MARCELO M. SUÁREZ-OROZCO (UNKNOWN BIRTHDATE) Founder of the Harvard Immigration Projects. He also is the Courtney Sale Ross University Professor of Globalization and Education, and codirector of immigration studies at New York University. He coauthored the book *Children of Immigration* and wrote numerous immigration-related scholarly articles such as "America's Immigration Advantage" and "Stranger Anxieties: U.S. Immigration and Its Discontents," which appeared in the *Harvard International Review.* The Harvard Immigration Projects study the impact immigrant students have on the U.S. educational system.

JAN VAN RIEBEECK (1619–1677) Leader of the first European colony in South Africa. The Dutch settlement, a business venture by the Netherlands government, was established to provide supplies to ships sailing the trade routes between Europe and Asia. It also led the way for other Europeans immigrating to South Africa.

CLAUDE WICKARD (1893–1967) U.S. secretary of agriculture (1940–45). The United States lacked sufficient domestic workers to meet the needs of its agricultural industries, and in 1942 he traveled to Mexico and met with government officials there, seeking to import Mexican nationals to work in American agriculture. The result was the Mexican Farm Labor Program Agreement between the U.S. and Mexican governments also known as the Bracero Program. The initial agreement provided migrant workers a guarantee of minimum housing, including laundry, bathing, toilet, and waste disposal facilities; a minimum wage of .30 cents per hour; and at least 30 days of work upon arrival in America. Within one year the agreement had been stripped of all its guarantees, meeting American farmers' single goal: an adequate labor force. The agreement also failed to meet U.S. labor needs so farmers continued to recruit Mexican migrant workers illegally, resulting in increasing illegal migration, human smuggling, and abuses of basic human rights that continued in 2006. The program was discontinued in 1964.

WILBUR ZELINSKY (1921–) One of the United States' most prominent cultural geographers and a professor emeritus at Pennsylvania State University. His migration theory "The Hypothesis of the Mobility Transition" was published in the *Geographical Review* (volume 61, no. 2) in 1971. The theory suggested patterns of migration might follow a series of much as occurs for demographic changes. According to the theory, there are five transitional stages of migration. The first stage is common in preindustrial societies where there is limited residential migration or movement between areas; in the second stage there is an increase in migration between rural and urban areas, long-distance migration, and emigration; in the third stage rural-to-urban migration continues along with a rapid increase in city-to-city migration; in the fourth stage rural-to-urban migration decreases while city-to-city migration increases as well as some migration of unskilled workers and highly skilled workers between countries; the final stage is more common in advanced societies and is primarily inter- or-intraurban migration due to advanced technologies reducing the need for people to migrate other than for some long-distance travel for jobs.

HANIA ZLOTNIK (UNKNOWN BIRTHDATE) Director of the United Nations Population Division. This United Nations division is responsible for monitoring a wide range of population-related topics, including international migration.

9

Organizations and Agencies

This chapter includes contact information for various organizations and agencies related to immigration and migration. Listings are arranged alphabetically in three categories: United States research organizations, legal agencies, and support groups; international organizations and agencies; and anti-immigration and migration organizations.

UNITED STATES ORGANIZATIONS AND GROUPS

American Civil Liberties Union
125 Broad Street, 18th Floor
New York, NY 10004
Phone: (888) 567-2258
URL: http://www.aclu.org

The American Civil Liberties Union (ACLU) advocates for immigrants, refugees, and noncitizens on numerous levels, including challenging unconstitutional legislation and laws. Among the materials available from the organization are publications, legislative documents, examples of immigration-related U.S. Supreme Court cases, and books about immigrants and immigration.

American Immigration Center
Phone: (800) 814-1555
URL: http://www.us-immigration.com/index.html

This private company provides one of the largest selections available of self-help immigration and citizenship documents and information. The company's stated objective is "to provide an informative, educational and self-help resource for basic U.S. immigration needs." Materials available from the company include immigration law books, and downloadable e-kits for U.S.

temporary work visas, U.S. green cards, immigration-related forms, and more. The site also contains answers to frequently asked immigration questions, a list of eligibility requirements, and a list of eligible countries.

American Immigration Lawyers Association
918 F Street, NW
Washington, DC 20004
Phone: (202) 216-2400
Fax: (202) 783-7853
URL: http://www.aila.org
E-mail: membership@aila.org

The AILA is a national association of more than 10,000 lawyers and law professors who practice and teach immigration law. Member attorneys represent U.S. immigrant families who have applied for permanent residency for spouses, children, and other close family members. They also represent U.S. businesses that sponsor highly skilled foreign workers seeking to enter the country either temporarily or permanently. Other groups represented by the AILA include foreign students, entertainers, and asylum seekers.

ASPIRA ASSOCIATION
1444 Eye Street NW, Suite 800
Washington, DC 20002
Phone: (202) 835-3600
Fax: (202) 835-3613
URL: http://www.aspira.org
E-mail: info@aspira.org

Founded in 1961, this association is the United States's only nonprofit organization dedicated entirely to the education and leadership development of Puerto Rican and Latino youth. In 2005 ASPIRA (from the Spanish verb *aspirar,* "aspire") served nearly 90,000 youths and their parents. It partners with over 200 universities, government agencies, and other Latino and non-Latino groups. The organization boasts that is youth members have a 95 percent high school graduation rate and 90 percent of its members go on to college.

Bureau of Population, Refugees, and Migration
U.S. Department of State
2201 C Street, NW
Washington, DC 20502
Phone: (202) 647-4000
URL: http://www.state.gov/g/prm

This organization is a division of the U.S. Department of State. Its responsibilities include developing policies on population, refugees and migration, and coordinating U.S. international population and migration policies within the U.S. government.

Center for Immigration Studies
1522 K Street, NW, Suite 820
Washington, DC 20005
Phone: (202) 466-8185
URL: http://www.cis.org
E-mail: center@cis.org

This pro-immigration think tank focuses on research and analysis of the economic, social, and demographic impact of immigration in the United States.

Lutheran Immigration and Refugee Service
122 C Street, NW, Suite 125
Washington, DC 20001
Phone: (202) 783-7509
Fax: (202) 783-7502
URL: http://www.lirs.org
E-mail: dc@lirs.org

The Lutheran Immigration and Refugee Service was established in 1939 in response to persecution by the Nazi government in Germany and the onset of World War II. Its original mission was helping Lutheran refugees escape from Europe. Today the organization provides assistance to refugees of all faiths and ethnicities. Between 1939 and 2005 LIRS has helped more than 330,000 refugees resettle in the United States. The group specializes in resettling refugee children and has expanded its outreach to include asylum seekers, undocumented workers, and other vulnerable immigrants.

National Immigration Forum
50 F Street, NW, Suite 300
Washington, DC 20001
Phone: (202) 347-0040
Fax: (202) 347-0508
URL: http://www.immigrationforum.org

The forum provides resources and tools for immigration and immigrant advocates, fact sheets, and current information about immigration legislation. It also provides links to newspaper articles, press releases, editorials, and other immigration-related materials. The forum was founded in 1982 with a goal of protecting immigrant rights through alliance building, advocacy, and public outreach efforts.

National Network for Immigrant and Refugee Rights
310 Eighth Street, Suite 303
Oakland, CA 94607
Phone: (510) 465-1984
Fax: (510) 465-1885
URL: http://www.nnirr.org
E-mail: nnirr@nnirr.org

Founded in 1986 by a group of immigrant community leaders, NNIRR evolved in response to opposition to proposed U.S. legislation that eventually was adopted as the Immigration Reform and Control Act of 1986. NNIRR works to document human rights abuses, challenge legislation, advocate for the rights of migrant workers, and provide a forum for immigrant community activists. Resources available from the NNIRR include fact sheets and links to other immigration- and migration-related Web sites.

New York Association for New Americans
17 Battery Place
New York, NY 10004
Phone: (212) 425-2900
URL: http://www.nyana.org

This association was created in 1949 by Jewish organizations in response to the aftermath of World War II in which thousands of Jewish refugees and other displaced persons were forced to live in refugee camps in eastern Europe. It set as its mission to bring these refugees and displaced persons to the United States. Since it inception NYANA has been on hand to help Jewish refugees from Cuba, Hungary, Iran, Syria, the former Soviet Union, and other countries resettle in America. It has also aided refugees from Southeast Asia, Vietnam, Haiti, Uganda, and Tibet. The organization also provides support and services to the general immigrant population.

Office of Immigration Statistics
U.S. Department of Homeland Security
425 I Street, NW, Room 4034
Washington, DC 20536
Phone: (202) 305-1613

URL: http://www.dhs.gov/ximgtn/statistics
E-mail: immigrationstatistics@hgs.gov

This organization collects immigration-related information that is used to create U.S. immigration policies and to help determine the effect of those policies on immigration.

Office of Refugee Resettlement
U.S. Department of Health and Human Services
Administration for Children and Families
370 L'Enfant Promenade, SW, 6th Floor East
Phone: (202) 401-9246
URL: http://www.acf.dhhs.gov/programs/orr

This division of the U.S. Department of Health and Human Services assists refugees in America in becoming financially self-sufficient.

U.S. Census Bureau
4700 Silver Hill Road
Washington, DC 20233
Phone: (202) 728-6829
URL: http://www.census.gov

This branch of the Department of Commerce gathers data about the people in the United States and the country's economy, which is used to track immigration and assimilation trends.

U.S. Citizenship and Immigration Services
1300 Pennsylvania Avenue, NW
Washington, DC 20229
Phone: (800) 375-5283
URL: http://www.uscis.gov/

Information about every aspect of immigration to the United States is available on this Web site. Among materials that can be accessed are forms for visas and green cards; information on laws and regulations; immigration handbooks, manuals, and policy guides; civics and citizenship study materials; resources for new immigrants; and the history of immigration law in America.

U.S. Customs and Border Protection
1300 Pennsylvania Avenue, NW
Washington, DC 20229

Phone: (202) 354-1000
URL: http://www.customs.gov

A division of the Department of Homeland Security, the Border Patrol is responsible for protecting America's borders and ports. Since 9/11 its emphasis has been on preventing terrorism.

U.S. Department of Homeland Security
Washington, DC 20528
Phone: (202) 282-8000
URL: http://www.dhs.gov

This federal agency is charged with protecting the United States from terrorist attacks, securing the country's borders and ports, and supervising the entrance and naturalization of aliens.

U.S. Immigration and Customs Enforcement
2675 Prosperity Avenue
Fairfax, VA 22031
Phone: (703) 285 6757
Fax (703) 285-6709
URL: http://www.ice.gov/index.htm

A branch of the Department of Homeland Security, ICE was created in 2003 by combining the law-enforcement divisions of the former Immigration and Naturalization Service and the U.S. Customs Service. Its stated mission is "to protect America and uphold public safety." ICE's far-reaching responsibilities include investigating employers and targeting illegal workers, identifying fraudulent immigration documents, enforcing ordered deportations of aliens, and more.

INTERNATIONAL ORGANIZATIONS AND GROUPS

Asian Migrant Centre
Phone: (852) 2312-0031
Fax: (852) 2991-0111
URL: http://www.asian-migrants.org/index.php?option=com_frontpage&Itemid=1

This Hong Kong-based organization works to promote the rights of migrant workers and their families in Asia. Additionally, it serves as a research, information, publishing, training, support, and action center for migrants.

December 18
René Plaetevoet, Director
Gaucheretstraat 164
1030 Brussels
Belgium
Phone: +32-2-2741435
Fax: +32-2-2741438
URL: http://www.december18.net/web/general/start.php?lang=EN
E-mail: info@december18.net

This online organization is named for the International Day of Solidarity with Migrants. Its stated mission is "to promote and protect the rights of migrants with dignity and respect as basic values." Among the materials available on the site are related documents such as articles from newspapers, magazines, and scholarly journals; books; statistics; fact sheets; and maps.

History of International Migration
Migration History
Leiden University
PO Box 9515
2300 RA Leiden
The Netherlands
Phone: +31 (0)71 527 2786
URL: http://www.let.leidenuniv.nl/history/migration

This Web site offers a wide selection of resources, such as documents and historical information related to international migration.

Institute for Migration and Ethnic Studies
University of Amsterdam
O.Z. Achterburgwal 237
1012 DL Amsterdam
The Netherlands
Phone: 31 20 525 3628
URL: http://www2.fmg.uva.nl/imes
E-mail: imes@fmg.uva.nl

The IMES is an interdisciplinary institute at the University of Amsterdam. Its research program promotes and integrates learning from different perspectives, including anthropology, sociology, communication and political sciences, social and economic geography, administrative law, and social and economic history.

Migrants Rights International
c.p. 135, route des Morillons
1211 Geneva
Switzerland
Phone: +41.22.9177817 / +41.22.7882873
Fax: +41.22.7882875
URL: http://www.migrantwatch.org/
E-mail: migrantwatch@vtx.ch

This group is a nongovernmental organization (NGO) with special consulting status with the United Nations Economic and Social Council. Its stated goal is promoting the human rights of all migrants. It was founded in 1994 during the United Nations International Conference on Population and Development in Cairo, Egypt, and is comprised of experts in the field of migration and migrant rights. Resources available from the organization include *Migrant News* and *MRI Bulletin,* both e-newsletters offer updates about related issues.

Migration Policy Institute
1400 16th Street, NW, Suite 300
Washington, DC 20036
Phone: (202) 266-1940
URL: http://www.migrationpolicy.org
E-mail: infor@migrationpolicy.org

The institute is a nonpartisan, independent think tank that studies migration and refugee policies at all governmental levels for communities worldwide.

Sans Papiers
URL: http://www.bok.net/pajol/index.en.html
E-mail: pajol@bok.net

This Web site is dedicated to advocating for the rights of undocumented Africans in France. It includes immigration reports from throughout western Europe and is offered in 11 languages. Information available on the site includes access to the College of Mediators who work on behalf of *sans papiers,* related articles and essays, and more.

Sin Fronteras
Calle Ortega 27-1
Colonia Coyoacán
Mexico City, CP 04000 Mexico
Phone: (52) 55-54-6335 or 55-54-6480

Fax: (52) 55-54-7180
URL: http://www.laneta.apc.org/sinfronteras/
E-mail: sinfronteras@laneta.apc.org

This not-for-profit, nongovernmental organization (NGO) was initiated in 1995 by a group of social activists and academics with the stated purpose of advocating for the "rights and well-being of refugees and migrants." Sin Fronteras provides information about legal and social assistance, public awareness, educational programs, and research materials.

Southern African Migration Project
Two St. David's Place
Parktown Johannesburg, South Africa
Phone: +27 (0) 11 717-3520
Fax: +27 (0) 11 484-2729
URL: http://www.queensu.ca/samp/
E-mail: msibi.n@pdm.wits.ac.za

According to the Southern African Migration Project (SAMP) Web site, this organization "conducts applied research on migration and development issues, provides policy advice and expertise, offers training in migration policy and management, and conducts public education campaigns on migration-related issues" relevant to South Africa. A wide variety of information is available about immigration policy, brain drain, xenophobia, HIV/AIDS, and migration and development in South Africa.

United Nations High Commissioner for Refugees
Case Postale 2500
CH-1211 Genève 2 Dépôt
Switzerland
Phone: +41 22 739 8111
URL: http://www.unhcr.org

This division of the United Nations is responsible for coordinating international actions to solve problems encountered by refugees, safeguard the rights of refugees, and provide services to refugees.

ANTI-IMMIGRATION ORGANIZATIONS AND GROUPS

American Border Patrol (Voices of Citizens Together)
2160 East Fry Boulevard, Suite 426

Sierra Vista, AZ 85635
Phone: (520) 803-7703
Fax: (520) 803-7730
URL: http://www.americanpatrol.com/

Founded in 1992 in response to the Los Angeles race riots, this group actively opposes illegal immigration and advocates greater security on the U.S.-Mexico border to control Mexican and illegal immigration. The group's founder, Glenn Spencer, supports maximum deportation efforts for all illegal immigrants and an English-only federal language policy. He further believes that the Mexican government is trying to reconquer its former territories in the American Southwest by sending large numbers of Mexicans to recolonize that land. The group's Web site is described as perhaps the most "directly negative and anti-immigrant" of any sites online.

American Immigration Control Foundation
PO Box 525
Monterey, VA 24465
Phone: (540) 468-2024
URL: http://www.aicfoundation.com
E-mail: aicfndn@cfw.com

This organization's key goal is developing an anti-immigration policy for the United States that is both workable and able to preserve traditional American values.

Americans for Immigration Control
PO Box 738
Monterey, VA 24465
Phone: (540) 468-2023
URL: http://www.immigrationcontrol.com
E-mail: aic@immigrationcontrol.com

From lobbying Congress to grassroots-level campaigning, this group is focused on regulating legal immigration and deterring illegal immigration. It supports legal reforms to reduce immigration to the United States, increasing funding for border patrol, establishing sanctions against employers who hire illegal immigrants, and opposing amnesty for illegal immigrants.

Border Guardians
128 Rainbow Drive, Suite 2893

Livingston, TX 77399
URL: http://www.borderguardians.org/index.php

This activist organization describes itself as "a group of American citizens who believe that defending America's sovereignty is the most important issue in the illegal immigration problem." It states it is fighting against the propaganda of "left-wing advocates of illegal immigration," including the U.S. and Mexican governments, the American Civil Liberties Union (ACLU), La Raza, and others. The Border Guardians' stated mission is to disrupt and deter illegal immigration by any legal means. Alternate goals are aiding the U.S Border Patrol, and standing in opposition to amnesty for illegal aliens, importing migrant workers, and outsourcing American jobs to other countries. Available on the Web site is access to related newspaper articles and the documentary *How to Burn a Mexican Flag,* which is offered for sale as a DVD.

Federation for American Immigration Reform
1666 Connecticut Avenue, NW, Suite 400
Washington, DC 20009
Phone: (202) 328-7004
Fax: (202) 387-3447
URL: http://www.fairus.org/site/PageServer

This organization supports the idea that U.S. immigration policies should be reformed to better serve the national interest, including improving border security, ending illegal immigration, and reducing annual immigration levels to 300,000 immigrants. The group advocates for a moratorium on all immigration except spouses and minor children of U.S. citizens and a limited number of refugees. Further, the group believes that immigrants negatively impact U.S. educational systems, health care, employment, crime rates, and government welfare programs. Access to articles and information about immigration as well as statistical data are available on the site.

Minuteman Project
PO Box 3944
Laguna Hills, CA 92654
Phone: (949) 587-5199
Fax: (949) 222-6607
URL: http://www.minutemanproject.com/
E-mail: info@minutemanproject.com

This activist group describes itself as "Americans doing the job Congress won't do. 'Operating within the law to support enforcement of the law.'" Its members take direct action to stop what they refer to as the "human flood of illegal immigrants" entering the United States at the U.S.-Mexico border. Members are recruited to patrol the border and report illegal immigrants to the U.S. Border Patrol. Critics of the group contend that the project is xenophobic and encourages vigilantism, but members claim they follow the law. The site includes access to published newspaper articles as well as hate mail the organization receives from opponents.

10

Annotated Bibliography

The resources in this annotated bibliography are divided into the following broad subjects areas:

International Immigration and Migration

United States

France

South Africa

Mexico

The Philippines

Each subject area is further subdivided into three categories: *Books, Articles and Reports,* and *Web Documents.* A final section lists immigration-related films and documentaries.

INTERNATIONAL IMMIGRATION AND MIGRATION

Books

Borjas, George J., and Jeff Crisp. *Poverty, International Migration and Asylum.* London: Palgrave Macmillan, 2005. This book examines the economic consequences of immigration and asylum migration, focusing on the economic consequences of legal and illegal immigration, and placing the study of immigration in a global context. It also includes case studies of various aspects of immigration and asylum in the United States, Argentina, Mexico, the Caribbean, Denmark, Sweden, and Iraqi asylum migrants in Jordan.

Castles, Stephen, and Mark J. Miller. *The Age of Migration: International Population Movements in the Modern World.* 3d ed. New York: Guilford Press, 2003. This book is described as a comprehensive and accessible introduction to the multiple aspects of population movements around the globe, from migration trends and policies to issues of immigrant incorporation and anti-immigrant politics. The authors also identify problems associated with migration and offer solutions.

Cornelius, Wayne A., James F. Hollifield, and Philip L. Martin, eds. *Controlling Immigration: A Global Perspective.* Palo Alto, Calif.: Stanford University Press, 2003. Contributors to this book examine case studies of immigration in receiving countries (the United States, Canada, and Autralia), countries resistant to immigration (France, Germany, the Netherlands, and Britain), and emerging receiving countries (Italy, Spain, Japan, and South Korea). Topics discussed include the ongoing immigration debate, the impact of the global market economy, and shifting from immigration control to migration management.

George, Sheba. *When Women Come First: Gender and Class in Transnational Migration.* Berkeley: University of California Press, 2005. In this book the author "sensitively exposes the emotional and psychic costs that are part and parcel of the immigrant pursuit of the American dream" by following the experiences of nurses from India who immigrate to the United States. Also touched upon is the challenge to the notions of manhood encountered by the husbands who follow the women.

Kapur, Devesh, and John McHale. *Give Us Your Best and Brightest: The Global Hunt for Talent and Its Impact on the Developing World.* Washington, D.C.: Center for Global Development, 2005. This book focuses on the consequences of the emigration of highly skilled workers from developing countries. It provides an analysis of the topic and offers creative policy recommendations related to brain drain for both sending and receiving countries.

Kingman, Mireille. *Nurses on the Move: Migration and the Global Health Care Economy.* Ithaca, N.Y.: Cornell ILR Press, 2005. The author shares personal stories of migrant nurses from countries, including South Africa and the Philippines, to discuss international nurse migration. Among the questions the book considers and attempts to answer are: Why do nurses decide to migrate? Is this migration voluntary or in some way coerced? When developing countries are faced with nurse vacancy rates of more than 40 percent, is recruitment by industrialized countries fair play in a competitive market or a new form of colonialization? What happens to these workers—and the patients left behind—when they migrate? What safeguards will protect nurses and the patients they find in their new workplaces?

Ozden, Calgar, and Maurice Schiff, eds. *International Migration, Remittances and the Brain Drain.* London: Palgrave Macmillan, 2005. This book is the first major work published by the World Bank's International Migration and Development Research Program. The volume contains case studies of the impact of remittances on poverty and expenditure patterns in select countries, including Mexico and the Philippines. The chapters discussing brain drain include one of the largest databases on brain drain, analyses of the topic, a discussion of brain waste, and the impact of skilled migration (brain gain) on productivity in destination countries.

Schierup, Carl-Ulrik, Peo Hansen, and Stephen Castles. *Migration, Citizenship, and the European Welfare State: A European Dilemma.* New York: Oxford University

Press, 2006. This book connects immigration and ethnic relations with the political and welfare state in Europe as it examines the problems associated with liberal antiracist policies. The authors carefully analyze the European Union's increasing policy involvement in international migration, immigrant integration, discrimination, and racism. The book draws on the analysis of related case studies from the United Kingdom, Germany, Italy, and Sweden to document the variety of Europe's social and political landscape.

Terry, Donald F., and Steven R. Wilson, eds. *Beyond Small Change: Making Migrant Remittances Count.* Washington, D.C.: Inter-American Development Bank, 2005. This book provides an overview of the importance of remittances, including how they improve the living conditions of poor families in receiving countries, how they help reduce the risks facing families spread across those countries, and how they can reduce poverty when used to finance investments in education, housing, and health care in the receiving countries. Research for the book draws on surveys, case studies, and cross-country and cross-region comparisons. While it targets remittances in Latin American and Caribbean countries, it also touches on remittances received by countries in Europe, Asia, and the Middle East.

The World in Motion: Short Essays on Migration and Gender. Geneva: World Health Organization, 2004. This book provides a set of preliminary but widely accepted understandings about issues of importance to immigrant women and those who advocate for them. It helps clarify the experiences of migrant women in various key areas, including labor migration, remittances, human trafficking, and immigration and identification.

World Migration 2005: Costs and Benefits of International Migration. Geneva: International Organization for Migration, 2005. Among the topics discussed in this book are where people are migrating today and why, what the implications are for the world's developing and industrialized economies, and the key issues facing policy makers in migrant origin, destination, and transit countries. Regional overviews include Africa and the Middle East, the Americas, Asia and Oceania, and Europe. Also discussed are migration-related development and migrant health and integration. Also included are data and statistics specific to international migration.

Articles and Reports

Castles, Stephen. "Confronting the Realities of Forced Migration." *Migration Information Source,* May 1, 2004. This article presents a brief background of forced migration in the past, then examines the topic and identifies who are forced migrants in the 21st century. It includes information about refugees, asylum seekers, those who have been displaced for a variety of reasons, and human trafficking and smuggling. The article concludes with a discussion about forced migration and the "Actual Global Crisis."

Deshingkar, Priya, and Sven Grimm. *Internal Migration and Development: A Global Perspective.* International Organization for Migration, February 2005. This report provides a response to the some of the basic questions related to voluntary internal migration, including migrations prompted by a search for employment, and permanent and temporary migration. It also addresses rural-rural, rural-urban, urban-rural, and urban-urban migration. Topics not covered in this report are forced migration due to development programs, wars and civil unrest, trafficking, and slavery.

Newland, Kathleen. "Migration as a Factor in Development and Poverty Reduction." *Migration Information Source,* June 1, 2003. This article considers the costs and benefits of migration from the perspective of poor countries of origin, including remittances, brain drain, and the impact of migration policies in rich countries.

World Economic and Social Survey 2004: International Migration. This detailed report released by the United Nations provides historical background information about migration in the 19th and early 20th centuries and then presents information about the topic during the 21st century, or what is defined as the period of globalization. Topics discussed include the economic impact of international migration on both countries of origin and destination, social integration of migrants, national policies and initiatives, and the future role of international migrants. The report also touches on international migration trends, temporary migration, and international migration management.

Web Documents

"Increasing International Migration Flows." *Migration: Earth,* Optimum Population Trust, 2006. URL: http://www.optimumpopulation.org/opt.more.migration.int.html. This document responds to several questions, including: Does migration affect the global ecosystem? Does mass international migration slow population growth? And, does mass international migration change ecological footprints? It takes the position that in the 21st century there are too many migrants, that migratory pressures may be expected to increase, and that receiving countries are unable to accept the increased flows of migrants.

International World History Project: World History from the Pre-Sumerian Period to the Present. URL: http://history-world.org/. There are more than 60 immigration- and migration-related essays available in the *World History Project,* including "History of America, Parts 3, 5 and 6"; "Establishment of Latin American States"; "British Dominions"; "Mexico: A Brief History"; and "Famine in Ireland."

UNITED STATES

Books

Bacon, David. *Communities without Borders: Images and Voices from the World of Migration.* Ithaca, N.Y.: Cornell ILR Press, 2006. This book, through photographs and transcribed oral histories, documents the experience of contemporary migrants. It follows the lives of migrants moving between Guatemala, Mexico, and the United States by vividly portraying their struggles to improve the lives of their families and themselves. The author draws on his experience as a photographer, journalist, and former labor organizer to take readers into the communities of these migrants and provide details of the "ties that bind them together."

Bode, Janet. *New Kids in Town: Oral Histories of Immigrant Teens.* Scholastic Paperbacks, 1995. In this book 11 teenage immigrants tell the compelling stories of their escapes from war, poverty, and repression to begin new lives in America.

Dinnerstein, Leonard, and David M. Reimers. *Ethnic Americans: A History of Immigration.* New York: Columbia University Press, 1999. This book provides a thoughtful and reasonably comprehensive analysis of immigrants in America and of ethnic experiences. It addresses the topics from both historical and contemporary perspectives, including immigrants in America during the colonial period, from 1789 to 1890, 1890 to 1920, and post World War II. It also discusses increasing immigration to the United States from Mexico, ethnic conflicts, restrictions placed on immigrants, and assimilation.

Fox, Jonathan, and Gaspar Rivera-Salgado, eds. *Indigenous Mexican Migrants in the United States.* San Diego: University of California, Center for Comparative Immigration Studies, 2004. This book explores the experiences of indigenous Mexican migrants in the United States, considering basic changes in how Mexican society is understood in the 21st century. The studies included present diverse perspectives on how sustained migration and the emergence of organizations of indigenous migrants influence social and community identity, both in the United States and in Mexico.

Gamboa, Erasmo. *Mexican Labor and World War II: Braceros in the Pacific Northwest, 1942–1947.* Seattle: University of Washington Press, 1999. Topics discussed in this book include the agriculture industry and migrant workers, the farm labor crisis that resulted from U.S. involvement in World War II, strikes by the Braceros workers, and the life and experiences of Braceros in the United States.

Garza, Encarnacion, Pedro Reyes, and Enrique T. Trueba. *Resiliancy and Success: Migrant Children in the United States.* Herndon, Va.: Paradigm Publishers, 2004. Rather than focusing on the negative, such as low-achievement levels, high attrition rates, and the academic failures of migrant students, this book presents the stories of successful high school and college students who come from migrant farm laboring families. Its goal is helping teachers, students, researchers, and policy makers understand factors that lead to success for minority language students.

Ngai, Mae M. *Impossible Subjects: Illegal Aliens and the Making of Modern America.* Princeton, N.J.: Princeton University Press, 2005. This book provides a historical perspective on immigration policy and practice for the period from 1924 to 1965. It explains how U.S. immigration laws were used as a tool to shape American racial policy, notably toward Asians and Mexicans, through the use of such concepts as "illegal aliens," "national origins," and "racial ineligibility to citizenship."

Rothenberg, Daniel. *With These Hands: The Hidden World of Migrant Farmworkers Today.* Berkeley: University of California Press, 2000. First-person narratives tell the stories of exploitation, low wages, stolen paychecks, and other abuses suffered by migrant agricultural laborers in the United States as they move from place to place, field to field. In addition to the words of the migrant workers, the book includes interviews with farmers, farm labor contractors, *coyotes* who smuggle illegal migrant workers into the country, government investigators, and union organizers.

Zolberg, Aristide R. *A Nation by Design: Immigration Policy in the Fashioning of America.* Cambridge, Mass.: Harvard University Press, 2006. This book is described as a thorough, authoritative account of American immigration history and the political and social factors that brought it about. The author profiles the changing opinions on immigration throughout American history and examines individually the roles played by business interests, labor unions, ethnic lobbies, and nativist ideologues in U.S. immigration shaping policy. How three different types of migration—legal migration, illegal migration to fill low-wage jobs, and asylum seeking—are shaping contemporary arguments over immigration to the United States is also discussed.

Articles and Reports

Borjas, George J. *The Impact of Immigration on the Labor Market.* Harvard University, January 2006. This report was prepared for the Conference on Labor and Capital Flows in Europe Following Enlargement, organized by the International Monetary Fund, the Joint Vienna Institute, and the National Bank of Poland. It specifically addresses the impact of immigration on the U.S. labor market and focuses on answering three key questions: What is the contribution of immigration to the skill endowment of the workforce? How do the employment opportunities of native workers respond to immigration? And, who benefits and who loses due to labor immigration?

Chishti, Muzaffar A., et al. *America's Challenge: Domestic Security, Civil Liberties, and National Unity after September 11.* Migration Policy Institute, 2003. This report describes and evaluates the impact of government policies on the United States's vulnerability to terrorism, on civil liberties of Americans, especially Arab and Muslim Americans, and on the sense of national unity. Among topics discussed in the report are how harsh measures taken against immigrants have not made Americans safer and how government immigration actions threaten the basic civil liberties of all Americans. In addition, the report offers alternative suggestions for immigration enforcement and enhanced domestic security.

A Description of the Immigrant Population. This report issued by the U.S. Congressional Budget Office in late 2004 was written to present the available facts and research on immigration to help provide necessary information as the agency prepared projections of the federal budget and the U.S. economy. It includes detailed information, data, and statistics about the foreign-born population in America, including how large it is, where the immigrants come from, where immigrants live, educational levels, places of employment and earnings, and poverty status. It also provides historical data about immigration to the United States dating back to 1821.

Dixon, David, Julie Murray, and Julia Gelart. *America's Emigrants: U.S. Retirement Migration to Mexico and Panama.* Migration Policy Institute, 2006. This lengthy report reviews and analyzes a growing phenomenon in the United States: American citizens leaving the country to live in other countries following retirement. The report addresses seven key themes: The size of the U.S.-born emigrant citizens aged 55 years and older grew notably in Mexico and Panama between 1990 and 2000 and data indicates the outflows of people in this age group is expected to increase; U.S. retirees contribute human and financial resources to their new communities and studies suggest the amount of capital is substantial; policies in the United States and destination countries can encourage or deter retirement migration; economic factors strongly influenced retirees' decisions to emigrate; most retirees gather extensive information about several countries before deciding to emigrate; how well retirees integrate into their new communities varies and most cite language as a barrier to adapting; and retirees help create jobs and other opportunities for the local citizens in destination countries but their presence also drives up the cost of real estate in the destination country.

Downes, Lawrence. "The Terrible, Horrible, Urgent National Disaster That Immigration Isn't." *New York Times,* June 20, 2006. This editorial carefully analyzes the immigration controversy in the United States that began in 2005. Downes touches on ideas presented in the popular media, such as "getting tough on immigration," the role "fear" plays in the discussion, and the cost of different proposed solutions to immigration problems. The author also discusses alternative methods for managing immigration, the potential costs at home and abroad, and future possibilities.

Meyers, Deborah Waller. "From Horseback to High-Tech: U.S. Border Enforcement." *Migration Information Source,* February 1, 2006. This article tells the story of the creation and evolution of the U.S. Border Patrol and law enforcement at the U.S.-Mexico border. It follows the development of the Border Patrol beginning in 1904 through 2005. Included is a timeline of events specific to border enforcement and data related to the apprehension of illegal border crossers from 1980 to 2003.

Three Decades of Mass Immigration: The Legacy of the 1965 Immigration Act. Released by the Center for Immigration Studies in September 1995, this report provides information about the act and a perspective of its impact on immigration 30 years after its passage. Included are comments and quotes related to the act made by the key players in 1965, both for and against the act. The report also contains a brief chronology of important immigration legislation passed in the United States, beginning with the Chinese Exclusion Act of 1882 and ending with the Immigration Act of 1990.

Web Documents

"2006 State Legislation Related to Immigration: Enacted, Vetoed, and Pending Gubernatorial Action." National Conference of State Legislatures, July 3, 2006. URL: http://www.ncsl.org/programs/immig/06ImmigEnactedLegis2.htm. In 2006, U.S. state legislatures introduced over 500 pieces of immigration-related legislation for consideration. Of those at least 57 were enacted in 27 states. This document lists each state that took legislative action and contains a brief description of each bill.

"Bracero Program," *The Handbook of Texas Online,* 2001. URL: http://www.tsha.utexas.edu/handbook/online/articles/BB/omb1.html. This article offers an overview of the U.S. Mexican Farm Labor Program Agreement with Mexico adopted in 1942 with a focus on its impact on Texas agricultural growers. The online handbook is sponsored by the Texas State Historical Association, the University of Texas Libraries, and the Center for Texas Studies at the University of Texas at Austin.

"Immigration from Mexico: Assessing the Impact on the United States." The Center for Immigration Studies, 2001. URL: http://cis.org/articles/2001/mexico/release.html. This study examines the costs and benefits for the United States of Mexican migrant workers entering the country. It includes detailed information about Mexican immigrants, including education levels, use of welfare, poverty and economic data, school-age population, impact on prices and wages, and second and third-generation immigrants.

Suárez-Orozco, Marcelo M. "Stranger Anxieties: U.S. Immigration and Its Discontents." *Harvard International Review,* 2006. URL: http://hir.harvard.edu/articles/1447. The author discusses the growing concern in the United States about the rapidly increasing growth of illegal immigration into the country and the competing immigration reform legislation passed by the U.S. House and Senate. The article also discusses immigration to the United States from a broader perspective, including historical and economic facts and the outlook for the future.

"U.S. Immigration and Naturalization Service—Populating a Nation: A History of Immigration and Naturalization." U.S. Customs and Border Protection, 2006. URL: http://www.cbp.gov/xp/cgov/toolbox/about/history/ins_history.xml. This article offers a history of the U.S. Immigration and Naturalization service from its inception through post 9/11. There are also links to other related articles available at this site.

FRANCE

Books

Freedman, Jane. *Immigration and Insecurity in France.* Burlington, Vt.: Ashgate Publishing, 2004. This book discusses the important place immigration issues occupy in French politics. It closely examines the debate over immigration in contemporary France, the development of immigration and nationality policies, and the discussions related to the integration of immigrants. Further, the book analyzes the headscarf affair and the resulting racism and anti-Islamic sentiment.

Hargreaves, Alec G. *Immigration, 'Race' and Ethnicity in Contemporary France.* New York: Routledge, 1999. This book discusses pressing and significant issues related to immigration in France, including the headscarf affair, evolution of an immigrant underclass, and reforming French immigration legislation and policies. Topics covered include politics, economics, social structures, and cultural practices specific to immigration and immigrants in France.

Laredo, Joe. *Foreigners in France: Triumphs & Disasters.* London: Survival Books, 2005. This book shares the true stories of expatriates living in France. It is described as an important new book for those planning to live, work, or buy a home in France.

Mandel, Maude. *In the Aftermath of Genocide: Armenians and Jews in Twentieth Century France.* Durham, N.C.: Duke University Press, 2003. France is the only Western European nation home to substantial numbers of survivors of the World War I and World War II genocides. With that in mind, the author discusses how changes in ethnic, religious, and national affiliations have been affected by these immigrants in recent history.

Sahlins, Peter. *Unnaturally French: Foreign Citizens in the Old Regime and After.* Ithaca, N.Y.: Cornell University Press, 2003. This book relates the story of the naturalization of foreigners in France from the sixteenth to the early nineteenth centuries. It provides a historical perspective on immigration, nationality, and citizenship in France and Europe.

Silverstein, Paul A. *Algeria in France: Transpolitics, Race, and Nation.* Bloomington: Indiana University Press, 2004. This book examines the Algerian presence in France through history and a variety of contemporary aspects, including immigration policy, colonial governance, urban planning, corporate advertising, sports, literary narratives, and songs. The author also investigates the connection between anti-immigrant racism and the rise of Islamist and Berberist ideologies in France.

Wolfreys, Jim. *Politics of Racism in France.* New York: St. Martins Press, 1998. In this book the author examines the ideology, structure, antecedents, and present activities of the National Front, a political party that actively opposes immigration to the country, particularly by Muslims from North Africa and the Middle East. The party also supports mandatory military service, reinstatement of the death penalty in France, and deportation of non-Europeans in France.

Articles and Reports

Blion Reynald, Catherine Wihtol de Wenden, and Nedjma Meknache. "France." *EU and U.S. Approaches to the Management of Immigration,* 2003. This lengthy and detailed report, one in a series of 18, was prepared for the Migration Policy Group with the support of the German Marshall Fund. It presents an analysis of immigration to France, including the country's immigration debate shifting from welcoming immigrants as workers to focusing on security, control, and repression of immigrants.

Guiraudon, Virginie. "Immigration Policy in France." *U.S.-France Analysis.* National Center for Scientific Research, January 1, 2002. This report analyzes French immigration policy, both historical and contemporary, and compares French legislation to U.S. immigration legislation.

Hamilton, Kimberly, Patrick Simon, and Clara Veniard. "The Challenge of French Diversity." *Migration Information Source,* November 2004. This article discusses 2004 legislation adopted by France in response to the Muslim headscarf controversy that banned the "wearing of ostentatious religious symbols in public schools." It provides background on French immigration policy and places policy in a contemporary context. Topics touched upon include the increase of asylum seekers arriving in France, a description of the French by nationality and origin, and discrimination of immigrants in France.

Murphy, Kara. "France's New Law: Control Immigration Flows, Court the Highly Skilled." *Migration Information Source,* November 1, 2006. This article discusses from a political point of view the immigration law passed by the French government in 2006.

Seljug, Affan. "Cultural Conflicts: North African Immigrants in France." *International Journal of Peace Studies* 2, no. 2 (July 1997). This article traces the history of North African immigrants in France, discusses Muslims in France and their experiences, and examines related conflicts such as the 1989 headscarf controversy in which Muslim girls were expelled from school for wearing headscarves to class.

Tapinos, Georges P. "Policy Responses to Population Ageing and Population Decline in France." September 29, 2000. This report was prepared for the Expert Group Meeting on Policy Responses to Population Ageing and Population Decline sponsored by the United Nations Secretariat, Department of Economic and Social Affairs, Population Division. Topics discussed include immigration as a method to meet the needs of the labor market and add to the populations.

Web Documents

"France. Immigration Law and Policy." *Legislationline,* 2006. URL: http://legislationline.org/?tid=131&jid=19&less=false. This document provides an analysis of the history of French immigration legislation through 2003. It also includes summaries of various articles published in 2005 related to the country's proposed new immigration bill.

Giguel, Anton. "French Immigration History," "French Immigration Policy." French Advisory Immigration Service. URL: http://homepages.uel.ac.uk/u0106050/. The information included in the documents on this Web site was created specifically for immigrants wishing to live in France. It focuses on the history of immigration in France and the European Union.

Peignard, Emmanuel. "Immigration in France." The Embassy of France in the United States, July 2001. URL: http://www.info-france-usa.org/atoz/immigration.asp.

Topics discussed in this article include the reasons people immigrate to France, facts and figures related to the number of foreigners and immigrants in France and their countries of origin, the integration of immigrants in French society, and France's immigration policies.

SOUTH AFRICA

Books

Abuse of Undocumented Migrants, Asylum Seekers, and Refugees in South Africa. New York: Human Rights Watch Africa, 1998. This book presents information about unpunished attacks and victimization of foreigners in South Africa by the South African police, the army, and by guards at detention facilities. It also addresses the overcrowded, substandard detention conditions for migrants awaiting deportation, treatment of refugees that fails to conform to international standards, and the country's lack of refugee legislation.

Crush, Jonathan, ed. *Transnationalism and New African Immigration to South Africa.* Kingston, Ontario, Canada: Queens University School of Policy, 2002. This book is described as a carefully researched, in-depth presentation of the experiences of cross-border migrant workers from neighboring African countries into South Africa. According to one review, the book "captures the high intensity of exchange between place of origin and destination, recognizes the importance of cultural identity and hybridity and provides avenues for challenging the assimilationist tendencies of immigration policies" in South Africa.

Elder, Glen S. *Hostels, Sexuality, and the Apartheid Legacy: Malevolent Geographies.* Athens: Ohio University Press, 2003. In this book the author examines male migrant worker hostels in South Africa. Once open to men only, the hostels have increasingly become home to "invisible" women migrants. The stories and experiences of 30 women living in one such hostel are shared in this book.

Jeeves, Alan H. *Migrant Labour in South Africa's Mining Economy: The Struggle for the Gold Mines' Labour Supply, 1890–1920.* Kingston, Ontario, Canada: McGill-Queens University Press, 2004. This book studies the origins of migratory laborers and discrimination in South Africa's emerging gold-mining industry. It refers to government records and the archives of private businesses to provide background about the industry, including recruitment practices, the struggle to control black African workers, the exploitation of workers, and the poor working conditions in the mines resulting in thousands of deaths.

Marx, Anthony W. *Making Race and Nation: A Comparison of the United States, South Africa.* Cambridge: Cambridge University Press, 1998. In this book the author uses a comparative historical approach to analyze the connection between race as a cultural and political category rooted in the history of slavery and colonialism and the development of three nation-states: South Africa, the United States, and Brazil.

Ramphele, Mamphela. *Bed Called Home: Life in the Migrant Labour Hostels of Cape Town.* Athens: Ohio University Press, 1993. South Africa's hostels were designed both to serve as temporary housing for Africans allowed to work in the country's "white-only" areas and to discourage permanent migration and family repatriation of the workers. This book documents the unsavory living conditions in the hostels, which have become permanent fixtures on the South African landscape. It also provides insight into the life of black African migrant workers by focusing on the idea of "space" as a social, physical, and political component of the hostels.

Truong, Thanh-Dom. *Poverty, Gender and Human Trafficking in Sub-Saharan Africa: Rethinking Best Practices in Migration Management.* New York: UNESCO, 2006. In this book the author discusses the profiles, strengths, and weaknesses of "best practices" in the fight against human trafficking in Sub-Saharan Africa. The book describes the connection among gender, poverty, and human trafficking. The work draws on a critical analysis of migration processes as they relate to human rights abuses.

Articles and Reports

Crush, Jonathan. "Regulating Migration in the 21st Century: A South African Perspective." South African Migration Project, July 6, 2000. This report was prepared for presentation at a panel discussion on the 21st-century challenges of migration. In the report the author makes the case that South African immigration policy up to 2000 continued to be governed by the apartheid-era Aliens Control Act and that the country's proposed new immigration bill should rescind and replace the act. The report also discusses obstacles that need to be overcome to enable South Africa to create a new policy adequate to the challenges of managing and benefiting from migration in the 21st century.

———. "South Africa: New Nation, New Migration Policy?" *Migration Information Source,* June 2003. In this article the author provides background about migration to South Africa beginning in the 1800s, specifically information related to cross-border labor migration from neighboring African countries. The article also discusses the country's immigration law enacted in 2002, authorized migrant movements between South Africa and other countries, refugees, and unauthorized (illegal) migration.

Klotz, Audie. "International Relations and Migration in Southern Africa." *African Security Review* 6, no. 3 (1997). This article discusses both illegal and legal migration to South Africa since 1994 and the end of apartheid. It also provides historical background about immigration in the country beginning in the early 1900s.

Maharaj, Brij. "Immigration to Post-Apartheid South Africa." *Global Migration Perspectives,* no. 1 (June 2004). Prepared for the Global Commission on International Migration, this lengthy report places migrant workers from neighboring African countries to South Africa in a historical context, provides demographic profiles of migrant workers, discusses reasons for migrants leaving their country of origin to work in South Africa, and how migrant workers are treated by South Africans. Also discussed are migrant workers and crime, welfare, health, social contributions, controls and deportation, and more.

Mattes, Robert, Jonathan Crush, and Wayne Richmond. "The Brain Gain: Skilled Migration and Immigration Policy in Post-Apartheid South Africa." *Migration Policy Series No. 20,* South African Migration Project. This report discusses the implications of the decline in immigration to South Africa and the increase in emigration from the country. The data in the report is based on a detailed survey and personal interviews of 400 skilled foreign nationals living and working in South Africa.

Posel, Dorrit. "Have Migration Patterns in Post-Apartheid South Africa Changed?" University of Natal South Africa, 2003. This report was prepared for the Conference on African Migration in Comparative Perspective held in Johannesburg June 4–7, 2003. It provides an overview of the migrant labor system in the country, notably the lack of evidence supporting the idea that "circular labor" (temporary workers filling jobs then returning to their homeland rather than remaining as permanent immigrants) ended or declined beginning in the 1990s.

Solomon, Hussein. "Turning Back the Tide: Strategic Responses to the Illegal Alien Problem in South Africa." *Monograph No. 4: People, Poverty and Peace, Human Security in Southern Africa,* May 1996. The increasing numbers of illegal aliens arriving in South Africa and the government's response are discussed in this article.

Web Documents

"Documented Migration, 2003." Statistics South Africa, Report No. 03-51-03 (2003). URL: http://www.statssa.gov.za/publications/statsdownload.asp?ppn=Report-03-51-03&sch=3352. This document produced by the South Africa government contains detailed and extensive migration statistics specific to documented immigration and self-declared emigration for the country from 1950 through 2003. Category breakdowns for documented immigrants include gender, age, occupation, country of previous permanent residence by occupation/birth/gender, and method of travel to and place of entry to the country. Categories for self-declared emigrants are similar, but they are specific to country of destination rather than country of origin.

History. South Africa Government Information. URL: http://www.info.gov.za/aboutsa/history.htm. This article traces the history of South Africa and provides information specific to events that led to immigration to and colonization of the country by the Dutch and British. It also discusses both the beginning and the end of apartheid.

"Johannesburg—Historical Background." The Economists.com, Cities Guide. URL: http://www.economist.com/cities/FindStory.cfm?CITY_ID=JOH&FOLDER=Facts-History. This article examines from a historical perspective the city of Johannesburg, South Africa, including its early days through the discovery of gold on a nearby farm. It discusses the impact immigrants who flocked to the area to find riches have had on the city, rising tensions between British and Dutch, how the treatment of black Africans eventually evolved into apartheid, and more.

MEXICO

Books

Bower, Doug, and Cynthia M. Bower. *The Plain Truth about Living in Mexico: The Expatriate's Guide to Moving, Retiring, or Just Hanging Out.* Boca Raton, Fla.: Universal Publishers, 2005. The authors, American emigrants living in Mexico, share their experiences and cover topics that include: Beginning the process of deciding whether Mexico is for you, evaluating locations and costs of emigration, avoiding being stereotyped as an Ugly American, finding a cure for culture shock before arriving in Mexico, and mastering Spanish before moving. Topics discussed also include safety in Mexico and the benefits of cheap living, travel, and medical care.

Byrnes, Dolores M. *Driving the State: Families and Public Policy in Central Mexico.* Ithaca, N.Y.: Cornell University Press, 2003. In this book the author focuses on a job-creation program established in 1996 by Mexico's president Vicente Fox when he was governor of the state of Guanajuato. The program, *Mi Comunidad,* was meant to reduce economic migration by Mexican nationals and became an important source of empowerment for small businesses in rural Mexico. A significant aspect of the program is the way it encourages former residents who have successfully migrated to the United States to invest in the *maquilas* (small businesses and factories) back home, thus helping create new jobs in Mexico.

Cohen Jeffery. *The Culture of Migration in Southern Mexico.* Austin: University of Texas Press, 2004. In this book the author examines the various factors that cause rural Oaxacans to migrate, the historical and contemporary patterns of their migration, the effects of migration on families and communities, and the economic, cultural, and social reasons why many citizens of southern Mexico decide to remain in their homeland rather than migrate.

Flores, Judith Leblanc. *Children of* la Frontera: *Binational Efforts to Serve Mexican Migrant and Immigrant Students.* Washington, D.C.: ERIC Clearing House on Rural Education and Small Schools, 1996. Described as one of the most comprehensive works to date on the subject, this book relies on practitioners and scholars to provide information about Mexican migrant and immigrant children, the political context within which they live and work in the United States, their educational needs, and efforts to meet those needs in the United States and Mexico.

Fomby, Paula. *Mexican Migrants and Their Parental Households in Mexico.* New York: LFB Scholarly Publishing, 2005. This book considers the factors associated with inception of migration careers, and asks how migration by selected children affects the social and economic organization of the parental household. The author writes from the perspective of migrants as adult children in their families of origin and shows that migrant-sending parental households in Mexico are distinctive in their composition, and that migrants continue to make significant economic contributions from abroad.

Guerin-Gonzales, Camille. *Mexican Workers and American Dreams: Immigration, Repatriation, and California Farm Labor, 1900–1939.* New Brunswick, N.J.:

Rutgers University Press, 1994. This book outlines the history of Mexican migrant laborers working on farms in rural California from 1900 to 1939. The author explores the connection between the Mexican immigrants' actual experiences and the American Dream, the exploitation of immigrants by their employers, and the deportation of thousands of Mexicans, both immigrants and naturalized citizens, during the Great Depression.

Martinez, Rubin. *Crossing Over: A Mexican Family on the Migrant Trail.* New York: Picador, 2002. In this book the author, a journalist, follows the journey of one Mexican family whose three sons, who were illegal migrants, died in a 1996 incident on the U.S.-Mexico border. Despite the loss of their sons, the family is determined to immigrate to America. The author reveals the effect emigration has had on them, the family members they leave behind, and their newly "adopted" country.

Articles and Reports

Blumenthal, Ralph, and Ginger Thompson. "Texas Town Is Unnerved by Violence in Mexico." *New York Times,* August 11, 2005, p. A18. This article discusses the rising problems associated with illegal immigration and illegal drug trafficking in the city of Nuevo Laredo, Mexico, and its U.S. sister city, Laredo, Texas and the impact on both communities.

Castillo, Manuel Ángel. "Mexico: Caught between the United States and Central America." *Migration Information Source,* April 1, 2006. Mexico's southern border with the Central American countries of Guatemala and Belize is the main route Central American nationals take in making their way into the United States. This article provides a historical background of the region, including early seasonal migrations by agricultural workers looking for jobs on Mexican farms and Guatemalan refugees in the 1970s and Mexico's related policies. It also addresses Central America in the 21st century, transit migration, illegal aliens and Mexico's deportation policies, and the future of Central American migration.

Hoyos, Melissa. "Hope. After 16 Years in the Shadows Two Sisters Win Legal Residency." *High Country News,* special edition, "The Trail North: Mapping Immigration's Human Landscape" 38, no. 9 (May 15, 2006). This article tells the story of two undocumented Mexican high school students who were brought illegally into the United States when they were babies, one by her uncle and the other by her mother and grandmother. It discusses the problems they have encountered "living in the shadows," such as fear of taking part in school activities, limited employment and future career opportunities, and the impact on their decision to attend college.

"The Immigrant's Trail." *High Country News,* special edition, "The Trail North: Mapping Immigration's Human Landscape" 38, no. 9 (May 15, 2006). This special edition of the magazine covers different aspects of illegal immigration from Mexico to the United States across the U.S.-Mexico border. In this article readers are introduced to the various topics associated with immigrants leaving Mexico and attempting to cross the desert Southwest border into the United

States. It also offers brief discussions of actions taken by the governors of Arizona and New Mexico, U.S.-Mexico border states where many of the immigrants attempt to cross.

Lettieri, Michael. "The Immigration Bomb Explodes." Council on Hemispheric Affairs, March 29, 2006. U.S.-Mexico relations specific to immigration and the increasing numbers of Mexican nationals entering the United States illegally are discussed in this report.

Marizco, Michael. "Abandonment. Plenty of Jobs, Not Enough Pay: Economic Forces Push Mexican Workers North." *High Country News,* special edition, "The Trail North: Mapping Immigration's Human Landscape" 38, no. 9 (May 15, 2006). This article discusses the reasons Mexican nationals are willing to risk their lives to make their way into the United States illegally. It discusses the impact the North American Free Trade Agreement has had on Mexico's economy and employment, and, through personal interviews with Mexican nationals still in their homeland, it discusses the benefit of remittances and the consequences of the immigrants' absence.

———. "Apprehension. On an 860,000-Acre Refuge, Wildlife Officers Face a Human Torrent." *High Country News,* special edition, "The Trail North: Mapping Immigration's Human Landscape" 38, no. 9 (May 15, 2006). The article, using personal interviews, tells the story of illegal immigration from the perspective of members of the U.S. Border Patrol covering the 860,000-acre Cabeza Prieta National Wildlife Refuge in southern Arizona where many illegal aliens attempt to enter the United States.

———. "Perseverance. An Immigrant's Journey: Dust, Flies, and the Long Walk." *High Country News,* special edition, "The Trail North: Mapping Immigration's Human Landscape" 38, no. 9 (May 15, 2006). In this article the author interviews immigrants still in Mexico as they prepare to make the dangerous journey across the border. Topics discussed include encounters with the U.S. Border Patrol, *coyotes* (human smugglers), and vivid descriptions of the hazards of the final walk across the desert into America.

"Mexico: HTAs, Fertility, Labor." *Migration News* 13, no. 4 (October 2006). Remittances paid by members of Mexico's HTAs (Hometown Associations), and the impact on the economy of the county's rapidly growing labor force and its high unemployment and low wages.

Smith, James. "Guatemala: Economic Migrants Replace Political Refugees." *Migration Information Source,* April 2006. In this article the author discusses historical migration trends and the impact Guatemalan refugees and economic migrants have on Mexico. It also touches on how Guatemala benefits from remittances paid by its migrant workers.

Thompson, Jonathan. "Contradiction. Fault Lines in the Land of Opportunity." *High Country News,* special edition, "The Trail North: Mapping Immigration's Human Landscape" 38, no. 9 (May 15, 2006). This article discusses the consequences of racial profiling in the United States in the struggle to control illegal immigration. It profiles one family of Mexican immigrants who came to America legally and are living in Greeley, Colorado, and the problems they encounter when they are grouped together with illegal aliens because they also are Mexican.

Web Documents

"The First Migrant Workers." The Farmworkers. URL: http://www.farmworkers.org/immigrat.html. This document tells the story of Mexican workers in the United States following the signing of the Treaty of Guadalupe in 1847, which transferred ownership of 45 percent of Mexico's territory (the region that now encompasses the states of Texas, New Mexico, Arizona, and California) to the United States. It follows the historical path of migrant Mexican workers through the late 1800s into 1929 and the Great Depression.

"Immigration." *Frontera NorteSur,* August–September 2006. URL: http://www.nmsu.edu/~frontera/immi.html. This document, produced by the University of New Mexico, provides commentary and insight on Mexico. This issue includes the subsections "Truncated American Dreams," "Mexican Deportations of Central Americans Continue," "The Border, Mexico Speaks Out on Guards, Gates and Gauntlets," and "The Fox Administration Backs President Bush."

"The Kamikazes of Poverty: Mexico's Immigration Problem." *The Economist.com,* January 29, 2004. URL: http://www.economist.com/world/la/displaystory.cfm?story_id=2388487. This article discusses the problems Mexico has encountered along its southern border with Guatemala. Rather than managing illegal aliens crossing the border to help in the war against terror, the government is struggling with economic migrants coming into the country by that route.

"Immigration." *Mexico Business Opportunities and Legal Framework.* URL: http://www.mexico-trade.com/citizen.html. This Web site provides information about Mexico's immigration law, including descriptions of the immigrant categories, the entry of business people under regulations set forth by the North American Free Trade Agreement, and naturalization of foreigners.

THE PHILIPPINES

Books

Choy, Catherine Ceniza. *Empire of Care: Nursing and Migration in Filipino American History.* Durham, N.C.: Duke University Press, 2003. To write this book the author conducted extensive interviews with Filipino nurses working in New York and other cities across the United States. This book combines the perspectives garnered from those interviews with others, including Philippine and American government and health officials, to reach the conclusions she presents, that is, that the origins of Filipino nurse migrations to America do not lie in the Philippines's independence in 1946 or the relaxation of U.S. immigration rules in 1965, but rather in the creation of an Americanized hospital training system during the period of early 20th-century colonial rule.

Corrigan, Jim, and Stuart Anderson, eds. *Filipino Immigration.* Broomall, Pa.: Mason Crest Publishers, 2003. This book provides an overview of immigration from the Philippines to the United States and Canada since the 1960s, when immigration laws were changed to permit greater numbers of people to enter these countries. The author also provides historical information about the Philippines and the difficulties Filipino emigrants have encountered over the years.

Espiritu, Yen Le. *Home Bound: Filipino American Lives across Cultures, Communities, and Countries.* Berkeley: University of California Press, 2003. Using transnational, historical, and feminist perspectives, the author provides insight into how race, gender, culture, and colonial legacies impact Filipino immigrants and Filipino Americans in the United States.

Karnow, Stanley. *In Our Image: America's Empire in the Philippines.* New York: Ballantine, 1990. This Pulitzer Prize–winning book tells the story of the United States's colonization of the Philippines. It focuses on the relationship between the two countries beginning with the United States acquiring the island nation from Spain in 1898, including America's efforts to re-create the Philippines "in our image."

Labor Migration in Asia: Protection of Migrant Workers, Support Services and Enhancing Development Benefits. Vol. 2. Geneva: International Organization for Migration, 2005. This book examines regulatory frameworks and allied measures to prevent abuses in recruitment and minimum standards in employment contracts and discusses pre-departure orientation programs in labor sending countries, including the Philippines. It also discusses training and development programs to help migrants choose better foreign employment options, migrant remittance flows and policy responses to improve remittance services and enhance the development impact of remittances, and ways in which governments can engage in facilitating and promoting international labor migration.

Parreenas, Rhacel Salazar. *Children of Global Migration: Transnational Families and Gendered Woes.* Palo Alto, Calif.: Stanford University Press, 2005. The author, who immigrated to the United States when she was 13 years old, discusses the problems she encounters now as a heterosexual adult on return visits to her country of origin in being mistaken for a man because of how she moves. In the book the role of gender in the formation of migrant transnational households is explored and the conflicting processes of gender is used as a base from which to examine the experiences of the children in these families.

Tadiar, Neferti Xina. *Fantasy Production: Sexual Economies and Other Philippine Consequences for the New World Order.* Hong Kong: Hong Kong University Press, 2003. In the book the author examines various phenomena that characterize the contemporary Philippines nation, including the mass migration overseas of domestic workers, the 'prostitution economy,' urban restructuring, and the revolt that ended the Marcos dictatorship.

Tyner, James. *Made in the Philippines: Gendered Discourses and the Making of Migrants.* New York: Taylor & Francis, 2004. In this book the author argues that migrants are socially constructed by the Philippines government's private, and nongovernmental/nonprivate organizations, which regulate labor migration, and how, in so doing, migrants become political resources.

Articles and Reports

Alburo, Florian A., and Danilo I. Abella. "Skilled Labour Migration from Developing Countries: Study on the Philippines." *International Migration Papers 51.* Geneva: International Migration Program, 2002. This study discusses brain drain in the Philippines since the 1970s. The article covers the loss of highly skilled physicians, teachers, engineers and others in the 1970s; the increasing outflow of mid-level professionals, including nurses, paramedics, and medical technicians in the 1980s; and the growth of communications industries in the 1990s, which led to another outflow of skilled workers from the Philippines such as electronic engineers and computer programmers and designers.

Asis, Maruja M. B. "The Philippines' Culture of Migration." *Migration Information Source,* January 2006. This article provides detailed insight into the culture of emigration from the Philippines, including the historical background, what it means to the country to be a labor exporter, how labor exporting works, protecting workers while they are overseas, remittances, and the future of economic migration in the country.

Iredale, Robyn, et al., eds. "Migration Research and Immigration Policy Making: A Study of Australia, the Philippines and Thailand." *International Social Science Journal* 56, no. 179 (2004). This report comprises a study investigating the connections between policymakers and migration researchers and the extent such connections impact development of migration policy. The study concludes that countries are increasingly influenced by public opinion on immigration, migration, and immigrants more so than by academic research on the subject.

O'Neil, Kevin. "Labor Export as Government Policy: The Case of the Philippines." *Migration Information Source,* January 1, 2004. In this article the author considers the history of economic migration from the Philippines and the government's role in emigration and its dependence on the remittances paid by the country's overseas foreign workers. Topics covered include government policy, protecting migrant workers while they are overseas, various policies to support migrants and encourage their repatriation, and assessing the success of the Philippines overseas foreign workers programs.

Palabrica, Raul. "Puzzling Inward Migration in the Philippines." *Philippine Daily Inquirer,* August 11, 2002. In this article the author addresses the influx of foreigners arriving in the Philippines, especially Chinese and Koreans, despite high unemployment in the country and increased labor migration by Filipinos.

See, Teresita Ang. "Influx of New Chinese Immigrants to the Philippines: Problems and Challenges." Manila, Philippines: Kaiser Heritage Center, May 13, 2004. In this report the author discusses the causes and consequences of the increasing numbers of Chinese immigrating to the island nation.

Tyner, James A. "The Global Context of Gendered Labor Migration from the Philippines to the United States." *American Behavioral Scientist* 42, no. 4 (1999), pp.

671–689. This article analyzes early labor migration from the Philippines—men going to the United States for work—and changes in the gender and destination of labor migrants in the 20th century as both women and men now migrate for employment in more than 130 countries.

Yeo, Gwen, et al. "Filipino American Elders through the Decades of the 1900s." *Cohort Analysis as a Tool in Ethnogeriatrics: Historical Profiles of Elders from Eight Ethnic Populations in the United States.* Stanford, Calif.: Stanford Geriatric Education Center, Stanford University School of Medicine, 1999. This study provides historical information about Filipino immigrants in the United States. It includes brief details about the impact on immigration of their status as U.S. nationals during the years the country was a U.S. territory, U.S. Filipino repatriation efforts, World War II, U.S. quotas on immigration from the Philippines, family reunification, and more.

Web Documents

Escobar, Pepe. "Will the Last One Leaving Please Turn Off the Lights." *Asia Times Online,* October 6, 2004. URL: http://atimes01.atimes.com/atimes/Southeast_Asia/FJ06Ae03.html. In this article the author discusses growing problems for overseas foreign workers from the Philippines, especially Filipino women working in Hong Kong who often are mistreated or exploited by their employers.

"Living and Working in the Philippines." Embassy of the United States in the Philippines, 2003. URL: http://manila.usembassy.gov/wwwha006.html. This document provides pertinent information necessary for U.S. citizens planning to enter the Philippines either for a short visit (21 days or less) or for those planning to immigrate to the country for an extended period.

"Online Guide About the Philippines History." URL: http://www.geocities.com/CollegePark/Pool/1644/timeline.html. This site offers information about the Philippines, including Spanish, American, and Japanese immigration to and colonization of the country from the precolonial period through the 1992 election of Fidel V. Ramos as the nation's 12th president.

"Philippine History." Pinas, 2005. URL: http://pinas.dlsu.edu.ph/history/history.html. An overview of Philippine history beginning with the country's first immigrants, who arrived 30,000 years ago, the Spanish invasion in 1564 and resulting colonization and influx of immigrants from Spain and other countries, and transfer of control of the islands to the United States in 1899 leading to increased immigration from America.

FILMS AND DOCUMENTARIES

Chatterton, John (narrator). *Death in the Mediterranean,* DVD. New York: The History Channel, 2004. Chatterton, an Italian journalist, discusses the mystery surrounding the disappearance of an unlicensed ferry attempting to smuggle 300 Indian, Pakistani, and Sri Lankan illegal immigrants to Italy. Only 29 passengers survived and they tell a vivid story of being forced onto a broken-down ferry piloted by a drunken captain, eventually to collide with a larger ship. With no wreckage found, the authorities derisively dismissed their account, until fishermen began to recover body parts in their nets.

Children of Chabannes, DVD. Directed by Lisa Gossels and Dean Wetherell. New York: Castle Hill Productions, 2000. This docudrama tells the story of how the people of Chabannes, a small village in France, take action to save the lives of 400 Jewish refugee children during World War II. The story is related through accounts of the children and townspeople who lived through the experience.

Chinatown: Strangers in a Strange Land, DVD. New York: The History Channel, 2000. Chinese immigration to America is traced back 150 years in this documentary. Topics discussed include what areas of China the immigrants came from and why, their contributions to the social and cultural fabric of the United States, and darker realities, such as the violence of Chinese gangs and gang wars.

Kurtis, Bill (narrator). *Investigative Reports: American Dream, American Nightmare*. New York: The History Channel, 2000. This documentary hosted by seasoned journalist and television news reporter Bill Kurtis turns a critical eye on the U.S. Immigration and Naturalization Service, described as "the most powerful uniformed police force in the United States."

Lost Boys of Sudan, DVD. Directed by Megan Mylan and Jon Shenk. New York: POV Films and PBS Television, 2004. This award-winning docudrama (San Francisco International Film Festival Best Documentary) tells the story of two orphaned Sudanese teen boys as they flee the violence in their homeland and make their way to America. It also relates their experiences with resettlement in the United States.

Patinkin, Mandy (narrator). *Ellis Island*, DVD. New York: The History Channel, 1997. Ellis Island was the gateway to America for millions of immigrants from the day it opened on December 31, 1890, until the day it was closed, November 12, 1954. In this documentary viewers are taken on a virtual tour of the historic facility, and historians discuss the policies implemented on the island, including Americanizing immigrants' names. Also included are immigrants' firsthand accounts of their experiences and interviews from the Ellis Island Oral History Project. Rare photographs and film footage also tell the stories of the many famous people who passed through Ellis Island's doors.

Quinn, Aidan (narrator). *The Irish in America*, DVD. New York: The History Channel, 1997. This documentary tells the story of the Irish immigrants to the United States and their impact on American society and culture. Included are portrayals of important historic Irish immigrants such as Andrew Jackson, boxer John L. Sullivan, and union organizer "Mother" Jones.

Rather, Dan (narrator) *Harvest of Shame*, DVD. Producer Edward R. Murrow. New York: CBS News, 1960. Seasoned television news journalist Dan Rather introduces this re-release of the 1960 documentary produced for television by legendary journalist Edward R. Murrow. This Peabody Award–winning documentary exposed the plight of migrant farm workers in America, and eventually led to changes in the laws protecting workers' rights.

Wallace, Mike. *Hispanics in America,* DVD. New York: the History Channel, 1999. Veteran CBS news anchor Mike Wallace discusses the impact of Hispanic immigrants in the United States. The film details the social and cultural changes that are tied to the rise of Hispanics in the United States, including the fears of some non-Hispanics that new arrivals are taking jobs from "real" Americans and driving up the cost of public services. Experts such as Roberto Suro, author of *Strangers among Us,* discuss the Hispanic experience in America today while other experts consider how the growing presence of Hispanics in America will shape the nation in the future.

Documentary Film Network is an independent project that bridges the gap between documentary filmmakers and viewers. This Internet site offers a selection of documentary films on a variety of topics, including immigration. Most of the films are downloadable free of charge. The films range in length from five minutes or less to one hour or longer. URL: http://www.documentary-film.net/.

Chronology

This chronology offers a list of significant events and dates relevant to international immigration and migration in the United States and the countries examined in the case studies: France, South Africa, Mexico, and the Philippines.

120,000–80,000 Years before the Present

- Research suggests that during this period the first notable movements of humans began with *Homo sapiens sapiens* moving into the Near East.

60,000–40,000 Years before the Present

- Archaeological evidence indicates human populations begin migrating into Australasia, Asia, and northwest into Europe.

35,000 Years before the Present

- Human migrations continue, spreading populations into the Americas, Oceania, Australia, and New Zealand.

5000 B.C.E.

- Indo-Europeans begin migrating out of the steppes region of Central Asia and spreading populations into Europe, the Middle East, and India.

4200–2900 B.C.E.

- Developments during this period, including domestication of the horse and invention of the wheel, make travel easier and are believed to have led to a mass migration of Indo-Europeans, who splintered into unique tribes and migrated to different locations. Based on language studies of varieties of Indo-European language, those identified as Aryans spread south into India. Others who spoke early Celtic, Germanic, and Italic languages migrated west into Europe, and people who spoke Greek and Persian languages migrated and settled in the regions between.

IMMIGRATION AND MIGRATION

ca. 1700 B.C.E.–1500 C.E.

- Bantu-speaking peoples from the area of modern-day Cameroon and Nigeria spread throughout the southern half of the African continent.

300–500 C.E.

- During the "Great Migration" the Visigoths, migrated from the Volga River region in Russia into what was then the Western Roman Empire. While the spark for the mass migration is uncertain, it led to the Germanic conquest of the Western Roman Empire and the eventual fall of that empire.

500–900

- A second "Great Migration" was probably caused by the continued expansion of Germanic tribes leading to the forced displacement of Slavic people in their path. Separate groups of Slavs migrated into an area between Germany and Poland, and south into Bohemia, Moravia, Slovakia, Hungary, and the Balkans. Other groups migrated north into Ukraine. Germanic migrations and invasions also pushed Turkish tribes living in the Roman Empire to migrate and settle in Greece, Syria, the Balkans, Palestine, Egypt, eastern North Africa, areas of Italy, and Turkey.

1219

- Mongol tribes leave Mongolia and take control of China, Turkistan, Afghanistan, Iran, Syria, Asia Minor, and sections of Russia and eastern Europe. The Mongol military migration forces Ottoman Turks to migrate from western Asia to Turkey and eastern Europe.

1400

- Through the mid-1400s Arabs and Muslims (Moors and Saracens) in North Africa migrate across the Straits of Gibraltar and invade Spain, causing the forced migration of 30,000 Spanish Christians to Damascus as slaves.

1492

- Spain is reclaimed by the Spanish leading to another forced migration as the Moors, who had occupied the country, fled back to North Africa and Jews living in Spain are forced out of the country and migrate to eastern Europe, Greece, and the Ottoman Empire.

1517

- Spanish explorer Francisco Hernández de Córdoba arrives in Mexico, opening the door to Spanish occupation of and immigration to the country.

Chronology

1521

- Spanish explorer Ponce de León establishes a settlement for Spain in Florida, which he discovered eight years earlier. The settlement fails, but it opens the door for others.
- Portuguese explorer Ferdinand Magellan becomes the first European to enter the Philippines. He claims the islands for Spain, paving the way for immigration to the country.

1550

- French immigrants arrive in North America and establish colonies near present-day Beaufort, South Carolina, and Jacksonville, Florida.

1565

- The first Spanish immigrants arrive in North America and establish a settlement at what is now St. Augustine, Florida.

1587

- English immigrants arrive in North America and establish "The Cittie" of Raleigh in North Carolina. The permanent colony was located near Roanoke Island, a failed English settlement established the previous year.

1598

- Juan de Oñate (1550–1630) settles the first colony in New Mexico at San Juan de los Caballeros, near modern-day Española.

1604

- French immigrants establish a colony near the St. Croix River in Maine, but poor conditions force them to migrate and reestablish the colony to the north in Port-Royal, Nova Scotia, Canada.

1607

- More English immigrants arrive in North America and establish Jamestown, a settlement in the Chesapeake Bay region of Virginia.

1620

- The Pilgrims, English Separatists, immigrate to the New World from Holland by way of England and establish a colony at Plymouth, Massachusetts.

1652

- The Dutch establish a colony in Cape Town South Africa as a supply station for ships traveling along trade routes between Europe and Asia. The colony opens the door for European immigration into South Africa.

IMMIGRATION AND MIGRATION

1683

- German Mennonites immigrate to North America and establish Germantown, a colony near Philadelphia, Pennsylvania.

1697

- The French government implements the Naturalization Tax, then attempts to identify foreigners living in France and charge them a residency fee. The effort failed, but 8,000 foreigners were counted living in the country.

1789

- France adopts the Declaration of the Rights of Man, laying the foundation for the country's future immigration policies and legislation.

1790

- The United States passes its first immigration-related law. The law allows naturalization only of "free white persons."

1798

- The United States passes the Alien and Sedition Acts, authorizing the president to deport foreigners believed to be dangerous.

1805

- The British annex the Cape Colony in South Africa from the Dutch and begin encouraging British citizens to immigrate to the colony.

1823

- Mexico wins independence from Spain and establishes the United Mexican States. Included in the country's territories are large swaths of America's Southwest that formerly belonged to Spain. Immigration of Americans to Mexico increases at this time fueled by Mexico's offer of land grants to families willing to settle in the country's northern territories. The only requirements for an immigrant to earn a land grant are converting to Catholicism and acquiring Mexican citizenship.

1830

- The United States passes the Indian Removal Act, leading to the forced migration of thousands of Native Americans from their homes in the Southeast to sparsely populated territories west of the Mississippi River. The migration became known as the Trail of Tears.

Chronology

1831

- French immigrants establish a settlement at Coatzacoalcos, Mexico. The settlement fails, but others established at Veracruz and Mexico City succeed.
- German immigrants develop the city of Mazatlán, Mexico, into a prosperous trading port at this time.

1845

- The Irish Potato Famine begins, triggering an influx of immigrants from Ireland to the United States. More than 500,000 Irish immigrate to the United States during the five-year famine.

1848

- ***February 2:*** Mexico and the United States sign the Treaty of Guadalupe Hidalgo, resulting in the United States acquiring most of Mexico's northern territories for $15 million. The lands include the states of California, Nevada, Utah, Arizona, New Mexico, and Colorado. Texas had secured its independence from Mexico about 10 years earlier so it was not part of the treaty. It also results in Mexico's population dropping by about 100,000 people, due not to emigration but to the change in borders, which now placed those people in the United States.

1849

- Gold is discovered in California, the United States, leading to a mass migration into the state. The discovery also triggers the first major Chinese immigration to the United States.

1851

- France begins keeping official government census records and tracking immigrants in the country.

1867

- Diamonds are discovered in South Africa's Vaal and Orange rivers region, triggering a mass migration of "tens of thousands of people," both white Europeans and black Africans into the area in search of wealth.

1868

- ***July 28:*** The Fourteenth Amendment to the U.S. Constitution, which states that "All persons born or naturalized in the United States, and subject to the jurisdiction thereof, are citizens of the United States and of the State wherein they reside . . . ," is ratified. Citizenship is denied to select groups, such as Chinese, by later governmental actions, including the Chinese Exclusion Act. This Constitutional amendment leads to unforeseen problems in the mid-2000s when millions of children born in the United States to illegal aliens are citizens and allowed to remain in the country while their parents face deportation.

1882

- The United States passes the Chinese Exclusion Act denying any further entry of Chinese immigrants into the country. The act also denies citizenship to Chinese immigrants already in America.

1886

- Gold is discovered in South Africa's Transvaal province near the city of Johannesburg. The discovery leads to another mass migration to the country by Europeans, Americans, Australians, and black Africans in search of riches.

1898

- ***October 1:*** The United States and Spain sign the Treaty of Paris, ending the Spanish-American War. Under terms of the treaty the United States acquires the Philippines from Spain for $20 million. As a U.S. territory, immigration from the Philippines to the United States increases.

1902

- With the encouragement of the British government 1,200 British nationals immigrate to South Africa, joining the more than 250,000 European immigrants already living there. The country also adopts its first culturally influenced immigration restrictions: a language requirement.

1903

- Chinese immigrants fleeing persecution in the United States establish the city of Mexicali in Mexico.

1905

- Korean immigrants arrive in Mexico and are sold by a Japanese slave trader to work on cactus plantations. Despite earning their freedom four years later the immigrants choose to remain in Mexico.

1906

- South Africa passes the Cape Immigration Act, which requires all immigrants to be able to fill out immigration forms in a European language and prove they have a means of support. The government applies a special tax to indentured Indian workers who fail to return to India.

- The United States requires all immigrants to speak and understand English before they can be naturalized.

1914–1918

- World War I leads to a decline in immigration.

1917

- Mexico adopts its Political Constitution of the United Mexican States. Still in effect in 2006, the constitution establishes the foundation for the country's future immigration laws.
- The United States designates Asia a "barred zone" and prohibits immigration from all Asian countries except Japan and the Philippines.

1924

- The U.S. government establishes the Border Patrol with the primary purpose of preventing Asian, Chinese, and European immigrants from entering the country illegally across the U.S.-Mexico border.
- The United States also adopts the Johnson-Reed Act, which establishes a nations-of-origin quota system that favors immigrants from northern Europe and bans immigration to the country by people ineligible for citizenship. The Japanese are primarily affected by the act.

1930

- South Africa amends its immigration laws to exclude Jews as a class of immigrants and establishes an immigration quota system that considers an immigrant's country of origin rather than reason for immigrating.
- The Great Depression takes hold worldwide, leading to a significant decrease in immigration and an increase in deportations of immigrants in nations affected by the depression.

1934

- ***March 24:*** The United States passes the Tydings-McDuffie Act, laying the foundation for the Philippines's independence and limiting to 50 the annual visas available to Filipinos wishing to immigrate to America.

1940

- ***September 28:*** The United States becomes involved in World War II, resulting in decreased immigration to the country.
- The Philippine government passes an immigration act known as the Commonwealth Act No. 613. The act establishes the country's Bureau of Immigration, defines immigrants, and establishes quotas for how many immigrants may enter the country each year.

1941

- ***December 7:*** The Japanese bomb Pearl Harbor, Hawaii, leading the United States to confine 120,000 Japanese immigrants and Japanese Americans in internment camps.

1942

- ***August 4:*** The Mexican Farm Labor Program Agreement (the Bracero Program) between the United States and Mexico is implemented. The program is intended to provide a labor force for the American agricultural industry. It is quickly abused by American farmers and leads to increased illegal migration into the United States by Mexican temporary laborers.

1945

- ***October 1:*** France adopts the country's first immigration law not tied to work, a decree based on the Declaration of the Rights of Man. The decree mandates a requirement of equality and integration of all immigrants regardless of nationality, religion, race, or culture. The decree is modified one month later and, by its terms, France is declared officially open to all immigrants and their families, and the National Office of Immigration is established.

1948

- Apartheid begins in South Africa. The restrictive policies of apartheid cause a decline in legal immigration to and an increase in emigration from the country.

1954

- The United States launches Operation Wetback, resulting in the deportation of more than 1 million Mexican immigrants and Mexican Americans. The program also puts in place sanctions against American employers who hire undocumented workers.

1964

- The Mexican Farm Labor Program Agreement (the Bracero Program) is ended due to increased mechanization of American farms and growing concerns about abuses of the program by American employers.

1965

- The United States passes the Hart-Cellar Act, which abolishes nation-of-origin quotas in effect since 1924. The act also institutes immigration criteria based on an immigrant's skills, profession, and family relationships with people already in the country.

Chronology

1966

- The United States passes the Cuban Refugee Act permitting more than 400,000 Cubans to enter the country.

1974

- France, responding to high unemployment in the country, officially closes its doors to all immigration by refusing to reissue residency permits to immigrants in the country and not authorizing entrance of immigrants for employment.
- Mexico enacts the General Law of Population clearly defining immigration into the country.
- The Philippine government passes the Labor Code of the Philippines, laying the foundation for the country's overseas employment programs, including establishing the Philippines Overseas Employment Administration.

1980

- ***April 15–October 31:*** The Mariel boatlift exodus brings more than 100,000 refugees fleeing Fidel Castro's regime in Cuba to the United States.

1989

- ***October:*** The headmaster of the Gabriel-Havez School in Creil, France, expels three Muslim female students for wearing Islamic headscarves to class, stating that wearing the scarves goes against a key provision of government policy calling for separation of church and state. After thousands of Muslims march in protest of the expulsions the girls are allowed to return to class.

1994

- Apartheid formally ends in South Africa with the rise to power of the African National Congress and election of Nelson Mandela as president. Growing unemployment in the country at this time, especially a lack of jobs for unskilled workers, increases xenophobia and pushes the South African government to close the country's doors to immigration.
- ***January:*** The United States, Mexico, and Canada launch the North American Free Trade Agreement. Although the goal of the agreement is to bring economic growth and improved living standards for the citizens of all three countries, Mexico's economy slips. Low-paying jobs and unemployment lead to increased illegal immigration into the United States by Mexican nationals.

1995

- South Africa adopts the Alien Control Amendment Act, which modifies the government's powers to deport illegal aliens, and the South African Citizenship

Act, which revises the country's requirements for residency and eventual citizenship of immigrants.

- The Philippines passes the Migrant Workers and Overseas Filipino Act to further regulate the country's overseas employment and to protect the welfare of Filipino migrant workers abroad. The act also establishes the Overseas Workers Welfare Administration.

1996

- ***September 14:*** An estimated 2,000 French nationals march through Marseilles protesting immigration and in remembrance of a French teen killed by an Arab youth. The marchers carry banners with slogans such as, "Immigration equals insecurity," and "France for the French."

2000

- South Africa's Refugee Act takes effect. The act prohibits asylum seekers from holding jobs, attending school, or opening a business until they are officially recognized as refugees.

2001

- ***October 26:*** The United States passes the Uniting and Strengthening America by Providing Appropriate Tools Required to Intercept and Obstruct Terrorism Act (PATRIOT Act) in response to the September 11 terrorist attacks on the country. The act uses immigration laws as one method of fighting terrorists and leads to the detention of more than 1,200 South Asian and Middle Eastern immigrants, mostly men.

2003

- South Africa passes an amended immigration law that allows South African businesses to hire highly skilled foreign professionals, but it prohibits hiring unskilled foreign workers.

2005

- ***January 1:*** France establishes the National Centre for Immigration History to recognize the role immigrants and immigration have played in the country.
- ***October 27:*** French police accidentally kill two teens of Arab nationality in a Paris suburb occupied primarily by immigrants. The event sets off rioting by large groups of foreign youth, most of them the children of North African and Arab immigrants. The riots continue for nearly three weeks and are described as the country's "worst urban violence in a decade."
- The Philippines government reinstates compulsory registration of foreign national workers and their family members. Registration requires that immi-

grants be fingerprinted and be in possession of a microchip-based identification card.

2006

- ***May 13:*** In France more than 11,000 immigrants march in Paris to protest the country's proposed new immigration law, claiming it promotes "selected immigration" and is "inhumane."
- ***March–May:*** During these months, thousands of Mexican immigrants in the United States, both legal and illegal, march and hold demonstrations in dozens of U.S. cities to protest the U.S. government's proposed changes to the country's immigration laws. Backlashes include rising anti-immigration sentiment among Americans and counterprotests that include burning Mexican flags in front of Mexican consulates in the United States.
- ***May 15:*** The United States announces Operation Jump Start, which will deploy more than 6,000 National Guard troops to assist the U.S. Border Patrol in controlling illegal immigration across the U.S.-Mexico border.
- ***June 17:*** Despite immigrant protests, the French Senate passes a new immigration law that favors immigration by highly skilled foreigners and restricts immigration by low-skilled or undereducated foreigners. It also requires that immigrants show they are able to support themselves, will make an effort to integrate into French society, and learn the French language.
- ***October 26:*** The United States passes the Secure Fence Act, which authorizes construction of a 700-mile-long fence at the U.S.-Mexico Border as a method to deter illegal immigration from Mexico into the United States.

2007

- ***March 13:*** During a meeting in Mexico, the country's recently elected president Felipe Calderon (elected December 1, 2006) chastised U.S. president George W. Bush for doing too little to reduce or eliminate the causes of illegal immigration from Mexico into America. Calderon also stressed the hardships caused in his country by the growing tide of Mexicans leaving the country for jobs in the United States.
- ***April 2:*** A comprehensive immigration bill introduced in the U.S. House of Representatives includes relief from the nonimmigrant intent requirement for some international students, increases the penalties for immigrants arrested for a variety of crimes, increases the number of border and immigration enforcement personnel, establishes an electronic employee verification system for employers and penalties for immigrants falsely attesting their right to work, and increases the number of available H-1B visas and green cards to 115,000.

- ***April 19:*** A Filipino immigration official working in a district office is recalled to the office in Manila after 20 Chinese immigrant laborers working in the Philippines were arrested and detained for working without legal permits.
- ***April 22:*** Immigration is a key issue in France's presidential election. In a run-off election May 6 between the top two winning candidates, Segolene Royal, a socialist sympathetic to immigrants, and Nicholas Sarkozy, who takes a more restrictive, anti-immigration position, Sarkozy is elected president.
- ***October:*** Despite efforts by the U. S. House and Senate to make changes to the country's immigration policies earlier in the year, the U.S. government failed to pass legislation or take further actions toward immigration reform as the year drew to a close.
- ***October 23:*** The French parliament passes a controversial immigration bill that includes requirements for language and cultural values exams and potential DNA testing for foreigners hoping to join relatives in France.

Glossary

This chapters offers a list of terms and their definitions relevant to international immigration and migration, including in the United States and the countries examined in the case studies: France, South Africa, Mexico, and the Philippines.

alien Also foreigner. A person in a country, either temporarily or permanently, that is not his or her country of origin.

apartheid The practice of racial segregation and political and economic discrimination in South Africa that led to large numbers of people emigrating from the country to other nations with less discriminatory policies.

asylum Protection granted to refugees by the country to which they have fled.

asylum seekers Someone who flees their homeland for a variety of reasons and applies for asylum in another country. They remain asylum seekers until their application for asylum is reviewed and considered by the receiving country and approved.

brain drain The consequences caused by the emigration of large numbers of highly skilled and educated people from one country to another country that offers improved employment, economic, and social opportunities.

brain gain The impact highly skilled and educated people have on the receiving country to which they emigrate from a country that offers fewer employment, economic, and social opportunities.

capital flight The loss of financial capital that is no longer invested in the country where its owner lives and earned it. For example, a country's investment in higher education is lost when the trained person emigrates.

citizenship The country in which a person is either born or is naturalized and in which that person has rights and responsibilities.

contract migrant worker A person working in a country not his or her homeland under arrangements with an employer in a destination country who establishes set limits on the length of employment and the specific job the person is hired for, for example, Filipinos participating in that country's overseas foreign worker programs.

coyote Smugglers from Mexico who get paid to transport Mexican migrant laborers and other immigrants, from Mexico or other nations, illegally into the United States across the U.S.-Mexico border.

cross-border workers Persons who commute between their country of origin, which is usually also their country of citizenship, to their place of employment in another country.

deport The legal act of removing a person from a country that is not his or her country of origin after he/she has been found removable for violating the country's immigration laws.

economic migrant A person who leaves his or her country of origin to seek work in another country where there are more opportunities for employment or where the wages are higher.

emigrant A person who leaves his or her homeland.

emigration The act of leaving one's country of origin to settle in or spend time in a different or destination country.

expatriate A person who becomes a permanent resident of another country.

family reunification The aspect of immigration that enables close family members of a person living in a country other than his or her homeland to immigrate for the purpose of joining that person and reunifying the family.

forced migration The act of forcing a person to leave his or her country of origin or region of residence to live in a new country or location, for example, Africans who were forced to other countries during the slave trade or Native Americans forced to leave their homes in the U.S. Southeast and migrate to land in the American West.

foreign national A person living in a country temporarily or who is a citizen of another country.

foreign retirees People who have retired from jobs and careers and have emigrated from their country of origin to live in another country due to lower costs of living or a better climate in the destination country.

globalization The development of a global economy that is marked by transnational flows of capital and human capital in the form of economic migrants.

guest-worker A person who is permitted to enter a foreign country on a temporary basis for the purpose of employment.

human smuggling The act of one person smuggling another person from his or her country of origin illegally into another country, usually for payment of a fee.

Glossary

illegal alien A person who enters a country without the proper legal documentation.

immigrant(s) A person who arrives in a new country to settle, usually permanently, after emigrating from his or her country of origin.

immigration The act of entering and remaining in a country of which one is not a native.

internally displaced person(s) A person or group of people forced to leave their homes for a variety of reasons, including wars, human rights violations, and natural or man-made disasters, but who remain in their country of origin rather than crossing borders to take up residency in another country.

inward migration Also return migration. The act of people migrating into a country or returning to their homeland following a period of time in another country.

irregular migration Leaving one's country of origin without going through the proper emigration procedures, or entering a destination country without the proper legal documentation or remaining in a destination country after one's visa has expired.

migrant(s) A person who moves regularly either within his or her country of origin or across borders to other countries in order to find employment.

migration The act of moving within one's country of origin or across borders to other destination countries periodically for employment or other reasons such as to escape inclement winter weather in northern climates.

nativism A sociopolitical policy of favoring the native population of a country over immigrants in the country.

North American Free Trade Agreement (NAFTA) The agreement that regulates the mutual trading relationship between the United States and Canada and establishes a similar relationship with Mexico. It has greatly increased illegal migration from Mexico into the United States.

nomad(s) People without an established place of residence who move from one location to another, usually seasonally and in long-established geographic patterns.

nonimmigrant A foreigner who enters a destination country temporarily for a specific purpose such as foreign students attending school, temporary workers, and exchange visitors.

outward migration The act of people leaving their homeland for economic or other reasons.

overseas foreign workers A term used by the Philippine government to describe the country's labor migrants.

pollero Loosely translated, chicken farmer. The term, like *coyote,* is used to describe a person who smuggles illegal immigrants into the United States from Mexico.

push-pull factors The factors in countries of origin and of destination that trigger immigration. Push factors in countries of origin may include poverty, unemployment, political instability or wars, and disruptive forces of nature such as hurricanes or tsunamis destroying an area. Pull factors in countries of destination may include ample employment opportunities, higher wages, or political stability.

quota The limits placed by a country's government on the number of people who may immigrate into the country each year.

refugee(s) A person who, due to well-founded fears of being persecuted for reasons of race, religion, nationality, political beliefs, or membership in a specific social group, leaves his or her country of origin for the safety of another country.

replacement population Immigrants in a country who provide a workforce to replace ageing native workers who are retiring or who help increase the declining populations in countries with low or negative birth rates among the native-born population.

remittances Money earned by migrant workers in a receiving country that is sent back to family members remaining in the country of origin.

repatriate People who have immigrated to another country and, after a period of time, return to their country of origin or citizenship.

resettlement The act of immigrants or refugees moving from their homeland and starting over in another country.

sans papiers The French term for a person in the country who lacks the necessary legal documents.

segregation The discriminatory act of separating or isolating a group of people based on race, class, or ethnicity, such as South Africa segregating black Africans during apartheid.

snakeheads Smugglers from China who get paid to transport migrant laborers and other immigrants illegally into South Africa and Pacific Rim countries.

temporary migrant workers People who enter a country legally for a short period of time to complete a job before returning to their homeland, such as Mexican Bracero workers who filled jobs on U.S. farms during the harvest seasons.

tourist(s) A person who travels to another country or location in his or her homeland for a short-term pleasure visit or a cultural experience.

trafficking The commercial trade of people who often are subject to illegal activities in the destination country or location such as sexual exploitation or involuntary servitude. Trafficking in humans is like the slave trade and generally involves physical force, coercion, fraud, or other types of intimidation or deception used against the person being trafficked.

transit country A country that migrants enter only for a short time as they continue on to their preferred destination country, for example, Guatemalan illegal immigrants entering Mexico on their way to the United States.

undocumented migrant A person who leaves his or her country of origin and enters another country without the proper documents.

visa overstayers People who enter a destination country legally on a visa but who fail to leave and return to their country of origin once the visa expires, thus becoming an illegal alien in the destination country where they have remained.

xenophobia An unreasonable fear or hatred of foreigners or strangers.

Index

Note: page numbers in **boldface** indicate major treatment of a subject. Page numbers followed by *f* indicate figures. Page numbers followed by *b* indicate bibliographic entries. Page numbers followed by *c* indicate chronology entries. Page numbers followed by *g* indicate glossary entries.

Index

Index

H

I

Index

Index

Index

Index

Index